# The Sustainable Fintech Revolution:

## Building a Greener Future for Finance

Kuldeep Singh
*Faculty of Management Studies, CMS Business School, Jain University (Deemed), Bengaluru, India*

Rebecca Abraham
*Huizenga College of Business and Entrepreneurship, Nova Southeastern University, Fort Lauderdale, USA*

Prasanna Kolar
*Koneru Lakshmaiah Education Foundation, India*

A volume in the Advances in Finance, Accounting, and Economics (AFAE) Book Series

IGI Global
PUBLISHER of TIMELY KNOWLEDGE

Published in the United States of America by
IGI Global
Business Science Reference (an imprint of IGI Global)
701 E. Chocolate Avenue
Hershey PA, USA 17033
Tel: 717-533-8845
Fax: 717-533-8661
E-mail: cust@igi-global.com
Web site: http://www.igi-global.com



Library of Congress Cataloging-in-Publication Data

Names: Singh, Kuldeep, 1990- editor. | Abraham, Rebecca, editor. | Kolar, Prasanna, 1994- editor.
Title: The sustainable fintech revolution : building a greener future for finance / edited by: Kuldeep Singh, Rebecca Abraham, and Prasanna Kolar.

Description: Hershey PA : Business Science Reference, [2023] | Includes bibliographical references. | Summary: "The Sustainable Fintech Revolution: Building a Greener Future for Finance explores how fintech can be used to promote sustainability in the financial industry. This book provides a comprehensive overview of the fintech ecosystem and its potential for advancing sustainability goals, including case studies of companies that have integrated sustainability into their business models. It also offers insights and recommendations for policymakers, regulators, financial institutions, and fintech companies on how they can promote sustainability in the financial industry. This book is ideal for academics and researchers in finance, technology, sustainability, and development studies, as well as practitioners in the fintech industry, policymakers and regulators, and NGOs working on sustainable finance and development issues"-- Provided by publisher.
Identifiers: LCCN 2023022581 (print) | LCCN 2023022582 (ebook) | ISBN 9798369300084 (hardcover) | ISBN 9798369300091 (paperback) | ISBN 9798369300107 (ebook)
Subjects: LCSH: Financial services industry--Technological innovations. | Sustainable development.
Classification: LCC HG173 .S839 2023 (print) | LCC HG173 (ebook) | DDC 332--dc23/eng/20230703
LC record available at https://lccn.loc.gov/2023022581
LC ebook record available at https://lccn.loc.gov/2023022582

This book is published in the IGI Global book series Advances in Finance, Accounting, and Economics (AFAE) (ISSN: 2327-5677; eISSN: 2327-5685)

British Cataloguing in Publication Data
A Cataloguing in Publication record for this book is available from the British Library.
All work contributed to this book is new, previously-unpublished material.
The views expressed in this book are those of the authors, but not necessarily of the publisher.
For electronic access to this publication, please contact: eresources@igi-global.com.

# Advances in Finance, Accounting, and Economics (AFAE) Book Series

Ahmed Driouchi
Al Akhawayn University, Morocco

ISSN:2327-5677
EISSN:2327-5685

## MISSION

In our changing economic and business environment, it is important to consider the financial changes occurring internationally as well as within individual organizations and business environments. Understanding these changes as well as the factors that influence them is crucial in preparing for our financial future and ensuring economic sustainability and growth.

The **Advances in Finance, Accounting, and Economics (AFAE)** book series aims to publish comprehensive and informative titles in all areas of economics and economic theory, finance, and accounting to assist in advancing the available knowledge and providing for further research development in these dynamic fields.

## COVERAGE

- Microfinance
- Finance and Accounting in SMEs
- Economics of Intellectual Property Rights
- Interest Rates and Annuities
- Risk Analysis and Management
- Investments and Derivatives
- Accounting Standards
- Applied economics
- Economics Geography
- Microeconomics

IGI Global is currently accepting manuscripts for publication within this series. To submit a proposal for a volume in this series, please contact our Acquisition Editors at Acquisitions@igi-global.com or visit: http://www.igi-global.com/publish/.

The Advances in Finance, Accounting, and Economics (AFAE) Book Series (ISSN 2327-5677) is published by IGI Global, 701 E. Chocolate Avenue, Hershey, PA 17033-1240, USA, www.igi-global.com. This series is composed of titles available for purchase individually; each title is edited to be contextually exclusive from any other title within the series. For pricing and ordering information please visit http://www.igi-global.com/book-series/advances-finance-accounting-economics/73685. Postmaster: Send all address changes to above address. 

## Titles in this Series

*For a list of additional titles in this series, please visit: http://www.igi-global.com/book-series/*

***Concepts and Cases of Illicit Finance***
Abdul Rafay (University of Management and Technology, Pakistan)
Business Science Reference • © 2023 • 273pp • H/C (ISBN: 9781668485873) • US $250.00

***The Importance of Entrepreneurship in Fostering Economic Progress***
Mohammed El Amine Abdelli (University of Western Brittany, France) Naima Bentouir (Ain Temouchent University, Algeria) and Esra Sipahi Döngül (Aksaray University, Turkey)
Business Science Reference • © 2024 • 300pp • H/C (ISBN: 9781668471272) • US $240.00

***Perspectives on the Transition Toward Green and Climate Neutral Economies in Asia***
Patricia Ordóñez de Pablos (The University of Oviedo, Spain) Mohammad Nabil Almunawar (Universiti Brunei Darussalam, Brunei) and Muhammad Anshari (Universiti Brunei Darussalam, Brunei)
Business Science Reference • © 2023 • 465pp • H/C (ISBN: 9781668486139) • US $325.00

***Revolutionizing Financial Services and Markets Through FinTech and Blockchain***
Kiran Mehta (Chitkara Business School, Chitkara University, India) Renuka Sharma (Chitkara Business School, Chitkara University, India) and Poshan Yu (Soochow University, China & Australian Studies Centre, Shanghai University, China)
Business Science Reference • © 2023 • 340pp • H/C (ISBN: 9781668486245) • US $265.00

***Circular Economy Implementation for Sustainability in the Built Environment***
Nicoleta Cobîrzan (Technical University of Cluj-Napoca, Romania) Radu Muntean (Transilvania University of Brașov, Romania) and Raluca - Andreea Felseghi (Technical University of Cluj-Napoca, Romania)
Business Science Reference • © 2023 • 300pp • H/C (ISBN: 9781668482384) • US $250.00

***Sustainable Growth and Global Social Development in Competitive Economies***
Andrei Jean Vasile (Petroleum-Gas University of Ploiesti, Romania & Romanian Academy, National Institute for Economic Research "Costin C. Kiriţescu", Romania) Mile Vasić (European Marketing and Management Association, Banja Luka, Bosnia and Herzegovina) and Predrag Vukovic (Institute of Agricultural Economics, Belgrade, Serbia)
Business Science Reference • © 2023 • 320pp • H/C (ISBN: 9781668488102) • US $250.00

IGI Global
PUBLISHER of TIMELY KNOWLEDGE

701 East Chocolate Avenue, Hershey, PA 17033, USA
Tel: 717-533-8845 x100 • Fax: 717-533-8661
E-Mail: cust@igi-global.com • www.igi-global.com

# Table of Contents

# Detailed Table of Contents



The emergence of fintech has made it possible for many unbanked individuals worldwide to obtain financial services through digital means. Recently, the COVID-19 health crisis has opened up new possibilities for digital financial services to speed up financial inclusion despite social exclusion. Many national governments have promoted its usage by lowering costs and boosting the transactional limits for digital transactions. In this research, the authors attempted to construct a model for the adoption of fintech in the context of rural India. The goal of this research is to identify the policies and initiatives that best promote the growth of the fintech ecosystem. They also make an effort to pinpoint the qualities of banking systems that are more likely to support fintech in order to collaborate effectively on financial inclusion. The methodology section of this work is built on the ISM-MICMAC technique.



In recent times, policymakers and scholars have directed their attention toward the notion of sustainability and green finance, coinciding with the growing global emphasis on environmental protection, climate change mitigation, and sustainable development. The integration of sustainability and green finance practices has emerged

The chapter aims to provide insight into the policy framework of green finance. The five-step roadmap begins with a vision whereby the reader is made aware of the concept of sustainability. India's initiative at the G20 summit of the UN Environment on the issue, thereby the first part, is concluded with a positive note on fairness and development. Similarly, a detailed analysis of the strategy undertaken at the national and international levels is discussed. Further, lead entities are enlisted along with the current state of ownership in some countries. No policy framework would be a good guide for policymakers and researchers to rely on if it is presented without including the essential requirements. To provide a sense of the change in green fintech, various examples have been curated related to green lending, crowdfunding, insurance, and ESG data providers. The comprehensive chapter is concluded by listing the essential metrics to evaluate the process of growth.



Promoting economic sustainability through the adoption of digital payment is of great significance for the long-term development of a country. Minimizing the environmental impact and promoting cost savings can lead to economic growth and development. This chapter examines the adoption of digital payment systems and its impact on sustainability initiatives. A survey of 450 mobile consumers in Karnataka revealed that awareness level towards digital payment systems is 93%, and UPI is the most preferred mode of digital payments, based on linear regression and using SPSS. It is also seen that time saved and ease of maintenance for each banking transaction has an impact on economic sustainability. All the respondents were aware of the components of sustainable development, and most were willing to contribute towards economic sustainability, though threat due to fraud is still a matter of concern for most of the users. This study provides insights into factors that promote economic sustainability in the context of adoption of digital payment systems.

Concerns about global instability and vulnerability have been raised by the massive economic crisis brought on by the COVID-19 pandemic. However, the COVID-19 epidemic and subsequent prolonged lockdowns have caused operational and financial difficulties for Indian institutions. Banks have devised a variety of measures to deal with the fallout from the epidemic, and as a consequence, clients have altered their financial behavior. The study takes a qualitative approach, analyzing the behaviors of gig workers via the lens of "expert mining." Researchers found that gig workers' employment uncertainty had the reverse effect on their behavior, making them more likely to sacrifice spending in lieu of saving for the future and significantly reducing on necessities such as livelihood spending and travel plan. In addition, the research found that there was a favorable association between the attitude towards the internet and the adoption of mobile banking among gig workers during Covid uncertainty.



The potential of financial technology to foster sustainable social entrepreneurship in India and contribute to the attainment of the United Nations' sustainable development goals (SDGs) has become increasingly apparent with the technological advances of the past few decades revolutionizing the way we live, work, and communicate. India, despite its rapid economic growth, encounters notable obstacles in realising the SDGs, such as poverty, inequality, and environmental deterioration. Conventional financial institutions have not effectively addressed these concerns. This chapter analyses the influence of financial technology (FinTech) on financial inclusion, the emergence of digital payments, blockchain technology, and their potential to facilitate social entrepreneurship that can lead to favourable social and environmental outcomes. The chapter delineates the challenges and opportunities that the FinTech industry offers to social entrepreneurship in India.

This chapter examines the network dynamics of green and dirty crypto currencies around Russia-Ukraine war of 2022. The war is acting as a catalyst for the growth and popularity of crypto currency market across the globe. The study uses price data of crypto currencies from the years 2021 to 2022. Based on the minimum spanning tree (MST), the study finds that network for the green and dirty crypto currencies is different before the war and during the war period. Furthermore, using the MST diagram, the study finds some key crypto currencies which play a significant role in the crypto networks. The study also makes use of dendrogram, to identify the clusters in the green and dirty crypto currency markets. This work has practical implications for crypto portfolio diversification during the war period.



India is the second-most populous country in the world, with a rapidly growing economy. Its population is highly tech-savvy and has a high level of adoption of digital technologies. The Indian government has taken several initiatives to promote digital transactions and financial inclusion. These initiatives have been instrumental in the growth of fintech in India. Fintech, or financial technology, is transforming the financial sector worldwide. Fintech solutions have led to the creation of new business models, streamlined operations, and enhanced customer experience. India is no exception to this trend, as it has witnessed a significant growth in fintech in recent years. The fintech ecosystem in India is highly diverse, consisting of startups, technology companies, banks, and non-banking financial companies (NBFCs). There are various challenges faced by fintech companies in India, such as lack of access to capital, regulatory hurdles, and competition from established players. This chapter proposal aims to provide a basic literature review on the development of fintech in India.

The Indian carpet industry, one of the country's most important sources of foreign exchange, is also well-known worldwide for its rich art and tradition. However, there is concern about innovation, financial inclusion, and sustainability. The current study explores the MANCHAHA initiative, a step taken by the Jaipur Rugs carpet industry toward sustainability, as well as its relevance and significance for other hand-craft or carpet industries. It also examines how it affects the financial inclusion of rug weavers. The single-case study method has been used in conjunction with the descriptive research design to conduct the study. The idea of innovation utilizing conventional methods is somewhat obsolete and underappreciated, but the company's MANCHAHA project disproved this preconceived notion.



Financial service firms are increasingly using financial technologies in order to offer bundle of financial services to the customers. In this process, the firms started adopting emerging technologies like AI, blockchain, bigdata, cloud computing, in their financial transactions and operations. The objective of this research is to provide bibliometrics such as top journals, top articles, most cited articles, most cited authors, top keywords, and so on related to sustainable finance research in order to provide future research directions to potential researchers. The appropriate articles, book chapters, conference papers, and reviews were identified from available sources using the search term "sustainable fintech" in the Scopus database, where 339 articles (as of 24-04-2023) from the years 2014 to 2023 were considered for bibliometric analysis using Vosviewer software. The study's future research paths will motivate researchers to conduct further research in the field of sustainable fintech.

The escalating climate catastrophe has made climate-sustainable development indispensable, the success of which relies on the sustainable adoption of innovative ideas and technologies. Against this backdrop, the FinTech industry saw the emergence of a novel FinTech model with a climate action motive, known as climate FinTech or green FinTech. This chapter contributes to the scanty climate FinTech literature by providing insights on the state of the art using an inductive qualitative methodology comprising a literature review, case research on Indian climate FinTech, and sentiment analysis of climate FinTech tweets. The chapter puts forward suggestions for the growth of the market, and the future implications. The results suggest that the climate FinTech landscape is made up of a multitude of business types and activities and this innovative yet impactful FinTech model is a promising proposition for countering climate catastrophe, especially using blockchain technology.

# Preface

In the nexus of financial innovation and environmental consciousness, a profound narrative unfolds through the collaborative effort of distinguished experts in the realm of fintech and sustainability. *The Sustainable Fintech Revolution: Building a Greener Future for Finance* stands as a testament to the critical juncture at which the financial and ecological spheres converge, beckoning for prudent action. The landscape of modern finance is undergoing a transformation, driven by the emergent paradigm of sustainability. Within these chapters, readers can embark on an intellectual journey that traverses the intricate terrains of green finance and transparency. The profound implications of sustainability disclosure come to light, amplifying how fintech plays a pivotal role in steering the trajectory toward a future marked by both financial prosperity and environmental integrity.

Fintech is still a relatively new industry, and it is still evolving rapidly. This means that there is a great deal of uncertainty about the future of sustainable fintech. However, the potential benefits of sustainable fintech are significant, and it is likely that this field will continue to grow in the years to come. One of the key challenges facing sustainable fintech is regulation. Financial regulators are still trying to figure out how to regulate fintech companies, and this can make it difficult for sustainable fintech companies to operate. However, it is important to remember that regulation can also be a force for good, and it can help to ensure that sustainable fintech companies are operating in a responsible manner. Another challenge facing sustainable fintech is data privacy. Fintech companies often collect a lot of data about their customers, and this data can be used to track people's spending habits and other personal information. This raises concerns about data privacy, and it is important for sustainable fintech companies to be transparent about how they collect and use data. It is important to consider the social impact of sustainable fintech. Fintech companies have the potential to make a positive impact on society by expanding access to financial services, reducing poverty, and promoting environmental sustainability.

In today's rapidly evolving world, the confluence of financial technology (fintech) and sustainability has emerged as a transformative force, reshaping the trajectory of both the financial industry and the global ecosystem. Against the backdrop of pressing environmental challenges, socioeconomic inequalities, and technological advancements, *The Sustainable Fintech Revolution: Building a Greener Future for Finance* takes its place as a beacon of insight, guiding readers through the intricate intersections of finance, technology, and sustainability. As humanity grapples with the urgent need to reconcile economic growth with ecological preservation, this book stands as a timely and indispensable resource. Traditional practices have often yielded adverse environmental consequences and exacerbated social disparities. Simultaneously, technology has emerged as a powerful agent of change, driving innovation and redefining the boundaries of possibility. The amalgamation of these two forces forms the bedrock of sustainable fintech—a frontier where financial ingenuity converges with environmental stewardship.

The significance of this book becomes apparent when examined against the backdrop of contemporary global challenges. Climate change, resource depletion, and social inequality have transcended regional boundaries to become shared planetary concerns. Governments, institutions, corporations, and individuals alike are reckoning with the imperative to address these challenges. In this context, finance—often viewed as a driver of economic growth—can no longer be disentangled from its broader societal and environmental impacts.

Sustainable development goals (SDGs) set forth by the United Nations chart a course toward a more equitable and environmentally conscious world. Yet, the path to realize these goals is fraught with complexity. This book steps into the multifaceted dimensions of sustainable fintech and illustrates how its principles align with the broader SDG agenda. By delving into the nuances of green finance, technological innovation, and inclusive economic systems, the book elucidates pathways that harmonize economic aspirations with ecological imperatives.

In the contemporary financial landscape, technology is a double-edged sword. While it has democratized access to financial services, its potential for misuse has also been realized through fraudulent schemes and exploitative practices. As the world becomes increasingly interconnected, the risks associated with financial misconduct multiply. This book's comprehensive analysis of financial fraud in the age of fintech contributes not only to academic discourse but also to the pragmatic pursuit of secure and transparent financial systems.

The COVID-19 pandemic has amplified the need for resilient financial ecosystems. The book's exploration of the pandemic's impact on gig workers' job insecurity and banking behaviors sheds light on the intricate relationship between external crises and financial decision-making. By contextualizing this research within the broader fintech framework, the book provides a foundation for understanding how technology can both alleviate and exacerbate the vulnerabilities exposed by such crises.

In the global arena, geopolitics and finance are intertwined in increasingly intricate ways. The examination of the Russia-Ukraine conflict in the context of green and dirty cryptocurrencies underscores the nuanced role of digital finance in shaping geopolitical dynamics. As nations grapple with the implications of digital currencies and the power they bestow, the book offers a window into the complexities of this landscape.

Furthermore, the comprehensive analysis of fintech in India holds relevance beyond national boundaries. India's journey exemplifies the dynamic interplay between fintech, policy, and financial inclusion—a model that offers valuable insights for emerging and established economies alike. As nations seek to foster financial access and innovation, the book's insights into India's experience serve as a guiding light.

At the heart of this book lies a call to action—a demand for recalibrating finance as an instrument of positive change. Through sustainable fintech, economic growth is interwoven with ecological sustainability. By showcasing the symbiosis between financial technology and sustainable practices, the book spotlights opportunities for innovation, collaboration, and reinvention.

In an era where financial systems extend their reach into every corner of the globe, the impact of this book transcends its pages. It reverberates in boardrooms, regulatory agencies, academia, and grassroots initiatives. It empowers readers to view fintech not merely as a tool for financial optimization, but as a conduit for building a more inclusive, equitable, and sustainable future.

The target audience of *"The Sustainable Fintech Revolution: Building a Greener Future for Finance"* encompasses a diverse spectrum of stakeholders whose interests converge at the crossroads of finance, technology, and sustainability. This book's multidisciplinary nature resonates with individuals and groups spanning academia, industry professionals, policymakers, entrepreneurs, students, and the environmentally conscious public. Through its comprehensive exploration of sustainable fintech, the book speaks directly to these varied groups, offering tailored insights and actionable knowledge.

At the heart of scholarly discourse, this book finds resonance among researchers, scholars, and academics from fields as varied as finance, economics, environmental studies, technology, and entrepreneurship. The nuanced exploration of topics such as sustainability disclosure, green finance, fintech innovation, and the interplay between technology and climate sustainability provides a treasure trove of primary and secondary research material. The academic community will find in-depth analyses, comprehensive bibliometric reviews, and qualitative insights that can serve as both foundations for new research and windows into emerging trends.

Within the rapidly evolving landscape of financial technology and sustainability, professionals across the finance, technology, and environmental sectors are positioned to benefit. Bankers, financial analysts, fintech entrepreneurs, technology architects, and sustainability officers will discover invaluable insights into the integration of sustainable practices within financial systems. This book illuminates the potential of fintech to drive green investments, mitigate financial fraud risks, and foster innovative solutions for a rapidly changing world.

Institutions tasked with shaping financial regulations and policies stand to gain from this book's comprehensive policy implications section. The discussion on green finance, sustainable development, and the role of fintech in economic inclusion presents policymakers with a nuanced understanding of the synergies between regulation, innovation, and sustainability. This audience can draw inspiration and guidance from the book's insights to craft policies that balance economic growth with environmental stewardship.

Startups and entrepreneurs exploring the fintech space will find this book a valuable guidepost. The discussion on sustainable social entrepreneurship, the transformative potential of digital payment systems, and the innovation-driven approach to financial inclusion offer a roadmap for those seeking to make a positive impact in the financial sector. The book's insights can help shape business strategies that resonate with contemporary sustainable aspirations.

Aspiring students and researchers in economics, finance, technology, and sustainability fields will find this book a vital resource for both academic pursuit and professional development. The accessible yet comprehensive treatment of complex topics provides a strong foundation for understanding the symbiotic relationship between finance, technology, and the environment. From undergraduate to postgraduate levels, students can draw upon this material for projects, theses, and coursework.

Global institutions such as the United Nations, World Bank, and regional development banks are invested in promoting sustainable practices worldwide. The book's alignment with the sustainable development goals and its exploration of the role of fintech in achieving these goals provide valuable perspectives for multilateral organizations working at the nexus of finance and development.

This book mainly contains fifteen chapters. The first Chapter provides a qualitative study on financial inclusion through fintech adoption, showcasing technology's transformative impact on underserved populations. The second chapter has discussed sustainability disclosure and green finance as drivers of a sustainable future by emphasizing transparency and ethical finance. The third chapter explores the growth of green investments through fintech innovations, showcasing technology's potential to align investments with environmental goals. The fourth chapter assesses financial inclusion progress via the rural banking system, shedding light on how fintech bridges the gap for marginalized communities. The fifth chapter focuses on financial fraud in the age of fintech, using bibliometric analysis to highlight emerging research agendas. In the sixth chapter, the future analysis of phygitalisation in India's financial services unveils technology's role in reshaping customer experiences. The seventh chapter highlights policy implications of green finance, advocating for balanced economic growth and environmental protection. Chapter eight discusses how the adoption of digital payment systems promotes economic sustainability by improving access and efficiency. The ninth chapter studies the effect of COVID-19 uncertainty on gig workers' job insecurity and financial behaviors, revealing insights into crisis-driven decision-making. Chapter ten narrates fintech's role in India's journey toward sustainable social entrepreneurship and achieving SDGs. In chapter eleven, the Russia-Ukraine conflict's impact on green and dirty cryptocurrencies unveils the nuanced role of digital finance in geopolitical contexts. Chapter twelve presents a systematic literature review of fintech in India, offering insights into the sector's evolution and potential. Chapter thirteenth explores financial inclusion and sustainable development of traditional practices through the 'MANCHAHA' program, spotlighting the socio-economic impact. The fourteenth chapter conducts a bibliometric analysis of a decade of sustainable fintech research, guiding future research directions. Finally, chapter fifteen explores the interconnection of fintech and climate sustainability through qualitative methodology, illuminating the path to environmentally-conscious financial decisions.

This book, through its meticulously curated chapters, embarks on a transformative journey that illuminates the uncharted territory where finance, technology, and sustainability coalesce. By converging innovative fintech solutions with the imperative of environmental stewardship, this compendium has the power to reshape the trajectory of the financial landscape. With a deepened understanding of sustainability disclosure, green investments, financial inclusion, and the challenges of fraud in the digital age, readers are empowered to navigate the complexities of this rapidly evolving realm. Through its comprehensive analysis of diverse themes and its multidisciplinary approach, the book generates a ripple effect that extends beyond its pages, cascading into boardrooms, regulatory chambers, academic institutions, and the broader public sphere. As a guiding compass for scholars, policymakers, industry leaders, and the environmentally conscious, this book propels a sustainable fintech revolution that transcends conventional boundaries, ushering in an era where finance becomes an ally in the pursuit of a greener, more equitable future.

*Kuldeep Singh*
*Faculty of Management Studies, CMS Business School, Jain University (Deemed), Bengaluru, India*

*Rebecca Abraham*
*Huizenga College of Business and Entrepreneurship, Nova Southeastern University, Fort Lauderdale, USA*

*Prasanna Kolar*
*Koneru Lakshmaiah Education Foundation, India*

# Chapter 1
# Financial Inclusion Through FinTech Adoption:
## A Qualitative Study

**Kuldeep Singh**
https://orcid.org/0000-0002-8180-4646
*Faculty of Management Studies, CMS Business School, Jain University (Deemed), Bengaluru, India*

**Khalid Hussain Alhamzi**
*Gulf College, Hafr Al-Batin, Saudi Arabia*

**G. Vinodini Devi**
https://orcid.org/0009-0006-4061-3604
*Koneru lakshmaiah Education Foundation, India*

## ABSTRACT

*The emergence of fintech has made it possible for many unbanked individuals worldwide to obtain financial services through digital means. Recently, the COVID-19 health crisis has opened up new possibilities for digital financial services to speed up financial inclusion despite social exclusion. Many national governments have promoted its usage by lowering costs and boosting the transactional limits for digital transactions. In this research, the authors attempted to construct a model for the adoption of fintech in the context of rural India. The goal of this research is to identify the policies and initiatives that best promote the growth of the fintech ecosystem. They also make an effort to pinpoint the qualities of banking systems that are more likely to support fintech in order to collaborate effectively on financial inclusion. The methodology section of this work is built on the ISM-MICMAC technique.*

DOI: 10.4018/979-8-3693-0008-4.ch001

## INTRODUCTION

Fintech is transforming how financial services are provided to low-income people and small enterprises (Demir, Pesqué-Cela, Altunbas, & Murinde, 2022; Ozili, 2018). Banks and their representatives, microfinance organisations, and informal systems have traditionally provided financial services; these sectors are often subject to be less competitive (Vo et al., 2021; Kling et al., 2020). However, they mostly rely on in-person interactions with financial service providers and cash transactions. These discussions serve as the foundation for credit monitoring and often serve as a means for individuals to acquire financial literacy (Morgan & Long, 2020; Lusardi & Mitchell, 2011). Although this situation is being changed by the introduction of fintech: with the creation of digital financial instruments accessible via computers or mobile devices, and hence, the need for face-to-face contact has significantly decreased (Haddad & Hornuf, 2019; Kurniasari et al., 2021). Basically, digital advancements and business model developments in the financial industry that are enabled by technology are included in fintech. These technologies have the potential to fundamentally alter the way that businesses today produce and distribute their goods and services, develop traditional industry structures, dissolve industry boundaries, encourage entrepreneurship, offer new financial entry points, and democratise access to financial services.

Researchers, practitioners, and policy makers all need to be aware of recent advancements in financial innovation and the advances in financial inclusion that have followed (Kurniasari et al., 2021; Krishna Priya & Anusha, 2019). Therefore, this study examines the enablers related to current financial innovations to find out how they affect various stakeholders, mainly those who were previously unbanked in terms of access to financial services. The population in developing countries who are bankable and unbanked has grown over the last ten years as a result of financial innovation in the shape of new distribution channels, products, and providers. On the other side, it may also be seen as new technology-driven companies that want to take on established financial institutions in the provision of financial services (Noreen et al., 2022; Joia & Cordeiro, 2021). In a broader sense, the term "fintech" refers to technological advancements in the financial services industry that are frequently linked to new business models, service providers, processes, and products. All of these developments have the potential to materially affect how financial services are provided, whether by market leaders or by up-and-coming players.

The remaining sections of the essay are organised as follows. The emphasis of the next part is on the historical context and the most recent wave of financial innovations that have benefited financial inclusion. The approach is covered in Section 3 together with expert mining and ISM-MICMAC. The ISM model, its results, and how they affect the economy are covered in Section 4. Theoretical and practical consequences are discussed in Section 5; conclusions are made in Section 6, along with suggestions for further research outcomes.

## LITERATURE REVIEW

Fintech is a relatively new financial sector where technology is used to improve financial functions (Gangopadhayay, 2009; Barik & Sharma, 2019). During the global financial crisis of 2008, improvements in e-finance and mobile technology for financial institutions gave rise to the fintech industry (Shihadeh & Liu, 2019; Siddiqui & Siddiqui, 2020). This movement is defined by the convergence of big data, artificial intelligence, social media, social networking, and e-finance innovation (Haddad & Hornuf, 2019; Kurniasari et al., 2021). In particular, the adoption and dissemination of financial technologies and their interactions with financial inclusion and prosperity are suggested as additional routes that may support the finance-development nexus in the large literature on innovation and technology diffusion (Krishna Priya & Anusha, 2019). Standard models often, meanwhile, assume that everyone has a bank account, omitting the coverage gap in the financial sector caused by the roughly 1.7 billion adults over the age of 15 who are not now a part of formal financial institutions (WHO, 2018) (Demir, Pesqué-Cela, Altunbas, & Murinde, 2022). More inclusive finance is a policy goal of many governments all over the globe as a way to boost savings and investment due to the productivity and equity-enhancing impacts of financial inclusion. Fintech offers a crucial transmission channel via which rising productivity and wider financial inclusion boost GDP per capita. It also creates the possibility for efficient policy tools aimed at promoting technology diffusion and the creation of fintech infrastructure and support (Demir, Pesqué-Cela, Altunbas, & Murinde, 2022; Demir, Pesqué-Cela, Altunbas, & Murinde, 2022; Chen & Yuan, 2021).

*Table 1. W-o-S and Google Scholar search analysis*

| S.No. | Keywords | Scholar-Google | W-o-S |
|---|---|---|---|
| 1 | Fintech and Financial Inclusion | 30 | 2 |
| 2 | Fintech | 8 | 3 |
| 3 | Fintech and Bank Regulations | 53 | 10 |
| 4 | Fintech Adoption and Financial Technology | 1 | 0 |
| 5 | Financial Inclusion and Fintech Strategies | 3 | 2 |
| 6 | Fintech and Access to finance | 2 | 1 |
| 7 | Digital Technology and Financial Inclusion | 1 | 0 |

## #W-o-S: WebofScience

According to the previous theories, poor individuals are unable to escape poverty because they have less access to formal financial services mainly due to flaws in the financial system, such as information asymmetries and transaction costs (Banerjee & Newman, 1993). Several cross-country studies, which generally define financial inclusion as families and businesses having access to and using formal financial services, imply that high levels of financial inclusion are beneficial. In the developing world, 80% of individuals have access to a cell phone. Mobile phones are actually more common in families than access to power or clean water (World Bank 2016; Demir, Pesqué-Cela, Altunbas, & Murinde, 2022). Although fintech developments are regarded as game changers for increasing financial inclusion, there are still several challenges to their broad adoption and usage. The technical and behavioural preconditions that affect how users behave in relation to financial technology are not completely understood in the literature currently in existence.

The authors of this study talk about how banking companies might help rural areas survive in the new tech era. According to this study, if banking companies begin to offer their financial inclusion and technical support to rural households, then these people will be able to use a variety of sources to raise money for different purposes, such as starting a new business, managing crops, farming, or engaging in other commercial activities. The framework for financial inclusion and fintech enablers, which are essential for rural India in its struggle against conventional banking and financial needs, are also provided in this paper.

*Table 2. Experts' profile*

| S.No | Domain | Profile | Experience |
|---|---|---|---|
| 1 | Rural Agricultural Cooperative Bank | Manager | 5 |
| 2 | Rural Agricultural Cooperative Bank | Senior Manager | 11 |
| 3 | Rural Agricultural Cooperative Bank | Manager | 9 |
| 4 | Banking Firm | Assistant Manager | 6 |
| 5 | Banking Firm | Senior Manager | 14 |
| 6 | Banking Firm | Regional Manager | 16 |
| 7 | Banking Firm | Senior Manager | 13 |
| 8 | Educational Institution | Professor | 18 |
| 9 | Educational Institution | Professor | 16 |
| 10 | Educational Institution | Associate Professor | 12 |
| 11 | Public Enterprise | Manager | 6 |
| 12 | Financial Institution | Policy advisor | 19 |

The study utilised the search results from Web-of-Science, and Scholar Google databases and find the previous studies by using 6 words, as indicated in Table 1, to find past work relevant to fintech and facilitators of financial inclusion systems that could aid rural families in dealing with such un banking situations.

*Table 3. List of enablers*

| Sr. No. | Enablers | References | Expert Mean Score |
|---|---|---|---|
| 1 | Financial Literacy | Lusardi & Mitchell, 2011 Morgan & Long, 2020 | 4.13 |
| h2 | Digital Financial Services | Bapat, 2022); Van & Phaladi, 2021 | 3.93 |
| 3 | Self-inclination for Fintech Adoption | Banna et al. 20212021); (Joia & Cordeiro, 2021); Demir et al. 2022 | 4.07 |
| 4 | Regulatory Frameworks | (Knaack & Gruin, 2017); (Ozili, 2021) | 4.00 |
| 5 | Networking with local Institution | (Dennissen et al., 2019); (Banna et al., 2022) | 3.93 |
| 6 | Fear of approaching formal institutions | (Banna et al., 2021); (Ozili, 2021); Shihadeh, 2019(Shihadeh, 2020) | 4.07 |
| 7 | Grievance and Complaints Mechanism | (Shah et al., 2019); (Barik & Sharma, 2019) | 4.00 |
| 8 | Government policies and strategies | (Noreen et al., 2022); (Mouna & Jarboui, 2022) | 4.00 |
| 9 | Access to deposit and credit services | Masau et al. 2018(Musau et al., 2018); (Kurniasari et al., 2021) | 4.07 |
| 10 | Effective financial inclusion delivery mechanism | (Vo et al., 2021); Mhalanga, 2020 (Mhlanga, 2020) | 4.33 |
| 11 | Penetration of Bank Branches | (Bapat, 2022); Ahmed & Mallick, 2019 (Ahamed & Mallick, 2019) | 4.13 |
| 12 | Promotion of a cashless economy | (Bayero, 2015); (Srouji, 2020) | 4.13 |

With the aid of the Boolean search approach, the search was carried out (AND, OR, NOT). This strategy was employed to collect pertinent research papers and to get rid of duplicate articles. The title has been thoroughly searched for all five keywords from 2000 to 2022. The search results made it clear that, substantial prior efforts had been made in relation to financial inclusion. It's interesting to note that a search for "fintech" turned up a significant publication that had been published within the previous ten years. This illustrates how crucial this topic is to modern research approaches. Using this method, we additionally made a filter to all research articles to identify those that addressed crucial elements that aid a banking system in addressing various financial inclusion issues. In order to determine the enablers that are essential for any financial institution's attempts to solve this issue, the researchers found thirty research papers. The study represents the researchers' initial attempt to look at hierarchical relationship between these enablers. The originality of this study lies in the prospect that, given the correct technical support, rural society could benefit from the functioning Indian banking system—a prospect that has not yet been investigated in mostly previous research articles.

## EXPERT MINING

In the current study, the enablers were chosen and the linkages between each enabler were discovered using the expert mining process. For this, the researchers made contact with academicians, social activists, bank personnel, and representatives of rural financial institutions. A total of 15 experts were chosen and engaged in discussions concerning all cited enablers in order to understand their views and obtain their insights (see Table 2). To evaluate the importance of enablers, the researchers developed questionnaires for each enabler they had found through a thorough literature review method, followed by an expert discussion.

Likert scale was used for the questionnaire, with one denoting "strongly disagree" and five denoting "strongly agree." Each scale item was created using words like "Enabler A is important to address the financial exclusion" and others of a similar nature. Although the number of experts may seem low, previous study has taken into account a similar number of experts for the same ISM-Micmac framework (Banerjee & Newman, 1993; Agrawal et al., 2017; Bux et al., 2020).

## DATA AND METHODOLOGY

Phase one comprised a thorough literature search to identify 12 enablers for this experiment. In phase two, the ISM-MICMAC methodology was employed to look at the enablers' placement in the hierarchical relationship model.

The researchers only chose as key enablers for whom the experts' mean scores for their importance in achieving financial inclusion were above 3.5. However, all 12 enablers in this study had a mean score above 3.5, therefore all were taken into account for further analysis (see Table 3).

## ISM AND SELF-STRUCTURAL-INTERACTION MATRIX

Building an SSIM matrix is the first stage in ISM-MICMAC modelling, as illustrated in Table 3, and it is primarily utilised to identify the linkages among all enablers. A binary coding structure serves as the basis of the SSIM matrix, which uses four symbols to indicate the relationships between enablers. The following four are the symbols used to determine the relationship among enablers:

V: we have to assign V if $i_{th}$ variable helps to achieve benefits for $j_{th}$ variable
A: we have to assign A if $j_{th}$ variable helps to achieve benefits for $i_{th}$ variable
X: we have to assign X if both variables ($i_{th}$ and $j_{th}$) are helping to achieve benefits for each other
O: we have assign O if there is no relationship between $i_{th}$ and $j_{th}$ variable

This study recognised 12 factors that made a hierarchical model viable. The VAXO technique encourages the development of an SSIM matrix table related to fintech and other enablers that aid in financial inclusion in the rural sector. Table 4 depicts the VAXO modelling.

*Table 4. SSIM matrix of financial inclusion enabler model*

| V | V-$_{12}$ | V-$_{11}$ | V-$_{10}$ | V-$_{9}$ | V-$_{8}$ | V-$_{7}$ | V-$_{6}$ | V-$_{5}$ | V-$_{4}$ | V-$_{3}$ | V-$_{2}$ | V-$_{1}$ |
|---|---|---|---|---|---|---|---|---|---|---|---|---|
| V-$_{1}$ | V | O | V | V | A | V | O | V | A | V | V | |
| V-$_{2}$ | V | A | V | V | A | V | O | V | A | V | | |
| V-$_{3}$ | A | O | A | A | A | O | O | A | A | | | |
| V-$_{4}$ | V | V | V | V | X | O | O | V | | | | |
| V-$_{5}$ | V | A | V | V | A | V | O | | | | | |
| V-$_{6}$ | O | O | O | O | O | V | | | | | | |
| V-$_{7}$ | V | A | A | O | A | | | | | | | |
| V-$_{8}$ | V | V | V | V | | | | | | | | |
| V-$_{9}$ | V | A | A | | | | | | | | | |
| V-$_{10}$ | V | A | | | | | | | | | | |
| V-$_{11}$ | V | | | | | | | | | | | |
| V-$_{12}$ | | | | | | | | | | | | |

The reachability matrix is constructed by transforming the symbols V, A, X, and O according to some fundamental rules shown in Table 5.

*Table 5. Rules to replace VAXO to get reachability-matrix*

| SSIM matrix | Reachability matrix | Reachability matrix |
|---|---|---|
| If the symbol is V | "i - j entry will become 1" | "j - i entry will become 0" |
| If the symbol is A | "i - j entry will become 0" | "j - i entry will become 1" |
| If the symbol is X | "i - j entry will become 1" | "j - i entry will become 1" |
| If the symbol is O | "i - j entry will become 0" | "j - i entry will become 0" |

As it was already mentioned, association might be a sign that a group of enablers are helping to achieve each other. But somewhere, transitivity can be seen as the property that if the first enabler is connected to the sixth one and the sixth enabler is connected to the ninth one, then the first symbol must be connected to the ninth enabler (see Table 7). The study is therefore producing the final reachability matrix after taking into account the transitivity issue.

*Table 6. Initial reachability matrix of Agri-food supply chain barrier model*

| V | V-1 | V-2 | V-3 | V-4 | V-5 | V-6 | V-7 | V-8 | V-9 | V-10 | V-11 | V-12 |
|---|---|---|---|---|---|---|---|---|---|---|---|---|
| **V-1** | 1 | 1 | 1 | 0 | 1 | 0 | 1 | 0 | 1 | 1 | 0 | 1 |
| **V-2** | 0 | 1 | 1 | 0 | 1 | 0 | 1 | 0 | 1 | 1 | 0 | 1 |
| **V-3** | 0 | 0 | 1 | 0 | 0 | 0 | 0 | 0 | 0 | 0 | 0 | 0 |
| **V-4** | 1 | 1 | 1 | 1 | 1 | 0 | 0 | 1 | 1 | 1 | 1 | 1 |
| **V-5** | 0 | 0 | 1 | 0 | 1 | 0 | 1 | 0 | 1 | 1 | 0 | 1 |
| **V-6** | 0 | 0 | 0 | 0 | 0 | 1 | 1 | 0 | 0 | 0 | 0 | 0 |
| **V-7** | 0 | 0 | 0 | 0 | 0 | 0 | 1 | 0 | 0 | 0 | 0 | 1 |
| **V-8** | 1 | 1 | 1 | 1 | 1 | 0 | 1 | 1 | 1 | 1 | 1 | 1 |
| **V-9** | 0 | 0 | 1 | 0 | 0 | 0 | 0 | 0 | 1 | 0 | 0 | 1 |
| **V-10** | 0 | 0 | 1 | 0 | 0 | 0 | 1 | 0 | 1 | 1 | 0 | 1 |
| **V-11** | 0 | 1 | 0 | 0 | 1 | 0 | 1 | 0 | 1 | 1 | 1 | 1 |
| **V-12** | 0 | 0 | 1 | 0 | 0 | 0 | 0 | 0 | 0 | 0 | 0 | 1 |

Six iterations have been run to evaluate each enabler's ordered level (see Table 8). In these rounds, the final reachability matrix was constructed using the reachability set (row-wise frequency of 1) and the antecedent set (column-wise frequency of 1) for each enabler.

*Table 7. Final reachability matrix with transitivity analysis*

| V | V-1 | V-2 | V-3 | V-4 | V-5 | V-6 | V-7 | V-8 | V-9 | V-10 | V-11 | V-12 | Driving Power |
|---|---|---|---|---|---|---|---|---|---|---|---|---|---|
| **V-1** | 1 | 1 | 1 | 0 | 1 | 0 | 1 | 0 | 1 | 1 | 0 | 1 | 8 |
| **V-2** | 0 | 1 | 1 | 0 | 1 | 0 | 1 | 0 | 1 | 1 | 0 | 1 | 7 |
| **V-3** | 0 | 0 | 1 | 0 | 0 | 0 | 0 | 0 | 0 | 0 | 0 | 0 | 1 |
| **V-4** | 1 | 1 | 1 | 1 | 1 | 0 | 1* | 1 | 1 | 1 | 1 | 1 | 11 |
| **V-5** | 0 | 0 | 1 | 0 | 1 | 0 | 1 | 0 | 1 | 1 | 0 | 1 | 6 |
| **V-6** | 0 | 0 | 1* | 0 | 0 | 1 | 1 | 0 | 0 | 0 | 0 | 1* | 4 |
| **V-7** | 0 | 0 | 1* | 0 | 0 | 0 | 1 | 0 | 0 | 0 | 0 | 1 | 3 |
| **V-8** | 1 | 1 | 1 | 1 | 1 | 0 | 1 | 1 | 1 | 1 | 1 | 1 | 11 |
| **V-9** | 0 | 0 | 1 | 0 | 0 | 0 | 0 | 0 | 1 | 0 | 0 | 1 | 3 |
| **V-10** | 0 | 0 | 1 | 0 | 0 | 0 | 1 | 0 | 1 | 1 | 0 | 1 | 5 |
| **V-11** | 0 | 1 | 1* | 0 | 1 | 0 | 1 | 0 | 1 | 1 | 1 | 1 | 8 |
| **V-12** | 0 | 0 | 1 | 0 | 0 | 0 | 0 | 0 | 0 | 0 | 0 | 1 | 2 |
| **Dependence Power** | 3 | 5 | 12 | 2 | 6 | 1 | 9 | 2 | 8 | 7 | 3 | 11 | **69** |

*Table 8. Iteration no. 1 to achieve the level for barriers*

| V | Reachability (Set of One) | Antecedent (Set of One) | Level |
|---|---|---|---|
| **V-1** | 1,2,3,5,7,9,10,12 | 1,4,8 | 7 |
| **V-2** | 2,3,5,7,9,10,12 | 1,2,4,8,11 | 6 |
| **V-3** | 3 | 1,2,3,4,5,6,7,8,9,10,11,12 | 1 |
| **V-4** | 1,2,3,4,5,7,8,9,10,11,12 | 4,8 | 8 |
| **V-5** | 3,5,7,9,10,12 | 1,2,4,5,8,11 | 5 |
| **V-6** | 3,6,7,12 | 6 | 4 |
| **V-7** | 3,7,12 | 1,2,4,5,6,7,8,10,11 | 3 |
| **V-8** | 1,2,3,4,5,7,8,9,10,11,12 | 4,8 | 8 |
| **V-9** | 3,9,12 | 1,2,4,5,8,9,10,11 | 3 |
| **V-10** | 3,7,9,10,12 | 1,2,4,5,8,10,11 | 4 |
| **V-11** | 2,3,5,7,9,10,11,12 | 4,8,11 | 7 |
| **V-12** | 3,12 | 1,2,4,5,6,7,8,9,10,11,12 | 2 |

Enablers are categorised at different levels as a result of the interactions between antecedents and reachability sets (see Figure 1).

## DISCUSSION

This research aimed to determine the variables that facilitate financial inclusion through fintech. The results of the study have been examined using the MICMAC technique, which categorises the enablers into four quadrants that are specifically named as autonomous, independent, dependent, and linkage criterion (see figure 2). In the first cluster that is autonomous, only one factor falls under this, which is related to the fear of approaching formal institutions having weak driving power and weak dependence. Although on RBI webpage in one report published on financial inclusion in 2008, it is mentioned that "People may have access to financial services but may not want to use them, according to frequent observations. Even if they don't use financial services, it is maintained that such voluntarily excluded individuals should be included in measures of access. Even among the 'voluntarily excluded,' however, this may actually be due to the fact that the services are too expensive, inappropriate for their needs, or because potential customers are afraid of being turned down outright.

Some of those who are "involuntarily barred" from services like loans pose a significant credit risk, making it difficult for lenders to responsibly provide for them" that shows the reasons why people may have fear of approaching formal institutions (Viswanathan, 2014). Because as per the model, fear is not related to any other factor impacting financial inclusion, the government and financial institution members should pay attention to it.

Although the factors belonging to the autonomous cluster have little impact on the outcome process, therefore they are typically excluded from the system. The second cluster is made up of elements with weak driving and strong dependence. In this study five factors, "Self-inclination for Fintech Adoption", "Grievance and Complaints Mechanism", "Access to deposit and credit services", "Effective financial inclusion delivery mechanism", and "Promotion of a cashless economy" came to the second cluster that is dependent cluster, which are having very high dependence and low driving force. In the ISM model all these enablers came at the top level, showing the importance and inclination for financial inclusion (Noreen et al., 2022; Musau et al., 2018; Ahamed & Mallick, 2019; Shihadeh, 2021). It demonstrates that government must concentrate on multiple strategies based on delivery mechanisms, grievance and complaints mechanisms, and access to deposit and credit services in order to enhance access to formal financial institutions (Musau et al., 2018). In the third cluster, that belongs to linkages elements, no enablers came to this cluster. However, the fifth enabler is part of the same driving and dependence force and has the potential to interact with other variables. In fourth cluster, that is based on independent criterion, five enablers, "Financial Literacy", "Regulatory Frameworks", "Digital Financial Services", Government policies and strategies", and "Penetration of Bank Branches" came to this cluster having a very high driving and less dependence force. All of these enablers were present at the base level of the ISM model, highlighting their significance as highly concentrable characteristics that enable a government to fulfil its goal of financial inclusion (Gangopadhayay, 2009; Kurniasari et al., 2021; Arun & Kamath, 2015; Pham & Doan, 2020).

*Figure 1. ISM model*

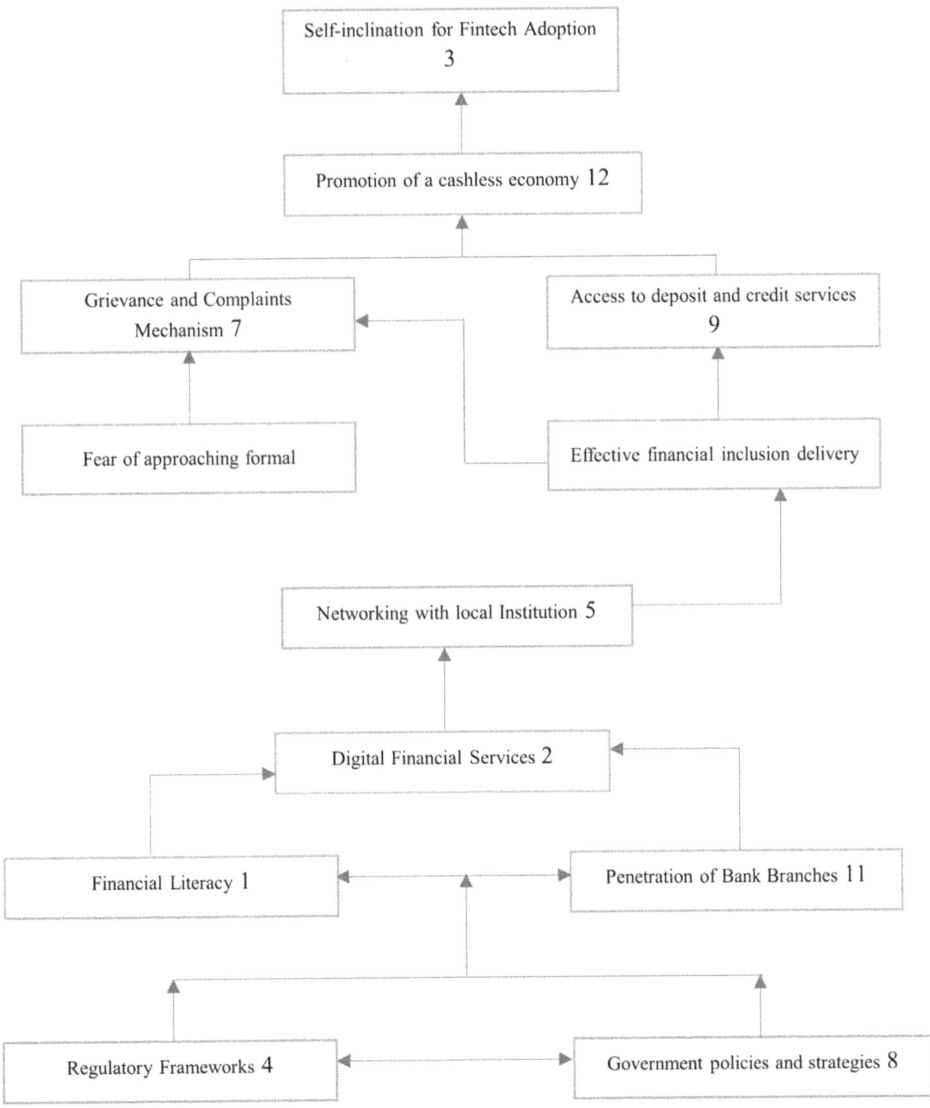

*Figure 2. MicMac model*

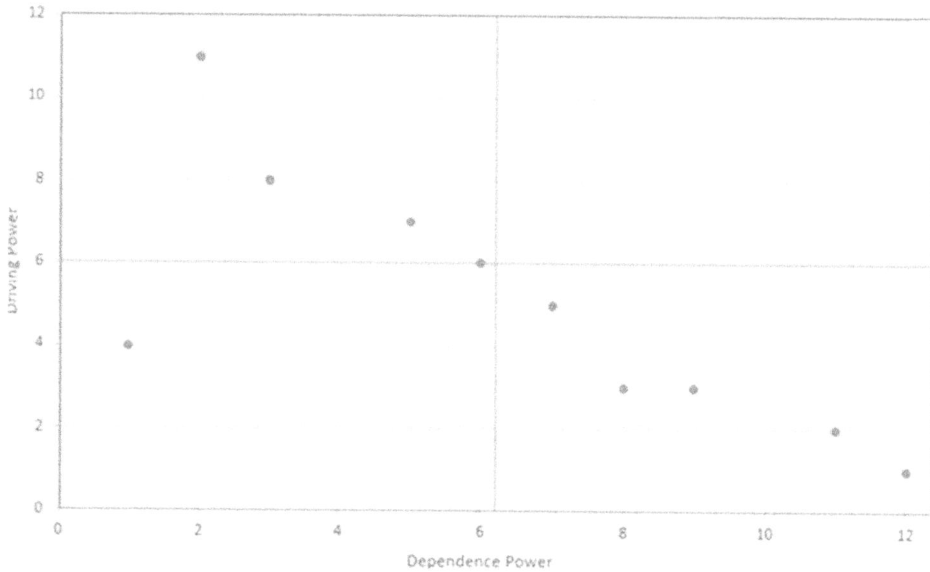


One of the key findings of the study is that fear is a significant factor that impacts financial inclusion through fintech. This finding is supported by previous literature that has identified fear as a major barrier to financial inclusion. For example, a study by Briones and Zhuang (2011) found that fear of banks and formal financial institutions was a major obstacle to financial inclusion among low-income households in the Philippines. Similarly, a study by Arora and Sood (2015) identified fear and lack of trust in formal financial institutions as major barriers to financial inclusion in rural areas of India. These findings highlight the importance of addressing fear and building trust among potential users of fintech in order to promote financial inclusion.

Another key finding of the study is the importance of government policies and regulatory frameworks in promoting fintech adoption and financial inclusion. This finding is supported by previous literature that has emphasized the critical role of government policies in promoting financial inclusion through fintech. For example, a study by Bose and Pal (2018) found that government policies such as financial literacy programs, subsidies, and incentives played a significant role in promoting the adoption of digital financial services in rural areas of India. Similarly, a study by Dehghanpour, Alipour, and Ahmadi (2020) found that regulatory frameworks and government policies were key factors influencing the adoption of fintech in Iran. These findings highlight the need for supportive government policies and regulatory frameworks to promote fintech adoption and financial inclusion.

The study also identified the importance of financial literacy as an enabler of fintech adoption and financial inclusion. This finding is supported by previous literature that has highlighted the critical role of financial literacy in promoting financial inclusion. For example, a study by Han, Kim, and Kim (2018) found that financial literacy was positively associated with financial inclusion among low-income households in South Korea. Similarly, a study by Chowa, Masa, and Ansong (2017) found that financial literacy was a significant predictor of financial inclusion among rural households in Ghana. These findings suggest that efforts to promote financial literacy may be an effective strategy for promoting fintech adoption and financial inclusion.

Finally, the study identified the importance of access to deposit and credit services as an enabler of fintech adoption and financial inclusion. This finding is supported by previous literature that has emphasized the critical role of access to financial services in promoting financial inclusion. For example, a study by Fanta and Yigermal (2018) found that access to financial services was a key determinant of financial inclusion among rural households in Ethiopia. Similarly, a study by Malaquias and Mendes (2019) found that access to credit was a significant predictor of financial inclusion among low-income households in Mozambique. These findings highlight the importance of efforts to expand access to deposit and credit services in promoting fintech adoption and financial inclusion.

## IMPLICATIONS

The findings of this study have significant practical implications for policymakers, financial institutions, and fintech companies in India and other developing countries. First, the government must take steps to address the fear of approaching formal financial institutions among the unbanked population. Providing financial education, building trust through community outreach programs, and simplifying financial products and services can help overcome this fear. Second, the government must focus on developing multiple strategies that provide access to formal financial institutions and promote a cashless economy to enhance the adoption of fintech. Third, financial literacy and regulatory frameworks must be established to create an environment conducive to the growth of fintech. Fourth, the government must provide policies and strategies that enable the penetration of bank branches and increase the use of digital financial services.

Fintech companies and financial institutions can also play a crucial role in promoting financial inclusion through fintech. Fintech companies can develop products and services that are tailored to the needs of the unbanked population, such as microfinance and mobile banking. Financial institutions can partner with fintech companies to develop and deliver these products and services. They can also collaborate with the government to develop policies and strategies that promote financial inclusion through fintech.

The study on the adoption of fintech in rural India has several theoretical implications that are relevant to the existing literature on financial inclusion, fintech, and the Indian economy. Firstly, the study highlights the importance of financial literacy in promoting the adoption of fintech among rural populations. Financial literacy has been identified as a key factor in promoting financial inclusion and enhancing individuals' capacity to access financial services (Aker & Mbiti, 2010). The study underscores the need for governments and financial institutions to invest in financial literacy programs that are tailored to the needs of rural populations, and that help to raise awareness about the benefits of fintech adoption.

Secondly, the study highlights the significance of regulatory frameworks in shaping the growth and adoption of fintech in rural India. Regulatory frameworks play a critical role in shaping the development of fintech ecosystems, and in ensuring that fintech solutions are safe, secure, and accessible to all (Shetty & Kulal, 2017). The study underscores the need for governments and regulators to design regulatory frameworks that are tailored to the needs of rural populations, and that help to promote the growth of the fintech ecosystem.

Thirdly, the study highlights the importance of digital financial services in promoting financial inclusion among rural populations (Demirgüç-Kunt & Klapper, 2012). Digital financial services have emerged as a key enabler of financial inclusion, and have the potential to reach populations that are otherwise excluded from traditional financial services (Ali et al., 2020). The study underscores the need for governments and financial institutions to invest in the development of digital financial services that are accessible, affordable, and tailored to the needs of rural populations.

Finally, the study highlights the role of government policies and strategies in promoting financial inclusion and the adoption of fintech. The study underscores the need for governments to design policies and strategies that are focused on enhancing access to financial services, and that help to promote the growth of the fintech ecosystem. The study also highlights the need for governments to collaborate with financial institutions, regulators, and other stakeholders in order to achieve these goals.

## CONCLUSION

The study's outcomes offer important recommendations for scholars, institution leaders, and policy makers. A hierarchical structure of self-inclination variables toward financial inclusion through fintech is provided in this study. It has been established that a number of factors influence one's propensity for financial inclusion because no such linking factors were discovered in the MICMAC analysis. Fintech-constrained allied elements are derived at the top level of the current ISM model, grievance redressal mechanisms, fear-related enablers are in the middle, regulatory and policy-related enablers are at the bottom of the model. Factors at the bottom level that are connected to policy areas have a strong driving force. This demonstrates that support from institutions and the government has a significant impact on individuals' propensity for financial inclusion. For the development of the ISM model, twelve financial inclusion-related factors have been identified in this study. Future research may potentially take into account more variables. Only expert mining was employed in the study to validate the criteria. Future researchers can therefore use structural equation modelling (SEM) in these experiments for further statistical validation since no statistical validation has been addressed.

## REFERENCES

Agrawal, A. K., Kumar, D., & Rahman, Z. (2017). An ISM approach for modelling the enablers of sustainability in market-oriented firms. *International Journal of Business Excellence*, *12*(1), 23. doi:10.1504/IJBEX.2017.083331

Ahamed, M. M., & Mallick, S. K. (2019). Is financial inclusion good for bank stability? International evidence. *Journal of Economic Behavior & Organization*, *157*, 403–427. doi:10.1016/j.jebo.2017.07.027

Aker, J. C., & Mbiti, I. M. (2010). Mobile phones and economic development in Africa. *The Journal of Economic Perspectives*, *24*(3), 207–232. doi:10.1257/jep.24.3.207

Ali, O., Ally, M., & Dwivedi, Y. (2020). The state of play of blockchain technology in the financial services sector: A systematic literature review. *International Journal of Information Management*, *54*, 102199. doi:10.1016/j.ijinfomgt.2020.102199

Arun, T., & Kamath, R. (2015). Financial inclusion: Policies and practices. *IIMB Management Review*, *27*(4), 267–287. doi:10.1016/j.iimb.2015.09.004

Banerjee, A., & Newman, A. F. (1993). Occupational choice and the process of development. *Journal of Political Economy*, *101*(2), 274–298. doi:10.1086/261876

Banna, H., Kabir Hassan, M., & Rashid, M. (2021). Fintech-based financial inclusion and bank risk-taking: Evidence from OIC countries. *Journal of International Financial Markets, Institutions and Money*, *75*, 101447. doi:10.1016/j.intfin.2021.101447

Banna, H., Mia, M. A., Nourani, M., & Yarovaya, L. (2022). Fintech-based Financial Inclusion and Risk-taking of Microfinance Institutions (MFIs): Evidence from Sub-Saharan Africa. *Finance Research Letters*, *45*, 102149. doi:10.1016/j.frl.2021.102149

Bapat, D. (2022). Exploring the relationship between lifestyle, digital financial element and digital financial services experience. *International Journal of Bank Marketing*, *40*(2), 297–320. doi:10.1108/IJBM-12-2020-0575

Barik, R., & Sharma, P. (2019). Analyzing the progress and prospects of financial inclusion in India. *Journal of Public Affairs*, *19*(4). doi:10.1002/pa.1948

Bayero, M. A. (2015). Effects of Cashless Economy Policy on Financial Inclusion in Nigeria: An Exploratory Study. *Procedia: Social and Behavioral Sciences*, *172*, 49–56. doi:10.1016/j.sbspro.2015.01.334

Bux, H., Zhang, Z., & Ahmad, N. (2020). Promoting sustainability through corporate social responsibility implementation in the manufacturing industry: An empirical analysis of barriers using the ISM-MICMAC approach. *Corporate Social Responsibility and Environmental Management*, *27*(4), 1729–1748. doi:10.1002/csr.1920

Chen, W., & Yuan, X. (2021). Financial inclusion in China: An overview. *Frontiers of Business Research in China*, *15*(1), 4. doi:10.118611782-021-00098-6

Demir, A., Pesqué-Cela, V., Altunbas, Y., & Murinde, V. (2022). Fintech, financial inclusion and income inequality: A quantile regression approach. *European Journal of Finance*, *28*(1), 86–107. doi:10.1080/1351847X.2020.1772335

Demir, A., Pesqué-Cela, V., Altunbas, Y., & Murinde, V. (2022, January). Fintech, financial inclusion and income inequality: A quantile regression approach. *European Journal of Finance*, *28*(1), 86–107. doi:10.1080/1351847X.2020.1772335

Demirgüç-Kunt, A., & Klapper, L. F. (2012). Financial inclusion in Africa: An overview. *World Bank Policy Research Working Paper*, 6088.

Dennissen, M., Benschop, Y., & van den Brink, M. (2019). Diversity Networks: Networking for Equality? *British Journal of Management*, *30*(4), 966–980. doi:10.1111/1467-8551.12321

Gangopadhayay, S. (2009). How Can Technology Facilitate Financial Inclusion in India? A Discussion Paper. *Review of Market Integration*, *1*(2). doi:10.1177/097492920900100206

Haddad, C., & Hornuf, L. (2019). The emergence of the global fintech market: Economic and technological determinants. *Small Business Economics*, *53*(1), 81–105. doi:10.100711187-018-9991-x

Joia, L. A., & Cordeiro, J. P. V. (2021). Unlocking the potential of fintechs for financial inclusion: A delphi-based approach. *Sustainability (Switzerland)*, *13*(21), 11675. doi:10.3390u132111675

Kling, G., Pesqué-Cela, V., Tian, L., & Luo, D. (2020). A theory of financial inclusion and income inequality. *European Journal of Finance*, doi:10.1080/1351847X.2020.1792960

Knaack P., & Gruin, J. (2017). *From Shadow Banking to Digital Financial Inclusion: Regulatory Framework Constestation between China and the FSB*. Academic Press.

Krishna Priya, P., & Anusha, K. (2019). Fintech issues and challenges in India. *International Journal of Recent Technology and Engineering*, *8*(3). doi:10.35940/ijrte.C4087.098319

Kurniasari, F., Gunardi, A., Putri, F. P., & Firmansyah, A. (2021). The role of financial technology to increase financial inclusion in Indonesia. *International Journal of Data and Network Science*, *5*(3), 391–400. doi:10.5267/j.ijdns.2021.5.004

Lusardi, A., & Mitchell, O. S. (2011). Financial literacy around the world: An overview. *Journal of Pension Economics and Finance*, *10*(4), 497–508. doi:10.1017/S147474721100448 PMID:28553190

Mhlanga, D. (2020). Industry 4.0 in finance: The impact of artificial intelligence (ai) on digital financial inclusion. *International Journal of Financial Studies*, *8*(3), 45. doi:10.3390/ijfs8030045

Morgan, P. J., & Long, T. Q. (2020). Financial literacy, financial inclusion, and savings behavior in Laos. *Journal of Asian Economics*, *68*, 101197. doi:10.1016/j.asieco.2020.101197

Mouna, A., & Jarboui, A. (2022). Understanding the link between government cashless policy, digital financial services and socio-demographic characteristics in the MENA countries. *The International Journal of Sociology and Social Policy*, *42*(5–6), 416–433. doi:10.1108/IJSSP-12-2020-0544

Musau, S., Muathe, S., & Mwangi, L. (2018). Financial inclusion, bank competitiveness and credit risk of commercial banks in Kenya. *International Journal of Financial Research*, *9*(1), 203. doi:10.5430/ijfr.v9n1p203

Noreen, M., Mia, M. S., Ghazali, Z., & Ahmed, F. (2022). Role of Government Policies to Fintech Adoption and Financial Inclusion: A Study in Pakistan. *Universal Journal of Accounting and Finance*, *10*(1), 37–46. doi:10.13189/ujaf.2022.100105

Ozili, P. K. (2018). Impact of digital finance on financial inclusion and stability. *Borsa Istanbul Review*, *18*(4), 329–340. doi:10.1016/j.bir.2017.12.003

Ozili, P. K. (2021). Has financial inclusion made the financial sector riskier? *Journal of Financial Regulation and Compliance*, *29*(3), 237–255. doi:10.1108/JFRC-08-2020-0074

Pham, M. H., & Doan, T. P. L. (2020). The impact of financial inclusion on financial stability in Asian countries. *Journal of Asian Finance, Economics and Business*, *7*(6), 47–59. doi:10.13106/jafeb.2020.vol7.no6.047

Shah, K., Mare, S., & Anderson, R. (2019). Understanding mobile money grievances from tweets. In *ACM International Conference Proceeding Series*. ACM. doi:10.1145/3287098.3287123

Shanker, S., & Barve, A. (2021). Analysing sustainable concerns in diamond supply chain: A fuzzy ISM-MICMAC and DEMATEL approach. *International Journal of Sustainable Engineering*, *14*(5), 1269–1285. doi:10.1080/19397038.2020.1862351

Shetty, K. U., & Kulal, A. (2017). Financial Inclusion through Mobile Banking in India. *SSRN 3768366.*

Shihadeh, F. (2020). The influence of financial inclusion on banks' performance and risk: New evidence from MENAP. *Banks and Bank Systems*, *15*(1), 59–71. doi:10.21511/bbs.15(1).2020.07

Shihadeh, F. (2021). Financial inclusion and banks' performance: Evidence from palestine. *Investment Management and Financial Innovations*, *18*(1), 126–138. doi:10.21511/imfi.18(1).2021.11

Shihadeh F., & Liu, B. (2019). Does financial inclusion influence the banks risk and performance? Evidence from global prospects. *Academy of Accounting and Financial Studies Journal, 23*(3).

Siddiqui, T. A., & Siddiqui, K. I. (2020). FinTech in India: An analysis on impact of telecommunication on financial inclusion. *Strategic Change*, *29*(3), 321–330. doi:10.1002/jsc.2331

Srouji, J. (2020). Digital Payments, the Cashless Economy, and Financial Inclusion in the United Arab Emirates: Why Is Everyone Still Transacting in Cash? *Journal of Risk and Financial Management*, *13*(11), 260. doi:10.3390/jrfm13110260 van Niekerk, M. G., & Phaladi, N. H. (2021). Digital financial services: Prospects and challenges. *Potchefstroom Electronic Law Journal*, *24*, 1–25. doi:10.17159/1727-3781/2021/v24i0a10744

Varma, A. (2019). Fintech Adoption Choices of Small Businesses: A Technology Organization Environment (TOE) Framework study. *Accounting and Finance Research*, *8*(2), 86. doi:10.5430/afr.v8n2p86

Viswanathan, R. (2014). RBI report on financial inclusion: A review. *Economic and Political Weekly*, *49*(9).

Vo, D. H., Nguyen, N. T., & Thi-Hong Van, L. (2021). Financial inclusion and stability in the Asian region using bank-level data. *Borsa Istanbul Review*, *21*(1), 36–43. doi:10.1016/j.bir.2020.06.003

# Chapter 2
# Sustainability Disclosure and Green Finance:
## Driving the Transition Towards a Sustainable Future

**Pooja Mishra**
*GLA University, India*

**Kishore Kumar**
*CHRIST University (Deemed), NCR Campus, India*

**Akanksha Singh Fouzdar**
*GLA University, India*

**Ankita Singh**
*Agra University, India*

## ABSTRACT

*In recent times, policymakers and scholars have directed their attention toward the notion of sustainability and green finance, coinciding with the growing global emphasis on environmental protection, climate change mitigation, and sustainable development. The integration of sustainability and green finance practices has emerged as a crucial strategy to address climate change, advance sustainable development goals issues, and build a resilient global economy in the face of pressing environmental challenges. The adoption of green finance and sustainability practices is no longer limited to developed economies. Many developing and under-developed countries are also taking a proactive approach to develop and implement a roadmap and framework for incorporating sustainability. In this chapter, the authors explore the notion of green finance, its crucial role in advancing sustainability, and the substantial consequences it can bring about for diverse businesses and stakeholders.*

DOI: 10.4018/979-8-3693-0008-4.ch002

## INTRODUCTION

The rising global focus on addressing climate change has led to heightened attention toward green finance (GF) in recent literature (Khan et al., 2022; Tariq & Hassan, 2023). The endorsement of the Paris Climate Agreement and the adoption of Sustainable Development Goals by international organizations and national governments respectively demonstrate a stronger dedication to environmental sustainability. Within this framework, it is essential not to disregard the efforts made by the Asian Development Bank (ADB), which actively participates in diverse initiatives aimed at fostering environmentally sustainable development throughout Asia and the Pacific area. One such initiative is climate change funding, a collaborative effort between the Asian Development Bank (ADB) and the Global Environment Facility (GEF). In this context, climate mitigation funding plays a vital role in the framework as it encompasses investment processes aimed at distributing funds to foster environmental sustainability in the region. According to UNEP, for a seamless transition toward sustainability, it is imperative to augment investments in renewable energy sources. In research focused on policymaking, the concept of sustainability has gained significant prominence as a guiding principle for desired outcomes. The Brundtland Report published in 1987 played a pivotal role in shaping this understanding and served as a primary source of inspiration (Commission on Environment, 1987). Consequently, green finance has emerged, emphasizing efficient allocation of resources, environmental sustainability, and prudent investments aimed at mitigating climate and investment risks. Green finance expands upon the concept of sustainability by incorporating environmental, social, and governance (ESG) concerns and risks (Naeem et al., 2022). Its primary objective is to promote investments in sustainable initiatives, thereby furthering the goals of sustainability (Green and Sustainable Finance, 2022).

However, in contrast to conventional financial practices, green finance prioritizes environmental sustainability by placing a strong emphasis on resource efficiency (Kumar et al., 2021). (Zhang et al., 2019) mentioned, the concept of GF is still evolving, leading to a lack of consensus among scholars regarding its precise definition. Further (Klein et al., 2019) mentioned, that green finance refers to the financial support provided for investments that yield positive environmental outcomes. The G20 defines GF as encompassing various financial instruments like green bonds, along with agreements, mechanisms, and environmentally friendly operational practices. It also involves disclosing these agreements to reduce carbon emissions, foster the development of climate-resilient infrastructure, and promote environmentally sustainable practices (Liu & Wu, 2023). However, different opinions exist among researchers regarding the potential outcomes of pursuing the green path for recovery. While some argue that embracing the green path aligns with the goals of sustainability, resilience, and immediate action, emphasizing the financial services sector's ability to drive the necessary change, others contend that following the green path may result in a recovery that is less sustainable, resilient, and urgent (Crona et al., 2021; Navickas et al., 2021). Therefore, a thorough examination of the literature is crucial to attain a well-rounded perspective and grasp the true economic implications of green finance. By undertaking a thorough review, one can achieve an equitable understanding of GF and its tangible influence on the organizations and economy. The existing literature broadly concurs that GF is allied with environmentally favorable results, including the reduction of carbon emissions and increased energy savings. Multiple studies and scholarly sources support the notion that financial investments directed toward green initiatives yield positive environmental outcomes (Crona et al., 2021; Klein et al., 2019; Liu & Wu, 2023; Zhang et al., 2019). In this chapter, we begin by presenting contextual information on sustainability and green financial instruments, including green bonds and green debt, while also exploring the motivations behind GF. Furthermore, we delve into an examination of the existing literature concerning sustainability disclosure, summarizing its trajectory, catalysts, and significance.

## CORPORATE SUSTAINABILITY

In recent years, the concept of "corporate sustainability disclosure" (CSD) has gained significant traction. It is increasingly recognized that businesses rarely operate in isolation from their surrounding environment. As organizations continuously engage with their environment, they exert influence on both society and the natural environment (Sreepriya et al., 2023). Consequently, growing apprehensions regarding the potentially significant environmental and social impacts of corporate operations have prompted worldwide demands for businesses to implement sustainable practices (Adams & Frost, 2008; Kumar et al., 2023). In this era of readily available information and evolving stakeholder expectations, businesses are embracing sustainability disclosure practices as a response to the mounting awareness and expanding knowledge among stakeholders (Zieba & Johansson, 2022). Lately, there has been considerable growth in the implementation of sustainability disclosure practices by businesses (Kumar & Prakash, 2020). Several factors have played a role in the significant acceptance and implementation of sustainability reporting in numerous countries. These factors include heightened awareness, the introduction of new laws and regulations, the pursuit of legitimacy, and a deeper comprehension of how sustainability disclosures impact corporate value and financial performance.

Further, the implementation of Global Reporting Initiative (GRI) also provides a global standard for sustainability reporting and facilitates the comparison of data across different organizations.

Moreover, multiple theories can be employed to comprehend the influence of sustainability disclosure on corporate value. One such theory is the institutional theory, which elucidates why companies engage in corporate social responsibility (CSR) and sustainability reporting initiatives. According to this theory, businesses participate in sustainability initiatives to conform to cultural and institutional standards, values, and beliefs. Similarly, the legitimacy theory argues that businesses must act in a manner that aligns with societal expectations due to a social contract between society and enterprises. Therefore, businesses report on their sustainability efforts to maintain the implied social compact and gain legitimacy for their survival. In line with the resource dependence theory, businesses strive to secure limited resources and rely on stakeholders for essential resources. Sustainability reporting is seen as a strategic tool to reduce dependency on resources, and stakeholders can impose conditions in this context. According to stakeholder theory, enterprises that engage with society at large through transparency in social, environmental, and governance aspects have the potential to generate long-term benefits, profitability, and value (Behl et al., 2022). Stakeholder theory provides implicit insight into how sustainability reporting serves as an indicator of business value. Hence, the resource dependence and stakeholder relationship theories contribute to understanding whether sustainability reporting can enhance business value. Further, the adoption of sustainability theories can aid in overcoming potential barriers from stakeholders when seeking funding to enhance business value.

## Sustainability Disclosure: An Indian Perspective

India has placed a strong focus on enhancing transparency and promoting social and environmental accountability in sustainability reporting especially in the past few decades. Reforms in the Indian business sector are driven by the recognition of structural changes and how enterprises utilize disclosure practices (Kumar et al., 2022). In the past, India has implemented various policies given in Figure 1 aimed at improving sustainability disclosure. One notable development was the implementation of the National Voluntary Guidelines (NVG) on social, environmental, and economic business responsibility, which were introduced by the Ministry of Corporate Affairs in 2011. Following this, SEBI made it mandatory to publish a Business Responsibility Report (BRR) for the top 100 listed companies in India based on market capitalization. The information disclosure of nine principles under NVGs was mandated by the government. Companies were also required to submit a corporate responsibility report as part of their mandated CSR (Corporate Social

Responsibility) spending, aiming to enhance the quality of disclosures. Additionally, the increased incorporation of GRI (Global Reporting Initiative) reporting standards in the Indian context in 2017 led to improved practices in sustainability reporting (Kumar & Prakash, 2019). This BRR disclosure rule was further extended for the top 500 listed companies in India in 2015 and for the top 100 companies in the year 2019. Further, SEBI (Securities and Exchange Board of India) introduced a new set of disclosure guidelines for sustainability in 2020. In a circular, SEBI outlined the framework for the business responsibility and sustainability report known as the Business Responsibility and Sustainability Report (BRSR), applicable to the top 1,000 companies based on market capitalization (Kumar et al., 2021). Mishra and Sant (2023) described BRSR as the most comprehensive framework for sustainability information disclosure at par with the other global standards of sustainability disclosure like the Global Reporting Initiative (GRI), Climate Disclosure Standard Board (CDSB), Sustainability Accounting Standards Board (SASB), etc. This represents another significant milestone in India's efforts to enhance sustainability disclosure requirements. These guidelines aims to standardize the disclosure of corporate sustainability parameters, enabling investors to make more informed investment decisions by accessing comparable and relevant information about corporate sustainability disclosure (CSD). Several empirical studies have highlighted that these reforms have significantly improved the corporate sustainability scenario in India. The following figure shows the evolution of sustainability disclosure-related reforms in India.

*Figure 1. Policies implemented to strengthen sustainability in India*

## Sustainability Disclosure and Firm Performance

Numerous factors have played a role in the current surge of global interest in sustainability. These encompass the European Union's dedication to transitioning towards renewable energy sources, a heightened recognition of climate-related risks, a worldwide emphasis on the relationship between finance and sustainability, and the introduction of regulations aimed at enforcing specific obligations for disclosing sustainability information (Adams & Frost, 2008; Kumar et al., 2021; Sreepriya et al., 2023). As a result, sustainability has gained prominence at the international level and is now recognized as a crucial factor for the long-term success of businesses. Moreover, businesses are recognizing the growing importance of integrating sustainability into their decision-making processes to foster value creation based on principles such as global responsibility, fairness, transparency, inclusiveness, and active stakeholder engagement. The initial findings regarding the impact of sustainability on business value have yielded conflicting results (Ameer & Othman, 2012). Some studies found a positive relationship, while some studies have identified a negative correlation between business social performance and financial performance, some findings suggest no significant influence on stock market performance attributable to sustainability reports (Ameer & Othman, 2012; Kumar et al., 2021; Sreepriya et al., 2023).

## GREEN FINANCE

### Green Finance Instrument

In response to the challenges posed by climate change, resource scarcity, and environmental pollution, the United Nations introduced the concept of "green" in the early 1980s. In this context, there have been calls from academics for financial institutions to take responsibility by making intentional investments to establish green finance within society. These investments are regarded as a means to incentivize businesses to adopt environmentally sustainable practices and attain sustainable outcomes over the long term (Lin et al., 2022). The roots of green finance can be traced back to the early 1970s, a time when the field was in its nascent stage and only a limited number of research articles were available for consultation (Fedorova, 2020). The academic discourse on green finance didn't attract substantial notice and momentum until the early 1990s. As the world grapples with sustainability challenges such as global warming and the exhaustion of natural resources, there's a growing acknowledgment of the need to infuse sustainable approaches into nearly every aspect of human existence (Kumar & Prakash, 2019; Riva et al., 2022). The current corpus of literature has thoroughly explored and detailed a wide variety of green financial tools (Fedorova, 2020; Klein et al., 2019; Liu & Wu, 2023; Naeem et al., 2022). Green financial instruments comprise a variety of financing methods, encompassing private loans, public bonds (such as corporate, municipal, and government bonds), private equity, publicly traded equity, investment funds, and other financial instruments. The primary objective of these mechanisms is to provide funding for projects that are environmentally and climate-conscious, including endeavors like renewable energy initiatives, recycling schemes, and the development of eco-friendly infrastructure. The primary goal of green financial tools is to support the transition to a carbon-neutral economy and contribute to activities focused on reducing the impacts of climate change. When it comes to eco-friendly financial offerings, it's evident that green bank loans and green bonds stand out as the most prevalent and influential options. These two instruments hold significant importance in the domain of sustainability (Gilchrist et al., 2021). Buchner et al. (2021) reported that the main origin of green finance in 2021 was derived from green debt through loans and bonds, constituting 61% of the overall total. Equity investment comprised 33% of the raised funds, while government and institutional grants contributed to 6% of the entire green finance landscape (Buchner et al., 2021). Additional widely recognized green financial tools encompass green derivatives (Little et al., 2015), green insurance (Mills, 2012), carbon tax (O'Mahony & O'Mahony, 2020), and carbon investing and pricing instruments (Hafner et al., 2020).

## Green Bonds

The inception of green bonds in 2007 was motivated by a group of Swedish pension funds aiming to contribute to projects targeting global warming but facing uncertainty regarding the means to raise funds for such initiatives (Yeow & Ng, 2021). They resorted to the World Bank, which came up with a brand-new financing strategy that had an adverse effect on the environment, leading to the issuance of the first green bond ever. According to a survey done by Statista since 2014, there has been a continuous upward trajectory in the global issuance of green bonds, with a consistent year-on-year increase. As depicted in Figure 2fig, the value of green bonds has experienced a significant surge in recent years. In 2014, green bonds with a total worth of approximately 37 billion dollars were issued. Subsequently, this figure reached a peak of around 582 billion dollars in 2021 (Statista, 2022). The global green bond market is estimated to be 90 trillion US dollars with which climate-aligned bonds account for 694 including Billion US dollars.

The expansion of the green bond market has been significantly driven by the introduction of corporate green bonds, issued by private companies instead of national banks. The market witnessed a substantial growth spurt just one year after the private sector's entry in 2013, with the market value nearly tripling (Tolliver et al., 2020; Yeow & Ng, 2021).

*Figure 2. The value of green bonds issued worldwide (2014-2022)*
*Source: Statista*

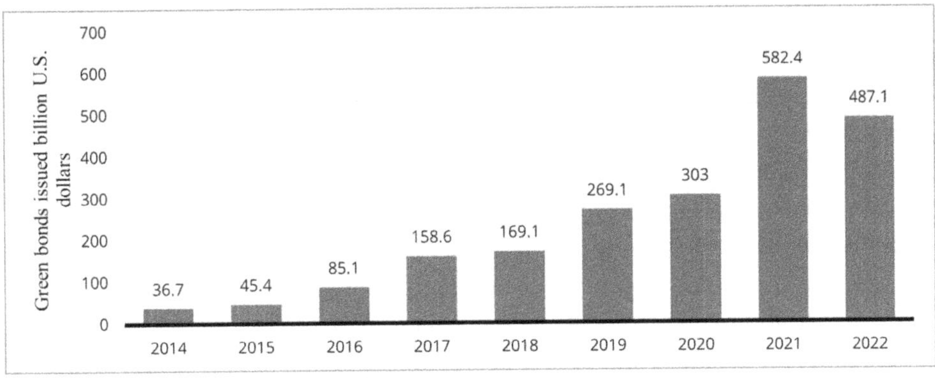


## Motivations for Adopting Green Finance

The increasing investor awareness and concern regarding climate-related issues have paralleled the development and adoption of green financial instruments. This expansion has been further facilitated by the implementation of global and regional environmental policies, resulting in a substantial growth of green finance practices. Following the signing of the Paris Climate Agreement in 2015, there has been a noticeable escalation in the expectations placed on governments, financial institutions, and businesses to prioritize environmental protection and address climate change concerns. (Tolliver et al., 2020) mentioned, the agreement has heightened the pressure for these entities to take decisive actions toward achieving sustainability and reducing greenhouse gas emissions. International and regional organizations, such as the United Nations, World Bank, International Monetary Fund (IMF), European Union, and G20, are exerting increasing pressure on their member countries and trading partners to embrace GF principles within their financial systems. These influential organizations are advocating for the integration of sustainability considerations, urging policymakers and financial institutions to align their strategies and practices with green finance principles (Bhandary et al., 2021). In response to these pressures, governments, financial institutions, and corporations are embracing environmental-focused reforms on a global scale. Consequently, after synthesizing the available literature (Bhandary et al., 2021; Hafner et al., 2020; Liu & Wu, 2023; Tolliver et al., 2020), we contend that two main drivers prompt firms to adopt green practices. Firstly, non-compliance with environmental policies exposes firms to direct financial penalties. Secondly, there is a potential loss of social capital and reputation, along with a surge in actual or perceived investment risk, for firms that fail to prioritize sustainability measures.

## Economic Effects of Green Finance

According to the Financial Action Facility of the United Nations Environment Programme, green finance is not merely an investment in environmentally-related sectors, but rather an investment in the environment itself. This perspective emerged at the turn of the twenty-first century, coinciding with the introduction and widespread promotion of the Equator Principles, which emphasize the importance of environmental considerations in financial decision-making (Contreras et al., 2019), underlined the necessity of adopting international frameworks and rules relating to sustainability, such as the Equator Principles, to support long-term sustainable development (Kumar & Prakash, 2020). According to scholars (Contreras et al., 2019; Kumar & Prakash, 2020), the prevailing view suggests that green finance has a positive economic impact by attracting external funding for green projects. (Kumar & Prakash, 2020) conclude that financial institutions play a crucial role in promoting green industries. Hence, it is imperative to gradually phase out high-pollution and high-energy consumption projects, while actively promoting environmentally friendly and ecological initiatives to establish novel mechanisms for economic development (Volz, 2018). Further, the Principle of Responsible Investment (PRI), which is strongly endorsed by the United Nations, stands as a prominent proponent of responsible investing. The PRI encompasses six guidelines for ethical investment and integrates the Environmental, Social, and Governance (ESG) framework into investment practices. The overarching objective of the PRI is to foster the development of a sustainable global financial system. Furthermore, there is a growing emphasis on the issuance of green financing products in emerging nations, alongside developed countries. In the period from 2012 to 2022 (Figure 3), China emerged as the leading emerging market issuer, having issued approximately 221,267 billion dollars worth of green bonds. India, Chile, Brazil, and Poland also ranked among the largest issuers in this category. These trends indicate a collective shift towards a sustainable future.

## Linkage Between Green Finance Disclosure and Firm Performance of the Organization

Irrespective of the approach taken to implement green finance, the issuer or borrower of these green instruments commits to utilizing the funds acquired specifically for "green projects."

Consequently, the efficacy of these instruments relies on the confidence of market participants in the proper allocation of funds for their intended purpose, as well as the actual sustainability performance of the projects being supported. Taking green bonds as an illustration, the key differentiating factor between a green bond and a

*Figure 3. Cumulative value of green bond issuance in emerging markets from 2012 to 2021, by country (in million U.S. dollars)*
*Source: Statista*

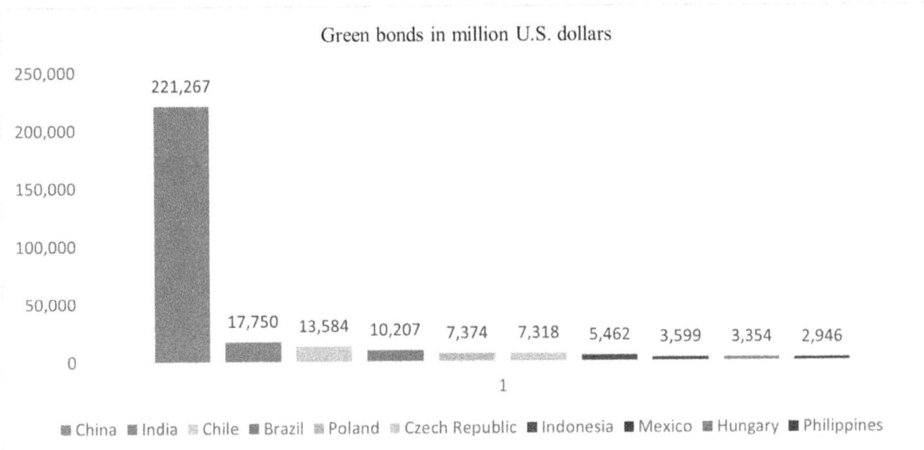


conventional bond is that the issuer explicitly declares the former as a green bond. Obtaining this designation ensures that the proceeds from the bond issuance will exclusively fund low-carbon and climate-resilient investment projects. As a matter of course, participants in the green finance market seek clear guidelines and standards to define the criteria for projects that qualify for the "green" label. Additionally, they require guidelines and frameworks to regulate the disclosure of how bond proceeds are utilized and the environmental, social, and governance (ESG) performance of the invested projects. These measures aim to ensure transparency and accountability in the green finance sector.

As investors' expectations regarding corporate sustainability continue to evolve, numerous businesses have embraced the "green" movement by issuing green bonds and aligning themselves with environmentally responsible practices. The actual value offered by green bonds has received comparatively less attention, primarily due to their status as a relatively recent addition to the realm of green financing mechanisms (Yeow & Ng, 2021). The primary objective of green bonds is to generate funds specifically for the financing of environmentally friendly initiatives and the development of green technologies. Furthermore, businesses that embrace environmentally friendly practices by issuing green bonds also benefit financially. Green bonds encourage companies to adopt greener methods across all aspects of their operations, leading to three key outcomes: (1) notable reductions in energy expenses, (2) enhanced efficiency, and (3) increased eligibility for government tax incentives (Ameer & Othman, 2012; Henisz et al., 2014; Schneider, 2011). Long-term cost reductions and tax benefits directly influence profitability, while enhanced efficiency ensures optimal output with minimal input. As a result, the adoption of green practices through the issuance of green bonds indirectly impacts corporate financial performance by incentivizing businesses to embrace sustainability, ultimately leading to increased profitability and higher financial valuation (Tan et al., 2022).

## NEXUS BETWEEN SUSTAINABILITY AND GREEN FINANCE

The interconnection between sustainability disclosure and green finance serves as a crucial connection that significantly contributes to fostering favorable transformations (Liu & Wu, 2023). Sustainability disclosure encompasses the transparent communication by corporations of their environmental, social, and governance (ESG) achievements to various stakeholders, such as investors, regulatory entities, and the broader public (Schumacher, 2022). This disclosure not only fosters accountability but also provides critical information for decision-making, enabling stakeholders to gauge a company's commitment to responsible business practices. Conversely, green finance relates to financial structures aimed at supporting ecologically sustainable ventures, encompassing actions that address climate change, curtail resource utilization, and advocate environmentally conscious approaches (Gilchrist et al., 2021; Tariq & Hassan, 2023). The intersection of sustainability disclosure and green finance is realized through various pathways. Primarily, sustainability disclosure offers vital insights to investors, aiding them in identifying enterprises in harmony with ESG principles (Behl et al., 2022; Schumacher, 2022). Consequently, this action stimulates investments that contribute to the advancement of environmentally friendly ventures. Secondly, the transparent presentation of sustainability information elevates a company's reliability, thereby diminishing potential risks for investors and lenders involved in supporting green projects. Thirdly, the practice of sustainability disclosure motivates companies to embrace and maintain conscientious conduct, ultimately bolstering their qualification for green funding. Fundamentally, the harmonious interaction between sustainability disclosure and green finance establishes a cyclical process encompassing accountability, investments, and favorable environmental outcomes. This underscores their mutual reliance on nurturing a future characterized by sustainability and resilience (Ameer & Othman, 2012; Kumar & Prakash, 2019; Zieba & Johansson, 2022).

The integration of sustainability and green finance assumes paramount importance in the context of addressing climate change and realizing sustainable development goals (Buchner et al., 2021; Lin et al., 2022). As climate change continues to escalate, posing unprecedented challenges to global ecosystems and economies, the need for concerted efforts to mitigate its impacts has become imperative (Bhandary et al.,

2021; Little et al., 2015). The convergence of sustainability principles with financial mechanisms, evident in the concept of green finance, arises as a potent approach to direct resources toward endeavors that emphasize environmental conservation, carbon mitigation, and sustainable methodologies (Naeem et al., 2022; Tariq & Hassan, 2023). By incorporating sustainability factors into financial choices, organizations can steer capital towards ventures that promote renewable energy, efficient resource utilization, and the restoration of ecosystems. This symbiotic relationship between sustainability and green finance not only advances the pursuit of climate resilience but also synergizes with the overarching Sustainable Development Goals (SDGs) (Contreras et al., 2019; Kumar & Prakash, 2020). Through targeted investment in sectors such as clean energy, sustainable infrastructure, and responsible consumption, the integration of sustainability and green finance serves as a substance for achieving several SDGs, including affordable clean energy, climate action, and responsible consumption and production. In essence, this fusion serves as a pivotal element that drives worldwide endeavors to counteract climate change, all the while cultivating a path of sustainable development that aligns environmental guardianship with economic advancement and societal welfare.

## CHALLENGES IN GREEN FINANCE AND SUSTAINABILITY

The primary concerns surrounding sustainability reporting revolve around achieving uniformity, comparability, and reliability. These challenges arise from the absence of a universally accepted set of standards that can serve as a consistent framework for reporting, as well as the relatively slow adoption of third-party assurance for such reporting. (Kumar et al., 2021) conducted an assessment of corporate sustainability reports of Indian companies to evaluate their reporting quality concerning corporate environmental performance. The findings indicate that the methodologies employed in these reports lack clarity and consistency. This suggests that conducting research based on cross-sectional data drawn from corporate sustainability reports may pose risks due to the challenges of comparability. Moreover, the lack of credible and comparable sustainability disclosure poses challenges to the effectiveness of green financial instruments, particularly due to the potential for opportunistic use of funds, known as greenwashing (Schumacher, 2022). Greenwashing refers to the practice of marketing products, services, and financial instruments as "green," "sustainable," "carbon neutral," or "net zero," even when they do not meet essential environmental, climate, or sustainability standards in ss

## CONCLUSION

This chapter examines the governance aspect that currently prevails in the GF market, along with the increasing recognition of green bonds as a viable vehicle for green financing.

This chapter further investigates green financial instruments, analyzes disclosure standards related to green finance, and explores the impact of GF on business performance and overall economic growth. We begin by providing an overview of the development of sustainability, sustainability disclosure, and several green financial initiatives. The literature highlights two primary initiatives for businesses to adopt green practices: firstly, the enforcement of environmental regulations imposes financial penalties on companies that violate these laws; secondly, businesses face the risk of losing social capital and damaging their reputation as the perception of investment risk increases. Further, as the prominence of green finance and public awareness regarding the environment continues to increase, the need for environmental disclosure is also escalating. Through our findings, it becomes evident that most studies agree on the positive correlation between a company's sustainability practices and its financial performance, while also revealing a negative association with its cost of capital. Moreover, green financial tools play a crucial role in facilitating businesses' access to funding and fostering innovation for environmental endeavors. In response, equity investors have taken steps to mitigate environmental risks in their portfolios by incorporating green companies, while corporate managers have also recognized the significance of climate-related risks when making strategic decisions at the firm level.

Various international bodies, regulators, financial institutions, and regional associations have developed their approach and framework for green finance and incorporating sustainability. The diversity in approach across these frameworks and approaches is a key bottleneck in developing the 'de facto' approach. It is imperative to establish a well-defined framework of guidelines for policymakers to adhere to when implementing sustainable practices related to GF. Because to the extent of our knowledge, there hasn't been a standardized set of GF policies that can be universally applied to all major nations, whether developed or developing. The lack of consensus on a clear definition of what constitutes 'greenness' makes it challenging to gather comprehensive data on GF (Cui et al., 2018). Moreover, it is imperative to establish a well-defined framework of guidelines for policymakers to adhere to when implementing practices related to green finance.

## REFERENCES

Adams, C. A., & Frost, G. R. (2008). Integrating sustainability reporting into management practices. *Accounting Forum*, *32*(4), 288–302. doi:10.1016/j.accfor.2008.05.002

Ameer, R., & Othman, R. (2012). Sustainability practices and corporate financial performance: A study based on the top global corporations. *Journal of Business Ethics*, *108*(1), 61–79. doi:10.100710551-011-1063-y

Behl, A., Kumari, P. S. R., Makhija, H., & Sharma, D. (2022). Exploring the relationship of ESG score and firm value using cross-lagged panel analyses: Case of the Indian energy sector. *Annals of Operations Research*, *313*(1), 231–256. doi:10.100710479-021-04189-8

Bhandary, R. R., Gallagher, K. S., & Zhang, F. (2021). Climate finance policy in practice: A review of the evidence. *Climate Policy*, *21*(4), 529–545. doi:10.1080/14693062.2020.1871313

Buchner, B., Naran, B., Fernandes, P., Padmanabhi, R., Rosane, P., Solomon, M., Stout, S., Strinati, C., Tolentino, R., Wakaba, G., Zhu, Y., Meattle, C., & Guzmán, S. (2021). *Global Landscape of Climate Finance 2021*. Climate Policy Initiative.

Contreras, G., Bos, J. W. B., & Kleimeier, S. (2019). Self-regulation in sustainable finance: The adoption of the Equator Principles. *World Development*, *122*, 306–324. doi:10.1016/j.worlddev.2019.05.030

Crona, B., Folke, C., & Galaz, V. (2021). The Anthropocene reality of financial risk. *One Earth*, *4*(5), 618–628. doi:10.1016/j.oneear.2021.04.016

Cui, Y., Geobey, S., Weber, O., & Lin, H. (2018). The Impact of Green Lending on Credit Risk in China. *Sustainability, 10*(6). doi:10.3390/SU10062008

Fedorova, E. P. (2020). Role of the State in the Resolution of Green Finance Development Issues. *Finansovyj Žhurnal — Financial Journal, 12*(4), 37–51. doi:10.31107/2075-1990-2020-4-37-51

Gilchrist, D., Yu, J., & Zhong, R. (2021). The Limits of Green Finance: A Survey of Literature in the Context of Green Bonds and Green Loans. *Sustainability, 13*(2), 478. doi:10.3390/SU13020478

Hafner, S., Jones, A., Anger-Kraavi, A., & Pohl, J. (2020). Closing the green finance gap – A systems perspective. *Environmental Innovation and Societal Transitions*, *34*, 26–60. doi:10.1016/j.eist.2019.11.007

Henisz, W. J., Dorobantu, S., & Nartey, L. J. (2014). Spinning gold: The financial returns to stakeholder engagement. *Strategic Management Journal, 35*(12), 1727–1748. doi:10.1002mj.2180

Khan, M. A., Riaz, H., Ahmed, M., & Saeed, A. (2022). Does green finance really deliver what is expected? An empirical perspective. *Borsa Istanbul Review, 22*(3), 586–593. doi:10.1016/j.bir.2021.07.006

Klein, A., Widge, V., Bergedieck, L., & Maheshwari, A. (2019, November 1). *Green Finance : A Bottom-up Approach to Track Existing Flows (Vol. 2) : Full Report.* World Bank. https://documents.worldbank.org/en/publication/documents-reports/documentdetail/788041573021878350/full-report

Kumar, K., Kumari, R., Poonia, A., & Kumar, R. (2021). Factors influencing corporate sustainability disclosure practices: Empirical evidence from Indian National Stock Exchange. *Journal of Financial Reporting and Accounting, 21*(2), 300–321. doi:10.1108/JFRA-01-2021-0023

Kumar, K., & Prakash, A. (2019). Examination of sustainability reporting practices in Indian banking sector. *Asian Journal of Sustainability and Social Responsibility 2019, 4*(1), 1–16. doi:10.1186/S41180-018-0022-2

Kumar, K., & Prakash, A. (2020). Managing sustainability in banking: Extent of sustainable banking adaptations of banking sector in India. *Environment, Development and Sustainability, 22*(6), 5199–5217. doi:10.100710668-019-00421-5

Lin, Z., Liao, X., & Jia, H. (2022). Could green finance facilitate low-carbon transformation of power generation? Some evidence from China. *International Journal of Climate Change Strategies and Management, 15*(2), 141–158. doi:10.1108/IJCCSM-03-2022-0039

Little, L. R., Hobday, A. J., Parslow, J., Davies, C. R., Grafton, R. Q., Little, L. R., Hobday, A. J., Parslow, J., Davies, C. R., & Grafton, R. Q. (2015). Funding climate adaptation strategies with climate derivatives. *CliRM, 8*, 9–15. doi:10.1016/j.crm.2015.02.002

Liu, C., & Wu, S. S. (2023). Green finance, sustainability disclosure and economic implications. *Fulbright Review of Economics and Policy, 3*(1), 1–24. doi:10.1108/FREP-03-2022-0021

Mills, E. (2012). The greening of insurance. *Science, 338*(6113), 1424–1425. doi:10.1126cience.1229351 PMID:23239720

Mishra, PSant, T. G. (2023). Examine the level of environmental, social and governance disclosure in sustainability report – a study of the Indian banking sector. International Journal of Innovation Science, (ahead-of-print). https://doi.org/10.1108/IJIS-08-2022-0136

Naeem, M. A., Karim, S., Rabbani, M. R., Bashar, A., & Kumar, S. (2022). Current state and future directions of green and sustainable finance: a bibliometric analysis. *Qualitative Research in Financial Markets*. doi:10.1108/QRFM-10-2021-0174/FULL/PDF

Navickas, V., Kontautiene, R., Stravinskiene, J., Bilan, Y., Navickas, V., Kontautiene, R., Stravinskiene, J., & Bilan, Y. (2021). Paradigm shift in the concept of corporate social responsibility: COVID-19. *Green, 3*(2), 138–152. doi:10.3934/GF.2021008

O'Mahony, T., & O'Mahony, T. (2020). State of the art in carbon taxes: a review of the global conclusions. *Green Finance, 2*(4), 409–423. doi:10.3934/GF.2020022

Riva, F., Magrizos, S., Rubel, M. R. B., & Rizomyliotis, I. (2022). Green consumerism, green perceived value, and restaurant revisit intention: Millennials' sustainable consumption with moderating effect of green perceived quality. *Business Strategy and the Environment, 31*(7), 2807–2819. doi:10.1002/bse.3048

Schneider, T. E. (2011). Is environmental performance a determinant of bond pricing? Evidence from the U.S. pulp and paper and chemical industries. *Contemporary Accounting Research, 28*(5), 1537–1561. doi:10.1111/j.1911-3846.2010.01064.x

Schumacher, K. (2022). *Environmental, Social, and Governance (ESG) Factors and Green Productivity: The Impacts of Greenwashing and Competence Greenwashing on Sustainable Finance and ESG Investing*. SSRN Electronic Journal. doi:10.2139/SSRN.4303609

Sreepriya, J., Suprabha, K. R., & Prasad, K. (2023). Does GRI compliance moderate the impact of sustainability disclosure on firm value? *Society and Business Review, 18*(1), 152–174. doi:10.1108/SBR-06-2022-0172

Statista. (2022). *Green bonds worldwide*. Statista. https://www-statista-com.eu1.proxy.openathens.net/study/108882/green-bonds-worldwide/

Tan, X., Dong, H., Liu, Y., Su, X., & Li, Z. (2022). Green bonds and corporate performance: A potential way to achieve green recovery. *Renewable Energy, 200*, 59–68. doi:10.1016/j.renene.2022.09.109

Tariq, A., & Hassan, A. (2023). Role of green finance, environmental regulations, and economic development in the transition towards a sustainable environment. *Journal of Cleaner Production*, *413*, 137425. doi:10.1016/j.jclepro.2023.137425

Tolliver, C., Keeley, A. R., & Managi, S. (2020). Drivers of green bond market growth: The importance of Nationally Determined Contributions to the Paris Agreement and implications for sustainability. *Journal of Cleaner Production*, *244*, 118643. doi:10.1016/j.jclepro.2019.118643

Volz, U. (2018). *Fostering Green Finance for Sustainable Development in Asia.* (ADBI Working Paper Series). Asian Development Bank Institute. www.adbi.org

World Commission on Environment. (1987). *Report of the World Commission on Environment and Development: Our Common Future Towards Sustainable Development 2. Part II. Common Challenges Population and Human Resources 4*. WCE.

Yeow, K. E., & Ng, S. H. (2021). The impact of green bonds on corporate environmental and financial performance. *Managerial Finance*, *47*(10), 1486–1510. doi:10.1108/MF-09-2020-0481

Zhang, D., Zhang, Z., & Managi, S. (2019). A bibliometric analysis on green finance: Current status, development, and future directions. *Finance Research Letters*, *29*, 425–430. doi:10.1016/j.frl.2019.02.003

Zieba, M., & Johansson, E. (2022). Sustainability reporting in the airline industry: Current literature and future research avenues. *Transportation Research Part D, Transport and Environment*, *102*, 103133. doi:10.1016/j.trd.2021.103133

# Chapter 3
# Growth of Green Investments Through FinTech Innovations

**R. Vinaya**
https://orcid.org/0009-0002-4526-8054
*School of Commerce and Management Studies, Dayananda Sagar University, India*

**Nisha Goyal**
https://orcid.org/0000-0002-7897-0635
*School of Commerce and Management Studies, Dayananda Sagar University, India*

## ABSTRACT

*In order to maintain a development that is harmonious with the environment while simultaneously maximizing profits, adopting green, sustainable, and responsible investments has become a goal for every company. This has resulted in numerous new trends in technology, financial management, and how businesses want to position themselves in the market through green investments. Fintech, with its digital transformation, ease of doing business, transparency, and expanded reach, plays an important role in this scenario. Fintech is developed as an alternative to traditional financial institutions and plays a critical role in long-term green investment. The aim of this study is to investigate the significance of green investment and its growth with Fintech innovations. The findings show that Fintech innovation increases the sustainability of financial businesses by encouraging green investment as well as green economic growth by raising the level of green finance development, which is crucial for most nations.*

DOI: 10.4018/979-8-3693-0008-4.ch003

## 1. INTRODUCTION

A serious ecological degradation occurring worldwide and the brisk economic growth occurring around it made "Green Growth" a high priority economic agenda in most of the nations around as they continue to expand their economy rapidly (He et al., 2020). "Green Growth" acts as a part of economic development that is environmentally sustainable, which ensures economic development alongside the environmental protection. In recent times due to unpredictable and complicated global economic scenario, there is a hindrance to this objective because of environmental deterioration, ecological devastation and compromised sustainable growth (Ghosh, 2022). In 1987, the United Nations Brundtland Commission put forth the concept of sustainable development, which was defined as "meeting the requirements of the present without jeopardising future generation's needs" (UN, 1987). Resulting over 140 nations have included sustainable growth targets in their agendas (UN, 2022).

Innovating environmental friendly products, managing trade-offs between optimal product & service performance, and improving social & environmental benefits are all made possible by sustainability. Saunila et al. (2018) state that increasing green innovation and attracting green investment should be industries' top priorities. Green innovation spans a broader variety of activities, such as the development of new notions, goods & services, processes or organizational structures to address environmental concerns. The term "Green Investment" is quite wide. It might be viewed as a standalone notion, a component of a bigger investing subject, or even closely related with other investment strategies that provide the financial resources required for green innovations.

In order for the country to move towards an economy which is financially sustainable along with exceptional economic growth, financial technology development is expected to be crucial. It gives retail investors ways to look into and invest in goods that support the twin goals of high-quality economic growth and sustainability of the environment (Nenavath and Mishra, 2023). The financial crisis that hit the world in 2008 made an emerging pattern in the financial industry focusing on the business model associated with digitalisation and FinTech (Pawłowska et al., 2022). Fintech is a multidisciplinary phrase that refers to the integration of two well-developed fields, namely financial technology and financial markets (Gupta et al., 2023). The Financial Stability Board (FSB) defines FinTech as "financial innovation brought about by technology that creates new business models, applications, processes or products that have a significant impact on financial markets, financial institutions or the way financial services are enhanced" (FSB, 2016). In accordance with the UN SDGs, the World Bank along with other global development institutions is promoting FinTech as an important facilitator for inclusive of finance along with alleviating poverty

(UNSGSA, 2018). By offering social bonds and green bonds, financial market has created a way for financing environmentally and socially conscious projects which are least preferred by conventional businesses. The major setback for this green initiative is the lack of ability to attract investors. FinTech helps to overcome this limitation by offering a platform for green investors and also by bringing household savings to the economy. FinTech with artificial intelligence has developed into a significant field of study, due to AI's increasing multidisciplinary interactions and integration with machine learning, data science, finance and economics. From very recent years, the next generation artificial intelligence has undergone a rapid development with its applicability to a wide range of applications in finance (Cao, 2022). With the popularity of tools like ChatGPT, Google Bard, etc., which is growing in demand, provided a wider scope for green investment through FinTech.

Previous researches have studied how innovation in finance influences sustainable development. However a limited research explained about how innovation in financial technology affects green investment development. FinTech innovation immediately results in the advancement of products & services in the financial sector that are environment friendly, which promotes the expansion of green investment. This is better understood theoretically and empirically via study. The present study contributes to the existing literature on green investments and to pool of knowledge available. Initially it contributes by highlighting the factors that influence green investment and examining the way green investment affects thorough high-quality economic growth. Secondly, it contributes in understand FinTech and its innovations to the growth of green investment. Further, it explores how green investments & FinTech innovation are related and provides a substantial & particular contribution to field of sustainable finance by explaining the promotion and acceptance of green investments in developing market economies using Fintech technologies.

## 2. THE METHODOLOGY

A thorough literature review is intended to synthesise present research articles, conference proceedings, working papers, or other available material in a certain topic. To understand the current state of green investment and the role that Fintech plays in boosting green investment, conceptual study method is applied here. In order for that, the study undertakes systematic literature review for reviewing of Green Investment and Fintech, by summarizing and synthesizing the findings of existing literature from various peer reviewed journal articles/ academic journals. This study draws on a number of articles, primarily from EBSCO, to conduct the research. At first, keywords were used in conjunction with Boolean operators to search within "TX All Text" using search phrases (1) Green Investment AND (2) Fintech or Financial technology or Fin Tech. The search results are further scrutinized using "search limiters" functionality of EBSCO.

We used a two-phase search procedure to find and select the appropriate papers (Figure 1). Search procedure is divided into two phase: (1) The initial search and (2) The selection & acceptance of appropriate articles. Below is a chronological explanation of this.

## Phase One: The Initial Article Search

The preliminary search entails using a suitable search engine to locate all journal papers on Fintech innovations and green investment. The EBSCO search tool was considered suitable because: (1) it automatically create citations using services through searches from library (Laing and James, 2023); (2) EBSCO is a leading provider of online research services to colleges, offering access to more than 400 databases and more than three billion records. (Collins, 2015).

The database was searched using advanced search modes. The search terms used are 'Green investment' and 'Fintech' or 'Financial technology' or 'Fin Tech'. The initial query resulted in 773 papers consisting of News, Academic journals, Magazines and trade publications. Further search limiters were added such as, the articles for the study was selected with the time frame 2008-23; the articles source type was restricted to academic journals; articles were limited to peer reviewed; The articles authored in any of the languages other English were also discarded. The results were cut down to 88 journal articles after applying search limiters.

## Phase Two: Article Selection and Acceptance

The content of the of 88 journal articles involved the screening of abstract and research objectives, further which reduced to 51 journal articles, which later involved screening of methodology, hypothesis, theoretical frameworks, findings and relevance to study. Even though 88 journal article had the term Green investment and Fintech but didn't address the objective of the study which involves Fintech innovations and its contribution in growth of green investment.

*Figure 1. Research methodology process*

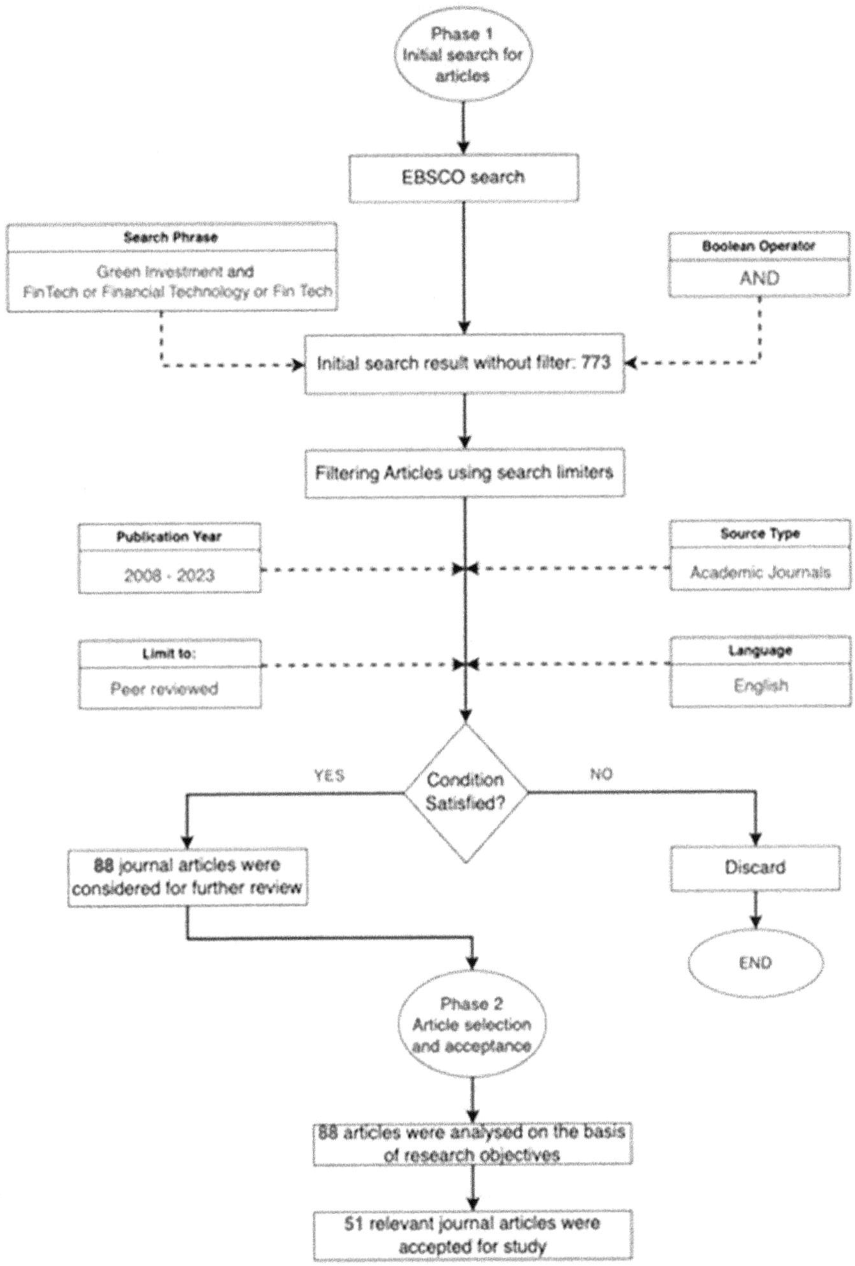

## 3. THEORETICAL BACKGROUND

### 3.1 Drivers of Green Investments

Due to climate change, global warming, and growing pollution, people are more aware of the need to preserve the environment, live in peace with it, and save the planet. Hence, more and more demands are generating for environmental friendly products & services and there is a scope for lot of innovations in this area. This consumer behavior change is one the key drivers of Green Investment. Coming to industries, Customers carefully regard and take into account corporate social responsibility (CSR) while choosing any product or service. (Wang et al., 2022). Hence, Environmental sustainability is becoming more important as the general public and investors are becoming more aware about the adverse consequences of changes in the climate. (MacAskill et al., 2021). Companies using environmental friendly resources and skills to meet consumer demands outperform their competitors in terms of overall performance and also have positive impact on society (Tian et al., 2023).

Government policies and regulations play a crucial role in green growth and investment. Green investment has become an economic policy's top concern, which creates need for new policies and plans. Sustainable Development Goals (SDG) of United Nations, which is slated for completion by 2030, has evolved into a crucial tool for advancing national policies all around the world. For developing countries, "United Nations Framework Convention on Climate Change" (UNFCCC) introduced "Green Climate Fund" (GCF) to implement sustainable finance. These funds are allocated to reduce emission of greenhouse gases and for contribution as green finance (Zheng et al., 2021). Some of the Asian counties have also created an environment for private sector to actively participate in sustainable development (Muganyi et al., 2021). With the aim of achieving a climate-neutral economy, decarbonizing the economy by 2050, switching to renewable energies, and promoting the circular economy, the European Union (EU) has adopted the EU Green Deal (Macchiavello and Siri, 2022). Additionally, both favorable and detrimental media attention might push highly polluting companies to satisfy the environmental needs of their stakeholders and so increase their innovative environmentally friendly technological skills (He et al., 2022). Green innovation plays a vital role in developing of environmentally safe products & processes by utilizing materials and skills which reduce emissions of hazardous substance which are harmful to environment, which is only possible through active participation of government and public in green investment. The firms are more likely to invest in green innovations only when it gives importance to sustainability in the economy, institutions, and society (Saunila et al., 2018).

Technology improvements, economies of scale, strong legislative support, and positive public perception have all contributed to the enormous growth of green investment in recent years (Luc and Benedict, 2013). According to (Zhao et al., 2021), Innovative renewable energy technologies are being developed in large part due to national energy regulations like Feed-In Tariffs (FIT). Hence, by offering a minimum fair price for products which are on-par with the market, it supports the growth of renewable energy resources. (Chitimiea et al., 2021) classifies green investment drivers into two factors: External drivers and internal drivers. External drivers include change in climate, behaviors of stakeholders & consumer, Target Market, Regulation & Legislation, and Incentives & Public financing. Internal drivers include Culture of organization, Preference of an investor, Efficiency gains, Reputation and financial performance.

## 3.2 Green Investments and Its Impact on Economy

The concept of Sustainable Development or Green Investment or Green Growth is not new. The idea of Green Growth was first manifested in "United Nations Economic and Social Commission for Asia and Pacific" (UNESCAP) in 2005 with an aim to bring in a model for sustainable development with less carbon emission concentrating mainly in developing countries of Asia (Zhou et al., 2022). There was a persistent misconception that sustainable development would hinder the economic growth of industrialized nations, even though it was already on the agenda of these nations. Countries gradually came to understand that it is actually the other way around over time. Investment towards green growth will help to boost the economy having a positive influence on environment and its development. It is a long-term objective to strike a balance between environmental risks and economic expansion rather than a short-term objective (Zhou et al., 2022). According to Internal Finance Corporation (IFC), green finance is an investment strategy that safeguards environment, ensures social justice, and promotes a country's economic prosperity (Zheng et al., 2021).

Innovations often arise when there is a need or a pressure. With institutional and economic pressures, green innovation can be driven at a rapid pace with social sustainability leading to economic development (Saunila et al., 2018). Green economic growth requires a variety of factors to be taken into account, which includes innovations in technology, economic variables, consumption of energy, upgrading of industries, and other factors affecting economic development (Zhang, 2023). Energy is the required input element in economic activities (Liu, 2022). Hence, any investment on energy sector will be having a greater impact on economic development. Similarly, agriculture plays a immeasurable role in an any economic development for which sustainable agriculture development is necessary which can be driven by green investment. In order to control agricultural sustainability, the European Union offers tools through its Common Agricultural Policy (CAP), which also estimates the sustainability elements (Environmental, Social and Economic) in European countries (Gernego et al., 2022). The economic component entails the development of financial benefits for sustainable entities, the social component supports local communities by providing infrastructure and bettering living conditions, one of the key focuses of Common Agricultural Policy (CAP) is environmental conservation, which is included in the environmental component (Gernego et al., 2022).

Recently, the mutual fund firms have begun to offer Green Mutual Funds, giving investors a platform to invest in green businesses. These are the most recent kinds of funding in the sector, and they haven't yet gained the necessary momentum. Green and alternate energy mutual funds are excellent ways to generate income along with benefiting the environment (Cavaliere et al., 2022). Zhou et al. (2022) discuss that a nation's contribution to green growth and lowering carbon emissions is highlighted by the Green Growth Index for that nation. The index would be built using a variety of variables from the fields of production, consumption, and the environment.

## 3.3 Fintech Innovations and its Impact on Green Investments

Various financial technologies applied to automate processes including typical labour-intensive non-routine, intellectual decisions, and more in the financial services industry are referred to as "Fintech". A few Fintech applications include payment systems, contract verification, trading, managing risks, quantitative handling of assets, financing, mobile banking, retention of customers, and investment banking (Das, 2019). Fintech benefits consumers, managers and companies to effectively control their financial processes and operations by applying technology which uses software and algorithms (Farahani et al., 2022).

The performance of enterprise with high pollutants can be regulated to minimize ecological issues by adoption of Fintech. Also Green growth and ecological sustainability can be boosted by introducing green loans and social bonds as part of green financing project. It also improves cash flow by enabling investors to invest in environmentally friendly products and process innovations, which raises the country's environmental performance (Tian et al., 2023). Fintech development such as switching to renewable energy sources for its operations can lowers $CO_2$ emissions, which in turn helps to achieve the United Nations SDG (Sustainable Development Goal) goals to achieve 45% fewer $CO_2$ emissions by 2030 from 2010 levels and to reach net zero emissions by 2050 (2015 Paris Agreement). Fintech may also be used to improve monitoring and management of the attainment and advancement of sustainable development goals.

For green economic development, the role of Green Finance and Fintech is very crucial (Zhang, 2023). By digitizing processes, enabling fewer paper work, paper bills, and needless bank visits for every transaction, Fintech promotes sustainability. Generally, investors are more susceptible towards the impact they create in society. If an investment results in a larger social and ecological impact, then they are willing to compromise on the return on investment. This is convincing evidence that given a chance, investors opt for projects which creates impact and it's time to make good use of it by promoting green projects. Green investments are also driven by return expectation of the investors in addition to environmental impact (Siemroth and Hornuf, 2023). Along with Fintech, Artificial intelligence (AI) has got potential to make an important contribution in achieving sustainable growth (Farahani et al., 2022).

## 4. FINTECH INNOVATIONS

A financial innovation is just like any other innovations in any other sector, i.e. a development of new product or service or a completely new process. Innovations in financial sector have been in place even before Fintech entered the market. E.g. ATM revolutionized financial innovation which simplifies customer life. Similarly online banking which offers convenient banking experiences for its customer at fingertips impacted positively on nature by reducing lot of paperwork and saving trees. Fintech leads to highest proficiency with least or minimum human involvement in its processes. Fintech innovations drastically change financial sector by replacing traditional financial services with convenient and cost-effective alternatives (Rabbani, 2022). Customer-centric services, payment settlement, and financial inclusion can be enhanced by Fintech (Jarvis and Han, 2021). Fintech is advancing rapidly in the fields of Crowdfundings, Peer to Peer lending, digital currency, mobile banking, Electronic wallet/Digital wallet, crypto currencies, Robo-advisors in portfolio diverseness, Insur-Tech, Reg-Tech, etc.

### 4.1 Crowdfunding

Sustainable entrepreneurship is growing and is responding to environment, social, and economic threats. But, it remains as a problem when seeking finance from conventional capital suppliers. Crowdfunding is providing an avenue for bridging any financing gaps (Bento et al., 2019). Crowdfunding offers alternative financing for individuals and small enterprises, pooling contributions for various projects from large number of individuals (Luo et al., 2022). It has the potential to provide funds for many causes, ranging from commercial enterprises to social movements (Gosain and Agrawal, 2021). Jarvis and Han (2021) classify crowd funding based on reward, donation, equity, and debt, which aims to democratize capital access and expand funders. It is attracting investors due to its unique characteristics where investors can select how their capital is being used (Siemroth and Hornuf, 2023). Entrepreneurs use voluntary disclosure of data techniques in their crowdsourcing campaign to advertise their goods to prospective sponsors and buyers (Rossolini et al., 2021). For sustainability projects, crowdfunding is a useful technique for raising money. After a campaign using crowdfunding, sustainability initiatives are 70% more likely to thrive (Bento et al., 2019).

## 4.2 P2P Lending (Peer to Peer)

P2P lending involves e-auctions in which individuals can lend money without bank or traditional financial institution intermediation (Liu et al., 2019). P2P platforms offer cost reduction for borrowers and investment opportunities, potentially leading to economic development in a country (Purkayastha and Tuzlukaya, 2020). Unsecured lending through P2P facilitators provides investors a long-term profitable consumer lending market (Namvar, 2014). Hence, the P2P lending platform enables investors to shift towards more sustainable future which in turn provides opportunities to new entrepreneurs to come up with green projects for sustainable development of an economy.

## 4.3 Digital Currency or Virtual Currency or Crypto Currency

Digital money is a decentralised payment system that operates on a well-defined network. It uses telecommunication network to transmit value among its users, along with it other networks can also be used such as Bitcoin, Ethereum, Ripple, EOS, Litecoin etc. (Khetwani and Jain, 2022). There are two tradable crypto currencies: coins and tokens. Coins have their own blockchains, whereas tokens are issued on some underlying platform, usually one that enables smart contracts (Hu et al., 2019). Block chain technologies or virtual currencies uses huge amount of energy for its processes, which are hazardous in nature. The carbon consumption can be reduced with use of alternate energy sources such as bio-fuel. To meet this goal, there is a need of green investments, where investors are willing to invest in carbon free energy production (Wang et al., 2023).

## 4.4 Mobile Banking

A mobile banking is an electronic method which has revolutionised financial transactions by employing authentication mechanisms that are customer friendly and secure (Jun et al., 2018). Mobile banking eases payments & money transfers and plays a significant role in mobile investment decision making such as life insurance policies, ETFs and etc., (Fan, 2022). Digital financing significantly helps green investments by promoting intra-firm funding and escalating market rivalry. And in stricter environmental and financial restrictions locations, regional firms have the larger impacts by E-Finance (Ding et al., 2023). Mobile banking facilities in converting the unproductive income into productive income by easy means of interface services provided by the service providers.

## 4.5 Robo-Advisors in Portfolio Diversification

Robo-advisors are cutting-edge technologies that employ machine learning algorithms to provide users with investment advice. As robo advisors replace human advisers with algorithms, they charge lower rates than conventional wealth management services, which make it an attractive choice for investors. Robo-advisory services provide financial advice, either as a complete service provider or as an entry path to a more personalized financial services program (Woodyard and Grable, 2018). Customers that value sustainability choose an automated Robo advisor that provides environmentally friendly investing solutions and select one for their portfolio. (Brunen et al., 2022).

## 4.6 InsurTech and RegTech

InsurTech combines the word's "Insurance" and "Technology". It is the application of technical advancements to increase productivity and minimize cost in the present insurance sector. (Mirza et al., 2021). Hence, it can be said that insurance sector has been leveraged by InsurTech. Fintech is a concern for the whole financial industry, although insurance companies are receiving less attention than banks and investment firms. There is a need for new insurance policies for green projects that can draw more and more sustainable investors in order to promote sustainable development. Insurance companies must also develop new policies that allow investors to choose how their premiums should be used.

The term 'RegTech' is an application of emerging mechanism to regulatory operations (Rambaud and Gázquez, 2022). RegTech have been in place for organisations in order to "respond to immediate business needs, drive operational efficiencies, and reduce costs in regulatory compliance and risk management." As a supervisory technology (SupTech), RegTech was developed to help regulators deal with the increasing number of new financial technology products based on cutting-edge technology, such as blockchains. (Verduyn and Lenglet, 2022). Global legislation has compelled organisations in the financial services industry. Companies have redesigned their legal reporting processes and relied on RegTech to assist them assure comprehensive adherence to the many regulations that they're subjected to. (Gordon, 2018). By simplifying regulations, enhancing risk oversight, streamlining the reporting of ESG indicators, and promoting transparency, RegTech greatly advances financial sustainability.

## 5. IMPLICATIONS AND FUTURE RESEARCH DIRECTIONS

The planet's environment has become inextricably intertwined with the economic system, with the influence of elements that promote change and consequences leading to macroeconomic measures producing a latest system known as "Green Economy" (Elimam, 2023). By expanding sustainable credit and sustainable investment, Fintech technologies support environmentally friendly finance and sustainable economic development (Zhou et al., 2022). Fintech networks money into sustainable channels and programs which can be developed to increase awareness of people's environmental impact as well as what individuals are able to do to decrease them (Nenavath and Mishra, 2023). Green investments' impact on the environment can help investors build credibility for being responsible (Su, 2021).

By looking at a firm's financial report and fundamentals online using mobile applications, one can invest in any company with ease. Another way to put it is that Fintech innovation boosts financial companies' sustainability by promoting green economic expansion and increasing green investment. Green investment decisions are based on what you're looking for in terms of returns which can be profits or sustainable development (Cavaliere et al., 2022). By establishing a dependable, long-term regulatory and legal environment, regulators have the ability to increase the returns on green investments. To encourage enterprises to swiftly embrace the digital age and enhance their financial health, the government ought to optimize the green taxing structure and increase enforcement of laws (Liu et al., 2023).

Firms encounter financial restrictions in their efforts to preserve environmental sustainability. Environmental sustainability involves a long-term and on-going process that requires significant commitment. It is challenging to avail capital for sustainable R&D activities by company's capital, it is where the external source of funding is required which can be achieved through Fintech innovations. The investors need not wait for government bonds to go green in future, rather with the help of peer to peer lending platform the investors can invest on environmentally-friendly, resource-saving, or climate-friendly activities. Fintech also develops solution for carbon trading, investment in renewable energies, and green mutual funds by using cutting edge technology provided through Fintech innovations.

Adopting merely a general term (such as "sustainable" or "ecological") to describe a product might reduce project's chances of success. Considering all, it would appear that crowdfunding investors are well aware of these problems and will not back companies that make a vague promise of sustainability (Corsini et al., 2023). Along with company fundamentals, a parameter called "Green Index" can be included which would indicate a company's overall contribution in either reducing environmental hazards or introducing innovative green products. The performance of enterprise with high pollutants can be regulated to minimize ecological issues by adoption of Fintech. There are different studies on constructing green growth index but there is a need of global green growth evaluation system with indicators reflecting countries contribution towards green growth and its direct impact on economic development.

The chapter provides a theoretical foundation for further research and there is scope to explore further on each of the currently available Fintech innovation to expand in the lines of Green investment.

## 6. CONCLUSION

The chapter exhibits that sustainable growth of the economy and the environment can be ensured by using green investment as a financial strategy. With its emphasis on innovation and technical agility, the Fintech sector has the potential to mobilise public as well as private capital to support scaling up green investment. Even while Fintech projects and infrastructure are developing more quickly in the private sector, Fintech will gradually takes a role in decision making of public and private sectors. Fintech contributes to sustainable development by promoting green investing, reducing transaction costs, and improving efficiency. Fintech's has the ability to drive financial inclusion with its user friendly interface, mobile applications, lower charges and no geographical boundaries making for greater accessibility. The financial sector and green economy sectors can interact using Fintech. The advancement of technology will streamline a number of operations. Though technological development has contributed to environmental degradation, it is also believed that it may one day provide solutions to a number of environmental issues. As Green investment is a driving force for sustainable development, it provides an opportunity for green products, such as sustainable bonds, sustainable insurance, green fund etc, by attracting investment through regulatory frameworks adopted through RegTech. An innovation in financial technology provides a path for free flow of household investment, through which the unproductive funds can be turned into productive capital. Without Fintech innovation, it would be impossible for borrowers and lenders to connect. Customer-centric services helps in meeting investor's expectations. In order to foster innovation and draw in more green investment, a transparent regulation is also essential Government should offer monetary incentives to encourage investors to make investments in the transition to sustainability, such as rebates or grants. Financial technologies is going to be a major driving factor for attracting green investments with its ease of use, transparency, lesser operational cost, advance technology, flexibility, efficiency, security, speed and convenience. Green investments and Fintech innovation studies are still in their infancy, and there is a dearth of empirical data.

## REFERENCES

Bento, N., Gianfrate, G., & Thoni, M. H. (2019). Crowdfunding for sustainability ventures. *Journal of Cleaner Production*, *237*, 117751. doi:10.1016/j.jclepro.2019.117751

Brunen, A.-C., & Laubach, O. (2022). Do sustainable consumers prefer socially responsible investments? A study among the users of robo advisors. *Journal of Banking & Finance*, *136*, 106314. doi:10.1016/j.jbankfin.2021.106314

Campbell-Verduyn, M., & Lenglet, M. (2022). Imaginary failure: RegTech in finance. *New Political Economy*, 1–15.

Cao, L. (2022). Ai in finance: Challenges, techniques, and opportunities. [CSUR]. *ACM Computing Surveys*, *55*(3), 1–38. doi:10.1145/3502289

Cavaliere, L. P. L., Dhaliwal, S., Dutta, M., & Ahamed, F. (2022). A Pathway towards Green India: Green Funds and Green Investment. *Journal of Positive School Psychology*, *6*(2), 4151–4156.

Chiţimiea, A., Minciu, M., Manta, A. M., Ciocoiu, C. N., & Veith, C. (2021). The Drivers of green investment: A bibliometric and systematic review. *Sustainability*, *13*(6), 3507. doi:10.3390u13063507

Collins, T. (2015). Library evolution, trends and the road ahead from the EBSCO lens. *Information Services & Use*, *35*(1-2), 99–107. doi:10.3233/ISU-150771

Corsini, F., & Frey, M. (2023). Exploring the development of environmentally sustainable products through reward-based crowdfunding. *Electronic Commerce Research*, *23*(2), 1183–1207. doi:10.100710660-021-09509-5

Das, S. R. (2019). The future of Fintech. *Financial Management*, *48*(4), 981–1007. doi:10.1111/fima.12297

Ding, Q., Huang, J., & Chen, J. (2023). Does digital finance matter for corporate green investment? Evidence from heavily polluting industries in China. *Energy Economics*, *117*, 106476. doi:10.1016/j.eneco.2022.106476

Elimam, H. (2023). Opportunities and Constraints Confronting Transformation Towards a Green Economy in the Developing Countries. *Economics and Business Quarterly Reviews, 6*(1).

Eyraud, LClements, BWane, A. (2013). Green investment: Trends and determinants. Energy Policy, 60, 852-865.

Fan, L. (2022). Mobile investment technology adoption among investors. *International Journal of Bank Marketing*, *40*(1), 50–67. doi:10.1108/IJBM-11-2020-0551

Farahani, M. S., Esfahani, A., Moghaddam, M. N. F., & Ramezani, A. (2022). The impact of Fintech and artificial intelligence on COVID 19 and sustainable development goals. *International Journal of Innovation in Management. Economics and Social Sciences*, *2*(3), 14–31.

Gernego, I., Urvantseva, S., & Sandulskyi, R. (2022). Green investment opportunities for sustainable agriculture. *Management Theory and Studies for Rural Business and Infrastructure Development*, *44*(2), 185–194. doi:10.15544/mts.2022.19

Ghosh, K. (2022). Green Finance Initiatives in India. *IUP Journal of Accounting Research & Audit Practices, 21*(2).

Gordon, M. (2018). Regulatory reporting: Success is found in a solid foundation. *Journal of Securities Operations & Custody*, *10*(1), 57–66.

Gosain, S., & Agrawal, N. (2021). Factors Affecting the Financial Success of Crowdfunding Campaigns: A Systematic Literature Review. *South Asian Journal of Management*, *28*(3).

Gupta, R., Kaur, H., & Kaur, M. (2023). Evolution of Fintech Ensuring Sustainability in Financial Markets: A Bibliometric Analysis. *International Management Review*.

He, Z., Cao, C., & Feng, C. (2022). Media attention, environmental information disclosure and corporate green technology innovations in China's heavily polluting industries. *Emerging Markets Finance & Trade*, *58*(14), 3939–3952. doi:10.1080/1540496X.2022.2075259

He, Z., Liu, Z., Wu, H., Gu, X., Zhao, Y., & Yue, X. (2020). Research on the Impact of Green Finance and Fintech in Smart City (2020) Complexity, 2020, art. no. 6673386. *DOI*, *10*, 6673386.

Hu, A. S., Parlour, C. A., & Rajan, U. (2019). Cryptocurrencies: Stylized facts on a new investible instrument. *Financial Management*, *48*(4), 1049–1068. doi:10.1111/fima.12300

Jarvis, R., & Han, H. (2021). Fintech Innovation: Review and Future Research Directions. *International Journal of Banking. Finance and Insurance Technologies*, *1*(1), 79–102.

Jun, J., Cho, I., & Park, H. (2018). Factors influencing continued use of mobile easy payment service: An empirical investigation. *Total Quality Management & Business Excellence*, *29*(9-10), 1043–1057. doi:10.1080/14783363.2018.1486550

Khetwani, K., & Jain, S. (2022). *An analysis on the awareness & insight of cryptocurrency.*

Laing, K., & James, K. (2023). EBSCO and Summon Discovery Generator Tools: How Accurate Are They? *Journal of Academic Librarianship*, *49*(1), 102587. doi:10.1016/j.acalib.2022.102587

Liu, H., Yao, P., Latif, S., Aslam, S., & Iqbal, N. (2022). Impact of Green financing, Fintech, and financial inclusion on energy efficiency. *Environmental Science and Pollution Research International*, *29*(13), 1–12. doi:10.100711356-021-16949-x PMID:34705207

Liu, Q., Zou, L., Yang, X., & Tang, J. (2019). Survival or die: A survival analysis on peer-to-peer lending platforms in China. *Accounting and Finance*, *59*(S2), 2105–2131. doi:10.1111/acfi.12513

Liu, Y. B., Deng, W. F., Luo, K., & Tang, M. Y. (2023). *Impact of Environmental Taxation on Financial Performance of Energy-Intensive Firms: The Role of Digital Transformation*. Hindawi.

Liu, Z., Song, J., Wu, H., Gu, X., Zhao, Y., Yue, X., & Shi, L. (2021). Impact of Financial Technology on Regional Green Finance. *Computer Systems Science and Engineering*, *39*(3), 391–401. doi:10.32604/csse.2021.014527

Luo, X., Ge, L., & Wang, C. (2022). Crowdfunding for microfinance institutions: the new hope? *MIS Quarterly, 46*, 1.

MacAskill, S., Roca, E., Liu, B., Stewart, R. A., & Sahin, O. (2021). Is there a green premium in the green bond market? Systematic literature review revealing premium determinants. *Journal of Cleaner Production*, *280*, 124491. doi:10.1016/j.jclepro.2020.124491

Macchiavello, E., & Siri, M. (2022). Sustainable finance and Fintech: Can technology contribute to achieving environmental goals? *European Company and Financial Law Review*, *19*(1), 128–174. doi:10.1515/ecfr-2022-0005

Mirza, A. A. I., Muhamed, N. A., & Kamarubahrin, A. F. (2021). Islamic Insurtech Conceptual Framework: A Proposal. Ihtifaz. *Journal of Islamic Economics, Finance, and Banking*, *4*(2), 131–143.

Muganyi, T., Yan, L., & Sun, H. P. (2021). Green finance, Fintech and environmental protection: Evidence from China. *Environmental Science and Ecotechnology*, *7*, 100107. doi:10.1016/j.ese.2021.100107 PMID:36160697

Namvar, E. (2014). An introduction to peer-to-peer loans as investments. *Journal of Investment Management First Quarter.*

Nenavath, S., & Mishra, S. (2023). Impact of green finance and Fintech on sustainable economic growth: Empirical evidence from India. *Heliyon*, *9*(5), e16301. doi:10.1016/j.heliyon.2023.e16301 PMID:37234625

Pawłowska, M., Staniszewska, A., & Grzelak, M. (2022). Impact of Fintech on Sustainable Development. Financial Sciences. *Nauki o Finansach*, *27*(2), 49-66.

Purkayastha, N. N., & Tuzlukaya, Ş. E. (2020). Determination Of The Benefits And Risks Of Peer-To-Peer (P2p) Lending: A Social Network Teory Approach. *Copernican Journal of Finance & Accounting*, *9*(3), 131–143. doi:10.12775/CJFA.2020.016

Rabbani, M. R. (2022). Fintech innovations, scope, challenges, and implications in Islamic Finance: A systematic analysis. *International Journal of Computing and Digital Systems*, *11*(1), 1–28.

Rambaud, S. C., & Gázquez, A. E. (2022). A RegTech approach to Fintech sustainability: The case of Spain. *European Journal of Risk Regulation*, *13*(2), 333–349. doi:10.1017/err.2021.62

Rossolini, M., Pedrazzoli, A., & Ronconi, A. (2021). Greening crowdfunding campaigns: An investigation of message framing and effective communication strategies for funding success. *International Journal of Bank Marketing*, *39*(7), 1395–1419. doi:10.1108/IJBM-01-2021-0039

Saunila, M., Ukko, J., & Rantala, T. (2018). Sustainability as a driver of green innovation investment and exploitation. *Journal of Cleaner Production*, *179*, 631–641. doi:10.1016/j.jclepro.2017.11.211

Siemroth, C., & Hornuf, L. (2023). Why Do Retail Investors Pick Green Investments? A Lab-in-the-Field Experiment with Crowdfunders. *Journal of Economic Behavior & Organization*, *209*, 74–90. doi:10.1016/j.jebo.2023.02.023

Su, X. (2021). Can green investment win the favor of investors in China? Evidence from the return performance of green investment stocks. *Emerging Markets Finance & Trade*, *57*(11), 3120–3138. doi:10.1080/1540496X.2019.1710129

Tian, H., Siddik, A. B., Pertheban, T. R., & Rahman, M. N. (2023). Does Fintech innovation and green transformational leadership improve green innovation and corporate environmental performance? A hybrid SEM–ANN approach. *Journal of Innovation & Knowledge*, *8*(3), 100396. doi:10.1016/j.jik.2023.100396

Wang, Z., Shahid, M. S., Binh An, N., Shahzad, M., & Abdul-Samad, Z. (2022). Does green finance facilitate firms in achieving corporate social responsibility goals? *Economic research-. Ekonomska Istrazivanja, 35*(1), 5400–5419. doi:10.1080/1331677X.2022.2027259

Woodyard, A. S., & Grable, J. E. (2018). Insights into the Users of Robo-Advisory Firms. *Journal of Financial Service Professionals, 72*(5).

Ye, W., Wong, W. K., Arnone, G., Nassani, A. A., Haffar, M., & Faiz, M. F. (2023). Crypto currency and green investment impact on global environment: A time series analysis. *International Review of Economics & Finance, 86*, 155–169. doi:10.1016/j.iref.2023.01.030

Zhang, Y. (2023). Impact of green finance and environmental protection on green economic recovery in South Asian economies: Mediating role of Fintech. *Economic Change and Restructuring, 56*(3), 2069–2086. doi:10.100710644-023-09500-0

Zhao, G., Zhou, P., & Wen, W. (2021). Feed-in tariffs, knowledge stocks and renewable energy technology innovation: The role of local government intervention. *Energy Policy, 156*, 112453. doi:10.1016/j.enpol.2021.112453

Zhou, G., Zhu, J., & Luo, S. (2022). The impact of Fintech innovation on green growth in China: Mediating effect of green finance. *Ecological Economics, 193*, 107308. doi:10.1016/j.ecolecon.2021.107308

## ADDITIONAL READING

Chen, M., Chen, R., Zheng, S., & Li, B. (2023). Green Investment, Technological Progress, and Green Industrial Development: Implications for Sustainable Development. *Sustainability, 15*(4), 3808. doi:10.3390u15043808

Gomber, P., Koch, J. A., & Siering, M. (2017). Digital Finance and Fintech: Current research and future research directions. *Journal of Business Economics, 87*(5), 537–580. doi:10.100711573-017-0852-x

Hinson, R., Lensink, R., & Mueller, A. (2019). Transforming agribusiness in developing countries: SDGs and the role of Fintech. *Current Opinion in Environmental Sustainability, 41*, 1–9. doi:10.1016/j.cosust.2019.07.002

Indriastuti, M., & Chariri, A. (2021). The role of green investment and corporate social responsibility investment on sustainable performance. *Cogent Business & Management, 8*(1), 1960120. doi:10.1080/23311975.2021.1960120

Liu, W., Sun, Y., Yüksel, S., & Dinçer, H. (2021). Consensus-based multidimensional due diligence of Fintech-enhanced green energy investment projects. *Financial Innovation*, *7*(1), 1–31. doi:10.118640854-021-00289-3

Senyo, P. K., & Osabutey, E. L. (2020). Unearthing antecedents to financial inclusion through Fintech innovations. *Technovation*, *98*, 102155. doi:10.1016/j.technovation.2020.102155

## KEY TERMS AND DEFINITIONS

**Carbon Footprint:** The amount of greenhouse gases emitted by the living creatures.

**Crowdfunding:** a way for raising a fund from large number of investors without involvement of traditional methods of banking or any financial institutions.

**Fintech:** the integration of technological advances in the financial sector to boost financial services and processes.

**Fintech Innovation:** Innovation in the financial sector which uses artificial intelligence and machine learning in its processes.

**Green Index:** an index which helps in measuring the organisations performance towards balance of nature.

**Green Innovation:** Innovations that aims at reducing negative impacts on the environment by at most utilization natural resources.

**Green Investment:** Investments that are made on sustainable products and services which aims at improving ecological balance.

**Sustainability:** The process of meeting the needs of current economy without impacting future growth.

# Chapter 4
# Financial Inclusion:
## An Assessment of Progress via Rural Banking System and Way Forward

**G. S. Vijaya**
https://orcid.org/0000-0001-9185-9862
*Faculty of Management Studies, CMS Business School, Jain University (Deemed), Bangalore, India*

**Divya Prabhu**
https://orcid.org/0000-0002-2880-4591
*Government First Grade College, Karkala, India*

**Sandhya M**
https://orcid.org/0009-0001-5552-9521
*Government First Grade College, Kaup, India*

**Jehad Aldehayyat**
*Al-Hussein Bin Talal University, Jordan*

## ABSTRACT

*Banking is essential for economic growth, but it often faces challenges in rural areas due to lack of knowledge, technology acceptance, education, and infrastructure. Rural Banking in India, with a universal presence, is still lagging behind in the developmental race. To achieve inclusive growth, the country should focus on overall growth without ignoring rural regions. However, rural areas are often the least focused on for providing hi-tech banking services or basic banking services. To achieve financial inclusion, technology can be integrated to provide basic banking services in remote or rural areas, with support from the government, banking regulators, bankers, and potential users. These aspects are covered in a lucid manner in this chapter by supportive facts and figures.*

DOI: 10.4018/979-8-3693-0008-4.ch004

## INTRODUCTION

"No one is left behind—today and tomorrow". Isn't this sustainability, in simple terms? By sustainable, we mean catering to the social, environmental, and economic needs of present and future generations. We are living on a planet whose resources are going to be depleted in the coming years if not utilized or conserved appropriately. In order to attain this objective, there is a need to bring everyone into the mainstream. The fruits of the efforts of every initiative must reach the last person in line. Sustainability is tied to social, economic, and environmental issues, but our concern here is focused on the economic matter linking it with the social and environmental factors influencing it. Out of the various possible means of attaining this objective, financial inclusion is one of them. Being financially inclusive, no doubt, makes a man take prudent financial decisions and achieve financial discipline, thereby leading to his economic well-being and prosperity. Development at an individual level like this is considered micro-level. However, when the inclusive growth of many such individuals happens at the macro level in the economy, the nation also starts to build itself. Factors such as easy access to resources, optimal usage of financial resources, quality of service, education or knowledge, a conducive social environment, developed infrastructure, etc. are needed to achieve financial inclusion and we must understand that Digital transformation is a socio economic change (Ajigini, 2023) (Bravo, 2023). However, in the context of our study, the achievement and progress of financial inclusion through technology-mediated banking are the centerpieces.

## FINANCIAL INCLUSION FOR SUSTAINABILITY: WHAT, HOW, AND WHY NOT?

Everyone would agree that there cannot be one single party or person who can solely be accounted for or responsible for contributing to sustainable growth. There are several parties whose involvement and actions can generate remarkable results that are clearly visible, quantifiable, and effective. The regulatory bodies of the Government, like the RBI (Reserve Bank of India), various financial service providers such as banks, post offices, insurance companies, non-banking financial entities, and people at large (individuals, small and big business enterprises in both rural and urban areas) are the major contributors and influencers to Sustainability. If there is any lapse from any of these parties, the sustainability circle breaks down or slows down its pace. This chapter shall describe more about these three parties with supportive facts and figures of progress and failures over the last few years studied from various genuine sources such as RBI publications, world bank data, global index reports etc and presented in lucid manner thereby attempt to provide an overview of the slow transformation and way forward.

The ensuing paragraphs will provide an overview of India's financial inclusion path as presented by the authors by means of their best possible talent on data literacy (Ajigini, 2023). It is vital to initially comprehend the present condition regarding Financial Inclusion using technological assistance in order to attain digital sustainability objectives. This chapter will encompass and emphasize the rate of technology adoption, the barriers that contribute to technological lag, and the concept of inclusion. The following sections in this study will also provide insight into the involvement of bankers and the participation of FinTech organizations in achieving success in Government welfare schemes and financial inclusion initiatives. In addition to examining the positive aspects, the study will also address the different challenges that hinder the progress of financial inclusion for banks, government entities, and the general population. The writers will present a framework in the concluding chapter, which is developed through extensive investigations, readings, and research. This framework aims to establish a model that may be utilized to attain sustained financial inclusivity and progress inside a nation.

## FINANCIAL INCLUSION JOURNEY: SMOOTH OR BUMPY ROADS?

Bringing a large group of people together through financial initiatives is not child's play. What India has achieved in terms of growth in financially inclusive concerns such as account opening and use of ATMs Access to credit, adoption of digital payments, etc. on a rapid scale is due to the big bet taken by the Government, Financial institutions, and Users on the technology aspect. Leveraging technology to align with the market, increasing the use of digital payment platforms post-demonetization, and growing FinTech have all been possible due to the tremendous financial inclusion initiatives and agenda. As per the India Digital Financial Inclusion report of 2019, despite the major efforts, the digital push is still not motivating close to 48% of the people in India who have accounts but have remained dormant (i.e., no deposits or withdrawals). This low level of usage and dormancy is due to lower access to technology, especially among low-income and rural populations.

*Figure 1. Showing savings, deposits, and rates sourced from NSO, annual bank accounts & RBI*

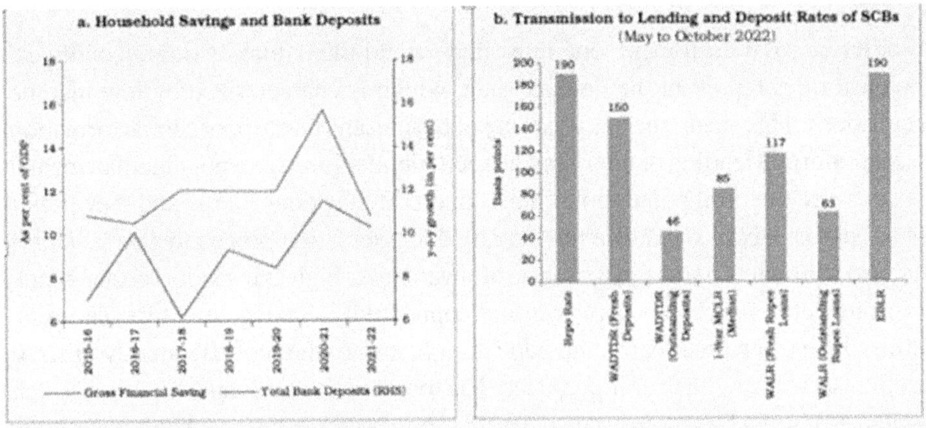


**Note:** WALR: Weighted Average Lending Rate; WADTDR: Weighted Average Domestic Term Deposit Rate; MCLR: Marginal Cost of Funds-based Lending Rate; EBLR: External Benchmark-based Lending Rate.
**Source:** NSO, Annual accounts of banks and RBI.

*Figure 2. Showing growth in borrowings sourced from annual bank accounts*

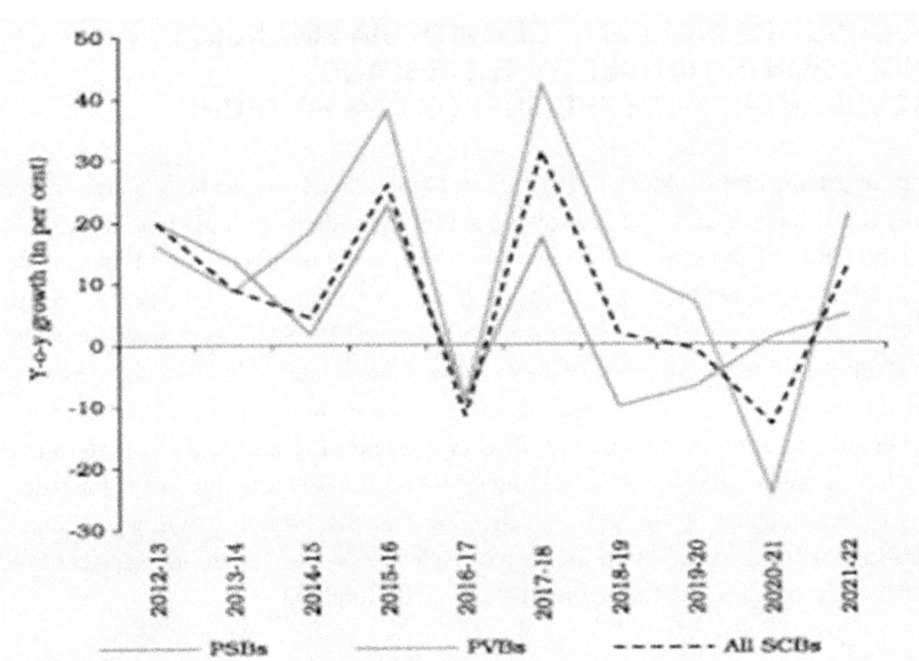


**Source:** Annual accounts of banks.

## DESCRIPTION OF THE NATURE OF RURAL BANK CONSUMERS

To describe rural customers, one must understand the nature of rural economies. The customers represent the demand side, which is characterized by low-income occupations. This means there is a scarcity of capital, and hence poor capital formation is seen. Informal lending or unorganized sector lenders are more popular than formal sectors since the rural population's need for credit may not be large and they prefer not to approach banks and face the lengthy documentation procedures and charges attached to them. There is also a lack of awareness, high transaction costs, a lack of infrastructure, and poor networks and connectivity. Savings and time deposits, jewelry loans, personal loans, and education loans are the most frequently utilized banking services by the rural populace. Customers utilize advanced services such as Demat, Mutual Funds, Insurance, BillPay, and NPS via Internet banking only on uncommon occasions. Due to their variable income, their savings and investment patterns (Barrachina, 2022 (IGI Global publishing)) are difficult to analyze but simple in nature: "They save when they earn and spend when they require."

## JOURNEY OF INCLUSIVE GROWTH VIA FINANCIAL INCLUSION INITIATIVES BY THE RBI AND GOVERNMENT WITH THE SUPPORT OF FINTECH

Before delving into an analysis of the Status of Inclusive Growth and potential future directions, it is important to acknowledge that individuals in India tend to possess a natural inclination towards saving. However, it is not necessary for all funds to be converted into investments or banking products. The data clearly indicates, as seen in Figure 1, that there is a significant disparity between Financial Savings and Deposits in Banks, despite the presence of a favorable interest rate on lending and deposits. Furthermore, there has been a significant increase in the level of borrowing within the country over the course of several years. (Refer to Figure 1 and 2). As we move further in deliberating as to how India's progression towards Financial inclusion has been attempted by the RBI and the Government through its unique schemes and supportive activities with the help of technology-driven banking services and FinTech companies, the following matters are highlighted:

## 5I AND RBI: BANKERS PARTICIPATION IN INCLUSIVE GROWTH: AN UNDERSTANDING AND APPRAISING OF WORK DONE

No doubt, even otherwise, banks have played a crucial role in connecting rural masses and providing benefits from the government to the common man. The banks have worked in various ways to contribute to financial literacy, financial inclusion, and thereby inclusive growth. At the operational level or branch level, right from the time a customer opens an account with them until the strategic level of framing products and services for different categories of customers, the banks have played a very significant role in the Indian economy.

The bank is leveraging technology for the sake of a quick and safe transfer of benefits to the final user. The Banks act like a bridge between the government and beneficiaries of welfare schemes. The Universal presence of banks with strong technology backup has enabled banks to deliver on their responsibilities pretty well. The monetary welfare schemes from the Government have been disbursed in large numbers, dealing with huge amounts, to different locations across the country only because of banks. From the point of view of rural banking, one of the concerns is the usage of banking services by the rural population. Even though Government schemes like Jan Dhan have created accessibility to banking services, they have been limited to only basic banking services. There is a huge gap with respect to the use of advanced functions that banks perform in comparison to such services in urban areas. Advanced services like Demat services, Mutual funds, Locker facilities, special kinds of deposits and credit facilities, etc. are not yet popular among the rural population. The authors are of the opinion that fulfilling this will make banking sector service complete in rural regions and raise their standard of living. However, the root cause of the problem is a lack of education or poor knowledge about these products and their usage in the rural region. Thus, there is a dire need to increase awareness and spread knowledge about the use and benefits of these advanced products and services offered by banks. In addition, technology acceptance is another crucial factor for success. The use of the digital payment system can truly help in winning this race. As envisaged by RBI Payments Vision 2025 as a recent initiative, the focus is on improving the digital environment based on technology built upon the five izs: integrity, inclusion, innovation, institutionalization, and internationalization.

**Instances of RBI initiatives towards the digital world:** UPI123Pay, launched in March 2022; UPI Lite, launched in September 2022; and Inter-operable Card-less Cash Withdrawal (ICCW) at ATMs are some of the revolutionary facilities supported by RBI that have facilitated fast payments and withdrawals, thereby preventing fraud, cloning, etc.

## DIGITAL BANKING PLATFORM: A NEED FOR INTERNATIONAL FINANCIAL INCLUSION

The world is a global market today. In this globalized era, businesses cannot afford to lose any deals that are complicated due to differences in currencies and subsequent delays in payments caused by the absence of a digital platform. Hence CBDC, i.e., Central Bank Digital Currency (CBDC), is one solution that can promote diversity in payment options and make international payments fast and cheap, thereby increasing financial inclusion in an international context. Post-pandemic, the central banks and governments of various countries are working to explore this option further through private cryptocurrency. Active research is going on on the potential of CBDCs, experimenting with the technology, etc., as revealed from the Bank for International Settlements (BIS) survey on CBDCs conducted in 2021. The days are soon going to come when Central banks will no longer be required to hold foreign currency accounts with other countries when digital currencies rule the world in the near future. International settlements are also going to happen in a fraction of a second! To make this possible, blockchain technology is surely going to contribute considerably. In addition, Neural networks, machine learning, artificial intelligence, and data analytics (Segall, 2022 IGI Global publishing) have the potential to be valuable tools for achieving global financial reach when applied and implemented effectively.

## CREDIT DELIVERY AND ITS EFFECT ON THE STATUS OF FINANCIAL INCLUSION

The RBI, as a true representative of the government, has been trying its best to offer and improve access to its basic financial products & services to spread awareness in finance- both personal or business including family businesses (Chagwesha, 2022 IGI Global publishing). The National Strategy for Financial Inclusion (NSFI) 2019–24 lays out the strategy and main goals of India's financial inclusion policies, with a focus on improving promoting financial literacy, digital financial inclusion, and also for strengthening the country's grievance redressal system..

Enhance Collateral free loans: In an amendment to the Credit Guarantee Fund for Micro Units (CGFMU) scheme carried out by the Government in July 2021, the amount of collateral-free loans to SHGs under the Deendayal Antyodaya Yojana-National Rural Livelihood Mission (DAY-NRLM) has been enhanced from Rs ` 10 lakh to Rs 20 lakh, as the RBI guidelines clearly stated not to charge any collateral. The entire loan (even if it goes below Rs 10 lakh) would be eligible for coverage under CGFMU. This is expected to encourage women's SHGs to seek a higher amount of loans. Now that the Government offers such a level of financial support to SHGs, more businesses are tending to commence in rural and semi-urban areas as well. The greater the creation of credit, the greater the economy's inclusive growth.

FinTech, for the above developmental schemes, can contribute to speeding up credit delivery. It can do so in India by partnering with banks, especially in rural areas. Lengthy banking procedures that are paper-based and expensive cannot encourage small businesses. One recent progress in this line is the digitalization of Agri-finance, which was jointly framed by the RBI and its Innovation Hub and is under experimentation in Madhya Pradesh and Tamil Nadu for delivering Kisan Credit Card loans in a digital manner. RBI's vision is to develop and provide such a standardized technological platform for easy credit to all segments, with special emphasis on rural and agricultural credit.

## CONTRIBUTION OF NBFCS TO INCLUSIVE GROWTH

One cannot ignore the contribution of the NBFC as a true supporter of India's economic growth. They supplement the banks when it comes to channels of credit intermediation. Over the years, NBFCs have gained a lot of significance, which is evident from the fact that they have three layers of framework, divided as the base layer, Middle Layer, and top layer, and the intensity of regulation increases as the layer progresses. NBFCs, as one of the parts of the financial sector, have grown not only in size but also in complexity. Their penetration in rural and semi-urban locations is also significant. To ensure strong association between banks and NBFCs in credit delivery to priority sectors, there is the facility of PSL classification, i.e., Priority Sector Lending. The PSL limit for loans against negotiable warehouse receipts (NWRs) or electronic NWRs (eNWRs) was increased from Rs `50 lakh to Rs 75 lakh per borrower to encourage their use and ensure a greater flow of credit to the farmers against pledge or hypothecation of agricultural produce (Source: RBI- Press release, 2021).

## GROWTH AND JOURNEY OF THE PAYMENT ECOSYSTEM IN INDIA—ALL THANKS TO RBI

The Indian payment ecosystem is globally renowned for its numerous payment systems, platforms, products, and services. In 2019, India was deemed a "leader" in 16 out of 40 indicators (See Figure 4), showing progress in large-value payment systems, rapid payment systems, online payment options, cross-border remittance channels, and declining check usage. However, the country faces challenges with its acceptance infrastructure, including ATMs and point-of-sale terminals. The initiative known as the Payment Infrastructure Development Fund was initiated in 2021 with the intention of enhancing the infrastructure for the acceptance of payments. The total number of payments increased by 63.8% during the fiscal year 2021–2022, and 99.9% of transactions were completed digitally. It is anticipated that this growth would result in an increase in economic activity. A look at the Figure 3 will give a better idea to the readers on the growth of Payment system in Value and Volume in the last 3 years.

*Figure 3. Chart showing components of payment systems*
*Source: RBI*

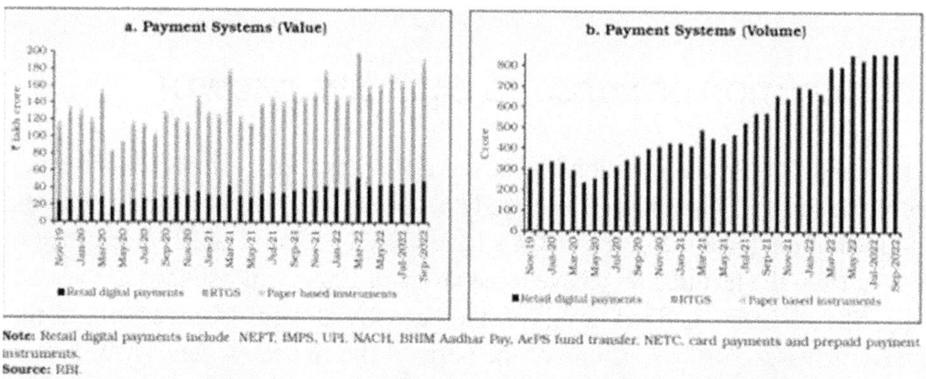


*Figure 4. Table showing payment system indicators*
*Source: RBI*

| Item | Volume (Lakh) | | | Value (₹ Crore) | | |
|---|---|---|---|---|---|---|
| | 2019-20 | 2020-21 | 2021-22 | 2019-20 | 2020-21 | 2021-22 |
| 1. Large Value Credit Transfers – RTGS | 1,507 | 1,592 | 2,078 | 13,11,56,475 | 10,55,99,849 | 12,86,57,516 |
| 2. Credit Transfers | 2,06,297 | 3,17,868 | 5,77,935 | 2,85,56,593 | 3,35,04,226 | 4,27,28,006 |
| 2.1 AePS (Fund Transfers) | 10 | 11 | 10 | 469 | 623 | 575 |
| 2.2 APBS | 16,747 | 14,373 | 12,573 | 99,048 | 1,11,001 | 1,33,345 |
| 2.3 ECS Cr | 18.3 | 0 | 0 | 5,146 | 0 | 0 |
| 2.4 IMPS | 25,792 | 32,783 | 46,625 | 23,37,541 | 29,41,500 | 41,71,037 |
| 2.5 NACH | 11,100 | 16,465 | 18,758 | 10,37,079 | 12,16,535 | 12,81,685 |
| 2.6 NEFT | 27,445 | 30,928 | 40,407 | 2,29,45,580 | 2,51,30,910 | 2,87,25,463 |
| 2.7 UPI | 1,25,186 | 2,23,307 | 4,59,561 | 21,31,730 | 41,03,658 | 84,15,900 |
| 3. Debit Transfers and Direct Debits | 6,027 | 10,457 | 12,189 | 6,05,939 | 8,65,520 | 10,34,444 |
| 3.1 BHIM Aadhaar Pay | 91 | 161 | 228 | 1,303 | 2,580 | 6,113 |
| 3.2 ECS Dr | 1.14 | 0 | 0 | 38,607 | 0 | 0 |
| 3.3 NACH | 5,842 | 9,646 | 10,755 | 6,04,397 | 8,62,027 | 10,26,641 |
| 3.4 NETC | 93 | 650 | 1,207 | 200 | 913 | 1,689 |
| 4. Card Payments | 72,384 | 57,787 | 61,783 | 14,34,813 | 12,91,799 | 17,01,851 |
| 4.1 Credit Cards | 21,773 | 17,641 | 22,399 | 7,30,894 | 6,30,414 | 9,71,638 |
| 4.2 Debit Cards | 50,611 | 40,146 | 39,384 | 7,03,920 | 6,61,385 | 7,30,213 |
| 5. Prepaid Payment Instruments | 53,941 | 49,366 | 65,783 | 2,14,860 | 1,97,095 | 2,79,416 |
| 6. Paper-based Instruments | 10,414 | 6,704 | 6,999 | 78,24,822 | 56,27,108 | 66,50,333 |
| **Total Digital Payments (1+2+3+4+5)** | **3,40,155** | **4,37,068** | **7,19,768** | **16,19,68,681** | **14,14,58,488** | **17,44,01,233** |
| **Total Retail Payments (2+3+4+5+6)** | **3,49,063** | **4,42,180** | **7,24,689** | **3,86,37,028** | **4,14,85,747** | **5,23,94,049** |
| **Total Payments (1+2+3+4+5+6)** | **3,50,570** | **4,43,772** | **7,26,767** | **16,97,93,503** | **14,70,85,596** | **18,10,51,565** |

**Source:** RBI.

The Composite Digital Payments Index (DPI) was introduced by the Reserve Bank in January 2021 to measure national payment digitization accurately (See Figure 5). The index is calculated semi-annually and considers five parameters: payment enablers, infrastructure demand, supply-side factors, payment performance, and consumer centricity. The RBI-DPI score increased substantially in March 2022, indicating the rapid adoption of digital payment methods as shown in the Figure 4 and 5. (Source: RBI Bulletin, 2021).

*Figure 5. Chart showing RBI DPI*
*Source: RBI*

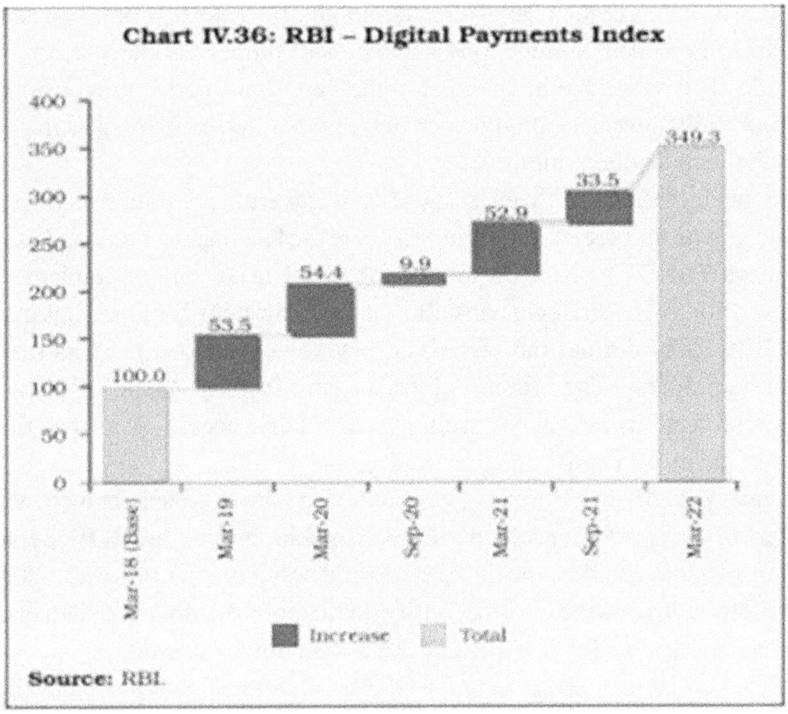


In 2014, the Reserve Bank of India developed guidelines for the National Payments Corporation of India and Bharat Bill Pay Limited's Bharat Bill Payment System (abbreviated as BBPS), which is an interoperable infrastructure for the payment of bills. The BBPS provides support for the payment of bills, it has a centralized mechanism for the resolution of customer complaints, and standardized rates for the convenience of consumers. The initial five billers to be included in the BBPS's scope and coverage were direct-to-home (DTH) television, electric and gas utilities, telephones, and water services. After some time, the scope was increased so that all categories of billers who create recurring bills are now eligible to participate as qualified participants. In September 2019, the BBPS ecosystem processed 1.10 crore transactions worth 1.900 crore. From 168 billers and the processing of 1.10 crore transactions worth Rs. 1.900 crore in September 2019, the BBPS ecosystem expanded to 20,519 billers and the processing of 9.49 crore transactions worth 16,582 crore in November 2022 (a substantial increase of 12000% in billers participation and roughly 870000& increase in transaction volume). Bharat Bill Payment Operating Units (abbreviated as BBPOUs) consisted of a total of 43 institutions and 10 non-banks by the end of November 2022. In May 2022, the minimum net worth threshold for non-bank BBPOUs was decreased from '100 crore to '25 crore in an effort to increase their involvement and align it with that of other non-bank participants in payment systems that handle client money and have a comparable risk profile. This was done in an effort to increase their participation (Suhr, 2023 IGI Global publishing) and align it with that of other non-bank players in payment systems that handle client funds.

Financial inclusion has been a significant government initiative to promote economic growth and social well-being. Despite the fact that the Pradhan Mantri Jan Dhan Yojana (PMJDY) and the Business Correspondent (BC) model implementation gave these initiatives a strategic boost, the National Strategy for Financial Inclusion (NSFI) 2019–2024 defines the vision and key objectives to expand its reach and maintain its progress. The primary objective is to increase financial literacy and consumer protection, as well as facilitate affordable access to formal financial services as mentioned earlier.

In January 2020, the Reserve Bank aimed to have a bank branch within 5 kilometers of every 500-household village or hamlet in rural areas. By September 2022, the objective could be met in 26 states and seven union territories. 99.97% of the identified villages were covered, with 40 villages remaining in Chattisgarh and Odisha and one Union Territory of Ladakh remaining uncovered.

The IMF's Financial Access Survey showed increased bank branch availability in India, despite rapid digitization(See Figure 6). However, global digitization has led to fewer branches (See Figure 8). India has the second-highest number of ATMs, but their availability remains minimal. PoS terminals and micro-ATMs with Aadhaar-enabled payment systems help bridge the gap. In 2021, the gender disparity in account ownership was expected to be eliminated (See Figure 7), and 43% of the adult population in India receive wages in currency, higher than in developing countries.

*Figure 6. Table showing the growth of commercial bank branches across countries*

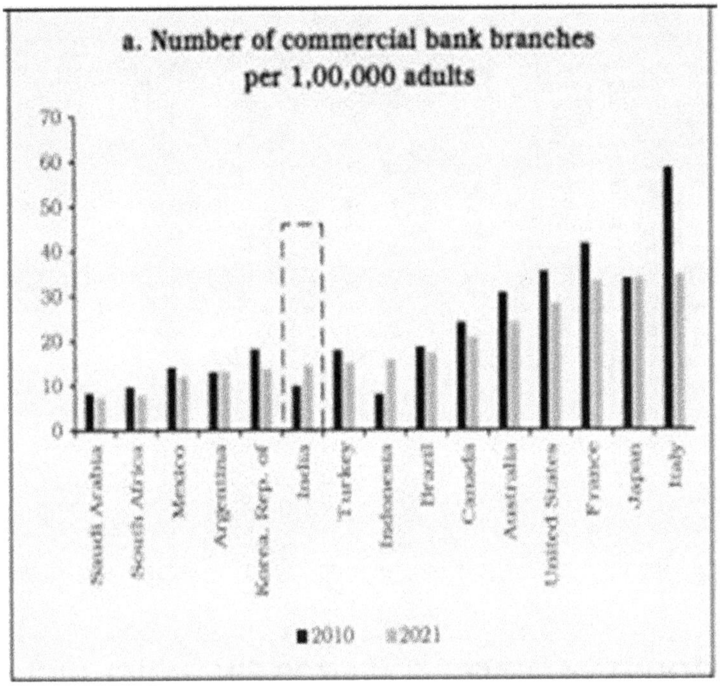


*Figure 7. Financial inclusion indicators*

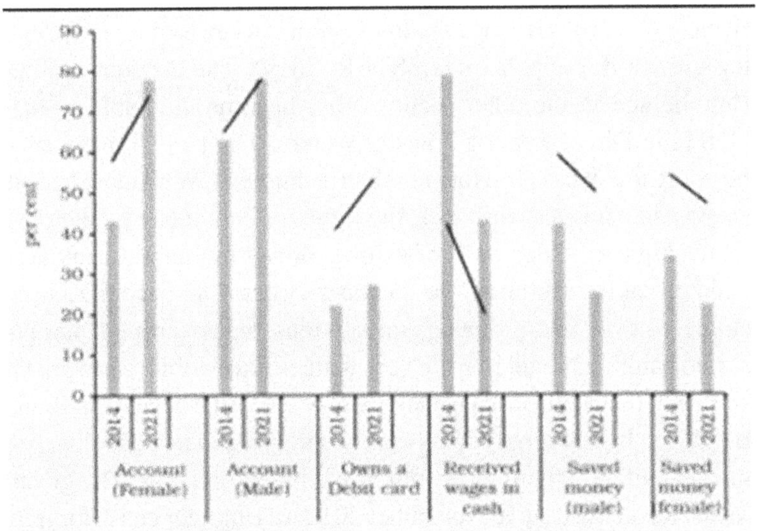


**Note:** Data as per cent of population above 15 years of age.
**Source:** Global Findex Database, World Bank.

*Figure 8. Table showing progress in financial inclusion*
*Source: RBI*

| Sr No. | Particulars | 2010 | 2015 | 2020 | 2021 | 2022* |
|---|---|---|---|---|---|---|
| 1 | Banking Outlets in Villages- Branches | 33,378 | 49,571 | 54,561 | 55,112 | 53,287 |
| 2 | Banking Outlets in Villages>2000-BCs | 8,390 | 90,877 | 1,49,106 | 8,50,406 | 18,92,462 ^ |
| 3 | Banking Outlets in Villages<2000-BCs | 25,784 | 4,08,713 | 3,92,069 | 3,40,019 | 3,26,008 |
| 4 | Total Banking Outlets in Villages – BCs | 34,174 | 4,99,590 | 5,41,175 | 11,90,425 | 22,18,470 ^ |
| 5 | Banking Outlets in Villages – Other Modes | 142 | 4,552 | 3,481 | 2,542 | 2,479 |
| 6 | Banking Outlets in Villages -Total | 67,694 | 5,53,713 | 5,99,217 | 12,48,079 | 22,74,236 ^ |
| 7 | Urban Locations Covered Through BCs | 447 | 96,847 | 6,35,046 | 4,26,745 | 12,95,307 ^ |
| 8 | BSBDA - Through Branches (No. in Lakh) | 600 | 2,103 | 2,616 | 2,659 | 2,661 |
| 9 | BSBDA - Through Branches (Amt. in Crore) | 4,400 | 36,498 | 95,831 | 1,18,392 | 1,20,464 |
| 10 | BSBDA - Through BCs (No. in Lakh) | 130 | 1,878 | 3,388 | 3,796 | 4,015 |
| 11 | BSBDA - Through BCs (Amt. in Crore) | 1,100 | 7,457 | 72,581 | 87,623 | 1,07,415 |
| 12 | BSBDA - Total (No. in Lakh) | 735 | 3,981 | 6,004 | 6,455 | 6,677 |
| 13 | BSBDA - Total (Amt. in Crore) | 5,500 | 43,955 | 1,68,412 | 2,06,015 | 2,27,879 |
| 14 | OD Facility Availed in BSBDAs (No. in Lakh) | 2 | 76 | 64 | 60 | 68 |
| 15 | OD Facility Availed in BSBDAs (Amt. in Crore) | 10 | 1,991 | 529 | 534 | 731 |
| 16 | KCC - Total (No. in Lakh) | 240 | 426 | 475 | 466 | 473 |
| 17 | KCC - Total (Amt. in Crore) | 1,24,000 | 4,38,229 | 6,39,069 | 6,72,624 | 7,10,715 |
| 18 | GCC - Total (No. in Lakh) | 10 | 92 | 202 | 202 | 96 |
| 19 | GCC - Total (Amt. in Crore) | 3,500 | 131,160 | 1,94,048 | 1,55,826 | 1,70,203 |
| 20 | ICT-A/Cs-BC-Total Transactions (No. in Lakh) # | 270 | 4,770 | 32,318 | 30,551 | 28,533 |
| 21 | ICT-A/Cs-BC-Total Transactions (Amt. in Crore) # | 700 | 85,980 | 8,70,643 | 8,49,771 | 9,05,252 |

**Notes:** 1. *: Provisional.
2. #: Transactions during the financial year.
3. ^: There is a significant increase in data reported by few private sector banks.
**Source:** FIP returns submitted by public sector banks, private sector banks and regional rural banks.

## AS THE COUNTRY MOVES TOWARDS FINANCIAL INCLUSION

India's digital financial inclusion has grown thanks to a lot of new ideas from both the public and private sectors. One of the main reasons for this is that the government has made it clear that access to the banking system is a key tool for reducing poverty and making growth more inclusive (mSTAR, 2019). The accounts opened under PMJDY (highlighted in the other sections) has become the pathway for transfer of all the DBTs ie Direct Benefit Transfer system. To open so many accounts so quickly, the government has put a lot of faith in technology. With more people getting internet access and using smartphones, the future of banking is likely to be digital. The goal is to skip over older ways of getting money by linking bank accounts to biometric identification (through the Aadhaar system) and mobile numbers. By giving licenses to new types of financial institutions, the government has pushed for a differentiated banking model in which companies like Mobile Network Operators (MNOs) while FinTechs can provide banking services under a Payment Bank license, and Micro Finance Institutions (MFIs) are encouraged to use technology to keep up with the market and help them grow into Small Finance Banks. The government's quick move to stop using cash in November 2016 was another cause for tremendous growth of digital payments. The state-owned businesses like State Bank of India (SBI), that have opened almost one-third of PMJDY accounts, still play a key role in providing direct banking services across India, the overall role of the government in the financial inclusion agenda has changed over the past four years. The government prioritizes technology-led infrastructure, like digital identification and payment technology, for the private sector to build on. (mSTAR, 2019)The Unified Payment Interface (UPI) has become the most common online payment method. The National Payments Council of India (NPCI) is in charge of it. Even though the number of new accounts has grown a lot, there is proof that India's push for digital finance isn't having much of an effect because accounts aren't being used much. 48% of people who have a bank account haven't put any money in or taken any money out of it in the last year. People with less access to technology, like those who are poor or live in rural areas, have more inactive accounts. A lot of work still needs to be done to make agent networks work, teach people about money, come up with the right goods for India's diverse population, and deal with the fact that people still want cash as a way to pay and jewelry and livestock as ways to save.

## PRADHAN MANTRI JAN DHAN YOJANA: A MUST-KNOW FOR ALL

The flagship financial inclusion program, PMJDY, aims to give unbanked and low-income people access to a variety of financial services, such as basic savings bank accounts, access to need-based credit, remittances, insurance, and pensions, by making good use of technology. The push for financial inclusion coincided with the implementation of two other significant Modi government initiatives: Digital India, made possible by the rapid expansion of cell phone and internet coverage, and Aadhaar, which provided each citizen with a distinct digital ID. The three parts of the drive toward digitally-led financial inclusion—PMJDY, Aadhaar, and Mobile—were called the J-A-M trio (Delhi, 2021).

The rate of increase in new PMJDY accounts has reduced in recent years after experiencing a high growth phase in the initial years of the program's existence. This is a sign that the program is getting closer to achieving its stated goal of providing access to financial services for all people. The PMJDY has been operational for eight years, which has resulted in an increase in the total deposit balances as well as an increase in the average deposit amount for each account. 56 percent of PMJDY account holders were females as of the end of August 2022, while 67 percent of PMJDY accounts were located in rural and semi-urban areas. If there are no customer-induced transactions in a PMJDY account for a period of two years, the account is regarded as inactive in accordance with the criteria that are currently in place. In August 2022, out of a total of 46.5 crore PMJDY accounts(See Figure 9), 81.2 percent were operational, which was an increase from 2017's figure of 76.25 percent. Only 8.2 percent of PMJDY accounts had anything in the way of a balance.

*Figure 9: Info on No. of PMJDY accounts*

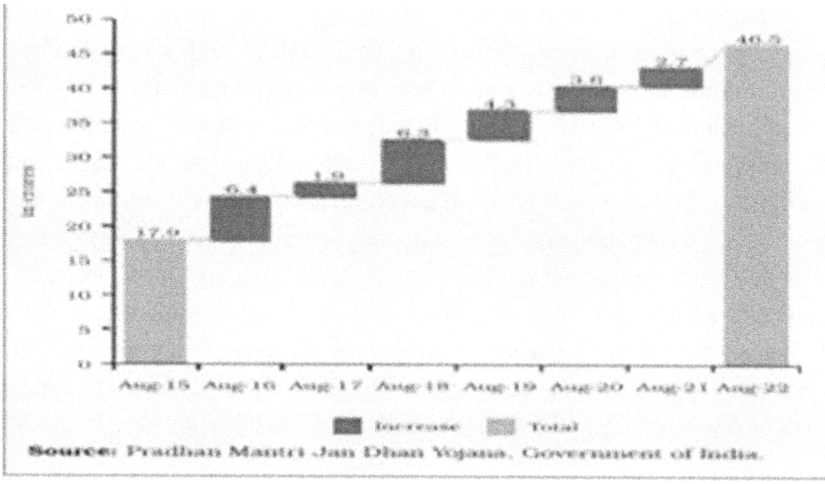

## THE INFOGRAPHS EXPLAINED

New bank branches opened by SCBs increased greatly during 2021–22, primarily in Tier 4, Tier 5, and Tier 6 centers. The share of Tier 2 and Tier 3 centers declined, but over half of the new branches were in Tier 1 and Tier 3 centers (See Figure 10). PSBs opened fewer new branches, but the share of rural areas increased to 20.8 percent in 2021–22, while urban and metropolitan areas declined from 63.6 percent to 52.6% (The Economic Times, 2023). In addition to the above, Global Findex data (Asli Demirgüç-Kunt, 2021) showed that the access gap between rich and poor (See Figure 11) has begun to close since 2014, with only 27% of the poorest Indians having a bank account compared to 41% of the richest (Asli Demirguc-Kunt, 2014).

About 197 million of the new accounts were in rural or semi-urban areas. PMJDY also seems to have helped narrow the gap between rural and urban account access in some ways. This is mostly due to the fact that most new accounts were opened in rural areas. In fact, this was the case for the vast majority of new accounts. Data from Financial Inclusion Insights showed that in 2014, 59% of Indians who lived in cities had access to a bank account, but only 52% of Indians who lived in rural areas did. But by 2017, this difference was no longer there: 79% of the rural population in India had a bank account, while only 76% of the urban population did.

*Figure 10. Opening up of new branches; growth in banking branches by SCBs; tier-wise break-up*

| Centre | 2018-19 | 2019-20 | 2020-21 | 2021-22 |
|---|---|---|---|---|
| Tier 1 | 2,194 (47.4) | 2,279 (52.4) | 1,541 (49.9) | 1,543 (47.7) |
| Tier 2 | 519 (11.2) | 367 (8.4) | 279 (9.0) | 235 (7.3) |
| Tier 3 | 712 (15.4) | 570 (13.1) | 481 (15.6) | 426 (13.2) |
| Tier 4 | 363 (7.8) | 355 (8.1) | 262 (8.5) | 293 (9.1) |
| Tier 5 | 373 (8.1) | 282 (6.5) | 178 (5.7) | 226 (7.0) |
| Tier 6 | 465 (10.1) | 500 (11.5) | 348 (11.3) | 509 (15.7) |
| **Total** | **4,626 (100.0)** | **4,353 (100.0)** | **3,089 (100.0)** | **3,232 (100.0)** |

**Notes:** 1. Figures in the parentheses represent proportion of the branches opened in a particular area *vis-à-vis* the total.

2. Tier-wise classification of centres is as follows: 'Tier 1' includes centres with population of 1, 00,000 and above. 'Tier 2' includes centres with population of 50,000 to 99,999. 'Tier 3' includes centres with population of 20,000 to 49,999. 'Tier 4' includes centres with population of 10,000 to 19,999. 'Tier 5' includes centres with population of 5,000 to 9,999, and 'Tier 6' includes centres with population of Less than 5000.

3. Data exclude 'Administrative Offices'.

4. All population figures are as per census 2011.

5. All the scheduled banks as on December 01, 2022, are considered for collating the data from 2018-19 onwards.

**Source:** CISBI, RBI. CISBI data is dynamic in nature and is updated based on information received from banks.

*Figure 11. Rich poor gap in access*

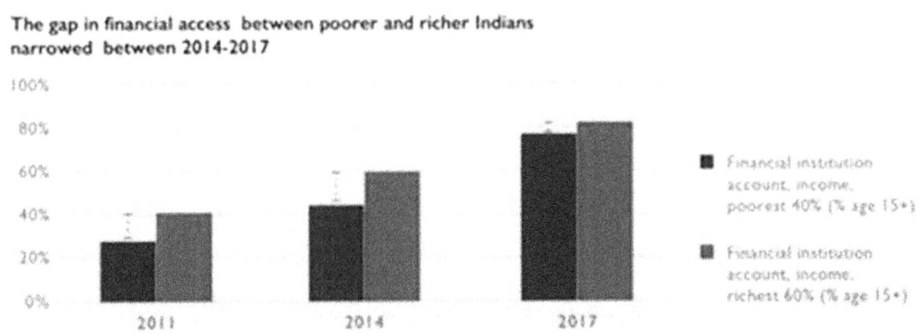

## TOWARDS GOING DIGITAL

Gone are the days when human beings only 'survived'. Today, the term 'living' has a wide meaning beyond breathing, surviving, sustaining, etc. People today are looking for better ways to pass their days, and economics also plays an impactful role. In other words, the world today is moving towards commercialization in whatever people do or act upon. This type of environment has given rise to the creation of business opportunities in literally everything we seek. Social media platforms like Instagram, Facebook, WhatsApp, etc. have been used to create opportunities, spread awareness, and also encash those opportunities. (Satpathy, 2015) (RBI, 2021-22). In this context, "Digital" is becoming a more and more relevant term and is becoming the talk of the town today. The digital world of Phonepe, GooglePay, Jan Dhan, FastTag, and other UPIs has troubleshooted several grass-roots problems in businesses and non-businesses as well. India has been witnessing numerous changes in people's lives, whether it was before, during, or after the pandemic (lockdown phase) in 2020, but one point to be noted is that the phase is faster than we have been thinking it to be. Banks, FinTechs, Payment Gateway providers, and government ministries have played a strong role in putting digital initiatives on the fast track. (The NPCI, 2023)

Based on a study conducted by NPCI (National Payments Corporation of India) in association with PRICE (People Research on India's Consumer Economy and Citizen Environment) in the year 2020, the report published by them in the year 2021 has provided interesting insights on the awareness and adoption of digital platforms by Indian households. The study revealed that the use of mobile phones has greatly contributed to pushing digital transactions throughout the country, irrespective of the region and income group (urban/rural, rich/poor, etc.). Thus, owning a smart phone is no longer considered a bottleneck for adopting digital payments. However, the point to be noted here is that the use of Banking apps has not been so popular among households. The table below highlights the same.

*Table 1. Showing digital payment methods: User share*

| Apps/ Digital payment channels used | Income Groups | | | Total |
|---|---|---|---|---|
| | Bottom 40% | Middle 40% | Top 20% | |
| PayTm, Phonepe type | 80 | 79 | 78 | 79 |
| UPI | 56 | 45 | 56 | 52 |
| Online shopping using Debit cards etc | 27 | 42 | 44 | 38 |
| Using Bank apps | 18 | 41 | 43 | 34 |

Source: NPCI Digital Payments Report, 2021

In addition to the above information, the report also showed that out of the 57% of low-income groups who have smart phones, only 5% of them use phones for banking-related matters. Among high-income groups, 90% of them have smart phones, but only 30% of them have been using phones for banking services. The study above also revealed that online banking is not so well developed, even though it has great potential. Also, awareness of the interoperability of the platforms is poor, which needs to be eradicated to increase digital adoption and thereby support financial inclusion (Demetriades, 2006) (Robert Cull, 2014). It can be very well contemplated that the bottom segments, i.e., low-income groups, especially the ones in rural segments, can be the drivers of digital transactions in the future.

## PAYMENT TO PERSON VIA DIRECT BENEFIT TRANSFERS (DBT)

The expansion of the government's Direct Benefit Transfer (DBT) program, which today channels 433 schemes from 56 ministries, has been in close correlation with implementation and growth of PMJDY. This DBT system is a government-led project that consists of many programs whose benefits are given directly to recipients and are generally distributed through state entities. With the help of other government programs, including fuel and fertilizer subsidies, insurance and pension plans, the Mahatma Gandhi National Rural Employment Guarantee Scheme (MGNREG) (Reich, 2021) (IMF, 2023) (RBI, 2021-22), and other benefits transfers has been able to grow synergistically. Receiving DBT payments into a bank account was likely the first time many individuals who used financial services for the first time between 2014 and 2018 used a digital financial service. The government's own statistics show that DBT is being received by more than 75 million PMJDY accounts. The challenge, on the other hand, comes in providing additional use cases that are convincing and in making the transition from the first stage of financial inclusion, access, to the second stage, active usage, which is explored in the following sections of this chapter.

## EFFECT OF THE DIGITAL REVOLUTION ON DBT: ANOTHER DRIVER FOR FINANCIAL INCLUSION

The DBT delivery system has been exceedingly successful owing to the adoption of digital payments in the country, especially during the pandemic. The survey report by NPCI showed that about 84% of households across all income groups received DBT cash support before lockdown, while the percentage rose to 85% overall post lockdown. However, in the case of low-income groups, the percentage was 79%

pre-lockdown and increased to 91% post-lockdown. It is clearly understood that the momentum towards adoption of digital payments in the rural and low-income segments has grown robustly over the years, but there is still more to go in enabling this growth towards achieving financial inclusion in a well-developed economic system. From this, it can be concluded that Indian rural and low-income groups have joined the march towards a digitally and financially inclusive India, but it is only a few who are adopting it.

Things required to be done to make the Indian rural consumer environment digitally safe and a cashless yet financially inclusive society include:

1. A high-quality push towards "how to use" is required. spread of awareness practically
2. Helplines for learning and problem solving
3. Safeguard features: stay safe guidelines (OTP sharing, passwords, unknown links, etc.)

## FINTECH REVOLUTION

FinTech companies include payment companies that facilitate P2P and retail payments through mobile wallets or UPI, such as Phone Pe, MobiKwik, PayTm and FreeCharge, and technology companies, such as Mswipe (RBI, 2021-22), that provide hardware for digital payments. In India, the growth of these enterprises has been tremendous over the years. Many of these payment FinTechs provided pre-paid purses, which were among the largest beneficiaries of demonetization. Even for minor financial transactions, the dearth of cash made digital the only viable option. The greatest aspect was that "the never-before-used digital service" population was also compelled to test out the digital mode. As a result, the volume of pre-paid instrument (PPI) transactions more than doubled between October 2016 and January 2017 (from 127 million to 296 million). Aadhaar's foundational digital infrastructure created opportunities for FinTech companies. With an increase in the number of smartphone users and the ability to sign up for digital payments through mobile devices, FinTech undoubtedly has a tremendous opportunity for business growth. FinTechs have also been able to expand in India as a result of the country's regulatory climate. In addition, it is evident that FinTech has revolutionized the government's operations, administrative procedures, and policies (Delhi, 2021). The increasing effectiveness of the Direct Benefit Transfer (DBT) system is a suitable example to use here. Also, numerous scholarships and the distribution of funds to the needy under the majority of programs have been digitalized and made more efficient than before. In summary, the FinTech revolution has made financial transactions quicker, simpler, greener, and better!

## CONTRIBUTION BY PAYMENT BANKS, RUPAY, UPI, AND OTHER PARTIES: WE CALL IT THE "FINTECH DRIVE"

In simple terms, **RuPay** is an Indian version of Visa or MasterCard that was launched in 2012. This was done to facilitate the use of newly opened PMJDY accounts for withdrawals and point-of-sale payments. As per the study conducted by MicroSave, of the total customers with PMJDY scheme bank accounts, 79% of them who were issued the card at the time of the launch (which comes to around 260 million cards), nearly half of the population did not really use it owing to difficulty traveling to the branch. This means that the receiving end has a problem or several other problems that hinder the usage or growth of digital payment platforms.

With an objective to encourage the entry of non-traditional financial service providers, i.e., telecom, FinTech, and postal platforms, into banking, **Payment banks** (Saon Ray, 2022) (RBI, 2021-22) came into existence in the country. It has also greatly contributed to digital financial inclusion, as explained in earlier sections. However, their participation was limited to only payments and debits and did not give much scope for the creation of credit, i.e., lending activities.

The Unified Payments Interface (UPI), launched in 2016, has significantly impacted India's digital payments growth since 2014. With low-cost interoperability and a Virtual Payment Address (VPA), UPI has experienced significant growth, surpassing debit cards and pre-paid instruments in monthly transaction volume. Between 2018 and 2019, UPI transactions increased by 450% (RBI, 2021-22) (TheWorldBankGroup, 2023). The widespread use of smart phones, particularly by low-income urban consumers, is one of the typical factors responsible for UPI's explosive rise. UPI transfers were initially expensive, with typical transaction values around Rs. 4,000. People started using UPI for smaller transactions as transaction volumes rose, converting from high-value payments to low-value purchases. As with debit cards (See Figure 12), the average UPI transaction size reached roughly Rs. 1,500 by 2018, indicating that UPI is quickly taking over as the preferred digital payment option for modest amounts.

The chart above (See Figure 12) shows the steady progress of UPI and the fall of other digital payment options between June 2016 and 2019.

*Figure 12. UPI vs others: The growth journey*

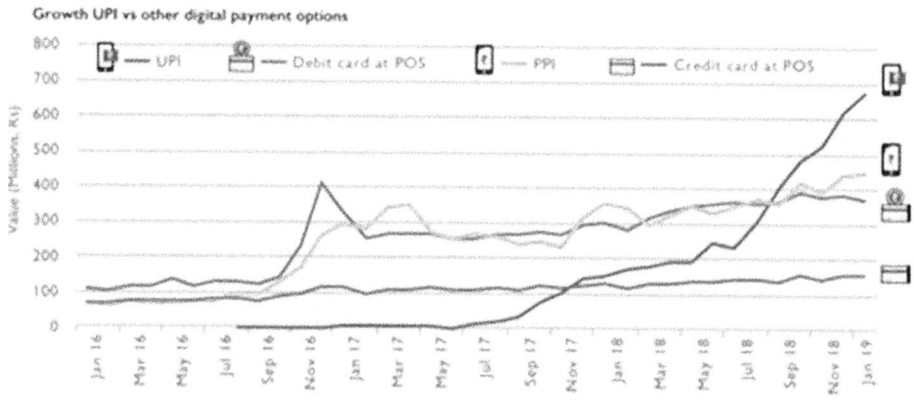


## A MOVE TOWARDS DIFFERENTIATED BANKING FROM 2014 TO 2018

This period in India witnessed the introduction of a new structure of differentiated banking through which even the most excluded populations, especially small businesses and low-income groups, could reap the benefits of accessing financial services. This innovation assisted in offering more customized or tailor-made solutions to specific market segments, unlike the large banks that offered all the services (MicroSave, 2022). Thus, this tier of banking could lead to servicing the payment vertical and also supporting banking services for poorer communities, as mentioned earlier. The catch here is that this has been possible only due to the leveraging of technology infrastructure in the country during this period. This stage encouraged FinTechs and MNOs to innovate and generate ideas to generate the movement of money in all possible legitimate ways, thereby greatly affecting the competitive structure of financial markets.

## WHAT NEXT?

From all the above information, it has been evident that Financial Inclusion and the digital revolution have greatly been influenced by each other and have contributed greatly towards sustainability ((NSO), 2020). However, there are certain loopholes, issues, and concerns that are highlighted in this section to conclude and give the reader a thoughtful closure to the true understanding of India's progress in sustainability via financial inclusion through digital banking channels and many more.

## THUMBS UP TO THE GOVERNMENT'S POLICY, BUT TO WHAT EXTENT HAS IT REACHED THE TARGET?

The policy and its implementation as regards technology, banking, and inclusion have been meticulously carried forward by the regulators (the government and RBI), but the following factors are the obstacles to this being reached out to the nation as a whole, irrespective of the region, class, and gender:

1. Poor penetration in rural areas: despite the huge success of PMJDY and other DBT systems, etc., India still lags behind in providing access to basic financial services to the rural class, especially the low-income groups. In addition, due to the excessive influence and presence of unorganized sectors, lenders, and financial service providers, certain categories and portions of the rural population have not greatly benefited from government initiatives. The nature of the rural population is also a hindrance. Such as those who are uneducated, those who are unemployed and staying at home in addition to not contributing to any economic activity, petty and daily wage earners, coolie workers, homemakers with little or no savings, etc do not willingly access financial service.
2. Geographic and infrastructural obstacles: Hilly regions with poor networks tend to also have poor infrastructure. Likewise, populations living in several other difficult locations in India have poor access to financial services. (Rajesh Barik, April 2019)

## GOVERNMENT AND BANKS ARE DOING THEIR JOBS, BUT ARE PEOPLE IGNORANT?: MATTER TO PONDER

The government and banking sectors are working hard towards the financial inclusion agenda, which has been very evident from the various schemes and positive actions explained earlier. But it looks like there is a lapse from the other party on the receiving end. The Indian population, by its nature, is very diverse and different. Their diversity is seen not only in food habits or attire but also in savings and investment styles. Lack of knowledge on effective money management, poor exposure to various financial markets, the fear factor, poor financial discipline and behavior resulting from low-income occupations, a lack of interest in IT-enabled banking services, etc. are some of the major reasons identified for this lapse. We Indians are savers by nature and blood. Our culture teaches us to save, not spend, but the above factors make our savings less resourceful. We do have saving potential but lack management skills to grow it efficiently. There are various other factors that prevent people from receiving the benefits derived from Banks and Government Schemes on Financial

Inclusion. The gender gap is one reason, while poor infrastructural facilities are another. (RBI, 2021-22)

Also, policymakers must understand that rural customers do not need complex offers from banks. All they need is acceptance of their ignorance and the openness of the bankers to cooperating with them and dealing with their problems. It is high time that banks stop pushing unwanted products on potential customers and offer them realistic and simple financial products that can make their economic lives better.

Nevertheless, the authors aim to emphasize a notable accomplishment of the nation that has garnered global astonishment in recent times. According to the source, India ranked first in terms of digital payment transactions, with China, South Korea, Thailand, and the UK following suit (Dethe, 2019) (Sachdeva, 2021). The globally recognized corporation Google has submitted a proposal to the United States' Federal Reserve, suggesting the use of India's National Payments Corporation of India (NPCI)-developed Unified Payments Interface (UPI) framework within the United States. The implementation of Aadhar in India has drawn attention from developed economies such as the US and the UK. These economies still heavily rely on traditional payment methods like card payments and cheques, while in contrast, Indian petty shops and micro shops prominently display UPI/PhonePe/Google Pay standees for bill payments. In contrast, China possesses digital payment platforms such as AliPay and WeChat that have similarities to the Unified Payments Interface (UPI), albeit with a higher degree of complexity than UPI. Also, according to a report published in 2021 on yourstory.com, India surpassed China by 25.5 billion real-time payments in the year 2020. Additionally, it has been projected that the nation's aggregate electronic transactions will surpass 50% by the year 2024. In a remarkable demonstration of technological advancement, India has successfully implemented mobile phone-based money transfers, a feat that was previously inconceivable in a country as diverse as India. Why are we still unable to achieve our sustainability goals?. With this backdrop, the subsequent parts will elucidate the pertinent issues for the readers.

## WHERE IS THE LOOPHOLE?

Overall, the lapse is greatly highlighted on the user's end, i.e., customers or the general public, for whom these services are offered universally.

The upcoming sections shall reflect upon the recommendations or suggestions to overcome the modalities observed in the policies of the Government, their implementation by the RBI and banks, and their final inclusive use by the customer or population as a whole.

1. Awareness first, Action next: Catch hold of a person randomly walking in any remote rural lane and ask him or her, "Do you know what insurance is?" or "Do you know how simple interest is different from compound interest?" or moving towards a more advanced part, ask him/her, "Do you know nationalized banks offer Atal Pension Yojana, which can guarantee you a fixed pension of Rs. 1000 to Rs. 5000 per month when you reach 60, and all you need to do is contribute Rs. 200–900 per month until you reach 60? Have you ever been told about it by banks?" Perhaps a person won't act upon it unless he knows what it is meant for and what the purpose or long- or short-term benefit of doing anything with money is. Thus, there is a strong need and a great push required to spread awareness through all possible means. For this, banks can follow the "Communication through community" idea. Identify well-known opinion leaders, young men and women of the locality, and school-going kids and make them a part of this Awareness campaign by titling them as Inclusion Ambassadors (Divya P., 2021) The focus here is that rural potential customers can be made aware of formal savings and its significance through their own kith and kin.
2. Grab support from the public: Banks can enter into partnerships, tie-ups, or MoUs with Education institutes through which they can make use of students to spread awareness and train people on things like the use of QR codes, PINs, OTPs, etc. This initiative would be termed **"Training the Trainer"** or "**Bank Ambassador**" (Divya P., 2021) and result in an effective linkage program. Educational Institutes can act as agents for Banks. The banks need not term this goal of "reaching the unbanked" as an expenditure; rather, they can consider it a Strategy to gain market share in the future. They can achieve this strategy successfully by entering into Memoranda of Understanding (MoU) or Collaborations with educational institutions in and around rural areas. With this, they can involve the student community in financial literacy and encourage them to run campaigns on behalf of the banks. It is a win-win situation for educational bodies, their students, local banks, and, of course, society. A Socially responsible bank would not only be appreciated by society but also gain an assured customer base for itself.
3. From "Cash in hand" to "Cash at the bank," followed by Active Usage: Awareness can lead to usage, and usage can convert cash in hand to cash at the bank. This means more focus should be given to increasing deposits and also credit and insurance in rural regions, thus creating quality assets for the banks and creating wealth. Apart from creating deposits and credit via banks, digital payment platforms and banking should also take this goal a step further by engaging the users in other banking and digital financial service functions like investing in pension schemes, mutual funds, insurance, loans for small

and medium businesses, and many other extended banking services. All in all, the use of banking should never stop, and the account should undergo activity at its best. And for this reason, expanding the role of Payment banks into lending and other advanced functions with proper regulations might be a great advantage to the public in general.

4. Improve and speed up the HOW (process improvement in banking): Procedures and policies must be simplified. Also, technology can be leveraged to make the initial and basic banking processes easy. For example, An application form or Withdrawal/Deposit slip may be made available in their Regional languages. Plus, at the time of Account opening, the customer may be asked to choose the language of further communication. If a Kannadiga opts for Kannada as his or her choice, all further letters, communications, mobile alerts, etc. can be sent in Kannada to him or her in all future scenarios (Technology can make this happen at low cost throughout the country). Lately, it has been seen that larger cooperative banks have taken the initiative to communicate with their stakeholders in Regional languages while sending SMS alerts, letters, etc. Hence, Commercial and other banks located in Rural regions could also do it as a Baby step to come closer to their rural customer base. This infrastructural change should come as a policy or rule via the government. The reason is that it requires a huge amount of capital investment for the technology development portfolio.
5. Customise offerings: There is "Fortune at the Bottom of the pyramid." Focus on the wider base of the pyramid. Rather than giving 1000 cr to one person by bank, why can't banks lend 100 loans of smaller denominations to small businesses? This option and the prudence to formulate tailor-made strategies for banks can be a boon (Prakash, 2020). The economics of low-balance savings accounts for banks are tough, but with a larger population utilizing this service, they can beat the heat.
6. Gender Gap reduction: there is a dire need to build a stronger gender focus into the next phase of financial inclusion programs. The system should lead to a more proactive approach to bringing women meaningfully into the financial system. There is still doubt about whether the financial system has been able to meet the true financial needs of the women's population in our nation (Saon Ray, 2022). Models based on bank accounts (which require physical travel) and smart phones can bias inclusion away from women, even when they do have adequate access to a bank account. With this regard, women centric financial institutions or communities should be encouraged to go digital like the SHGs. Furthermore, community based finance models must be developed and ensure that even the DBT women beneficiaries are covered to channel the money to their accounts.

7. Varied needs of rural profile: Rural customers' needs vary from those of urban customers. All they need are simplified, affordable, and useful products that make them financially disciplined and wise. Banks should offer products that encourage rural people to visit banks often. Providing zero balance accounts, high-interest rate time deposits, maintenance-free products, white-labeled ATMs, Online or SMS-based banking, etc. are some of them. Besides, the bankers should guide the customers in using the products efficiently.

All said and done, the chapter encompasses the progress, challenges and concerns of achieving financial inclusion in the Indian scenario (Rajesh Barik, April 2019). The authors express their overall deliberations in the following framework (See Figure 13) that would summarise the whole chapter in one in simple.

*Figure 13. A final framework of recommendation in a nut shell*

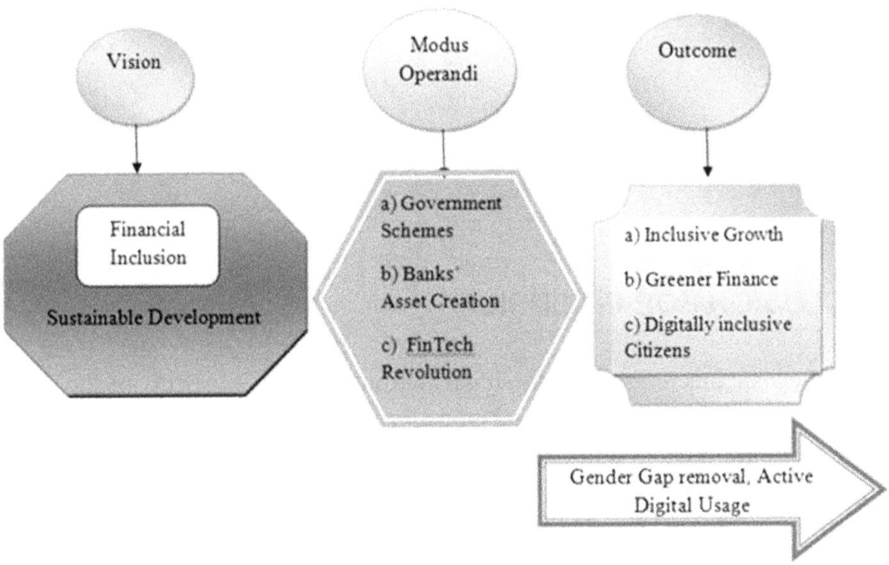


## FINALLY, WHAT CAN *WE* DO?

We live by capital, not by added value, so environmental protection is necessary (Phu, 2023 IGI Global publishing) . For achieving sustainable economic growth, the end users, i.e., the citizens of the country, play an inevitable role. Money can create more money only when it moves from one hand to another (AmericanEconomicReview, 2013). We, as end users, are required to do only THREE simple things:

Embrace technology,
Be aware of government efforts to provide access to financial services and
Actively utilize financial services, mainly banking.

*Figure 14. Technology by all, for all*

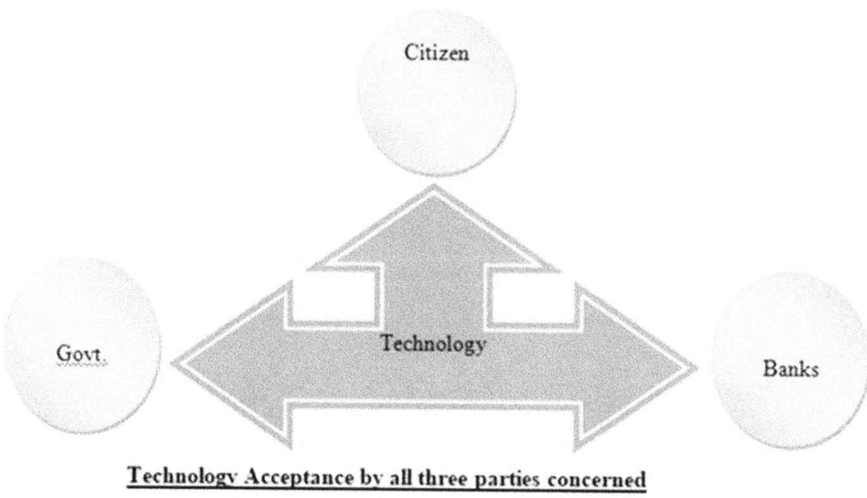


## CONCLUSION FOR INCLUSION

The chapter is expected to take the reader through relevant aspects of the digital revolution in the country and financial inclusion initiatives taken by the government, which must have created an impression of how significant the policies are in the overall progress of economic activities. Financial inclusion may be a costly affair, but it is worth the cost. A well-developed financial system supported by advanced digital technology (See Figure 14) optimally embraced by the citizens of the country both in rural and urban regions can definitely lead to economic sustainability (Beck, 2016). Our country is close to achieving this. A new and permanent partnership between the government, banks, and the nation's People will promote and make this achievement possible.

## REFERENCES

Ajigini, O. A., & Chinamasa, T. J. W. (2023). Modelling Digital Transformation Within the Financial Sector: A South African Perspective. [IRMJ]. *Information Resources Management Journal, 36*(1), 1–20. doi:10.4018/irmj.320642

American Economic Review. (2013). Why Don't the Poor Save More? Evidence from Health Savings Experiments. *The American Economic Review, 103*(4), 1138-71.

Asli Demirguc-Kunt, L. K. (2014). *Global Financial Index Report*. World Bank. https://pubdocs.worldbank.org/: https://thedocs.worldbank.org/en/doc/681361466184854434-0050 022016/original/2014GlobalFindexReportDKSV.pdf

Asli Demirgüç-Kunt, L. K. (2021). *The Global Findex Database- Financial Inclusion, Digital Payments and Resilience in the Age of Covid19*. World Bank Group.

Barrachina, M. D., & Baporikar, N. (2022). (IGI Global publishing)). Comparative Analysis of Factors Influencing Informal Investors of Spain and the United States. *International Journal of Applied Behavioral Economics, 11*(1), 1–14. doi:10.4018/IJABE.311051

Beck, T. (2016). Financial Inclusion –measuring progress and progress in measuring. *Fourth IMF Statistical Forum "Lifting the Small Boats: Statistics for Inclusive Growth."* IMF.

Bravo, E., & Ostos, J. (2023). Rational or Emotional User: The Dual Processing Approach to Understanding Continuance Usage. *Information Resources Management Journal, 36*(1), 1–20. doi:10.4018/IRMJ.325241

Chagwesha, M. (2022). Intergenerational Leadership Practices in African Family Firms: A Bibliometric Analysis. *International Journal of Applied Management Sciences and Engineering* 9(1), 1-13. doi:10.4018/IJAMSE.312850.

Delhi, P. (2021). *Press Release*. PIB. https://pib.gov.in/: https://pib.gov.in/PressReleaseIframePage.aspx?PRID=1778084

Demetriades, S. H., & Hook Law, S. (2006). Finance, Institutions and Economic Development. *International Journal of Finance & Economics, 11*(3), 245–260. doi:10.1002/ijfe.296

Dethe, A. (2019). *Not just Google, the world is watching India's UPI*. BFSI. https://bfsi.economictimes.indiatimes.com/news/editors-view/not-just-google-the-world-is-watching-indias-upi/

Ghodoosi, B. T.-S., Torrisi-Steele, G., West, T., & Li, Q. (2023). (IGI Global Publishing)). An Exploration of the Definition of Data Literacy in the Academic and Public Domains. *International Journal of Adult Education and Technology, 14*(1), 1–16. doi:10.4018/IJAET.325218

MicroSave. (2022). *Library.* MicroSave. https://www.microsave.net/library/

mSTAR. (2019). *India Digital Financial Inclusion Report- Journey Map.* USAID, fhi360.

NSO. (2020). *Sustainable Development Goals National Indicator Framework Progress Report* . GoI, Ministry of Statistics & Programme Implementation .

Phu, G. N. (2023). Factors Affecting the Use of Best Available Techniques and the Impact on Business Sustainability. *International Journal of Asian Business and Information Management, 14*(1), 1–18. doi:10.4018/IJABIM.325651

Prakash, P. (2020). Financial Inclusion Plan- Progress and Prospects. *IJRAR, 7*(1).

Rajesh Barik, P. S. (2019). Analyzing the progress and prospects of financial inclusion in India. *Journal of Public Affairs.*

RBI. (2021-22). *Trend and Progress of Banking in India.* New Delhi: RBI.

Reich, G. (2021). People love digital banking but will they surrender all their data? *The Financial Brand.* https://thefinancialbrand.com/news/open-banking/people-love-digital-banking-but-will-they-surrender-all-their-data-12189
1/

Robert Cull, T. E. (2014). Financial Inclusion and Development: Recent Impact Evidence. *Focus Note, 92*, 1.

Sachdeva, M. (2021). India Ranks 1st in Digital payment transactions globally. *In Shorts.* https://inshorts.com/en/news/india-ranks-1st-in-digital-paym ent-transactions-globally-report-1617259436829

Saon Ray, P. M. (2022). *Digital Financial Inclusion and Literacy from a G20 Perspective.* Asian Development Bank Institute.

Satpathy, I. B., Patnaik, B. C. M., & Das, P. K. (2015). Banishing Financial Untouchability of the Poor through PMJDY- A Tryst with New Destiny. *Mediterranean Journal of Social Sciences.* doi:10.5901/mjss.2015.v6n2p184

Segall, R. S., & Sankarasubbu, V. (2022). Using Open-Source Software for Business, Urban, and Other Applications of Deep Neural Networks, Machine Learning, and Data Analytics Tools. *International Journal of Artificial Intelligence and Machine Learning*, *12*(1), 1–28. doi:10.4018/IJAIML.307905

Suhr, H. C. (2023). Designing Audience Participation and Gamification in Intermedia Performance: Conceptual Framework and Theoretical Implications Post COVID-19. *International Journal of Art, Culture, Design, and Technology*, *12*(1), 1–13. doi:10.4018/IJACDT.316966

The Economic Times. (2023). Banks open more branches to cash in on credit growth. *The Economic Times*. economictimes.indiatimes.com: https://economictimes.indiatimes.com/industry/banking/finance/banking/banks-open-more-branches-to-cash-in-on-credit-growth/articleshow/97330007.cms

# Chapter 5
# Financial Fraud in the Age of FinTech:
## A Bibliometric Analysis for Future Research Agendas

**Bhartrihari Pandiya**
*National Forensic Sciences University, India*

**Priyanka Yadav**
*National Forensic Sciences University, India*

## ABSTRACT

*Fintech is a vast domain that includes a wide range of activities, from data security to financial service delivery, which helps companies automate their business operations and introduce the latest financial products and services. The problem of financial fraud has a significant impact on the finance sector and needs behavioral understanding from the perspective of both the fraudster and the consumer. The purpose of the chapter is to identify and analyze the various aspects of financial fraud in the age of Fintech and highlight the emerging research areas and trends. Co-occurrence and co-citation analyses were used to identify emerging trends and research directions related to fraud detection in Fintech research. The cluster analysis revealed five clusters which have been explained further. The research employs thematic clusters that identify fundamental, various themes based on their centrality and density. These themes and streams are intended to guide researchers, scholars, policymakers, and practitioners towards more precise, distinctive, and important areas of focus.*

DOI: 10.4018/979-8-3693-0008-4.ch005

## 1. INTRODUCTION

The financial sector has consistently faced an enduring struggle with financial fraud, leading to substantial economic losses, reputational harm, and the erosion of trust among stakeholders (Roszkowska, 2021). The issue of financial fraud exerts a substantial influence on the financial sector and needs behavioral understanding from the perspective of both the fraudster and the consumer. It can cause a loss of trust in the industry, lead to economic instability, and affect the cost of living. The conventional methods like auditing, which rely on manual techniques, are not very effective and accurate in tackling this issue because it is a complex problem. However, data mining-based techniques have demonstrated their usefulness in detecting minor abnormalities in vast sets of data. The financial industry has been impacted in a significant manner with the creation of machine-readable data, which has been made possible by the continuous advancement in computational power and storage. With the rapid advancement of Fintech, which encompasses various technologies such as mobile banking, online payments, blockchain, and artificial intelligence, new opportunities for financial fraud have emerged (Bhat et al., 2023; Hoang et al., 2022). The advent of fintech innovations has transformed conventional financial systems, offering increased convenience and efficiency. Nevertheless, these innovations have also brought forth new vulnerabilities and risks that can be exploited by fraudulent individuals (Luo et al., 2021). The intersection of finance and technology has given rise to a multifaceted and ever-changing landscape in which both traditional and emerging forms of financial fraud coexist. This necessitates a comprehensive understanding and the implementation of effective countermeasures. It's crucial to note that financial fraud can have significant repercussions on the stability of financial systems (Pacelli et al., 2022). Through the examination of financial fraud, we can pinpoint weaknesses, assess risks, and formulate strategies to protect the integrity of financial markets, institutions, and economies. Financial fraud can also lead to substantial economic losses, affecting individuals, businesses, and governments. By examining the economic impact of fraud, researchers can provide insights into its consequences, helping policymakers and organizations develop strategies to mitigate its effects. Financial fraud can have far-reaching social implications. It can lead to job losses, pension fund erosion, and damage to social welfare programs (Mosteanu and Faccia, 2020). Understanding these broader societal impacts can inform efforts to protect vulnerable populations and promote social justice. Thus, this was the motivation behind choosing this as the research work as it has huge implications in many areas.

## 1.1 Current Trends in Financial Fraud

The various areas which are evolving are of various natures like fraud schemes, technological advancements, regulatory developments, and emerging trends. The current scenario in the area of fraud in Fintech is quite varied (Mehrban et al., 2020). As deepfake technology becomes increasingly sophisticated, concerns are rising regarding its potential application in financial fraud (Cross, 2022). Research in this field can focus on comprehending the implications of deepfakes on identity theft, authentication systems, and devising countermeasures to identify and prevent synthetic identity fraud. Additionally, the role of artificial intelligence (AI) in fraud detection is noteworthy, as AI and machine learning algorithms play a progressively significant role in this domain. Consequently, there is a need for research aimed at developing AI models that are explainable, providing transparent and interpretable outcomes. Such models would enable stakeholders to comprehend the rationale behind fraud detection decisions. There is a growing focus on behavioral biometrics and user profiling where the use of behavioral biometrics can be explored, such as keystroke dynamics, mouse movement, and user profiling, can contribute to enhancing fraud detection capabilities (Sharma and Elmiligi, 2022). Research has focussed on developing robust models that analyze user behavior to identify suspicious activities and distinguish legitimate user actions from fraudulent ones. There are frauds in Decentralized Finance (DeFi) because of the rise of blockchain and decentralized finance (Dos Santos et al., 2022). A greater comprehension of the distinct fraud hazards linked to DeFi platforms is essential. This includes recognizing the risks related to smart contract weaknesses, manipulation of liquidity pools, and scams within decentralized exchanges. In the area of Social Engineering and phishing attacks, the human element remains a significant vulnerability in the Fintech ecosystem (TN and Kulkarni, 2022). Exploration of the psychology behind social engineering techniques and phishing attacks, focusing on user awareness, education, and effective interventions to mitigate these fraud vectors is required. As Fintech continues to evolve, new services and models are emerging such as P2P lending, advisory through robots, crowdfunding, and digital wallets. Research can examine the specific fraud risks and challenges associated with these emerging services, including regulatory gaps, consumer protection issues, and fraud detection mechanisms. On a global level, cross-border fraud and jurisdictional challenges are there since Fintech transcends geographical boundaries, posing unique challenges for cross-border fraud investigations and regulatory enforcement (Omarova, 2020). Thus, exploration of the complexities of cross-jurisdictional cooperation, legal harmonization, and the role of international frameworks in combating financial fraud in a globalized Fintech landscape is required. The ethical implications of fraud detection technologies are also recent areas. The usage of innovative technologies for detection of fraud raises ethical considerations related to privacy, bias, and algorithmic accountability. There is a need for research which can focus on ethical frameworks and guidelines to ensure responsible deployment and usage of fraud detection technologies, balancing the need for security with individual rights and societal values.

## 2. LITERATURE REVIEW

The existing research landscape on financial fraud in the Fintech age includes a extensive variety of studies that explore various aspects of fraud, its detection, prevention, and mitigation within the context of emerging financial technologies. The various themes and topics in the field have been reviewed. In the area of fraudulent activities in Fintech, studies have examined specific types of financial fraud prevalent in Fintech, including identity theft, payment fraud, insider fraud, money laundering, cyber fraud, and fraudulent investment schemes (Goecks et al., 2022). There have been researches which have focussed on fraud detection and prevention and reviewed developing advanced techniques and tools for fraud detection and prevention in Fintech, such as machine learning algorithms, data analytics, behavior-based authentication, biometrics, and blockchain technology (Gai et al., 2018; Chang et al., 2020). The literature on aspect of consumer vulnerability and scam awareness highlights the vulnerabilities of consumers in the Fintech ecosystem and investigates factors influencing their susceptibility to scams and fraudulent activities (Mogaji & Nguyen, 2022). It explores consumer behavior, decision-making processes, and awareness campaigns. There are various regulatory and legal frameworks and challenges posed by Fintech-related financial fraud and explored the effectiveness of existing legal frameworks. They have also proposed regulatory interventions and policy recommendations to mitigate fraud risks. Certain studies have targeted the trust and security aspect in Fintech exploring the role of trust and security in fostering user confidence and adoption of Fintech platforms (Roh et al., 2022; Kadyan et al., 2022). This includes research on user perceptions, security measures, privacy concerns, and the impact of security breaches on trust. The necessity for cooperation among financial institutions, technology companies, regulatory bodies, and law enforcement agencies to address financial fraud in the Fintech sector is substantial. This entails conducting research on information exchange, fostering public-private partnerships, and promoting collaborative endeavours.

The literature on financial fraud in the age of Fintech has experienced substantial growth in recent years as in the Figure 1 below, reflecting the increasing importance of the topic. Researchers have disseminated their discoveries through academic journals, conference proceedings, and industry reports. Within this realm of publication, a wide array of disciplines has made contributions, including finance, computer science, information systems, law, and criminology. The global perspective in research on financial fraud in the era of Fintech is evident, with contributions originating from various geographical regions. The existing body of literature concerning financial fraud amid the rise of Fintech embodies a multidisciplinary approach, amalgamating insights from finance, technology, law, and behavioral sciences (Gomber et al., 2018). The research landscape increasingly emphasizes the comprehension of fraud patterns, the development of advanced detection techniques, and the resolution of regulatory and consumer protection challenges (Jabłonowska et al., 2018; Garz et al., 2021). Nevertheless, there are still gaps to be addressed and opportunities for further exploration.

Accordingly, the objectives of the research work are -

1. To identify and analyze the various aspects of Financial Fraud in the age of Fintech and how literature has evolved in this research context
2. To highlight the emerging research areas and trends in Financial Fraud in the age of Fintech, thus providing suggestions for future research

## 3. METHODOLOGY

### Bibliometric Analysis

Given the growing prevalence and impact of financial fraud in the era of Fintech, it becomes imperative to conduct a thorough examination of the existing research within this field. Employing a bibliometric analysis offers a methodical and quantitative means to evaluate the state of knowledge, pinpoint research gaps, and unveil emerging trends. Through the scrutiny of scholarly literature related to financial fraud in the Fintech era, scholars can glean insights into the central themes, research methodologies employed, and the geographical dispersion of research endeavors. This type of analysis not only facilitates the recognition of extensively explored areas but also highlights domains warranting further investigation. Additionally, it serves as a tool for identifying potential cross-disciplinary collaborations and contributes to shaping the direction of future research agendas. The purpose of this research is to offer an summary of current research in the area of AI in banking. There is a need for reviewing the qualitative and quantitative research in order to organize the previous findings related to usage of AI in banking for risk assessment and mitigation. Bibliometric analysis can be of help in such cases where the present literature can be analyzed (Liu et al., 2015; Sun and Grimes, 2016) because it provides a systematic and transparent understanding of the research (Aria and Cuccurullo, 2017). The initial introduction of this concept involved a scientific method aimed at observing the evolution of a research area over time, adopting a multidisciplinary approach (Pritchard, 1969). These analyses help in the identification of impact on the basis of author data, research domain data, journal data, and emerging themes (Sarin et al., 2020). VOSviewer is one of the useful software which helps in conducting bibliometric analysis (Van and Waltman, 2011). Kumar et al. (2022) conducted bibliometric assessment technique to evaluate the development of Fintech documents from the perspectives of the variety of documentts produced in this field, development of yearly publishes with important indexes, leading journals and publishers, top-cited papers, largest number of papers produced from top nations, and frequently used keywords. Hence, bibliometric analysis was conducted to identify the research themes in the field. This study will also employ bibliometric analysis to explore recent trends in AI in banking for risk assessment and mitigation. It will help to showcase qualitative and quantitative analysis. The various emerging research areas will also be highlighted leading to upcoming research angles.

For the bibliometric analysis, SCOPUS database was considered for performing a literature search. The final search query which was used was as follows: TITLE-ABS-KEY ("FINTECH" AND "FINANCIAL FRAUD") AND (LIMIT-TO (SUBJAREA, "BUSI") OR LIMIT-TO (SUBJAREA, "DECI") OR LIMIT-TO (SUBJAREA, "ECON") OR LIMIT-TO (SUBJAREA, "SOCI")) AND (LIMIT-TO (LANGUAGE, "English")).

The number of total data points collected was 107. A full record of the bibliographical information, all citation information, abstract and related information was downloaded as a CSV file for further analysis. The description of the bibliometric data, most cited authors, subject-wise division, country wise analysis, etc. was done which showed the results respectively. Through an extensive bibliometric analysis of the current research concerning financial fraud in the era of Fintech, this study seeks to offer a valuable reference tool for researchers, policymakers, and professionals. It offers insights into current research trends, identifies knowledge gaps, and highlights potential future research agendas to effectively tackle financial fraud in the evolving landscape of Fintech.

## 4. RESULTS

The description of the year wise analysis, country wise analysis, and subject area wise analysis was done which showed the results respectively from Figure 1 to Figure 3. The bibliometric data analysis showing the co-occurrence keyword analysis has been depicted in this section.

*Figure 1. Documents year wise*

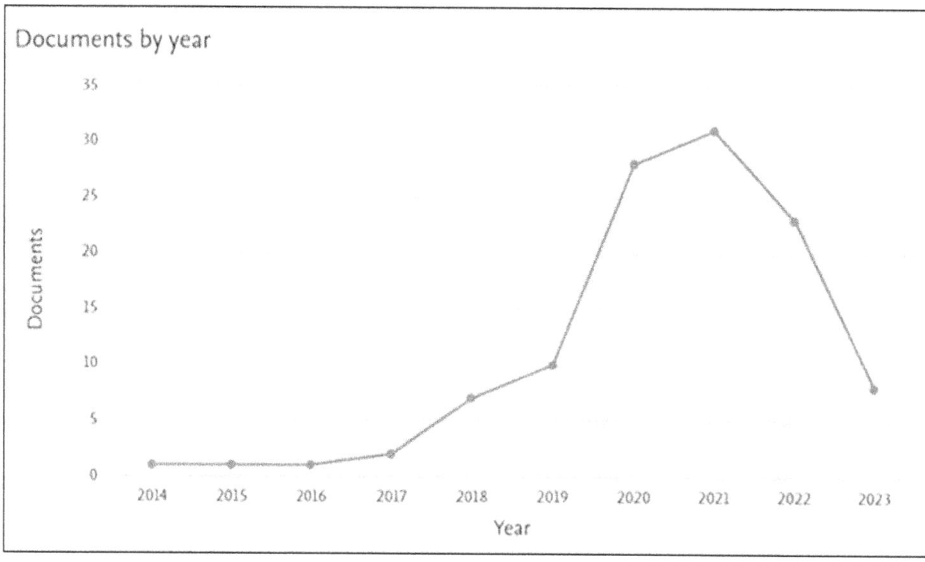


*Figure 2. Documents country wise*

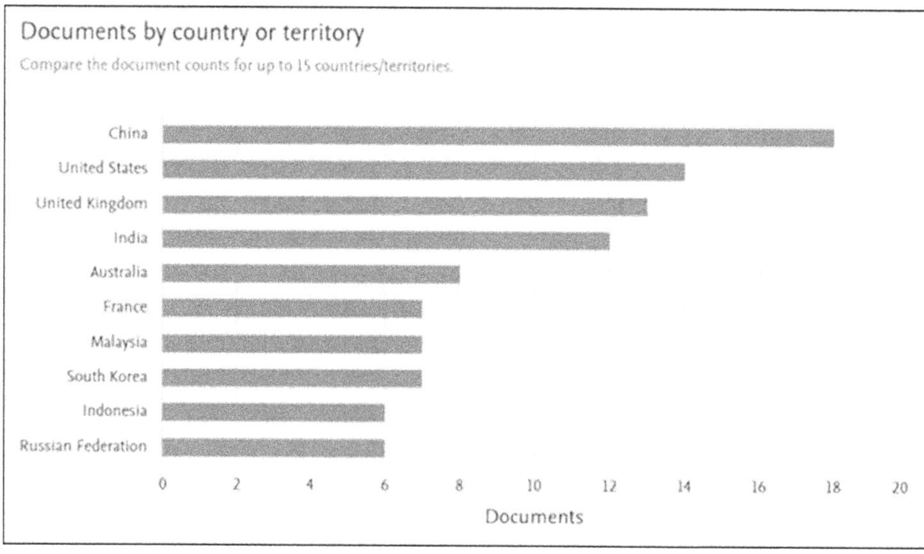

*Figure 3. Documents subject area-wise*

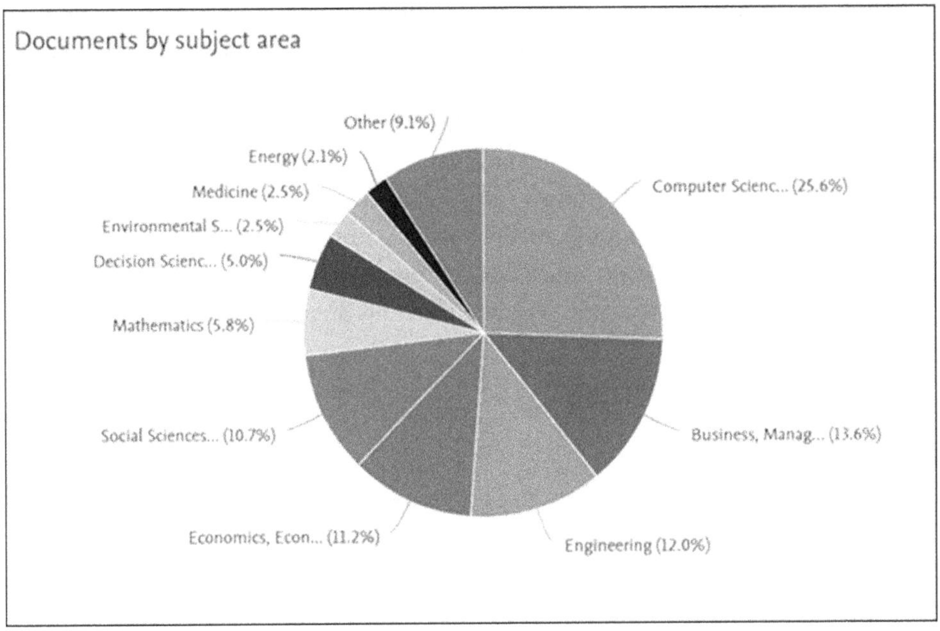


*Figure 4. Co-occurrence keywords*

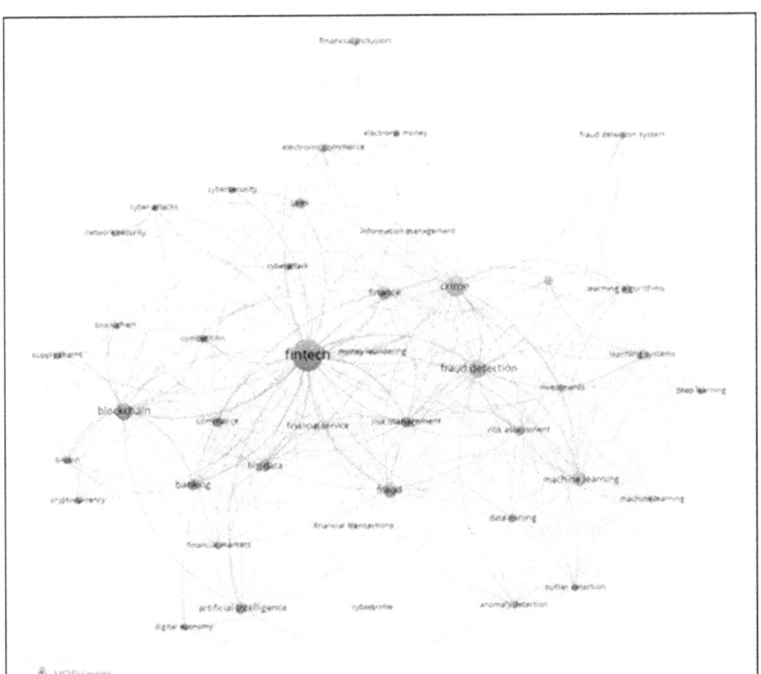

In Figure 4, the network analysis of co-occurring keywords is presented, revealing the identification of macro clusters following the bibliometric analysis. The co-occurrence diagram displays different colors indicating the connections with associated keywords within each cluster. There are five distinct colored clusters, namely Yellow, Red, Green, Blue, and Violet. Among these, the keyword 'Fintech' appears as the largest, suggesting its centrality as the main theme, with the remaining keywords being related to it. The utilization of an optimization algorithm, as described by Kumar et al. (2020), aids in detecting communities within extensive networks by combining nodes based on heuristics. The analysis of keyword co-occurrence provides valuable insights across various research areas and their application in specific domains.

In co-occurrence network analysis, the keywords are classified into four clusters like this:

**Cluster-1** (Red Cluster) - Co-occurrence keyword Fintech is the central theme around which the other keywords are placed. Other major themes are blockchain in which keywords like cryptocurrency and bitcoin are there. Risk management, digital economy and supply chains are also included in the cluster. The availability of big data in banking and commerce is also shown in the cluster.

**Cluster-2** (Yellow Cluster) - Co-occurrence keywords like information system and cybercrime in the financial services is shown here. Also, there keywords such as money laundering in cyber transactions is present. There can be more research correlating other variables in this cluster.

**Cluster-3** (Green Cluster): Keywords like crime and fraud detection are the major clusters which are connected to other keywords like risk assessment and fraud detection system. Keywords which are related to latest Information technology like deep learning, data mining, learning algorithms, machine learning and detection of anomaly are evident in the cluster. Mapping investments with learning systems can be an area of exploration.

**Cluster-4** (Blue Cluster): This cluster has keywords which summarizes the various attacks in the area of finance leading to crime. Keywords like Cyber-attack and cyber security are the keywords which are connected to bigger keywords like Frauds and Finance. This cluster has a great potential for the research work.

**Cluster-5** (Violet Cluster): The last cluster includes keywords electronic market, electronic money and how it is connected to financial inclusion. The sales and financial inclusion aspect is dependent on the dissemination of the electronic market and to what extent it has reached to the populace.

## 5. CONCLUSION

The bibliometric analysis on financial fraud in the age of Fintech highlights several key findings that provide insights into the existing research landscape and identify directions for future research agendas. The analysis revealed the summary of the existing landscape in the researches done. The basis for the presentation of the overall summary is understanding and interpretation of the published research papers in the area. The research on financial fraud in the age of Fintech is multidisciplinary, encompassing fields such as finance, computer science, law, and behavioral sciences. It covers themes such as fraud detection, prevention, consumer vulnerability, regulatory frameworks, trust, and industry collaboration. The various emerging themes include synthetic identity fraud, explainable AI for fraud detection, behavioral biometrics, social engineering, and ethical implications of fraud detection technologies. There is a huge scope for interdisciplinary collaboration as highlighted in various literatures, emphasizing the integration of multiple disciplines such as finance, computer science, law, behavioral sciences, and criminology. Collaborations can lead to comprehensive insights, innovative solutions, and effective fraud prevention strategies. In the era of Fintech, tackling financial fraud is exceedingly crucial, given the swift technological progress and the growing dependence on Fintech platforms. Financial fraud presents substantial risks to individuals, businesses, and the overall stability of the financial ecosystem. By conducting research and implementing effective measures, the interests of consumers can be safeguarded, enhance trust in Fintech services, protect financial systems, and promote the responsible and secure adoption of Fintech innovations. The analysis has thus provided the roadmap for future research on financial fraud in the age of Fintech. It is crucial for researchers, policymakers, regulatory bodies, financial institutions, and technology providers to collaborate and prioritize efforts to combat financial fraud. Only through comprehensive research, interdisciplinary perspectives, and robust policies the evolving challenges. The bibliometric analysis on financial fraud in the age of Fintech highlighted several key findings that provide insights into the existing research landscape and identify directions for future research agendas.

## 6. THEORETICAL IMPLICATIONS AND FUTURE RESEARCH

The dynamic landscape of financial fraud in the age of Fintech presents several emerging areas and topics that require further exploration. There is a huge need for interdisciplinary collaborations as fostering collaborations between researchers from finance, computer science, law, behavioral sciences, and other relevant disciplines to leverage their expertise and develop holistic approaches to combat financial fraud in

Fintech will help to research the subject better. An upcoming area identified is real-time fraud monitoring and response as there is a need to investigate the development of real-time fraud monitoring systems that can detect and respond to emerging fraud patterns quickly, minimizing financial losses and reducing the impact on victims (Uyyala and Yadav, 2023). The design should also be human-centered based on design principles to develop user-friendly interfaces, intuitive security features, and efficient educational resources that enable individuals to make well-informed choices and safeguard themselves from fraudulent activities are essential. It is crucial to thoroughly assess the strength of data privacy and security measures while evaluating the influence of evolving data protection laws like the General Data Protection Regulation (GDPR) and other regional frameworks on fraud prevention methods (Wylde et al., 2022). Additionally, identifying approaches to maintain a balance between privacy and the effectiveness of fraud detection strategies is imperative. Also, addressing the challenge of explainability and transparency in machine learning models used for fraud detection, ensuring stakeholders understand the underlying factors influencing fraud decisions and building trust in automated fraud detection systems. A broader scope would be in the area of behavioral economics and fraud prevention where leveraging insights from behavioral economics and decision-making theories to design interventions and nudges that encourage users to adopt secure behaviours, can help in making informed financial decisions, and protect them against fraud. A lot of global collaboration in research and information sharing is required in the area of fraud prevention strategies, considering the global nature of Fintech and financial fraud. By addressing these emerging research areas and future directions, researchers can contribute to the expansion of effective countermeasures, regulatory frameworks, user-centric approaches to combat monetary fraud in the age of Fintech, ultimately promoting the integrity and security of the financial ecosystem. The exploration of interdisciplinary collaborations and integration of multiple disciplines is crucial for comprehensive research on financial fraud in the age of Fintech. By bringing together diverse fields such as finance, computer science, law, behavioral sciences, and more, researchers can gain deeper insights, develop innovative solutions, and address the complex challenges associated with financial fraud.

## 7. MANAGERIAL IMPLICATIONS

There are a few managerial implications which have been presented in this section. There is a need to develop regulatory frameworks that are flexible and adaptable to keep pace with the rapid evolution of Fintech and emerging fraud risks. Encourage continuous monitoring and updates to address new fraud schemes and technological advancements. This can be done through collaborations with various stakeholders leading to information sharing. Collaboration may involve regulatory entities, financial establishments, and technology providers coming together to exchange information, share best practices, and pool intelligence pertaining to financial fraud. There is a huge need to promote international cooperation to address cross-border fraud challenges effectively. Also, establishing regulatory sandboxes or innovation hubs is the need of the hour which would facilitate responsible experimentation and foster the development of secure and innovative Fintech solutions. This would help to monitor and assess the potential risks associated with new technologies and business models. Users are very naïve and thus financial literacy programs are required to be implemented comprehensive. These educational efforts in the realm of finance have the capacity to equip consumers with the essential knowledge and skills required for securely navigating the Fintech landscape. There is a need to educate users about common fraud schemes, secure online practices, and responsible use of Fintech services. The research also reveals that there is a need for user-centric designing. Thus, Fintech providers should be encouraged to adopt user-centric design principles, ensuring that user interfaces, security features, and privacy settings are intuitive, transparent, and empower users to protect themselves against fraud. There should be a mandatory reporting and disclosure for Fintech firms for reporting incidents of financial fraud promptly and transparently to regulatory authorities. This establishment of disclosure requirements for data breaches and security incidents will enable users to take appropriate actions to mitigate potential harm. There should be collaboration between public and private Sectors to combat financial fraud along with platforms for sharing threat intelligence, coordinating responses, and conducting joint research and development initiatives. The work should be collaborative for developing industry-wide standards, certifications, and best practices for data security, fraud prevention and confidentiality in the Fintech ecosystem. Existing and upcoming Fintech firms should adopt these standards voluntarily and establish mechanisms for independent audits and certifications. These policy implications and recommendations derived from existing research aim to create a secure and resilient Fintech ecosystem that safeguards against financial fraud while promoting innovation, consumer trust, and financial inclusion. Policymakers and regulatory entities hold a pivotal responsibility in moulding the regulatory framework and establishing a setting conducive to combating financial fraud in the Fintech era.

## REFERENCES

Aria, M., & Cuccurullo, C. (2017). bibliometrix: An R-tool for comprehensive science mapping analysis. *Journal of Informetrics, 11*(4), 959–975. doi:10.1016/j.joi.2017.08.007

Bhat, J. R., AlQahtani, S. A., & Nekovee, M. (2023). FinTech enablers, use cases, and role of future internet of things. *Journal of King Saud University-Computer and Information Sciences, 35*(1), 87–101. doi:10.1016/j.jksuci.2022.08.033

Chang, V., Baudier, P., Zhang, H., Xu, Q., Zhang, J., & Arami, M. (2020). How Blockchain can impact financial services–The overview, challenges and recommendations from expert interviewees. *Technological Forecasting and Social Change, 158*, 120166. doi:10.1016/j.techfore.2020.120166 PMID:32834134

Cross, C. (2022). Using artificial intelligence (AI) and deepfakes to deceive victims: The need to rethink current romance fraud prevention messaging. *Crime Prevention and Community Safety, 24*(1), 30–41. doi:10.105741300-021-00134-w

Dos Santos, S., Singh, J., Thulasiram, R. K., Kamali, S., Sirico, L., & Loud, L. (2022, June). A new era of blockchain-powered decentralized finance (DeFi)-a review. In *2022 IEEE 46th Annual Computers, Software, and Applications Conference (COMPSAC)* (pp. 1286-1292). IEEE.

Gai, K., Qiu, M., & Sun, X. (2018). A survey on FinTech. *Journal of Network and Computer Applications, 103*, 262–273. doi:10.1016/j.jnca.2017.10.011

Garz, S., Giné, X., Karlan, D., Mazer, R., Sanford, C., & Zinman, J. (2021). Consumer protection for financial inclusion in low-and middle-income countries: Bridging regulator and academic perspectives. *Annual Review of Financial Economics, 13*(1), 219–246. doi:10.1146/annurev-financial-071020-012008

Goecks, L. S., Korzenowski, A. L., Gonçalves Terra Neto, P., de Souza, D. L., & Mareth, T. (2022). Anti-money laundering and financial fraud detection: A systematic literature review. *Intelligent Systems in Accounting, Finance & Management, 29*(2), 71–85. doi:10.1002/isaf.1509

Gomber, P., Kauffman, R. J., Parker, C., & Weber, B. W. (2018). On the fintech revolution: Interpreting the forces of innovation, disruption, and transformation in financial services. *Journal of Management Information Systems, 35*(1), 220–265. doi:10.1080/07421222.2018.1440766

Hoang, T. G., Nguyen, G. N. T., & Le, D. A. (2022). Developments in financial technologies for achieving the Sustainable Development Goals (SDGs): FinTech and SDGs. In *Disruptive technologies and eco-innovation for sustainable development* (pp. 1–19). IGI Global. doi:10.4018/978-1-7998-8900-7.ch001

Jabłonowska, A., Kuziemski, M., Nowak, A. M., Micklitz, H. W., Pałka, P., & Sartor, G. (2018). Consumer law and artificial intelligence: Challenges to the EU consumer law and policy stemming from the business' use of artificial intelligence-final report of the ARTSY project. *EUI Department of Law Research Paper*, (2018/11).

Kadyan, S., Bhasin, N. K., & Sharma, M. (2022). Fintech: Review of theoretical perspectives and exploring challenges to trust building and retention in improving online Digital Bank Marketing. *Transnational Marketing Journal*, *10*(3), 579–592.

Kumar, T., Vaidyanathan, S., Ananthapadmanabhan, H., Parthasarathy, S., & Ravindran, B. (2020). Hypergraph clustering by iteratively reweighted modularity maximization. *Applied Network Science*, *5*(1), 1–22. doi:10.100741109-020-00300-3

Liu, Z., Yin, Y., Liu, W., & Dunford, M. (2015). Visualizing the intellectual structure and evolution of innovation systems research: A bibliometric analysis. *Scientometrics*, *103*(1), 135–158. doi:10.100711192-014-1517-y

Luo, D., Mishra, T., Yarovaya, L., & Zhang, Z. (2021). Investing during a Fintech Revolution: Ambiguity and return risk in cryptocurrencies. *Journal of International Financial Markets, Institutions and Money*, *73*, 101362. doi:10.1016/j.intfin.2021.101362

Mehrban, S., Nadeem, M. W., Hussain, M., Ahmed, M. M., Hakeem, O., Saqib, S., & Khan, M. A. (2020). Towards secure FinTech: A survey, taxonomy, and open research challenges. *IEEE Access : Practical Innovations, Open Solutions*, *8*, 23391–23406. doi:10.1109/ACCESS.2020.2970430

Mogaji, E., & Nguyen, N. P. (2022). The dark side of mobile money: Perspectives from an emerging economy. *Technological Forecasting and Social Change*, *185*, 122045. doi:10.1016/j.techfore.2022.122045

Mosteanu, N. R., & Faccia, A. (2020). Digital systems and new challenges of financial management–FinTech, XBRL, blockchain and cryptocurrencies. *Quality - Access to Success*, *21*(174), 159–166.

Omarova, S. T. (2020). Technology v technocracy: Fintech as a regulatory challenge. *Journal of Financial Regulation*, *6*(1), 75–124. doi:10.1093/jfr/fjaa004

Pacelli, V., Miglietta, F., & Foglia, M. (2022). The extreme risk connectedness of the new financial system: European evidence. *International Review of Financial Analysis*, *84*, 102408. doi:10.1016/j.irfa.2022.102408

Pritchard, A. (1969). Statistical bibliography or bibliometrics. *The Journal of Documentation*, *25*, 348.

Roh, T., Yang, Y. S., Xiao, S., & Park, B. I. (2022). What makes consumers trust and adopt fintech? An empirical investigation in China. *Electronic Commerce Research*, •••, 1–33. doi:10.100710660-021-09527-3

Roszkowska, P. (2021). Fintech in financial reporting and audit for fraud prevention and safeguarding equity investments. *Journal of Accounting & Organizational Change*, *17*(2), 164–196. doi:10.1108/JAOC-09-2019-0098

Sarin, S., Haon, C., Belkhouja, M., Mas-Tur, A., Roig-Tierno, N., Sego, T., & Carley, S. (2020). Uncovering the knowledge flows and intellectual structures of research in Technological Forecasting and Social Change: A journey through history. *Technological Forecasting and Social Change*, *160*, 120210. doi:10.1016/j.techfore.2020.120210

Sharma, M., & Elmiligi, H. (2022). Behavioral biometrics: Past, present and future. *Recent Advances in Biometrics*, 69.

Sun, Y., & Grimes, S. (2016). The emerging dynamic structure of national innovation studies: A bibliometric analysis. *Scientometrics*, *106*(1), 17–40. doi:10.100711192-015-1778-0

TN, N., & Shailendra Kulkarni, M. (2022). Zero click attacks–a new cyber threat for the e-banking sector. *Journal of Financial Crime*.

Uyyala, P., & Yadav, D. C. (2023). The advanced proprietary AI/ML solution as Anti-fraudTensorlink4cheque (AFTL4C) for Cheque fraud detection. *The International journal of analytical and experimental modal analysis, 15*(4), 1914-1921.

Van Eck, N. J., & Waltman, L. (2011). Text mining and visualization using VOSviewer. *arXiv preprint arXiv:1109.2058.*

Wylde, V., Rawindaran, N., Lawrence, J., Balasubramanian, R., Prakash, E., Jayal, A., & Platts, J. (2022). Cybersecurity, data privacy and blockchain: A review. *SN Computer Science*, *3*(2), 127. doi:10.100742979-022-01020-4 PMID:35036930

# Chapter 6
# Future Analysis of Phygitalisation for Financial Services in India

**Ashwani Sharma**
https://orcid.org/0000-0002-3345-4979
*Dewan Institute of Management Studies, India*

**Reenu Kumari**
*Meerut Institute of Engineering and Technology, India*

## ABSTRACT

*The financial services industry has witnessed a significant transformation due to technological advancements from physical to digital and changing customer behavior and response towards financial services, leading to the adoption of phygitalisation. This combination of digital and physical channels aims to give a consistent experience to clients. Prior to government financial institutions, private financial institutions in India, such as ICICI Bank, HDFC Bank, and Axis Bank, had adopted innovative phygital strategies. This chapter analyzes the factors, challenges, and opportunities associated with phygitalisation in India's financial services industry. It employs a narrative review approach, including a review of the existing literature and research questions. This finding offers financial institutions a competitive advantage. However, challenges such as technological, regulatory, and cultural factors may need to be addressed. Overall, the future of phygitalisation in financial services in India appears promising.*

DOI: 10.4018/979-8-3693-0008-4.ch006

## INTRODUCTION

Passive reactions to arising patterns are not sufficient for businesses to achieve seriousness in a constantly changing business world. Every organization should enthusiastically seek cooperative energies that exist between guaranteeing that their clients are exceptionally engaged and fulfilled, other than staying up with innovation multiplication seen around the world (Mustajbasic, 2018). The achievement of sustainable development mainly focuses on the progress of the Indian economy. Thus, there is a need to include the maximum number of participants from each section of society. The progress of the country's economy struggles due to lack of awareness of financial literacy among the rural population, and accessibility of formal credit for the majority of the population is absent, which is a serious major obstacle for economic progress (Babu, 2005).

These diversifications are based on their culture, color, income, status, and gender, but one point that remains common is health problems and diseases (Sharma, Kumari, & Goel, 2022). The entire world is also diversified on the basis of the user interface of any services, but one thing that is financial needs remain the same. Globally, the financial service industry is changing rapidly from physical to digitalization. In this current transactional period, the phygital idea arises as an approach to guaranteeing that the client's actual world is associated with the computerized ecosystem via improved technology (Truong, 2019)

In recent years, the financial services industry of India has undergone a significant transformation as a proof of technological progress and varying customer behavior. With the increase in the usage of digital channels, customers now expect a seamless experience across all channels, which include physical and digital. To meet these expectations of the customers, financial institutions have been adopting the combination of physical and digital channels that we called as phygitalisation, which integrates physical and digital channels to provide a seamless customer experience. In India, the concept of phygitalisation is on rise, this concept works on both sides for those customers who need physical interaction with product and service and also want convenient and fast service as on digital platforms for payments and transactions. Several financial Institutions already work on this concept to serve the better customer service. For instance, HDFC Bank, one of India's leading private banks, has successfully amalgamated its physical and digital channels, ensuring a seamless customer experience. Other financial Institutions, such as ICICI Bank and Axis Bank, have also used phygital strategies.

During these current scenarios banks are working in a very serious and competitive environment. To support their activities, banks should thus separate themselves by reliably giving outstanding client experience. The perception of customers regarding the quality and experience provided by businesses is crucial for their survival (Mbaabu, 2020).

Changing customer behavior and expectations, technological advancements, and regulatory requirements are the basic drivers to adoption of phygitalisation of financial service in India. Due to the increasing acceptance of online channels and the emergence of fintech startups in India, there is a need to adopt changes to sustain competition among financial institutions. The basic objective of this research chapter is to analyze the future of phygitalisation for financial services in India that include drivers, challenges, and opportunities connected with this industry for phygitalsation. The study related to phygitalisation of financial services in India therefore, is important in order to deliver knowledgeable points concerning the result of phygitalisation of financial services in India.

## RESEARCH OBJECTIVE

The analysis of the future of financial services phygitalisation in India is the main objective of the research. The basic research questions are necessary to analyze this study.

## RESEARCH QUESTIONS

1. What are the phygitalisation drivers in the financial services Sector in India?
2. Reason to change the customer experience in financial services in India through phygitalisation?
3. What are the challenges associated with implementing phygitalisation in financial services in India?
4. What is the future of financial phygitalisation services in India?

## LITERATURE REVIEW

The rapid change in technology has significantly influenced the financial service area around the world. In India, the idea of "phygitalisation" has acquired prominence, combining physical and digital elements to improve client experience and smooth out financial services. This literature review aims to provide knowledge of future analysis phygitalisation for financial services in India.

There are different types of people in India and their literacy rate also differs from each other but the majority of people in rural India are less technical and that's why they do not completely access the financial services physically and digitally and this point is beneficial for financial inclusion. Demirguc-Kunt *et al.* (2018) define financial inclusion as the provision of accessible and affordable financial products and services that cater to the needs of individuals and organizations in terms of payments, savings, transactions, insurance, and credit. These services are delivered through a system that prioritizes transparency and fairness.

In recent years, consideration of phygitalisation has gained and several reports have been published and studies conducted on this subject. According to a Deloitte report, the utilization of online channels in financial services has expanded significantly over the years, and the clients now expect a consistent performance across all channels (Deloitte, 2018). This report also focuses on the importance of physical and digital channel combination to serve better and improved service to customers as their expectations.

One more report conducted by PwC says that the adoption of phygitalisation in the financial services industry is a reaction to changing client behavior and expectation (PwC, 2020). These studies further highlight the main points, improved client's experience, and increased efficiency and reduced cost, of phygitalisation.

For instance, Belghiti et al. (2017) conducted a study that specifically examined the conceptualization of the phygital shopping experience. This inductive research aimed to understand the nature of the phygital shopping experience by conducting a comparative analysis of two stores situated in Paris, France. In exploring the realm of phygital retail within the mobile-commerce platform in India, Duhan and Singh (2019) conducted a study. On the other hand, Mustajbasic (2018) investigated the design aspects of an e-market center and a Swiss market phygital store. The phygitalisation of financial services in India could be different from other countries and its operation style of working also varies from other countries, it is compulsory to conduct this study in order to analyze the phygitalisation in India.

VanTichelen and Coeurderoy (2019) for instance, analyzed the job and chances of phygital in the advanced omni-direct procedure in the present progressively cutthroat business setting. This field of research highlighted a crucial gap between digital channels and manual channels within an omni-channel framework. Consequently, the adoption of phygital channels was identified as a potential solution to bridge this gap.

Moreover, despite the fact that the investigations by Kathari (2019) gave an outline of the utilization of phygital banking and it was also investigated by Gupta, Gupta, and Indoriya (2020), they zeroed in on the Indian financial area. In Kathari's (2019) study, the focus was on exploring the advantages of phygital banking in the Indian financial sector. The research revealed that a few banks had recognized the opportunity to enhance their financial model and were offering phygital services by transforming their branches and improving the online experience. Similarly, Gupta, Gupta, and Indoriya (2020) conducted a comprehensive literature review to examine recent trends in the Indian financial industry. The study unveiled a significant surge in the adoption of the phygital banking model, indicating a positive trajectory. However, it is important to note that the findings of these studies cannot be automatically generalized to the entire Indian financial sector due to variations in contextual factors.

These reviewed studies provide a methodology gap. The above-mentioned studies normally use a desk examination method where existing literature on the phygital conception was studied. Therefore, the evaluation of the phygital financing model's effectiveness can only be accomplished by analyzing the answers to the research questions stated in the aforementioned research objectives.

The research is depending up on a review of existing literature, including reports, articles, and academic journals. The information gathered from the writing audit and reports examined utilizing subject examination. The examination includes identifying examples and topics in the information and interpreting their significance. The narrative format findings are presented and supported by review from the literature. Transitioning from the literature review, we will explore drivers, challenges, and opportunity associated with phygitalisation in financial service in India.

## 1. Drivers of Phygital Financial Service in India

There are following drivers of Phygital Financial Service

- ***Customer Expectations and Demands:*** Phygital services fulfill customer expectation through providing flexible and easily accessible digital facilities. Now consumers also expect all the financial facilities should be used physically as well as digitally (Accenture, 2021).
- ***Technological Advancements:*** Through digital transformation financial services are provided digitally and for the advancement financial institutions adopted mobile banking app, UPI, biometric authentication, digital transactions etc for the payments (PWC, 2020).
- ***Improved Customer Experience:*** Current business scenario is too hectic so it is not easy to take a leave from the workplace so at that time phygital services are opted by most of the consumers. Physital services are combining the best aspects of physical and digital services and customers take initiative in digital transactions. The flawless experience enhances customer satisfaction and loyalty. Now, In India around 90% banking transactions are started in digital form and consumers are not interested to visit financial institutional branches so they prefer internet banking, mobile banking, UPI, Pay tm, ATM etc. In the branches physical transactions are only in single digit (Times of India, 2023).

- ***Cost Efficiency:*** By digital divide can significantly reduce the operational cost in financial institution services as compared to physical branch system cost. Phygital helps shift certain day to day transactions to digital platforms so financial institutions can properly use resources and reduce other excess expenses (McKinsey & Company, 20221).
- ***Financial Inclusion:*** Rural population has not taken advantage of the full banking system so through digital platforms they enable financial services to reach near to each customer. This helps in enhancing financial inclusion and empower rural underserved communities (World Bank, 2017).
- ***Data Analytics and Personalization:*** Though the vast use of digitalization in banking systems generates vast amounts of data which reveal the behavior, preference and needs. Financial institutions offer recommendations, target marketing and customized financial solutions which will be enhance the overall consumer experience (Ernest & Young, 2021)
- ***Competitive Advantage:*** In the digital era Fintech startups are allowed traditional banking to advance banking with the help of phygital services. Incorporating phygital services empower traditional banks competitively and upgrade related to changes in technology in financial sectors. This approach also allowed physical and as well as digital accessibility of digital transactions through digital platforms (Forbes, 2022).

## 2. Phygitalisation Changing the Customer Experience in Financial Services in India

- Through phygitalization, customers experience the best of both worlds by seamlessly blending the convenience of digital technology with the human touch and functionality of digital instruments. This fusion enables the creation of a personalized customer journey that caters to their unique needs and preferences, resulting in an unparalleled customer experience.
- In India after the adaptation of phygital in various sectors customer experience is better as compared to traditional method of transaction. There are some notable aspects that are recognized in changes in customer experiences like customer open accounts, avail banking services by digital channels, enhanced online shopping, accelerated account setup and provide customers with hassle free experience.
- Furthermore, Phygitalisation has benefited to expansion of self-digital service options and through this service customers can play various transactions such as shopping, bill payment, fund transfer, account management etc by mobile app and online platforms. This handiness empowers customers to have great control over their digital financial services activities.

- Through, phygitalisation has also reform in customer support and engagement. In India, financial institutions are leveraging virtual assistants and Chabot's to provide instant and personalized assistant to customers. The AI powered tools are played major role in address common queries, product suggestion & recommendation and guide to customer for the take a better step for the payment on write place and product, thereby it make process too simple which enhancing the overall customer experience.
- Additionally, the integration of physical touch points with digital platforms has improved customer engagement. For instance, interactive kiosks and smart branches equipped with self-service machines enable customers to access services like cash deposits, withdrawals, and account inquiries easily. These blended experiences create a sense of convenience, combining the speed and efficiency of digital channels with the assurance and personal touch of physical interactions.
- Overall, phygitalisation is revolutionizing the customer experience in financial services in India by offering convenience, accessibility, and personalized interactions. It empowers customers with greater control over their financial activities, reduces friction in processes, and enhances engagement through innovative digital solutions. Financial service providers in India are increasingly leveraging this trend to cater to evolving customer expectations and stay ahead in the competitive market landscape.
- Phygitalisation, the integration of physical and digital experiences, is reshaping the customer experience in financial services in India. This convergence of physical and digital channels has led to a more seamless and personalized journey for customers, offering convenience, accessibility, and enhanced engagement.
- Digital onboarding is one way phygitalisation is altering the customer experience. Customers no longer need to physically visit banks in order to open accounts or access financial services thanks to digital channels. In addition to streamlining the account setup process and giving clients a hassle-free experience, this has greatly reduced paperwork. According to a report by KPMG, digital onboarding has improved customer experience and increased customer satisfaction in India's financial services sector (KPMG, 2022).
- Digital transformation in the banking sector is an ongoing and transformative process that influences both the external and internal landscape through the redesigning of internal procedures and established methodologies. The drivers behind this transformation are manifold, including the provision of services in remote areas devoid of physical branches, differentiation from competitors, and the reduction of operational expenses. Nonetheless, despite the undeniable benefits, there remains a significant level of uncertainty and

skepticism surrounding the widespread acceptance and adoption of digital technologies within the banking industry (Kitsios, Giatsidis & Kamariotou, 2021).

- In conclusion, phygitalisation is transforming the customer experience in financial services in India. It offers a seamless blend of physical and digital interactions, enabling convenient onboarding, self-service options, personalized support, and engaging touchpoints. These changes have contributed to improved customer satisfaction, increased adoption of digital channels, and enhanced customer engagement within the financial services sector in India.

## 3. Challenges Associated With Implementing Phygitalisation in Financial Services in India

Some challenges associated with the phygitalisation of financial services, along with text references supporting each challenge:

- ***Security and Privacy Concerns:*** The integration of physical and digital elements in financial services introduces new security and privacy risks. Cyber security threats, data breaches, and the potential compromise of sensitive customer information are significant concerns. Financial institutions must prioritize robust security measures and data protection protocols (Accenture ).
- ***Regulatory Compliance:*** Phygitalisation brings complex regulatory challenges, as financial institutions need to comply with regulations that govern both physical and digital channels. Meeting requirements related to data privacy, customer protection, and anti-money laundering can be particularly challenging in the context of phygital services. (Deloitte, 2018).
- ***Technology Integration:*** Integrating physical and digital systems requires overcoming technological hurdles. Legacy infrastructure, siloed systems, and compatibility issues may hinder the seamless integration of phygital services. Financial institutions must invest in modernizing their technology infrastructure and ensuring interoperability across channels (McKinsey & Company, 2022).
- ***Talent and Skill Gap:*** The implementation of phygital services necessitates a skilled workforce that possesses both banking expertise and digital competencies. However, there may be a shortage of talent with the necessary skills to manage and operate in a phygital environment. Financial institutions should focus on attracting, retaining, and up-skilling talent to bridge this skill gap. (PwC, 2020)

- ***Customer Adoption and Education:*** Transitioning from traditional banking to phygital services can face resistance from customers who are accustomed to traditional methods. Ensuring customer adoption requires effective change management strategies, customer education, and addressing concerns related to security, privacy, and convenience. (Ernest & Young, 2021).
- ***Digital Divide:*** The digital divide, characterized by unequal access to digital infrastructure and technology can impede the widespread adoption of phygital services. Disparities in internet connectivity, digital literacy, and technology access may exclude certain segments of the population from benefiting fully from these services. Financial institutions need to address these inequalities to ensure inclusive access (World Bank, 2017).
- ***Balancing Personalization and Data Privacy:*** Phygitalisation enables personalized services based on customer data analysis. However, striking a balance between personalization and customer privacy is critical. Financial institutions must handle customer data transparently, with strong data governance, privacy policies, and explicit consent mechanisms in place (Deloitte, 2018).

These challenges require careful consideration and proactive measures to overcome them and realize the full potential of phygital financial services.

## 4. Future of Phygitalisation in Financial Services in India

- Phygitalisation helps in reshaping the customer experience in India financial institutions. As the country emphasizes digitalization, financial institutions are leveraging phygital strategies to increase the interest of consumers in digital transactions.
- On the basis of PwC, India report (2021), Phygitlaisation is revolutionizing in all kinds of sectors and it makes convenience for all and easy accessibility of digital services. With the help of phygitalisation consumers can access digital services from anywhere and anytime through digital channels. There are so many platforms customers can use when going for the digital transactions like mobile banking app, Paytm, UPI, and others. On the basis of phygitlaization we can check customer behavior and preference so that we can provide customized solutions that meet individual needs and encourage the overall customer behavior and experience (EY India, 2021).
- Digital transformation within the financial sector entails leveraging technology to enhance business operations, elevate customer experiences, and foster the development of innovative products and services (IBEF, 2023). By 2025, Key digital sectors such as digital communication services,

electronics manufacturing, IT, business process management could witness a doubling GDP level in India; it will reach an estimated range of US$ 355-435 billion (IBEF, 2023).

- As mentioned in Times of India (2023), the Boston Consulting Group has forecasted that the market of digital payment will increase more than 3 times from $3 trillion to $10 trillion by the year 2026.
- The "India Stack," India's digital infrastructure, has become a subject of debate and research due to its significant role in the country's thriving Open Banking transformation. In the coming years, financial services providers will strive to integrate themselves with innovative solutions, aiming to generate enhanced opportunities. A prime illustration of this trend is insurance companies offering cost-effective insurance plans for airline or railway tickets. Likewise, banking institutions are offering enticing interest rates, flexible EMI options, or buy-now-pay-later services on e-commerce platforms, effectively embedding their financial services within the products and services offered by other entities.

## CONCLUSION

In conclusion, the analysis of the future of financial services phygitalisation in India shows a promising position. The phygital strategies adopted by financial institutions in India are driven by customer expectations, cost efficiency, technological progressions, enhanced customer experience, financial inclusion, data analytics, personalization, and the pursuit of a competitive benefit. However, the execution of phygitalisation faces a few difficulties, including security and protection concerns, administrative compliances, technology coordination, ability and expertise gaps, client adoptions and education, digital separation, and balancing personalization and information protection.

Notwithstanding these difficulties, the future of phygitalisation in financial services in India seems promising. It is altering the client experience by offering comfort, availability, customized associations, and further developed commitment. The coordination of physical and digital channels empowers consistent onboarding, self-services choices, customized help, and connecting with touch points. Financial Institutions in India are utilizing phygitalisation to meet advancing client expectations, increment in digital adoption, and upgrade consumer loyalty.

Looking forward, the future of phygitalisation in financial services in India will keep on developing as innovation technology and client preferences change. The digital transformation of the financial industry, combined with the government or public authorities' attention on digitalization, sets open doors for development and innovation. As India's digital infrastructure extends and online payment volumes increase, financial institutions will additionally coordinate phygital arrangements, offering many advanced benefits and embedding financial contributions inside different products and services.

To make the phygitalisation, banks and other financial institutions will deal with several criticisms or challenges and these challenges are highly followed regulations, high technology, more security and skilled employees, etc. To overcome these challenges and successfully implement phygitalisation, it is crucial to take certain initiatives. First initiative to require protection of consumer information and apply robust security measures to prevent cyber threats and breaches. Moreover, financial institutions must invest in technologies and cyber security systems to project customer data. This includes various tools, encryption protocols, multi factor authentication, information dictation system & regular audit to protect and save data of consumers.

At the end of this chapter, it is evident that phygitalisation in India, especially in financial institution services, is causing changes in customer behaviors, experiences, and expectations. By implementing phygital strategies, financial institutions can become more competitive and gain several advantages. This, in turn, leads to increased customer satisfaction and long-term success in the digital era.

## REFERENCES

Babu, G. R. (2005). *Financial services in India*. Concept Publishing Company.

Belghiti, S., Ochs, A., Lemoine, J. F., & Badot, O. (2017). The phygital shopping experience:An attempt at conceptualization and empirical investigation. In *Academy of Marketing Science World Marketing Congress* (pp. 61-74). Springer, Cham.

Deloitte. (2018). *Rise of Phygital Banking*. Deloitte. https://www2.deloitte.com/content/dam/Deloitte/in/Documents/financial-services/in-fs-phygital-banking-noexp.pdf

Demirguc-Kunt, A., Klapper, L., Singer, D., & Ansar, S. (2018). The Global Findex Database 2017: Measuring Financial Inclusion and the Fintech Revolution. World Bank Publications. 10.1596/978-1-4648-1259-0

Duhan, P., & Singh, A. (2019). *M-commerce: Experiencing the Phygital Retail*. Apple Academic Press. doi:10.1201/9780429487736

Economic Times (24, Nov, 2021). *World of phygital banking will be way forward: Bankers*. accessed on 6 July 2023

Ernst & Young (2021), *Why digital, ecosystem-enabled banking transformation is the way forward* accessed on 21 June, 2023

FinTech Mmagazine (2020), *The Phygital touch: fusing digital and physical in finance.* accessed on 12 June 2023

Forbes (2022), *How Banks can compete in the Post –Neobank Era* accessed on 14 July 2023

Gupta, P., Gupta, P., & Indoriya, N. (2020). New trends of Indian banking industry. *Studies in Indian Place Names, 40*(1), 311-319.

IBEF(2023), *Digital Transformation Shaping the Future of the Finance Industry*, India Brand Equity Eoundation. Accessed On 22, June 2023).

Kathari, S. (2019). Phygital banking: A game changer in Indian banking sector. *International Journal of Innovative Technology and Exploring Engineering*, *8*(9), 289–292. doi:10.35940/ijitee.H7283.078919

Kitsios, F., Giatsidis, I., & Kamariotou, M. (2021). Digital transformation and strategy in the banking sector: Evaluating the acceptance rate of e-services. *Journal of Open Innovation*, *7*(3), 204. doi:10.3390/joitmc7030204

KPMG (2022), *Customer on boarding - a key tool in the fight against financial crime. The benefits of getting it right from the beginning*. accessed on 15 July, 2023

Mbaabu, M. K. (2020). *Phygital Banking and Customer Experience in Commercial Banks in Kenya* [Doctoral dissertation, University of Nairobi].

Mckinsey & Company (2022), *McKinsey's Global Banking Annual Review*. Retrieved on 10 July, 2023)

Moravcikova, D., & Kliestikova, J. (2017). Brand building with using phygital marketing communication. Journal of Economics. *Business and Management*, *5*(3), 148–153.

Mustajbasic, A. (2018). *Introducing an e-marketplace and phygital store to the Swiss market.*

Phadke, S. (2020). *FinTech future: The digital DNA of finance*. Sage Publications Pvt. Limited. doi:10.4135/9789353885687

PwC. (2020). *The Future of Banking: From Digital to Phygital*. PWC. https://www.pwc.in/assets/pdfs/publications/2020/the-future-of-banking-from-digital-to-phygital.pdf

Sharma, A., Kumari, R., & Goel, N. (2022). Universal Health Coverage (UHC): Case Study on World's Health Emerging Strategy after the COVID-19 Pandemic. In Handbook of Research on Global Networking Post COVID-19 (pp. 328-341). IGI Global.

Shashikala, K. (2019). Digital disruption in the banking industry. *International Journal of Social and Economic Research*, *9*(3), 56–61. doi:10.5958/2249-6270.2019.00019.9

Times of India. (30 April, 2023), *The future of financial services in India* Monica Hovespain in Voices, Economy, TOI accessed on 22 July, 2023.

Truong, P. (2019). *Insight and its importance in the transactional marketing era.*

Van Tichelen, B. (2019). *The role and opportunities of Phygital in the digital omni-channel strategy*. Louvain School of Management.

WEFORUM. (2020), *Phygital: a banking strategy for the new isolation economy.* World Economic Forum. Accessed on 12 July, 2023

# Chapter 7
# Policy Implication of Green Finance

**Rashmi Shukla**
https://orcid.org/0000-0003-4237-8864
*Indian Institute of Management, Raipur, India*

**Charul Sawai**
*Daulat Ram College, Delhi University, India*

## ABSTRACT

*The chapter aims to provide insight into the policy framework of green finance. The five-step roadmap begins with a vision whereby the reader is made aware of the concept of sustainability. India's initiative at the G20 summit of the UN Environment on the issue, thereby the first part, is concluded with a positive note on fairness and development. Similarly, a detailed analysis of the strategy undertaken at the national and international levels is discussed. Further, lead entities are enlisted along with the current state of ownership in some countries. No policy framework would be a good guide for policymakers and researchers to rely on if it is presented without including the essential requirements. To provide a sense of the change in green fintech, various examples have been curated related to green lending, crowdfunding, insurance, and ESG data providers. The comprehensive chapter is concluded by listing the essential metrics to evaluate the process of growth.*

DOI: 10.4018/979-8-3693-0008-4.ch007

## INTRODUCTION

The road to a hundred miles begins with one conscious step followed by another strategic one. As we embark on the journey of change towards a greener future, technology-led financial services proved to have the potential to march the transition. With an increase in transactions, peer-to-peer lending seems a potent solution for financing the green project. Leveraging new emerging technologies such as blockchain technology, artificial intelligence, machine learning, and others provides a safety net for capitalising on such projects. The boom in information technology is supporting society's choice of being green and sustainable.

*"UPI has reached a scale where on an annual basis $1.5 trillion worth transactions are done and the average settlement time is 2 seconds" (G20 Summit, 2023) -Ashwini Vaishnaw, Union Minister for Electronics and Information Technology*

The transition in proceedings of the financial system has been tremendous. The amalgamation of technology and finance has freed the past constraint of financial inclusion and accessibility (Varga, 2017). Digital penetration has increased the interaction of banking customers to mobile devices and online websites from 32% before the pandemic to 50% (Accenture Banking, 2022). With Financial liberalisation set on the sail to accelerate efficiency and accessibility in the financial ecosystem, the flow of capital has increased manifold. Fintech in India recorded an estimated transaction value of USD 33 billion in 2016, which was further expected to be more than double, approximately USD 73 billion by 2020, with a 22% CAGR at five years on the basis (KPMG Fintech India, 2016).

Fintech has leapfrogged past constraints. But whether this digital penetration is plausible with Green Finance seems a cause of concern. Research suggests that with fintech 4.0, technological innovation such as Blockchain, Big Data, Internet of Things (IoT), and Cryptocurrency adds another feather to fintech, thereby promoting financial inclusion and supporting economic growth (Nassiry, 2018). Technology has proven to be a catalyst for remarkable achievements and unprecedented growth. By incorporating environmental considerations into digital payment infrastructure, we can address the pressing need for sustainability while also fueling economic development. Several examples, such as Alipay in China, Impakt in Switzerland, and Bettervest in Germany (GDFA Green Fintech Taxonomy, 2022), showcase how technology can enable the integration of green features to contribute to a more sustainable financial ecosystem. Similar growth has been seen in the area of digital Investment, Insurance, Banking Services and Risk Analyst. Mapping these changes would provide a better understanding. The spillover created with fintech innovation has been acknowledged by investors and corporate firms, thereby bringing the

Government and activists to the forefront to channelise the path towards sustainable growth. Moreover, It is well said that " *There can be no Plan B because there is no Planet B"* (Schoenmaker and Schramade, 2019). The Secretary General of the UN is highlighting the pressing need and concern of carrying the capacity of the earth, which is in distress and requires immediate action.

Thereby, it is being outlined that planning the policy frameworks streamlines the execution. This chapter is intended to provide the reader with an overview of changes that have enabled green finance so far in various ways for fintech. The roadmap of change entails following the framework beginning with evaluating fundamental drivers, defining the objectives, aligning the national strategic interest with international compliance, remapping the digital innovation, outlining the setbacks and trajectory regulation and lastly, evaluating the progress in the internalising sustainable finance (UN Environment, 2017).

## BACKGROUND

The evolution of fintech is not about a new trend that became popular; rather, it is a clear reflection of the advancement of technology, such as cloud computation, big data, machine learning, blockchain, etc, that is being utilised by financial institutions. Buckley, Arner, and Barberis were the first scholars to assess this phenomenon in 2015. Innovation in technology is shaping the business models of the startup. The early days of fintech, from 1866 to 1987, laid its foundation. Interconnectedness and increased globalisation were the first change. This marked fintech 1.0, followed by advancements in the banking sector. Digital banking has then become ubiquitous. The new innovations in financial services, followed by the credit boom, expedited the process of financial liberalisation, and as a result, the financial crisis of 2008 took place. This phase was fintech 2.0. Following this, the current phase is fintech 3.0. Technology-driven financial institutions are no new to the financial system, along with traditional brick-and-mortar banks (Vagra, 2017). On the other hand, carbon emissions by 2015 crossed 30,000 million metric tonnes worldwide (US EPA, 2022). The issue of net zero carbon became the need of the hour. Soon, the sustainable development goal 2030 was formulated in 2015, postulating the essential aim to be achieved by 2030. Net-zero carbon is one such target.

The way energy consumption is taking place is the major factor deterring the environment. To counter this, renewable and eco-friendly energy started gaining popularity. The concept of green and clean energy became the new manifesto of change. Environmentalists become the forerunners in promoting the cause. Followed by giant companies establishing solar and hydroelectric plants. To name a few, Adani and Tata are in India. Waste management is another factor challenging the carrying capacity of the earth. Worldwide-generated plastic waste accounted for only 2 million metric tonnes per year in 1950. While the annual production has roughly tripled since then, hitting 460 million metric tonnes in 2019 (Ritchie, 2018).

Leveraging electric vehicles is in line with the goal of reducing carbon emissions. Such green projects have become prominent. With ease of payment, accessibility, and robo-advisors with minimum cost, fintech is the new means of financing green projects. The first taxonomy of green fintech and data landscaping was proposed by Green Digital Finance Alliance (GDFA) and Swiss Green Fintech Network in 2022, highlighting major green fintech in areas of crowdfunding, digital payment, digital investment, insurance etc. The Sustainable Finance Working Group has been working on this issue, particularly during G20 meets. In addition to this, it took 8 years for fintech to become the fifth-largest bank in the United States, with an estimated value of $1 billion and 12 million customers (Accenture Banking, 2022). Europe has also made a high jump in terms of the number of fintech financing green projects. To name a few, German-based Bettervest, Swiss-based Invoya, etc. In Asia, Alipay has made significant strides towards environmentally conscious behaviour. So,

With such a transition taking place, this policy implication chapter highlights the initiative taken at various levels, categorically presented in the form of a policy framework beginning with a vision followed by strategy and concluding with measures to evaluate the policy.

## 1. VISION

It's never too late to begin; the change necessitates the need and wants to translate the supply. Few have realised the need earlier as per their advancement and level of impairment injected to the ecosystem for instance, Europe was the first one to introduce green bonds in 2007 and stands ahead from the rest in financing green investment via green bonds as of 2021. While others are still speculating about the change that demands sustainable growth with rational expectations. This section elaborates the vision of nations particularly India and that of fintech in envisaging green finance. In the beginning five principles of sustainable development are laid down to develop the holistic understanding of the common framework of Sustainability.

*"Sustainable development is the development that meets the needs of the present, without compromising the ability of future generations to meet their own needs".*

*Table 1. Carrying capacity (Schoenmaker & Schramade, 2019; Steffen et al, 2015) briefs the threshold limit of the earth*

| Earth system | Control variable | Planetary Boundary | Current value and trend |
|---|---|---|---|
| Climate Change | Atmospheric carbon dioxide concentration; parts per million (ppm) | At most 350 ppm | Maximum 350 ppm<br>Maximum 399 ppm and increasing (worsening) |

## 1.1 Comprehensiveness

Sustainable development takes a holistic approach encompassing space and time. It recognizes that sustainability is for both environmental and human systems, inclusive of local and global perspectives. Consider Table 1, which shows the climate change has exceeded the planetary boundary and reciprocates the need for a comprehensive plan. It recognises the interdependence of several elements, including social, economic, and environmental ones. Without compromising its ability, it seeks to achieve a balance between the needs of the present generation and those of future generations (UN, 1987).

Compressiveness is well tuned with India's vision. According to Hardeep Singh Puri, the current minister of Housing and Urban Affairs & Petroleum and Natural Gas in India, who has been a Civil Servant too, visualises Economy and Ecology in an integrated approach and quotes, *"India is demonstrating that economy and ecology are not at odds with each other, but in fact, fundamentally intertwined"* (G20 Summit, 2023). Keeping the lens of SDG 2030 convergent, India is working to create a holistic framework. Whether it's the agriculture sector or the construction sector, climate affects each one of us inexorably. Moreover, with the advent of carbon emissions, it has been exceeding the carrying capacity of Earth, which demands attention. Various collaborations have been working on this. One such collaboration is the G20, whose first summit addressed climate change in 2008. Ever since then, the climate has been a key topic for discussion. Lately, the discussion is on the circular economy.

Also, India's Presidency at G20, 2023 paved the way for addressing the concern towards the Environment. Resonating the vision of the Honourable Prime Minister of India on the Circular economy. Four key initiatives were proposed:

1. G20 knowledge exchange on Circularity in the Steel Sector
2. A step in becoming more conscious; Extended Producer Responsibility
3. Transition to a Circular Bio economy

4. Establishing the Resource Efficiency and Circular Economy (RECE) industry coalition

## 1.2 Connectivity

Sustainability recognizes that the world's challenges are systemically interlinked. Moreover, it is either prospered or sunk into unobligated debt. It acknowledges that actions in one area can have far-reaching consequences in other areas. For example, environmental degradation in one region can affect ecosystems and resources globally. This understanding emphasises the importance of considering the broader impacts of decisions and actions and promoting integrated approaches to problem-solving.

*"Vasudhaiva Kutumbakam " One Earth, One Family and One Future* with this tagline, India envisages to grow with Global Sustainability and Economic Development. Thus, being connected with the global fraternity. In internalising the potential of its goal, it endeavours to create Digital Public Infrastructure (DPI), Cybersecurity, and Digital Skilling. The Digital Economic Working Group has been working to create safe, secure and globally accessible solutions and protocols in this sphere. The three priorities in the area of the Digital Economy include (G20 Summit, 2023):

1. DPI resources, experiences, and learnings in the direction of a global DPI repository
2. A toolkit for cyber education and awareness was created, and it was agreed that cooperation was required to ensure a secure and resilient cyberspace.
3. The creation of a toolbox to assist nations in creating upskilling and reskilling initiatives on digital skills during Indonesia's presidency

Promoting the economy to the digital economy further augments the process of transition of financial institutions to fintech in the Indian ecosystem.

## 1.3 Equity

Sustainable development emphasises a fair allocation of resources and property rights, undermining the reality of Capitalist driven nations. Further suggesting that the allocation is for the present and for the coming endowed generation. It recognizes the importance of addressing social and economic inequalities, ensuring access to basic needs, and promoting social justice. Equity involves considerations of fairness, inclusivity, and the recognition of human rights.

## 1.4 Prudence

Prudence in sustainable development entails supporting the ecology, which is the giver without any demand but requires tenderness when greed becomes reckless. Proper regulation would perhaps provide a safety net. The responsibility is vested in the hands of citizens. No framework would support the ecology if everyone is not held accountable. Prudent decision-making considers long-term consequences and aims to minimise negative impacts while fostering sustainable practices and resource management.

## 1.5 Security

The goal of sustainable development is to nurture both the present and future generations with a safe, healthy, and high quality of life. It involves initiatives to conserve natural resources, secure basic requirements, and promote resilience in the face of challenges like climate change, extreme weather, and societal upheavals. Promoting secure livelihoods, alleviating vulnerability, and creating conditions that support the holistic well-being of individuals and communities must be prioritised in order to attain security through sustainable development.

The above five principles of sustainable development goals are holistic. It is an integrated approach in tackling the social, economic and environmental issues and its impact is affixed SDGs. SDG 13 addresses the issue of climate change. Leveraging fintech in financing the green projects makes the financing steady and convenient. Further the section talks about the initiative at the G20 Summit. Also, one example is quoted to elaborate the vision of one such fintech.

### 1.5.1 G20 Sustainable Finance Working Group 2023

In order to identify the bottlenecks of green finance and boost private capital in green investments, the Green Finance Study Group was officially established in 2016. Later, the group's activity was diversified by including a Sustainable Development feature in 2018, followed by the name being changed to the Sustainable Finance Working Group (G20 Summit, 2023). The newly established Sustainable Finance Working Group came into existence during the G20 meeting led by the Italian Presidency and co-chaired by the US and China in 2021. The proceedings of the group are towards climate change and aligning the International Financial Institution with the Paris Agreement (SFWG, 2023). More specifically related to following areas:

1. Mechanisms for timely and adequate resource mobilisation for climate finance
2. Enabling finance for the sustainable development goals

3. Capacity building of the ecosystem for financing towards sustainable development.

*"The financial system is transitioning to create, value and transact financial assets in ways that shape real wealth to serve the long-term needs of an inclusive and more sustainable economy"* (UN Environment Inquiry 2015, 2016). As per KPMG's Survey of Sustainability Reporting 2022, the largest of 250 companies by revenue, taking the reference from the 2021 Fortune 500 rating, the concern for ESG remains alike (KPMG Singapore, 2022). Inclining the business model towards a more sustainable and eco-friendly ecosystem. Stretching the need of the present in a more accountable and reliable way. 32% of consumers are highly engaged with adopting a more sustainable lifestyle (Climate Fintech Rise, 2021; Deloitte). The positive externality shadows the shift in behavioural consumption and production.

For instance, Accenture, an Information and Technology and Consultancy firm, sets the objective whose prospects are as follows:

- By signing the UNGC business ambition for the 1.5° pledge, which complies with the Paris Climate Agreement and the standards and guidelines of the science-based targets (SBT) initiative, the business is dedicated to holding global warming below 1.5° Celsius in 2020.
- It has also invested in carbon removal techniques based on nature as part of its sustainability initiatives. These investments are anticipated to reduce carbon emissions by roughly 13 million metric tonnes over the following 20 years, addressing the company's remaining emissions and helping it achieve its carbon neutrality targets. (Accenture 360°, 2022).

Had achieved a remarkable statistic, with 97% of its location operating with renewable energy. Adding to this, there has been a significant reduction of carbon emissions by 68% compared to its baseline. Had made a headwind by completing Ethics and Compliance training for 98% of its employees.

Thus, Fintech is unbundling the priorities of firms. Information-intensive and time-sensitive niches its flexibility (Lee, Y.J. Shin, 2015). The broad range of activities, including Mobile Payment, Wealth Management, P2P Lending, etc., encapsulate the service at disposal. Thus, for a healthier tomorrow, Sustainability takes charge in every possible aspect of the business to accelerate the consciousness towards the ecosystem and delve into a safe present as well. From production to disintermediation and financing, the responsibility is laid down in the hand of the user at each stage. So, Fairness and Development with accountable governance agile the progress towards Green Finance. Supporting the Global/ National initiative with faith in accomplishing the set target.

Further, the next section aims to lay the foundation for the strategies that are undertaken at the national and international levels.

## 2. STRATEGY

More inclusive and comprehensive collaboration is required. For low Carbon Emission and Climate Resilience: Green asset, Green Investment and Green tagging streamlines the risk. Further, Strategy can be conceptualised as Nationally and Internationally driven in the following way:

### 2.1 Nationally Driven

From the lens of the Government, usually, the five-year plan includes the strategic policy for the nation. Inclusive of major programmes, the schemes to implement. Which also includes policy considerations and deliberations on the past work, allocation of funds and resources to the sub-areas. So, with Sustainability taking upfront, new opportunities seem to realign. The Fiscal Space of government is a crucial factor in promoting green finance by regulation and incentivisation. Its essentiality is equalised in creating an impetus for its functioning. However, this is not alike for financial companies, more generally privately owned entities seek to maximise profit. But, a change has been seen in recent years: fintech companies have been incorporating ESG frameworks in their business model. The nature of the growth of green fintech startups is not alike. For instance, with the sudden increase in the pool of Unicorn startups in India, **green fintech** remained skewed. While **green startups** have stood out in many other ways. The majority of its green startups are EV manufacturers and Solar Grid energy providers. India's first electric vehicle, also an Unicorn, came in 2019 Ola Electric. Supported by Tata Group and funded $2 million to augment its growth. In Northern India, stubble burning is a major issue in winter. So, Takachar, founded by Vidyut Mohan and Kevin Kung, created an innovative machine to use agriculture left over and convert it into fertiliser and fuel. The initiative-driven startup won accolades by Prince William and the Royal Foundation in October 2021 and won the inaugural Earth Shot Prize (P, 2021).

Extending this section, by assessing the strategies of India and Europe in accordance with green finance.

### Case A: India

*India is a bright spot in the global economy. - Narendra Modi, Prime Minister of India* (G20 Summit, 2023)

### Initiative

With a population of 1.4 billion, greenhouse gas amounted to 3.9 billion carbon dioxide, which is equivalent to tonnes. Paving its way to becoming the third largest emitter in the world (Hussina, Dill, 2023). In order to mitigate such a correlated relationship, the National Action Plan on Climate Change (NAPC) in 2008, the National Clean Energy Fund (NCEF) in 2010, and the Indian Renewable Energy Development Agency (IREDA) in 1987 were established (Aggrawal, 2023).

Moreover, with the emergence of Fintech in India, it is creating a silver lining growth well above the traditional financial institutions. KPMG's report took into reference the Fintech 100 (2021); there has been a shift from North America and Europe to Asia Pacific as a new productive ground for fintech. A total of \$3.18 billion fund was raised in 2019-20, whereby the distribution is highly unequal, centred on the top 10 companies by equity funding in India. Adding to this, Payment service accounted for \$1 billion itself in November 2019 (RBI Bulletin, 2020). It has also taken significant steps forward in the field of Green Finance. Becoming the second largest issuer of green bonds worth \$10 billion (Climate Fintech Rise, 2021). As per the Ministry of New and Renewable Energy's report analysing the financial constraints, India requires Foreign Direct Investment (FDI) ranging from INR 15,000 crores to INR 20,000 crores annually in renewable energy alone. Currently, the US \$196.98b amount of funds is dispensed as per Invest India (Saha, n.d). The first Sovereign Green bond in India was introduced on 25th January 2023, worth \$980 million, nearly after its draft relating to the mobilisation of sovereign green bond for green infrastructure(Hussina, Dill, 2023).

### Key Actors

Government and regulatory actions have significantly impacted the situation. For instance, the Reserve Bank of India, the nation's central bank, has added the funding of small renewable energy projects to the requirements for banks' priority sector lending. Additionally, the government-backed Indian renewable energy development agency made history in May 2016 by becoming the country's first green bank (Climate Fintech Rise, 2021). Additionally, the Reserve Bank of India has introduced regulations requiring banks and non-banking financial institutions (NBFIS) to accept "green deposits". The objective is to ensure that the funds are utilised for various purposes such as efficient energy with minimum cost, eco-friendly means of commute, versatility among the citizens, clean water and waste management, Green construction and protection of biodiversity in every way possible. In March, the Securities and Exchange Board of India (SEBI) introduced a specific category of mutual funds called ESG (Environmental, Social, and Governance). This allows asset management companies in India to launch multiple ESG funds. As reporting on ESG parameters improves, the enhanced rigour and transparency will contribute to increased investor confidence (Saha, n.d). Greenko Group is the largest green bond issuer working in the domain of green energy, such as Solar and wind power projects (Hussina, Dill, 2023).

### Green Energy

Gradually, CleanTech is making strides in mitigating adverse environmental effects through substantial energy efficiency innovations. As renewable energy's portion of India's electricity grid continues to expand, there is a rising demand for clean power technologies, which is attracting both startups and investors to this sector. Approximately 20 percent of all start-ups in incubators across India are now centred around various aspects of sustainability, as reported by the Climate Collective Network (Climate Fintech Rise, 2021).

### Future Prospect

However, the field of green finance is still in its infancy, with green bonds making up just 0.7% of all bonds issued in India since 2014 (according to the latest data). Significant obstacles still stand in the way of widespread adoption and awareness, primarily due to insufficient information and coordination among different stakeholders. Climate FinTech companies are nowadays gaining prominence, whose existence is no new to ponder, but adoption seems challenging.

## Case B: Europe

The Fintech sector in Europe has rapidly transitioned from being a peripheral player to a central and influential part of the European financial landscape. In each of the seven largest European economies, namely France, Germany, Italy, the Netherlands, Spain, Switzerland, and the United Kingdom, there is now at least one fintech company among the top five banking services institutions in terms of market value. Notably, Germany and the Netherlands each have three fintech companies within their top five, and the primary banking services institution in the Netherlands held the position of the largest fintech in Europe based on market valuation in mid-2022 (Mckinsey Global Payments, 2020). Along this line of prominent leadership of London, UK, various initiatives have been taken to remap with sustainable development. The 25-Year Environment Plan seeks to promote a good healthy environment by mitigating the risk associated with it, which seeks to protect cities, rural landscapes, and biodiversity. Creating an impetus similar to Green Brexit. The UK Government plans to launch Green Saving Bonds through the medium of National Saving and Investment (HM Government, 2018). In order to finance a country's economic potential, the private sector is essential. Its ability to effectively mobilise its resources underpins its necessity. So, the UK Government plans to generate more than £1 billion a year by 2030 to help nature's recovery in England, starting with at least £500 million raised privately each year by 2027. Towards net zero emissions (Department for Environment, food & rural affairs UK, 2023). Following are some actions taken by UK:

### *UK Infrastructure Bank*

To assist the UK Government in endorsing net zero carbon by 2050, UK Infrastructure Bank was established in 2021. Reinforces partnerships with the private sector and local government across the UK. Over the initial five years, the Treasury has allocated a total of £22 billion in public funds to the Bank, enabling it to offer loans, equity investments, and guarantees for infrastructure projects. Out of this £22 billion allocation, the Treasury has allotted up to £5 billion as equity, £7 billion can be borrowed either through the Debt Management Office or private markets, and an additional £10 billion can be utilised as guarantees for various projects (HM, 2023).

### *Net-Zero Alignment*

The UK government has been working diligently to phase out the carbon emissions. Its ambition to become a net zero financial centre seems evident from its action. The release of the transition plan task force in April (2022) mandates the standard for private entities in the process of climate transition plans.

### *Taskforce on Nature-Related Financial Disclosures (TNFD)*

Introduction of the task force on climate-related financial disclosure (TCFD), which is the subsidiary of the financial stability board makes the UK standout from the rest in the queue due to its amalgamation of the policy in the law. This policy mandates companies to reveal data related to a financial contribution to climate and associated risks and opportunities. Further, the task force on nature-related financial disclosures (TFND) is under policy framing and deliberation.

### *UK's International Climate Finance (ICF)*

Being ahead in the race of transitions provides an impetus for the UK to act as an Assistor for the developing countries. Formally it's been done at the UK 's International Climate Finance initiative by the UK. Further, it envisages doubling its financial support between 2021 and 2026. (Anderson, 2023)

Till now, we have been discussing the actions at the national level. But, since sustainability demands connectivity and integrity, International driven initiative stands important. Upcoming section elaborates a few such actions.

## 2.2 Internationally Driven

Various institutions have been set up to review and keep track of sustainability. Disclosure of information penetration is not only bounded within the sphere of sustainability but it also tracks revenue associated with green businesses. A foundational background of Institutions, Data disclosing councils and Instruments. Some international initiatives as per UN Environment and World Bank Initiative are as follows:

### 2.2.1 The Sustainability Accounting Standard Board (SASB)

The Sustainability Accounting Standard Board (SASB) is responsible for managing this affair (UN Environment, 2017). The SASB Standards empower organisations to disclose sustainability information tailored to their specific industry, addressing the risks and opportunities that influence their overall value. In August 2022, the responsibility for maintaining these standards shifted to the International Financial Reporting Standard, IFRS Foundation following its merger with the Value Reporting Foundation (VRF), a global nonprofit organisation that previously oversaw these standards. The key environmental, social, and governance challenges that have the biggest effects on financial performance and enterprise value within 77 various industries are identified by the SASB standards. These standards were meticulously developed through a thorough and open process that included evidence-based research, open participation from businesses, investors, and industry professionals, as well as independent oversight and approval by the SASB standards board. International investors largely recognise the importance of the SASB standards and its increase in membership to 185 members representing 50% of global asset management (UN Environment, 2017). The first asset management firm in India to have endorsed the un-backed principles for responsible investment is Kotak Mutual Fund (Jain, 2020).

The PRI (Principle Responsible Investment) is built upon six guiding principles:

1. Environmental, Social, and Governance (ESG) variables are taken into account during the investment analysis and decision-making processes.
2. Being a proactive owner and incorporating ESG factors into ownership practices.
3. Asking the companies in which investments are made for the necessary disclosure on ESG issues.

4. Encouraging the concepts' acceptance and application inside the investment industry.
5. Collaborating to increase the beneficial effect of the principles' application.
6. Reporting on actions and development in placing the ideas into practice.

By adopting these principles, signatories commit to integrating ESG factors into their investment strategies and engaging with companies to improve their ESG performance. The PRI initiative has gained global recognition and serves as a framework for responsible investment practices across various sectors and geographies.

## 2.2.2 Sustainable Stock Exchange (SSE)

Stocks are an integral instrument in financing, the disclosure by a corporation. A sustainable stock exchange is a space or market where stocks from publicly traded firms can be traded, with an emphasis on environmentally conscious and ethical business practices. By adopting these principles, these exchanges want to foster accountability, transparency, and long-term value generation. Environmental, social, and governance (ESG) considerations into their listing requirements, disclosure guidelines, and trading rules make it more comprehensive. Sustainable Stock Exchanges encourage listed firms to disclose pertinent ESG data, such as their corporate governance practices, social policies, and environmental effect. These exchanges help investors distribute cash to companies that are sustainable and responsible while enabling them to make better selections.

Key objectives of sustainable stock exchanges include:

1. **Enhancing transparency**: By requiring ESG disclosure from listed companies, sustainable stock exchanges promote transparency and enable investors to assess a company's environment conscious behaviour.
2. **Encouraging responsible investment**: Sustainable stock exchanges aim to attract responsible investors who prioritise ESG factors in their investment decisions, leading to capital flow towards companies with strong sustainability practices.
3. **Supporting environmentally sound development goals**: by highlighting businesses that have a beneficial impact on social and environmental consequences, these exchanges assist in advancing sustainable development goals.
4. **Fostering dialogue and collaboration**: Sustainable stock exchanges facilitate dialogue among listed companies, investors, regulators, and other stakeholders to share best practices, encourage collaboration, and drive continuous improvement in sustainability performance.

Examples of sustainable stock exchanges include the Nasdaq Sustainable Bond Network, the Johannesburg Stock Exchange (JSE) in South Africa, and the Hong Kong Stock Exchange's ESG Reporting Platform. These exchanges are part of a global network committed to advancing sustainable finance and responsible investment practices. SSE now includes 60 stock exchanges, representing 70% of equity markets that are listed and 30,000 firms with a market size of $55 trillion (UN Environment, 2017). Significant understanding has been shown. From the above analysis of the UK, London's steady jump in Green Finance is quite evident also a notable fact that London was awarded with Stock Exchange of the Year in 2020 at Environment Finance Sustainable Investment (LSEG, 2020). As per KPMG Singapore (2022), the number of companies reporting sustainability and ESG issues is highest in Asia 89% of companies reporting the same, while in Europe, 82% in 2022. In June 2016, the Singapore Exchange in Asia enacted "Comply or Explain" environmental performance and policy reporting rules, requiring compliance from all listed companies by 2018. In 2016, China launched a large number of public and private green bond indexes to complement the 19 existing green equity indices (UN Environment, 2017; UN Environment Inquiry, 2017c), all of which are in line with a low carbon emission and climate resilience framework.

### 2.2.4 International Financial Institution

*Architect Of New Hope*: IFI is a financial institution established by two or more countries following international law. Usually, it is governed by a national government with international stakeholders. Major IFIs are IMF, World Bank, Asian Development Bank etc. Promoting banking and financing services with emerging needs and changing policy perceptive. Facilitate Financial Infrastructure, acts as Advisor and Support the functioning via Credit Bureau, Registries, Payment systems and Remittances. Initiation of a new policy framework, especially in the case of sustainability where the risk outweighs the possible long-term subsistence, backed by IFIs strengthens the management and robust the execution.

*Assistor*: Assisting investors in making innovative transactions, sustainable and profitable.

*Well heading Global knowledge and Convention*: By improving the flow of information IFI, Voluntary Guidance, label Schemes, Scaling up expansion and providing the mandatory requirement (UN Environment, 2017).

### 2.2.5 Green Digital Finance Alliance (GDFA)

Another collaboration of committed financial institutions and stakeholders, was created in 2017 at the World Economic Forum. To uphold the potential of digital finance in promoting environment sustainability. Interaction is shaped by leading Financial Institutions and Experts on a timely scaled basis.

## 3. REQUIREMENT

After having an understanding about the nature and strategy of the policy. In this section essential requirements are disclosed. Information symmetry is a prerequisite for the smooth implementation of any policy. Europeans embarked on infusing information symmetry in their system by means of transactions. Thus, this section provides a layout of changes taking place which are further required to increase in number.

### 3.1 Disclosure

Disclosure refers to information available to the public (UN Environment, 2017). The form of transfer may vary as per the regional propensity. For the success of any Sustainable pilot project, the inclusion of public finances plays an important role. Also, Low Carbon Emission and the concern of the circular economy are being dispatched by private fintech. Ant Financial Services Group, an entity of Alibaba Company, a prominent online operating mobile platform, is a member of the GDFC. The tranquillity of Alipay lies in the understanding of the pressing need for sustainability. One of its pilot projects aimed at promoting green consumption via the use of social media, big data, and mobile payments. A threefold approach involves preparing a virtual profile of carbon saving/ usage, providing data for saving carbon and at last planting trees to reward the carbon saving. With an estimate of 200 million people joining voluntarily and resulting in carbon emissions of 1,50,000 tons (UN Environment, 2017). Barclays report Rise (2021), suggests that 70% of adults in the UK expressed due concern for climate change but were helpless, unsure about the action plan. Mere concern does not yield the desired result. Thus, Alipay's initiative has encouraged consumers to be more responsible and to contribute without knowing the technical Where, How ? framework of Sustainability. Ever since the early Chinese Revolution of 1949, the march of support by Chinese citizens towards its nation development has been profound and tradition still prevails.

There are various types of Green Financial Instruments enabling a safe future. Various companies have initiated environment conscious behaviour by reporting the eco-friendliness of their services while inculcating positive and rational spending by consumers.

## 3.2 Green Digital Payment

There has been a significant jump in instant digital payment transaction rate globally from 40% to 60% with an infection on S-curve. More specifically, in countries like India, Spain, UK, China and Thailand usage rate has been doubled while in Singapore and Australia, it is increasing approximately by 50% year on year (Mckinsey Global Payment, 2020). Digital Payment services are leveraging Open Banking Infrastructure for furnishing credit. Moreover, it capitalises on the transaction with minimal cost and deterrence. With API (Application of Programming Interface) set on the floor, the accessibility has been comprehensive. The Green feature is incorporated in the Digital Payment app by external sources (GDFA Green Fintech Taxonomy, 2022). Integration ensures the evaluation of carbon footprint simultaneously on each transaction. ESG data vendors such as S&P Trucost stimulate the inception of related green pilot projects. *"Highly empowered consumers seek and champion brands that commit to sustainability"* (Climate Fintech Rise, 2021; Forrester). Structural transformation is shaping the needed change in the behaviour of consumers and producers. Keeping an eye on carbon emissions regulates consumption and accelerates consciousness towards the environment.

PAY GREEN

1. Swiss payment platform
2. Encourages online transactions of shopping. Also, accounts for carbon emissions associated with each transaction.
3. The Cost of emissions is charged to the emitter and not to the consumer

DACONOMY

1. Swedish fintech banking start-up
2. Also known as a DO card. Tracks and puts a price on carbon emission on each transaction and displays it on the mobile app.
3. Thereby handing the decision in the hand of the consumer whether to go ahead with the purchase or find some alternative (GDFA Green Fintech Taxonomy, 2022)

## 3.3 Green Digital Investment Solutions

Green Digital Investment is optimising Automated and Algorithm driven platforms, Monitoring the investment and Assessing and Managing the portfolio allocation (GDFA Green Fintech Taxonomy). Driven by Robo Advisor business model and providing sustainable investment options. Its applications are customised to promote green finance and use the resources optimally. As per Accenture Banking (2022), an estimated amount of investment of $150 TN by Bank of America is required to achieve Net Zero Carbon Emission within 30 years. Moreover, the major data vendors are MSCI[1] (Morgan Stanley Capital International), Refinitiv[2], RepRisk[3]. In addition to this, though the US accounts for the largest number of fintech startups, Europe dominates in Green Finance (IIFG, 2021). US$100 trillion is required to achieve the SDG goal 2030 between now and 2030, or US$8 trillion annually, as per World Economic Forum (WEF). Complementing this, until 2030, US$23 trillion financing will be required if mobilising a Sustainable Capital Market is by 21 emerging markets as per IFC. However, this allocation does not seem to be the endpoint of the trouble. Fiscal space is hindering the allocation of investment. Thereby, a reduction in sustainable investment from 60% to 40% in emerging economies of the world could be witnessed (SFWG, 2018).

INYOVA

1. Inyova is a Swiss Investing platform
2. Suggests automated investment advice and provides a list of companies based on selected impact areas (Water, Energy, Circular Economy) aligned with the values of the investors.
3. Easy to use by individuals, professionals and asset managers

FNG

1. Global Wealth Management Platform
2. Provide automated customised sustainable solutions like ESG reporting, aggregation data visualisation and preference setting.
3. Equipped with robo- advisor. Accept the savings which can be invested later aligned with green values. (GDFA Green Fintech Taxonomy, 2022)

## 3.4 Digital ESG-Data

*"Global ESG assets are on track to exceed $53 trillion by 2025"*. Bloomberg Intelligence (Climate Fintech Rise, 2021). Some ESG data providing companies leverage Open Source Data due to its cost- effectiveness. Some use Geolocation of Asset to monitor the impact while in other cases fintech grip Geosat[4] to detect pressure of methane in the atmosphere by absorption of radiation in the shortwave infrared.

Sentinel-one[5] and Sentinel-two[6] are commercial satellites using high-resolution data granularity with high acquisition costs (GDFA Green Fintech Taxonomy, 2022). Monitoring, Collecting, Analysing, Validating, Attesting, Reporting opaque the responsibility of fintech in this domain.

SATELLIGENCE

1. Dutch Fintech
2. Provides automated Satellite based information for financial services to monitor deforestation
3. Uses Statistical Tool Bayesian Iterative for evaluating alternatives and a wide range of possibility
4. Solutions are based on Machine Learning algorithm like Random Forest or Gradient Technique

## 3.5 Green Digital Crowdfunding and Syndication Platforms

With the use of crowdfunding fintech, a network of people can direct the creation of new products and media while also making money for charitable causes and for venture capital (lee, shin 2017; International trade administration, n.d.). Crowd investors leverage Cloud Computing and Artificial Intelligence into real assets such as trees, renewable energy etc (GDFA Green Fintech Taxonomy, 2022). Also, transitions in the business model enable crowdfunding for artistic purposes and for igniting start-up ecosystems (Pawlowska, Staniszewska, Grzelak, 2022).

BETTERVEST (GDFA Green Fintech Taxonomy, 2022)

1. German Fintech
2. Uses Big Data and Cloud Computing to assist fundraisers to reach various nodal of renewable energy venture
3. Accept funds as little as EURO50. Thereby, reducing the cost and carbon dioxide; economically viable too.

RAISE NOW

1. Swiss Fintech NGO
2. Provides fundraising solutions to donors at flexible ease. Encompasses board range of automated data.
3. Rapid, Transparent and accountable

## 3.6 Green Digital Risk and Insurance

Uses Artificial Intelligence, IoT data capabilities and Satellite to detect climate vulnerability and physical risk associated with it. Insurance mitigates the risk by providing a safety net and also shields by providing signals through sensors(GDFA Green Fintech Taxonomy, 2022).

CELSIUS PRO

1. Swiss Insure - Tech Company
2. Specialises in providing Insurance solutions to help its clients worldwide mitigate extreme weather and natural catastrophes
3. Uses Third party data and is flexible with proof evidence of loss.

## 3.7 Information Asymmetry

Information asymmetry is not favourable. Relevant Information is needed to ensure alignment, measurement and valuation of assets. Moreover, Information Asymmetry leads to moral hazard and adverse selection. Deviation from the most efficient allocation of resources. The creditworthiness of the initiatives lies in the following rating:

***ESG Rating***: Rating Agency involved in assigning score escapes board area related to Environment, Social and Corporate Governance such as work factors, equality within the company, good business environment, Cybersecurity, Information Security etc.

*Table 2. List of popular ESG Index (Hemanth, 2023). Highlighting the major ESG Index along with its distinct component included.*

| S.no | ESG Index | Description |
|---|---|---|
| 1. | Bloomberg ESG Disclosure Score | ● This statistic appraises a company's environmental, social, and governance (ESG) data transparency and disclosure, demonstrating its dedication to tackling ESG issues.<br>● The score is derived from information provided by companies and external ESG providers, encompassing a wide range of firms, regions, and sectors. |
| 2. | S&P Global Ratings ESG Evaluation | ● This assessment appraises a company's ESG performance through a **sector-specific** questionnaire, examining its adherence to ESG principles.<br>● This evaluation encompasses diverse firms, regions, and sectors, with companies furnishing responses to the questionnaire, offering insights into their ESG practices. |

*continues on following page*

*Table 2. Continued*

| S.no | ESG Index | Description |
|---|---|---|
| 3. | CDP | ● CDP, formerly known as the Carbon Disclosure Project, evaluates a company's involvement in mitigating climate change and its transparency regarding climate-related matters.<br>● Employing a sector-specific questionnaire, CDP focuses on climate change, forest conservation, and water protection, enabling a comprehensive evaluation of companies. |
| 4. | FTSE Russell's ESG Ratings | ● This gauges a company's performance in environmental, social, and governance aspects, relying solely on publicly available data. These ratings cover a broad spectrum of firms, regions, and sectors, offering a comprehensive analysis of ESG performance. |
| 5. | ISS Governance Quality Score | ● This score identifies corporate governance risks by assessing a company's management structure, shareholder rights, remuneration practices, and audit processes. Covering all types of firms, regions, and sectors, it provides a comprehensive evaluation of governance-related risks. |
| 6. | MSCI | ● The purpose of MSCI's ESG ratings is to assess how effectively a company handles ESG risks and opportunities that have a substantial financial impact.<br>● Based on their exposure to ESG risks and how well they manage those risks in relation to their peers, these ratings, which use a framework-based approach, distinguish market leaders from those that fall behind. |
| 7. | Sustainalytics ESG Risk Ratings | ● Sustainalytics ESG risk ratings assess a company's exposure to serious industry hazards as well as how well it tackles those risks. Encompassing firms, regions, and sectors, these ratings offer valuable insights into ESG risk management practices. |
| 8. | RobecoSAM Corporate Sustainability Assessment | ● Leveraging a variety of data sources, such as company-provided information, media reports, ngo data, scientific databases, news, and media coverage, this assessment measures a company's environmental, social, and governance performance alike the scores mentioned above. It includes businesses from different industries and geographical areas also. |
| 9. | Thomson Reuters ESG Scores | ● This company's score is no different from the above mentioned key categories, but it also incorporates management practises, shareholder practices, corporate social responsibility strategy, workforce policies, human rights, community engagement, and product responsibility factors in determining the score. |

### 3.7.2 Credit Rating

Credit rating is an analysis of the credit risk linked with a financial product or financial institution (Economic Times, 2023). With the purpose of determining their capacity to repay loans. Popular credit rating agencies, including Standard & Poor's and Moody's investor service, offer thorough analyses.

### 3.7.3 Credit Bureau

Credit bureaus collect information on individual consumer, financial entities to determine how creditworthy they appear (Investopedia, 2022). Three main credit Bureaus are Equifax, Experian, Transllnion.

## 4. LEAD ENTITIES

The major entities working to establish a green financial system includes Public Entity, Private Entity and Partnership. In some countries the prime leaders work in either of the following spheres. Depending upon the outreach, key actors work.

### 4.1 Public Entity

Financial regulators, particularly central banks, are responsible for ensuring the overall stability of the financial system. They set monetary policies, regulate banking activities and oversee the functioning of financial markets. In the context of capital market development, central banks often collaborate with capital market regulators to establish rules and regulations that promote transparency, investor protection, and efficient market operations. Finance ministries also play a significant role in the development process. They formulate policies, create a supportive legal framework, and coordinate efforts with other regulatory bodies to facilitate the growth of capital markets. In Azerbaijan, Georgia, Indonesia, Sri Lanka, Ukraine, and many other countries, financial regulators such as central banks, finance ministries, and capital market regulators work together to lead the development process (SBFN Toolkit, 2023). They establish regulations, monitor compliance, and implement policies that foster the growth and stability of capital markets .

### 4.2 Private Entity

Industry associations, private sector entities, or coalitions may in some instances, serve as the leaders of the development process roadmaps. This approach often involves collaboration among different private sector entities, such as businesses, industry representatives, and professional organisations, to collectively design and implement development strategies. Australia and New Zealand provide examples where private sector coalitions and platforms have taken the lead in designing roadmaps. These coalitions bring together stakeholders from various industries, sectors, and organisations to develop shared goals and strategies for economic development.

## 4.3 Public - Private Partnership

The involvement of both public and private entities in the roadmap development process is important as it ensures a comprehensive and inclusive approach. It allows for the inclusion of diverse perspectives, expertise, and resources from different sectors, leading to more holistic and continuous development strategies without the insufficiency of funds. Platforms or interagency working groups that represent key public and private sector players have driven development strategy processes in certain nations, for example, Thailand, Morocco, and Mongolia

For instance, Ireland

*"This roadmap sets out targeted measures with a view to Ireland being a leading sustainable finance centre by 2025, informed by extensive research and stakeholder engagement. It outlines how public-private sector collaboration will develop talent, prepare industry, leverage digital solutions, enhance the enabling environment, and promote and communicate Ireland's sustainable finance priorities and capabilities" (SBFN Toolkit, 2023).*

One notable instance is the collaboration between the Shenzhen Green Finance Committee, Energy Blockchain Labs, the International Institute Of Green Finance, and the China Emissions Exchange in China. They are currently piloting the utilisation of blockchain technology and IoT chips integrated into green assets to digitise the process of green certification and verification. This initiative aims to enhance transparency and efficiency in the green finance sector. Another example is the green asset wallet, which was authorised by the German Ministry for economic affairs and development and developed by Stockholm green digital finance. This project brings together a consortium of financial institutions, research institutes, and fintech partners. Their objective is to create a blockchain platform that enables cost-effective and immutable validation of green investment claims and verification of the environmental impact of such investments. These initiatives showcase how blockchain technology is being leveraged in the realm of sustainable finance to streamline processes, ensure credibility, and facilitate the transition towards a greener economy. The participation of diverse stakeholders emphasises the importance of cross-sector collaboration in generating innovation and achieving sustainable finance goals (SFWG, 2018).

## 4.4 Stakeholders

1) *Financial regulators:* This includes Central Banks, Commercial Banks, Capital Market Regulators, Insurance Regulators, and Pension Fund Regulators.

They play a crucial role in setting regulatory frameworks and standards for sustainable finance. For instance, in India, RBI the financial regulator has played a key role in augmenting lending to green projects. Indian Renewable Energy Development Agency is India's first green bank, established in May 2016 (Climate Fintech Rise, 2021).

2) *Government agencies:* Ministries, treasuries, national planning agencies, and national statistics offices contribute to policy-making, planning, and data collection related to sustainable finance.
3) *Elected officials:* Parliamentary subgroups or committees focused on sustainability issues can have an impact on shaping sustainable finance policies and regulations. The civic body of Ghaziabad Nagar Nigam UP, is the First Indian local government who has issued green bonds in 2021 worth US$20 million (Hussina, Dill, 2023).
4) *Financial sector industry associations:* Associations representing various sectors such as banking, microfinance, capital markets, insurance, sustainable finance, and fintech can provide expertise and advocacy for sustainable finance initiatives.
5) *Financial institutions:* Banks, microfinance institutions, stock exchanges, insurance firms, asset managers, mortgage businesses, and guarantee companies are all examples of financial organisations and are key players in implementing sustainable finance practices and financing sustainable projects.
6) *Private companies and networks:* Chambers of commerce, corporations, small and medium-sized enterprises (SMEs), and startups contribute to sustainable finance through their business practices, investments, and innovations.
7) *International organisations*: Development finance institutions, international organisations, and NGOs provide guidance, expertise, and funding for sustainable finance initiatives at a global scale.
8) *Service providers:* Rating agencies, credit information companies, and advisory firms support the implementation and evaluation of sustainable finance practices. For instance, Signatories to major flagship programs such as the Equator Principles (EP) for financial institutions, Guidelines on how to apply green finance are offered by the Principles for Responsible Investment (PRI), the United Nations Environment Programme (UNEP), and the statement of commitment by financial institutions on sustainable development (RBI Bulletin, 2021).
9) *Civil society organisations*: Labour unions, independent research institutes, and community-based organisations raise awareness, advocate for sustainability, and engage in dialogue around sustainable finance.

## 5. METRIC

Evaluation of policy is crucial in ascertaining the impact of specific policy. So, following are the few metrics which would help to determine how far the implication of policy has reached.

1) *Green Financing Volume*: This metric measures the total amount of financing directed towards environmentally sustainable projects, including renewable energy, energy efficiency, green infrastructure, and clean technologies. It provides an indication of the scale of investments in the green sector.
2) *Green Bonds Issuance:* Green bonds are securities that are issued specifically to finance environmentally beneficial projects. Monitoring the amount and growth of green bond issuance can provide information about the expansion of green finance activities.
3) *Environmental Impact Indicators:* These indicators measure the environmental outcomes of financed projects. They evaluate aspects such as reduced greenhouse gas emissions, energy savings, water conservation, waste reduction, and biodiversity conservation. By evaluating these impacts, progress can be measured in terms of tangible environmental benefits.
4) *Climate Finance Flow:* This metric tracks the flow of funds towards climate-related projects, including mitigation and adaptation measures. It assesses the mobilisation of financial resources to address climate change challenges.
5) *Green Portfolio Composition:* Examining the composition of financial institution portfolios can reveal the proportion of investments allocated to green or sustainable assets. It helps assess the alignment of investment strategies with environmental objectives.
6) *Environmental Risk Assessment:* This metric evaluates the extent to which financial institutions incorporate environmental risk factors into their decision-making processes. It entails evaluating exposure to risks associated with the climate, such as those that are physical (such as natural disasters) and those that are transitional (such as policy changes or technological advancements).
7) *Sustainability Reporting:* The adoption and quality of sustainability reporting by financial institutions and corporations can indicate their commitment to transparency and disclosure of environmental impacts, risk management strategies, and sustainability performance.
8) *Green Job Creation:* Employment generated from the establishment of green industries, namely renewable energy, energy efficiency, and sustainable agriculture, provides insight into the socioeconomic impact of green finance efforts.

9) *ESG Integration:* ESG (Environmental, Social, and Governance) standards are used to assess how well businesses perform on the measures of sustainability and ethical values. The incorporation of ESG factors into investment and other financial instruments can indicate progress in incorporating sustainability considerations.
10) *Policy and Regulatory Frameworks:* Monitoring the development and implementation of policies, regulations, and standards related to green finance can reflect progress in creating an enabling environment for sustainable finance activities.

## CONCLUSION

The chapter portrays the layout of the transition taking place in the fintech sector. To achieve SDG by 2030, sustainability has left no stone unturned to become an integral part of work for any entity. With Fintech commanding the change and opening new doors of opportunities, financing sustainable projects has been steady. The change required for heading to versatile innovation is taking place at EMDC (Economically more developed countries). ‘*The business of business is business*’ With this saying, Friedman, a Monetarist Economist, is highlighting the concern that the welfare of society is being compromised because companies aim to maximise their profit at the cost of the welfare of the society (Schoenmaker and Schramade, 2019). A similar view has been proposed by the New Keynesian Economist, whereby companies aim to maximise their profit at the cost of consumer surplus. However, this is not a concern in this chapter. This issue is encapsulated in the area of Corporate Social Responsibility. This chapter studied the impact from the lens of environmental sustainability. In addition, the chapter also provided a bird’s-eye view of how companies are utilising their financial services driven by technology to align their action towards sustainability. Namely, green crowdfunding, green insurance etc. The roadmap begins with describing the vision of green finance. Further, elaborates on India’s framework in G20. The strategies being used at national and international levels. The requirement in the process of implementing green finance is, for instance, the disclosure of information. Followed by introducing the lead entities and stakeholders, thereby ending with the measures/ metrics to evaluate the success. The implication of the policy framework would provide fintech companies, researchers and policymakers in comprehending the transition. The future maker and taker are the carriers of change. The dormant firms are the cause of disturbance in balancing the efficient allocation of resources in green finance. While the carrying capacity of the earth is being challenged, the distress seems intolerant. Unsettled practices may undermine the growth of developed nations.

## REFERENCES

G20 Argentina. (2018). *Sustainable finance synthesis report*. UN. https://unepinquiry.org/wp-content/uploads/2018/11/G20_Sustainable_Finance_Synthesis_Report_2018.pdf?showiframe=true

Accenture. (n.d.). *Let there be change*. 360° Value Report. https://www.accenture.com/content/dam/accenture/final/corporate/corporate-initiatives/sustainability/document/360-Value-Report-2022.pdf

Aggrawal, S. (2023). How green finance is paving the way for India's sustainable future. *Times of India Blog*. https://timesofindia.indiatimes.com/blogs/voices/how-green-finance-is-paving-the-way-for-indias-sustainable-future/

Anderson, K. (2023). *The UK's Green Finance Strategy: principles, objectives and steps*. Greenly. https://greenly.earth/en-gb/blog/ecology-news/the-uks-green-finance-strategy-principles-objectives-and-steps

CBI. (2022). *Sustainable debt global state of the market 2022*. Green Finance Platform. https://www.greenfinanceplatform.org/sites/default/files/downloads/resource/cbi_sotm_2022_03b.pdf

Department for Environment, Food, and Rural Affairs. (2023). *Green Finance Boost for Nature in the UK*. GOV.UK. https://www.gov.uk/government/news/green-finance-boost-for-nature-in-uk#:~:text=The%20 government%20has%20 set%20a,to%20 achieving%20our%20Environment%20 Targets.

GDFA. (2022). *A Green Fintech Taxonomy and Data Landscaping*. Interim Report. https://www.greenfinanceplatform.org/sites/default/files/downloads/resource/GreenFintechTaxonomyDataLandscaping-v5%20.pdf

HM. (2023). *A Green Future: Our 25 Year Plan to Improve the Environment*. HM Government. https://assets.publishing.service.gov.uk/government/uploads/system/uploads/attachment_data/file/693158/25-year-environment-plan.pdf

*Home*. (n.d.). IFRS. https://www.ifrs.org/issued-standards/sasb-standards/

Hussain, F. & Dill, H. (2023). *India incorporates green bonds into its climate finance strategy*. World Bank Blogs. https://blogs.worldbank.org/climatechange/india-incorporates-green-bonds-its-climate-finance-strategy

G20. (2023). India's G20 Halfway Milestone. *G20 Secretariat NEWSLETTER*. G20. https://www.g20.org/content/dam/gtwenty/gtwenty_new/document/G20_Newsletter%20English_May%202023_D8.pdf

Investopedia. (2022). *Basics of what a credit bureau is and does, plus major ones.* Investopedia. https://www.investopedia.com/terms/c/creditbureau.asp

Jain, S. (2020). *Financing India's Green Transition*, 338. ORF. https://www.orfonline.org/wp-content/uploads/2020/01/ORF_IssueBrief_338_FinancingGreenTransition_NEW27Jan.pdf

Kalia, C. (2020).*Green Finance is gaining traction for net zero transition in India.* EY US - Home.https://www.ey.com/en_in/climate-change-sustainability-services/green-finance-is-gaining-traction-for-net-zero-transition-in-india

KPMG. (2016). *Fintech in India, A global growth story*. KPMG. https://assets.kpmg.com/content/dam/kpmg/pdf/2016/06/FinTech-new.pdf

KPMG. (2022). *Enabling tomorrow: The emergent ESG Fintech ecosystem.* KPMG. https://assets.kpmg.com/content/dam/kpmg/sg/pdf/2022/11/enabling-tomorrow-the-emergent-esg-fintech-ecosystem.pdf

Lee, I. & Shin, Y. (2017). Fintech: Ecosystem, business models, investment decisions, and challenges. *Iran Arze*. https://iranarze.ir/wp-content/uploads/2019/01/E10696-IranArze.pdf

LSEG. (2020). *London leads the world's Sustainable Finance Ecosystem.* LSEG. https://www2.lseg.com/sustainablefinance

Mckinsey & Company. (2020). *The 2020 Mckinsey global payments report.* McKinsey. https://www.mckinsey.com/~/media/mckinsey/industries/financial%20services/our%20insights/accelerating%20winds%20of%20change%20in%20global%20payments/2020-mckinsey-global-payments-report-vf.pdf

Nassiry, D. (2018).*The role of fintech in unlocking green finance: policy insights for developing countries.* ADB. https://www.adb.org/sites/default/files/publication/464821/adbi-wp883.pdf

Nicholls, A. (n.d.). *Policies, Initiatives, and Regulations Related to Sustainable Finance.* Asian Development Bank. https://www.adb.org/sites/default/files/institutional-document/691951/ado2021bp-policies-initiatives-regulations.pdf

P., V. (2021). 11 Indian Green Startups working for the climate. *Medium.* https://medium.com/climate-conscious/11-indian-green-startups-working-for-the-climate-583169f83862

Pawłowska, M., Staniszewska, A., & Grzelak, M. (2022). *Does fintech promote the sustainable development of renewable energy enterprises?*

Reserve Bank of India. (2020). *FinTech: The Force of Creative Disruption*. RBI. https://rbidocs.rbi.org.in/rdocs/Bulletin/PDFs/7FINTECHEED4C43FC31D43C9B9D7F8F31D01B08E.PDF

Reserve Bank of India. (2021).*Green Finance in India: Progress and Challenges.* RBI. https://rbidocs.rbi.org.in/rdocs/Bulletin/PDFs/04AR_2101202185D9B6905ADD465CB7DD280B88266F77.PDF

Rise. (2021). *Rise FinTech Insights climate fintech*. Barclays. https://rise.barclays/content/dam/thinkrise-com/documents/Rise-FinTech-Insights-climate-fintech-2021-DIGITAL.pdf

Ritchie, H. (2018). *Plastic Pollution*. Our World in Data. https://ourworldindata.org/plastic-pollution

S. B. F. N. Network. (2023). *Developing sustainable finance roadmaps*. Sustainable Banking and Finance Network. https://www.sbfnetwork.org/wp-content/assets/toolkit/SBFN_Sustainable_Finance_Roadmap-Toolkit_Guide.pdf

Schoenmaker, D. & Schramade, W. (2019). *Principles of Sustainable Finance*. Oxford University Press.https://papers.ssrn.com/sol3/papers.cfm?abstract_id=3282699

SFWG. (2018). *Third Sustainable Finance Working Group (SFWG)*. DEA. https://dea.gov.in/sites/default/files/Third%20Sustainable%20Finance%20Working%20Group%20%28SFWG%29.pdf

UN Enviornment. (2017). *Roadmap for Sustainable Finance*. World Bank. https://sustainabledevelopment.un.org/content/documents/245112128312112017153333RoadmapforaSustainableFinancialSystem.pdf

US EPA. (2022). *Climate Change Indicators: Global Greenhouse Gas Emissions*. EPA. https://www.epa.gov/climate-indicators/climate-change-indicators-global-greenhouse-gas-emissions

Vagra, D. (2017). *Fintech, the new era of financial services*. Research Gate. doi:10.14267/VEZTUD.2017.11.03

## KEY TERMS AND DEFINITIONS

**Carbon Emissions:** The release of carbon that adds to the greenhouse gas group is known as carbon emission. The release may vary from the end use to the procurement process. Post industrialization carbon emissions have been exponentially increasing. The ill effects of its emissions are air pollution, respiratory issues, ozone layer depletion, air quality issues etc.

**Carbon:** Carbon is the sixth element in the periodic table. It is non-metal implying it is brittle, non-malleable, and non-ductile and insulator. With a density of 2.2g and a melting point of 3,550 °C. It supports life on earth and is an important component in the dietary chart of humans.

**ESG:** This refers to environmental, social and corporate governance. It emphasises well-being, inclusive of nature, the social sphere and the regulations associated with it. So, Whether the model of governance is capitalist or democratic ESG index is essential for determining the holistic development

**Fintech:** This refers to financial institutions incorporating technology in their business model. The financial instrument includes digital lending, digital insurance, digital payment etc. Leveraging Blockchain, Internet of Things (IoT), Big data, Machine Learning and Artificial Intelligence.

**Green Finance:** This refers to financing the transactions for sustainable projects such as investment in solar energy, green bonds etc. With the advent of fintech green investment suggestions are provided by automated tools such as Chabot.

**Net Zero Carbon:** This is a target that is proposed under this sustainable development goal of 2030. Net zero carbon refers to the reduction of carbon emissions in every possible way of its release. This step is aligned with attaining a sustainable livelihood.

**Sustainable Finance:** This refers to financing the transaction in a conscious way that does not hinder the wellbeing of the present and the future stakeholders. Investment at the cost of distress is not sustainable. It emphasises positive externality.

## ENDNOTES

1 *Besides stock, fixed income, and real estate indexes and tools for multi-asset portfolio analysis, MSCI is a prominent global provider of ESG and climate products.*

2 *The London Stock Exchange Group's subsidiary Refinitiv (Thomus Reuter) is a provider of infrastructure and data for the financial markets globally.*

3 *In the field of ESG data science, reprisk is a pioneering leader. Only ESG research company to combine skilled analysts with cutting-edge machine learning.*

4 *US Navy Geodetic satellite is carried 800 km and with 108-degree inclination orbit. It carried an altimeter that became successful in measuring the distance from satellite to the sea surface with a relative precision of approximately five km (NASA).*

5 *first of the satellite constellation for the copernicus mission run by the European space Agency (ESA). gives a constant sampling of the open ocean and provides wind and wave information. Application of wave energy is crucial to enhancing shipping efficiency.*

6 *For the best convergence and data delivery, the space segment consists of a constellation of two identical satellites in the same orbit, 180 degrees apart. Every five days at the equator, they together cover the whole terrestrial surface of the planet, big islands, interior waters, and coastal waters (ESA).*

# Chapter 8
# Promoting Economic Sustainability Through the Adoption of Digital Payment Systems

**Rajesh Shankaranarayana**
*Indian Institute of Management, Tiruchirapalli, India*

**Shalini Ramaswamy**
*Jain University (Deemed), India*

**Chaya Bagrecha**
*Jain University (Deemed), India*

**Kiran Hiremath**
*Presidency University, India*

**Madhavi A.**
*Jain University (Deemed), India*

## ABSTRACT

*Promoting economic sustainability through the adoption of digital payment is of great significance for the long-term development of a country. Minimizing the environmental impact and promoting cost savings can lead to economic growth and development. This chapter examines the adoption of digital payment systems and its impact on sustainability initiatives. A survey of 450 mobile consumers in Karnataka revealed that awareness level towards digital payment systems is 93%, and UPI is the most preferred mode of digital payments, based on linear regression and using SPSS. It is also seen that time saved and ease of maintenance for each banking transaction*

DOI: 10.4018/979-8-3693-0008-4.ch008

*has an impact on economic sustainability. All the respondents were aware of the components of sustainable development, and most were willing to contribute towards economic sustainability, though threat due to fraud is still a matter of concern for most of the users. This study provides insights into factors that promote economic sustainability in the context of adoption of digital payment systems.*

## INTRODUCTION

Digital payments are transactions that happen online or through other digital platforms without a physical exchange of money. Both the parties in the transaction, the payer and the payee, use electronic means to exchange money. The government of India has taken several measures to promote digital payments in our country. According to Statista (2022), the goal of "Digital India" is to establish a "digitally empowered" "Faceless, Paperless, Cashless" economy. The evolution of digital payments in India dates back to 1980s much before internet was introduced. At that time, there was no internet infrastructure in our country and only credit card and debit card were used by people instead of cash. Later in 1990s internet become quite popular and e-commerce sector began to grow. With the introduction of National Electronic Fund Transfer (NEFT) & Real Time Gross Settlement (RTGS) in 2005, and Immediate Payment Service (IMPS) in 2010, the digital fund transfer became very popular. But the problem was the interoperability with each other. Roy & Sahoo (2016) explains the areas of improvement in the existing payment systems - specifically the risks and other challenges faced in India. To overcome this issue, Unified Payments Interface (UPI) was introduced by National Payment Corporation of India (NPCI) in 2016. UPI is considered to be the most advanced, real time payment systems in India. According to Thakkar J et. al (2022), UPI has been a game changer in digital payment ecosystem in India. The author also talks about the strategies initiated by the government to increase the usage of UPI in India. Rastogi et al (2021) talks about how UPI is contributing to the Indian economy by not only supporting the financial literacy but contributing to the financial inclusion of the poor. Mahesh A et.al (2021) talks about the remarkable growth of UPI in the recent past and how customers have shifted to the paperless and contactless payment system. Naranje (2023) explains the rapid growth in popularity of digital payments in India. He also mentions the government's role in being pro-digital which is encouraging people to adopt digital payments.

According to Statista (2023), more than 72 billion digital transactions were recorded across India during the financial year 2022. The market for digital payments is expected to reach a total transaction value of US$180.40 billion in 2023. By 2027, it is anticipated that the overall transaction value will increase by 15.56% each year (CAGR 2023–2027), totalling US$321.70 billion.

The volume of digital payments got a major fillip due to demonetization in 2016 and Covid pandemic in 2020. Jose (2023) explains the tremendous change in the payment system witnessed in our country and also the after effects of demonetization and Covid-19 pandemic that led to changing demographics which paved the way for a sustainable economic growth.. Singh et al., (2023) found that there is a significant increase in the number of people shifting to digital payment mode for all their financial transactions. More than 76% of the respondents showed the intention to use fintech payment services during pandemic. Manocha et al., (2019) found that demonetization made a significant impact in rising the number of digital payments in the country. There is a transformation from cash economy to digital, cashless economy creating a digitally empowered nation. Contrary to this is the study conducted by Sandeep Kaur et al (2020), where the authors analysed the impact of demonetization on digital payment by conducting an event study. Eight indicators of digital payment like credit card, debit card, RTGS, NEFT, M-wallet, M-banking, IMPS and PPI cards were analysed for a period of 49 months and it was observed that there was no significant impact of demonetization on the digital payment system in India. Similar findings were seen in the study conducted by Kanchan K (2018). The author observed that there was a sudden growth in the digital transactions in the next month of demonetization. This phenomenon was due to the temporary cash crunch in the economy. After few months there was a decline in the usage of digital payments due to the availability of cash in the market.

Growth of digitalization and the use of internet has contributed enormously to the transformation of the Indian economy. The country is able to connect well with global players in all aspects. Despite the various opportunities that digital payment system has offered, there are quite a few challenges faced by the people while shifting to digital payments in India. Kajol K et al., (2022) did a literature review on the digital financial transactions and the factors that influence its adoption. Some of the challenges like cost, perceived threat of danger due to fraud, complexity in usage, resistance to change and privacy concerns were observed among the respondents. Khando et al., (2022) explains the key challenges into social, economic, legal, technical and awareness. The social challenges can be related to social influences, culture, satisfaction, trust, loyalty etc. Economic challenges are cost, tax and security implications, inflation, sustainability, government stability etc. Technical challenges include infrastructure, privacy, access to internet, speed, fraud, disruptive technology, safety and reliability issues. Legal issues include legitimacy issues and regulatory issues. Awareness challenges are lack of knowledge and education, insecurity resistance to change etc.

This study provides insights into the awareness level of customers on digital payment system, specifically understanding the reasons for digital payment adoption and also its impact on the economic sustainability of the customers. Two research questions are explored in the present study.

- What is the awareness level of customers towards digital payments and reasons for such adoption?
- What is the impact of digital payments on the economic sustainability of customers?

## THEORETICAL BACKGROUND AND HYPOTHESES

### Research Framework

This study considers various factors like awareness level, reasons for adoption and digital payment's impact on economic sustainability. While there are many more factors which this study has not considered, the above mentioned factors are well established in the literature.

### Awareness

Awareness refers to the knowledge or perception about the digital payment system. Several studies have been conducted in India in various urban cities, rural India, among the youth and other age groups and models have been developed to find and analyse the extent of awareness about digital payments. Vinitha et at., (2017) explains the necessity of creating awareness among the respondents to strengthen their adoption towards e payment systems. Thakker J et al., (2023) analyses the initiatives taken by the Indian government to increase the usage of UPI and found that there is a significant impact of age and occupation of women on the awareness about the UPI and its configuration in the city of Pune. Though the digital payments are quite common in the urban cities, it is yet to percolate in rural India. Nath et al., (2022) found in his study that rural Assam is not digitally literate which is hindering the people to accept the adopt digital payments. Social and infrastructure barriers are also stopping them from becoming digitally literate. Age of the respondent is an important factor to analyse the awareness level about digital payment. Kaur et al., (2023) conducted a study to find the awareness level among the youth towards digital payment in Delhi, NCR region and it is disheartening to find that lot of youth are still not completely aware about the digital payment and technical glitches is one of the factor that is stopping them from adopting digital payments. Nikitha et al., (2023) found that demonetization and covid pandemic has been two important factors which has led to increase in the awareness about digital payments among the respondents in Karnataka.

Several research can be found where authors have developed models to analyse the digital payment awareness, adoption, implementation in developing economies. Gupta S et al., (2023) developed an e-payment adoption model to examine the consumer awareness towards digital literacy and digital engagement. The study was conducted on tech savy respondents and found that awareness has positive effects on the consumer empowerment. Kumar et al., (2023) applied unified theory model named stimulus-organism-response (S-O-R) theory to explore and analyse the preferences of consumers for using online payment services. There are several factors that influences the happiness, satisfaction and behaviour intention of consumers. The study found that awareness about the digital payments is an important factor for consumer satisfaction. The hypothesis could thus be stated as below:

**H1**: UPI is more popular compared to any other mode of digital payment

## Reasons for Adoption

Adoption is a process of acceptance, integration and usage. Researchers have found several reasons like demonetization, covid pandemic, government initiatives like launch of UPI, penetration of smart phones and affordable internet connection for the adoption of digital payment systems. Jain S (2023) found in his study that demonetization and Covid pandemic gave thrust for the forceful and sudden adoption of digital payments in India. Apart from this, NPCI launched by Government of India, promoted the single window mobile payment system which made the entire payment process simpler and easier compared to other modes of payment. Parvathy B et al., (2023) explains the reasons for the fast adoption of digital payments is the usage of smart phones, availability of affordable internet connection which in turn has made the all the digital payment applications literally cost-free. The study found that most of the users are happy with the service provided by the cost-free digital payment applications but disappointed with security issues. Vinitha et al., (2017) found factors such as perceived use, perceived ease of use, perceived risk and trust influencing the consumer's intention to adopt digital payments. In the process of adoption, consumers come across several challenges or impediments. Similar study was conduced by Kanchi S (2023) in Pune city where Technology Acceptance Model (TAM) was used to analyse the adoption of digital payment system. Level of education plays a major role in the adoption due to which it is very low among the hawkers in Pune city. Another research on TAM model is undertaken by Gupta S K et al., (2023) to analyse the behavioural intentions of tourists towards the adoption of digital payments using mobile wallets. Partial Least Square Structural Equation Modeling (PLS-SEM) technique is applied to test the TAM model. Predictor variables such as perceived value, perceived enjoyment, compatibility and social influence and mediating variables like service satisfaction and service trust were used to check their impact on outcome variables, behavioural intention. The findings of the study indicate that there is significant impact of predictor and mediating variables on the outcome variable towards the use of digital payments.

Gupta S et al., (2023) analyses the challenges faced by consumers in the process of decision making toward adoption of e-payment system. Factors such as digital awareness, digital literacy and digital engagement determines the adoption of e payment systems. The study used purposive sampling methods among the respondents in India who used digital payment services. The authors developed e adoption model to do the analysis. Singh S (2023) uses technology diffusion model to analyse the pattern and rate of adoption of UPI and also explore the future trend in India. It was found that UPI is gradually decreasing the share of other modes of digital payment systems and also reducing the reliance on cash transactions. But using UPI comes with various challenges like security issues, infrastructure woes, failed or delayed transactions, daily transaction limits etc.

## Trust in Usage of Digital Payment

Trust is defined as belief or something that is safe and reliable. Research shows that there are several factors that influence the digital payment adoption. One of the key factors in consumer trust in digital payment adoption. Mondego et al., (2020) asserts that trust play a vital in the adoption of new payment system. The objective of this study is to identify the factors that influence the consumer trust in mobile payment systems. The findings show that behavioural and organizations factors have a significant impact on the consumer trust toward mobile payment system. Similar study was conducted in India by Palak k et al., (2020) to check the relationship between trust-based factors and consumer's behaviour intention to use electronic payments. The findings indicate that trust acts as a significant determinant of digital adoption in India. Al-Sabaawi et al., (2023) investigated the factors influencing the use of e payment in Iraq. The study is based on Unified Theory of Acceptance and Usage of Technology model (UTAUT). The findings of the study indicates that trust as one of the factors affect the intention to accept e payment system. Rouibah K (2016) presented online trust model with four external factors and three endogenous variables. Propensity to trust is one of the external factors and consumer trust is one of the endogenous variables. The findings revealed that consumer trust is one of the most important drivers of online payment adoption.

## Economic Sustainability

Economic sustainability is defined as " *the practice of conserving natural and financial resources to create long-term financial stability*" (indeed.com 2022). Another definition goes like "*Economic sustainability refers to practices designed to create the long-term economic development of a company or nation while also managing the environmental, social, and cultural aspects of its activities. It is about balancing economic growth and generating profit with the impact on the environment and people*" (prysmiangroup.com). It is incorporated in the United Nations Sustainability Development Goals (SDGs) which guides countries for creating a long-lasting impact on the environment and people. Jeronen, E. (2020) has given definitions on economic sustainability based on various approaches. One of the approaches refer to maintaining sustainable economic growth and production efficiency without harming the environment.

"*Are digital payments more sustainable?*" (medium.com) explains how digital payments are key to achieve sustainability. Digitization helps in reducing the card foot prints, improves environmental impact and increases the efficiency in financial management. Digitization is key to financial inclusion and financial inclusion in turn is key to combat poverty and aids in achieving sustainable development goals. Research has been undertaken in several countries to analyse the interrelationship between digital payments, financial inclusion and sustainability. Lee (2023) undertook a study with a sample of 29 low- and middle-income Asian countries to check whether digital payment system promotes financial inclusion and contributes green environment. The study also focuses on understanding the awareness of consumers toward the implementation of green recovery technologies. Niankara (2023) analyses the influence of financial inclusion on the digital payment solutions within the regional economy of Gulf Cooperation Council. Salman D et al., (2023) conducted a study in Egypt to analyse the effect of digital financial inclusion on the green economy. The findings of the study shows that implementation of digital financial services significantly brings down the carbon emission in the long run. Xu R et al., (2023) explains the role of digital inclusive finance (DIF) in promoting green economy in developing countries. The study was conducted using DIF index on Chinese listed companies. The authors asserts that government supervision is necessary to achieve high quality development in green technology innovation. Very few studies have been found in Indian context with respect to economic sustainability and digital payments. Meghana K et al., (2018) analyses the impact of digital payment system on the economic sustainability of a township in Gujrat. The authors have developed a conceptual framework where it is found that there is significant impact of digital payment on economic sustainability – increased productivity, reduced cost and time, convenience, better money management, rise in total revenue to retailers and finally consumers are financial empowered. The study used UTAT model and found that consumers are leading a healthier life with reduced stress, better money managers and have accepted digital payment system as a culture and life style. The hypotheses could thus be stated as below:

**H2a**: Economic sustainability is impacted by availability of digital payment systems
**H2b**: Economic sustainability is impacted by safe and secure transactions
**H2c**: Economic sustainability is impacted by time saved for performing each digital transaction
**H2d**: Economic sustainability is impacted by ease of maintenance for banking transaction activity
**H3**: Safe and secure transactions lead to trust in digital payment systems

## RESEARCH METHODOLOGY

### Operationalization and Data Collection

The variables such as awareness, reason for adoption and economic sustainability used in the study were operationalized by validating them from prior research. A structured questionnaire was developed to measure the awareness of respondents on digital payments, reasons for adoption of digital payments and impact of digital payments on economic sustainability.

The data was collected randomly from many parts of Karnataka state by posting it online. 468 responses were collected with 450 usable sample size. The data so collected was analysed using IBM SPSS 24.0. Linear regression was used to test the hypotheses - measure the awareness level, reasons for adoption and impact on economic sustainability.

### Descriptive Statistics

The sample respondents of this study constituted the general public residing in the state of Karnataka. The sample comprises of 450 respondents with different socio-economic characteristics. The age of the respondents ranged from 18 to 60 years where a large group of respondents were in the group ranging from 18-30 years at 72.5%. The gender breakdown showed 63.6% men and 36.4% women. The occupation of the respondents varied in terms of students, employees, businessman and homemakers or others where a large group of respondents belonged to employees at 46.89%. Majority of the respondents are using digital payments at 93%. The modes of digital payments used by the respondents were credit card, debit card, UPI payments and internet banking where most of the respondents chose UPI payments at 59.78%. Most of the respondents use digital payments daily at 64.3%. Respondents used digital payments for online or in-person shopping, restaurants, movie booking and online fund transfer of which online or in-person shopping stood first at 48.2%.

## RESULTS

### Awareness

Two questions were asked in the survey to check the awareness about the digital payments. The first question was to determine how respondents get to know about the digital payments. The options given were Banks, advertisements, news and friends and relatives. As per the findings most of the respondents got to know from advertisements at 45.5% followed by friends and relatives at 27.5%, banks at 16.5% and news at 10.5%. The second question was to check the awareness on various modes of digital payments. The findings showed that majority of the respondents are aware of UPI payments like phone pay at 57.1% followed by mobile banking at 18.6%, net banking at 14.6% and debit and credit card payment at 10.3%. It can be concluded that all the respondents have heard and are aware about the digital payment system.

It is also observed from the data that more than 50% of the users of digital payment system have concerns on threat of scam and 16% of the users do not fully trust the system but use it for digital payments. This serves as a precaution that digital payment providers need to consider during the design.

### Economic Sustainability

Economic sustainability is measured in terms of time saving for performing each transaction, how safe and secure are the digital payment modes, 24/7 availability and ease of maintenance of banking transactions. Based on the survey data collected, it is seen that 65.2% respondents saved time due to digital payment usage, 61.5% respondents felt safe and secured using one of the digital payment modes, 81.4% respondents opined that the financial transactions can be done 24/7 and at any time, 61.3% respondents felt that it is easy to track and maintain all the financial transactions due to digital payment systems.

## DISCUSSION AND MAJOR FINDINGS

### Awareness

Table 1 and Table 2 shows the results of linear regression to test Hypothesis 1.

*Table 1. ANOVA test for testing awareness of mode of digital payments*

| ANOVA[a] | | | | | | |
|---|---|---|---|---|---|---|
| Model | | Sum of Squares | df | Mean Square | F | Sig. |
| 1 | Regression | 6.027 | 4 | 1.507 | 17.857 | .000[b] |
| | Residual | 38.562 | 457 | 0.084 | | |
| | Total | 44.589 | 461 | | | |
| a. Dependent Variable: Electronic_payment_Usage=Yes | | | | | | |
| b. Predictors: (Constant), Credit_Card, UPI, Debit_Card, Internet_Banking | | | | | | |

*Table 2. Regression test for testing awareness of mode of digital payments*

| Coefficients[a] | | | | | | |
|---|---|---|---|---|---|---|
| Model | | Unstandardized Coefficients | | Standardized Coefficients | t | Sig. |
| | | B | Std. Error | Beta | | |
| 1 | (Constant) | 0.621 | 0.040 | | 15.575 | 0.000 |
| | UPI | 0.311 | 0.037 | 0.365 | 8.332 | 0.000 |
| | Debit_Card | 0.011 | 0.032 | 0.016 | 0.354 | 0.724 |
| | Internet_Banking | -0.015 | 0.029 | -0.023 | -0.513 | 0.608 |
| | Credit_Card | 0.029 | 0.032 | 0.039 | 0.880 | 0.379 |
| a. Dependent Variable: Electronic_payment_Usage=Yes | | | | | | |

As can be seen in table 2, UPI is the preferred mode of digital payments, supporting hypothesis 1. The findings are aligned with the previous finding of Gupta D et al., (2020) and Thakker J et al., (2023).

## Economic Sustainability

Table 3 and Table 4 shows the results of linear regression to test Hypothesis 2.

*Table 3. ANOVA test for measuring economic sustainability*

| ANOVA[a] | | | | | | |
|---|---|---|---|---|---|---|
| Model | | Sum of Squares | df | Mean Square | F | Sig. |
| 1 | Regression | 1.873 | 4 | 0.468 | 5.010 | .001[b] |
| | Residual | 42.716 | 457 | 0.093 | | |
| | Total | 44.589 | 461 | | | |
| a. Dependent Variable: Electronic_payment_Usage=Yes | | | | | | |
| b. Predictors: (Constant), Safe_secure, Availability, Maintenance_ease, Time_saving | | | | | | |

*Table 4. Regression for testing factors for measuring economic sustainability*

| Coefficients[a] | | | | | | |
|---|---|---|---|---|---|---|
| Model | | Unstandardized | Coefficients | Standardized Coefficients | t | Sig. |
| | | B | Std. Error | Beta | | |
| 1 | (Constant) | 0.777 | 0.037 | | 21.100 | 0.000 |
| | Availability | 0.038 | 0.037 | 0.049 | 1.027 | 0.305 |
| | Time_saving | 0.090 | 0.034 | 0.139 | 2.668 | 0.008 |
| | Maintenance_ease | 0.061 | 0.032 | 0.096 | 1.922 | 0.055 |
| | Safe_secure | -0.019 | 0.031 | -0.029 | -0.598 | 0.550 |
| a. Dependent Variable: Electronic_payment_Usage=Yes | | | | | | |

As can be seen in table 4, time saved for performing each digital transaction has a significant impact on economic sustainability (less than 5% significance), supporting hypothesis H2c. It is seen that ease of maintaining banking transaction, at 10% significance level, has an impact on economic sustainability, hence supporting H2d partially. The findings are aligned with the previous findings of Meghana K et al., (2018). It is also seen that availability of digital payment systems and safety and security of digital payments is not significant, hence H2a and H2b is not supported. This finding contradicts the finding by Meghana K et al., (2018).

With hypothesis H2b not supported and 16% of the users who use digital payments not having trust, hypothesis H3 is also not supported. This is in contradiction to previous research findings by Mondego et al., (2020), Palak k et al., (2020), Al-Sabaawi et al., (2023) and Rouibah K (2016).

Table 5 illustrates the summarized hypotheses testing.

*Table 5. Summary of hypotheses testing*

| | *Hypotheses* | *Supported?* |
|---|---|---|
| H1 | UPI is more popular compared to any other mode of digital payment | Yes |
| H2a | Economic sustainability is impacted by availability of digital payment systems | No |
| H2b | Economic sustainability is impacted by safe and secure transactions | No |
| H2c | Economic sustainability is impacted by time saved for performing each digital transaction | Yes |
| H2d | Economic sustainability is impacted by ease of maintenance for banking transaction activity | Partially |
| H3 | Safe and secure transactions lead to trust in digital payment systems | No |

## Implications

The unprecedented growth in value and volume of digital payment transactions in India shows that there is a gradual change in the behaviour of the consumers towards cashless and paperless economy. The present study highlights the awareness, acceptance and reasons for adoption of digital payment system in Karnataka. The government of India has taken several initiatives to promote digitization and achieve the sustainability goals. For the emerging economy, promoting such technology driven initiatives will help to achieve economic growth and development. There are certain areas, where the adoption of digital payments is not to the fullest extent due to various challenges like, infrastructure woes, illiteracy, resistance to change, security threat and socio-cultural barriers. The government agencies and financial institutions should work together to strengthen the application of financial services and technology methods and strive to expand the coverage of digital payment services. Authorities should give special attention to create awareness data privacy, security and fraud detection and provide a risk-free digital payment system to the consumers. Overall, the behaviour of consumers towards the adoption of digital payments is positive and encouraging. What makes these consumers to continue to use digital payments and stay loyal to the payment modes? The government agencies, financial institutions, technology providers and application developers should strive to meet and increase the satisfaction level of the consumers. As more and more consumers are adopting the digital payment systems, the service providers should ensure and respond to their needs and promptly resolve their issues. This will further increase the usage of digital payments and within few years, the government's vision of 'Digital India' can be accomplished.

## CONCLUSION

Promoting economic sustainability through the adoption of digital payment is of great significance for the long-term development of a country. Minimizing the environmental impact and promoting cost savings can lead to economic growth and development. This paper examined the adoption of digital payment systems in Karnataka and its impact on the sustainability initiatives. Using a survey of 450 mobile consumers in Karnataka it is seen that UPI is the most preferred mode of digital payment. It is also seen that saving of time for each transaction and ease of maintenance for each banking transaction has an impact on economic sustainability. All the respondents are aware about the components of sustainable development and most are willing to contribute towards economic sustainability, though threat due to fraud is still a matter of concern for most of the users. This study provides insights into factors that promote the economic sustainability in the context of adoption of digital payment systems in Karnataka.

### Limitations and Scope for Future Research

Although the present study has given insights into the awareness, acceptance and adoption of digital payments, there are several other factors which can be considered to conduct this study. Models can be developed and used to analyze digital payment systems Kumar R (2023). There are certain limitations with respect to sample size, area chosen and time frame. If the sample size can be increased and the area of study can be expanded to other state of India at different time period, the results will vary. By introducing new variables into this study, there is profound scope for future researchers to address these areas. Further, this paper focused only on consumer perspective towards digital payment system. However, analyzing the perspective of the service providers, technology providers, application developers and financial institutions is worthy of attention.

## REFERENCES

Al-Sabaawi, M. Y. M., Alshaher, A. A., & Alsalem, M. A. (2023). User trends of electronic payment systems adoption in developing countries: An empirical analysis. *Journal of Science and Technology Policy Management, 14*(2), 246–270. doi:10.1108/JSTPM-11-2020-0162

Naranje, A. G. (2023). Future Of Digital Payment System in India: An Overview. *International Journal for Multidisciplinary Research International Conference on Multidisciplinary Research & Studies.*

Lee, C. C., Chen, P. F., & Chu, P.J. (2023). Green recovery through financial inclusion of mobile payment: A study of low- and middle-income Asian countries. *Economic Analysis and Policy, 77*, 729-747. doi:10.1016/j.eap.2022.12.012

Deepankar, R. & Amarendra, S. (2016). Payment Systems in India: Opportunities and Challenges. *Journal of Internet Banking and Commerce, 21*(2).

Gupta, S., & Prusty, S. (2023). Does consumer empowerment influence e-payment systems adoption? A digital consumer-centric perspective. *Journal of Financial Services Marketing*. doi:10.105741264-023-00238-4

Gupta, S. K., Tiwari, S., Hassan, A., & Gupta, P. (2023). Moderating Effect of Technologies into Behavioural Intensions of Tourists toward Use of Mobile Wallets for Digital Payments: TAM Model Perspective. *International Journal of Hospitality & Tourism Systems, 16*(1).

Jain, S. (2023). A study on Digital Payment System and its Future Feasibility in India. *International Journal of International Institute of Management Studies, 2*(1).

Jeronen, E. (2020). Economic Sustainability. In S. Idowu, R. Schmidpeter, N. Capaldi, L. Zu, M. Del Baldo, & R. Abreu (Eds.), *Encyclopedia of Sustainable Management. Springer*. Online. doi:10.1007/978-3-030-02006-4_197-1

Jose, S. (2023). Impact of Demonetization and Pandemic on Digital Payments Usage. *International Journal of Science and Research, Volume 12*(3). https://ssrn.com/abstract=4383173

Kajol, K. Singh, R., & Paul, J. (2022). Adoption of digital financial transactions: A review of literature and future research agenda. *Technological Forecasting and Social Change, 184*. doi:10.1016/j.techfore.2022.121991

Kanchi, S., Joglekar, S., & Manjare, R. (2023). Study of Technology Adoption and Perceived Usefulness of Digital Payment of the hawkers in Pune City. *Rabindra Bharati University Journal of Philosophy*.

Kanojia, P. & Lal, M. (2020). *Impact of Trust on Customer Adoption of Digital Payment Systems*. doi:. doi:10.4018/978-1-7998-2398-8.ch002

Kathial, K. (2018). Impact of Demonetization on Digital Transactions in India. *Asian Journal of Management*, *9*(1), 281–287. doi:10.5958/2321-5763.2018.00042.2

Kaur, H., & Mehta, R. (2023). A Study on the Adoption of Digital Payments by Indian Youth. In *ICASDMBW 2022: Proceedings of the International Conference on Application of AI and Statistical Decision Making for the Business World, ICASDMBW 2022*, (p. 247). European Alliance for Innovation. 10.4108/eai.16-12-2022.2326162

Khando, K., Islam, M. S., & Gao, S. (2022). The Emerging Technologies of Digital Payments and Associated Challenges: A Systematic Literature Review. Future Internet, 15(1), 21. MDPI AG. doi:10.3390/fi15010021

Kumar, R., Singh, T., Mohanty, S. N., Goel, R., Gupta, D., Alharbi, M., & Khanna, R. (2023). Study on online payments and e-commerce with SOR model. *International Journal of Retail & Distribution Management*. doi:10.1108/IJRDM-03-2023-0137

Mahesh, A. & Bhat, G. (2021). Digital Payment Service in India - A Case Study of Unified Payment Interface. *International Journal of Case Studies in Business, IT, and Education (IJCSBE), 5*(1), 256-265. doi:. doi:10.5281/zenodo.5091207

Manocha, S., Kejriwal, R., & Upadhyaya, A. (2019). The Impact of Demonetization on Digital Payment Transactions: A Statistical Study Proceedings of International Conference on Advancements in Computing & Management (ICACM). *SSRN*. https://ssrn.com/abstract=3446558 or doi:10.2139/ssrn.3446558

Meghana, K., & Tripathi, S. (2018). Digital Payment System for Economic Sustainability. A Case Study of Gujarat Narmada Fertilizers and Chemicals Ltd in India. *Scientific Quarterly 4*(44). doi: www.oamquarterly.polsl.pl doi:10.29119/1899-6116.2018.44.8

Mondego, D. Y., & Gide, E. (2020). Exploring the factors that have impact on Consumers'trust in Mobile Payment Systems nn Australia. *JISTEM-Journal of Information Systems and Technology Management, 17*, e202017009. doi:10.4301/S1807-1775202017009

Nath, H., & Boro, D. (2022). Use and Awareness of Digital Payment in Rural Areas: Special reference to Lakhimpur District, Assam. *IJFANS, 11*. www.ijfans.org, Vol.11, Iss. 7

Niankara, I. (2023). The impact of financial inclusion on digital payment solution uptake within the Gulf Cooperation Council Economies. *International Journal of Innovation Studies, 7*(1), 1-17. doi:10.1016/j.ijis.2022.09.004

Nikhitha, U., & Shalini, R. (). Adoption of digital payment system: A study conducted in the state of Karnataka. Intern*ational Research Journal of Modernization in Engineering Technology and Science 5*(4).

Parvathy, V., & Durairaj, D. (2023). Upi System: Utilisation and User Reaction toward Cost-Free Digital Payment Platform among Mobile Payment Users in Chennai. *Resmilitaris, 13*(3), 357-369.

Rana, N. P., Luthra, S., & Rao, H. R. (2023). Assessing challenges to the mobile wallet usage in India: An interpretive structural modelling approach. *Information Technology & People, 36*(4), 1533–1554. doi:10.1108/ITP-07-2021-0535

Rastogi, S., Panse, C., Sharma, A., & Bhimavarapu, V. M. (2021). Unified Payment Interface (UPI): A Digital Innovation and Its Impact on Financial Inclusion and Economic Development. *Universal Journal of Accounting and Finance., 9*(3), 518–530. doi:10.13189/ujaf.2021.090326

Rouibah, K., Lowry, P. B., & Hwang, Y. (2016). The effects of perceived enjoyment and perceived risks on trust formation and intentions to use online payment systems: New perspectives from an Arab country. *Electronic Commerce Research and Applications, 19*, 33–43. doi:10.1016/j.elerap.2016.07.001

Kaur, S. & Walia, N. (2020). Impact of demonetization on digital payments in India – Event study methodology. *Pacific Business Review International, 13*(4).

Singh, A. K., & Sharma, P. (2023). A study of Indian Gen X and Millennials consumers' intention to use FinTech payment services during COVID-19 pandemic. *Journal of Modelling in Management, 18*(4), 1177–1203. doi:10.1108/JM2-02-2022-0059

Singh, S. K., Singh, S. S., & Singh, V. L. (2023). Predicting adoption of next generation digital technology utilizing the adoption-diffusion model fit: The case of mobile payments interface in an emerging economy. *ACCESS Journal: Access to Science, Business, Innovation in Digital Economy, 4*(1), 130-148. doi:10.46656/access.2023.4.1(10)

Thakkar, J., & Thakkar, P. (2023). Digital Payments Revolution: A Study of Awareness, Acceptance, and Usage of Unified Payments Interface Technology Among Selected Women in India. *2022 OPJU International Technology Conference on Emerging Technologies for Sustainable Development (OTCON)*, Raigarh, Chhattisgarh, India. 10.1109/OTCON56053.2023.10114004

Vinitha, K. & Shanmugam, V. (2017). Factors Influencing Consumer's Intention to Adopt Digital Payment-Conceptual Model. *Indian Journal of Public Health Research & Development*. doi:. doi:10.5958/0976-5506.2017.00181.4

Xu, R., Yao, D., & Zhou, M. (2023). Does the development of digital inclusive finance improve the enthusiasm and quality of corporate green technology innovation? *Journal of Innovation & Knowledge*, *8*(3), 100382. doi:10.1016/j.jik.2023.100382

# Chapter 9
# A Study on the Effect of COVID-19 Uncertainty on Gig Workers' Job Insecurity and Banking Behavior

**Kuldeep Singh**
https://orcid.org/0000-0002-8180-4646
*Faculty of Management Studies, CMS Business School, Jain University (Deemed), India*

**Vedantam Seetharam**
*Faculty of Management Studies, CMS Business School, Jain University (Deemed), India*

**Nimisha Singh**
*Indian Institute of Information Technology, Allahabad, India*

## ABSTRACT

*Concerns about global instability and vulnerability have been raised by the massive economic crisis brought on by the COVID-19 pandemic. However, the COVID-19 epidemic and subsequent prolonged lockdowns have caused operational and financial difficulties for Indian institutions. Banks have devised a variety of measures to deal with the fallout from the epidemic, and as a consequence, clients have altered their financial behavior. The study takes a qualitative approach, analyzing the behaviors of gig workers via the lens of "expert mining." Researchers found that gig workers' employment uncertainty had the reverse effect on their behavior, making them more likely to sacrifice spending in lieu of saving for the future and significantly reducing on necessities such as livelihood spending and travel plan. In addition, the research found that there was a favorable association between the attitude towards the internet and the adoption of mobile banking among gig workers during Covid uncertainty.*

DOI: 10.4018/979-8-3693-0008-4.ch009

## INTRODUCTION

The COVID-19 pandemic has caused a significant economic downturn, with adverse effects on the global economy, causing instability and vulnerability. The pandemic has impacted individuals in different ways, with those in unsteady employment positions likely to be among the most adversely affected. Insecurity regarding employment leads to inferior psychological and physical health, a more negative outlook towards work, and lower levels of life satisfaction. With extended lockdowns and social distancing measures in place, banks in India have faced disruptions in their operational activities and financial aspects, leading to the implementation of various strategies to manage the impact of the pandemic. These strategies have resulted in a shift in consumer banking behavior, with an increased emphasis on internet and mobile banking services.

The gig economy has grown rapidly over the past decade, driven by technological advancements and changing employment patterns. The banking industry has also experienced significant technological advancements that have impacted the marketing strategies of banks, particularly in the area of digital banking. As a result of the shift towards digital banking, traditional banking models are being challenged. Banks are now delivering multi-channel services to their customers through telephone, Internet, and mobile interfaces. In order to meet rising customer expectations, banks are focused on discovering and retaining customers while also increasing profitability. This trend is not limited to traditional customers, as gig workers are becoming increasingly comfortable with technology and the Internet. As a result, Malaysia's financial industry has recognized the importance of digitizing its operations.

The COVID-19 pandemic has caused a significant shift in the approach of policymakers, leading to unprecedented levels of advice, legislation, and influence on individuals, businesses, and organizations. In the past, policymakers had focused on minimizing individual avoidance actions during outbreaks to avoid imposing substantial economic costs without necessarily reducing transmission. However, due to the high mortality rate associated with COVID-19, policymakers have taken on the responsibility of imposing extreme national packages of social distancing and business closures to prioritize reducing transmission and mortality from the disease, rather than risking the potential substantial economic impacts that may result from individual avoidance behavior (Keogh-Brown et al., 2020).

During the COVID-19 pandemic, micro-organizations with fewer than ten employees and self-employed individuals without employees were particularly affected. These groups make up the informal economy, which includes all economic activities conducted by workers and economic units that are not fully covered by formal arrangements (Chirumbolo et al., 2021).

## HISTORICAL PERSPECTIVE

When assessing the growth of specific scientific research, the quantity of academic papers published is a crucial metric. Statistical analysis reveals that, between 2020 and 2022, 31 research papers were published on the topic of Covid and Freelancers. In comparison, a search for Covid and Job Insecurity resulted in 409 research findings, while a search for Covid and Banking produced 199 research findings (See Fig 1-3).

*Figure 1. Search results for COVID and freelancer keyword in WebofScience search engine*

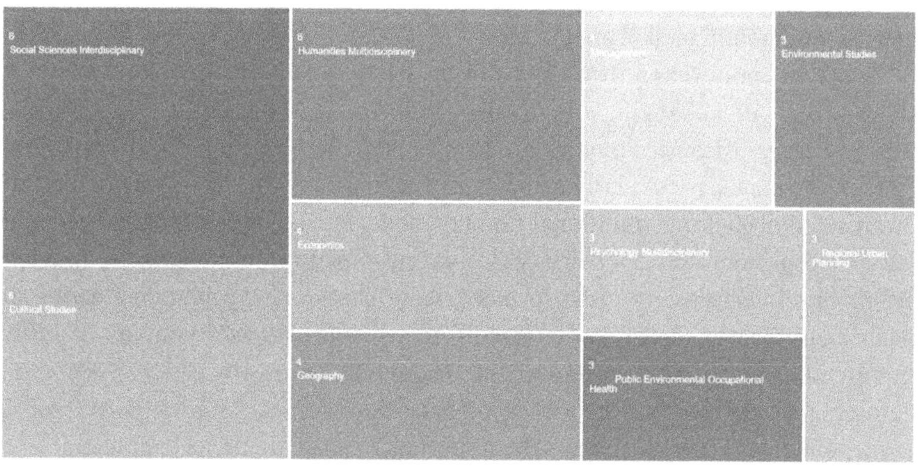


Figures 2 and 3 depict the growth trend of published articles in the field of Covid, job insecurity, and banking during the pandemic, as indexed in Web of Science journals. The data clearly shows an increasing trend in the number of articles being published since the start of the pandemic. Notably, the field of gig workers had the lowest share of publications, with only 31 records, suggesting the need for more research in this area.

Figure 1 shows the web of science categories with the highest co-occurrence among Cultural Studies, Humanities, Multidisciplinary Economics, Geography, Management, Environmental Studies, Psychology, Multidisciplinary, Public, Environmental Occupational Health, Regional Urban Planning, Urban Studies, Communication Environmental Sciences, Architecture, Business Computer Science, Information Systems, Health Care Sciences, Services, Health Policy Services, Immunology, Industrial Relations, Labor Medicine Research, Experimental, Psychiatry, Psychology Applied Sociology, and Women Studies in the most frequency.

*Figure 2. Search results for COVID and job insecurity keywords in WebofScience search engine*

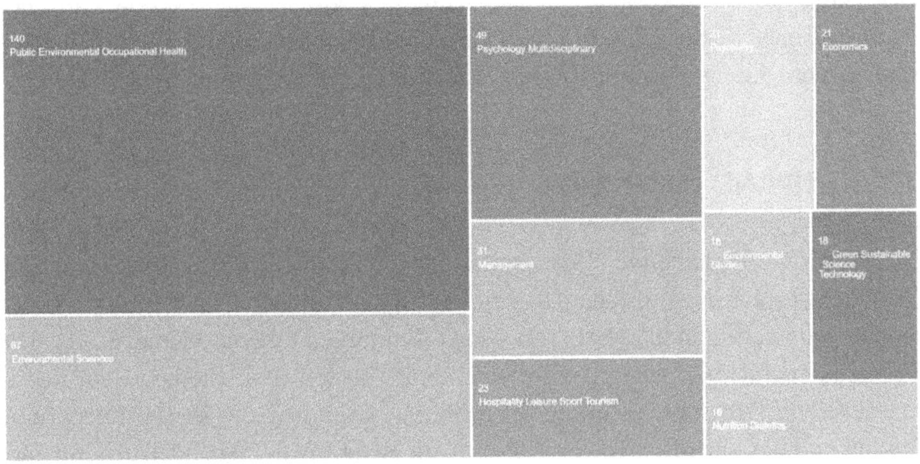


*Figure 3. Search results for COVID and banking keywords in WebofScience search engine*

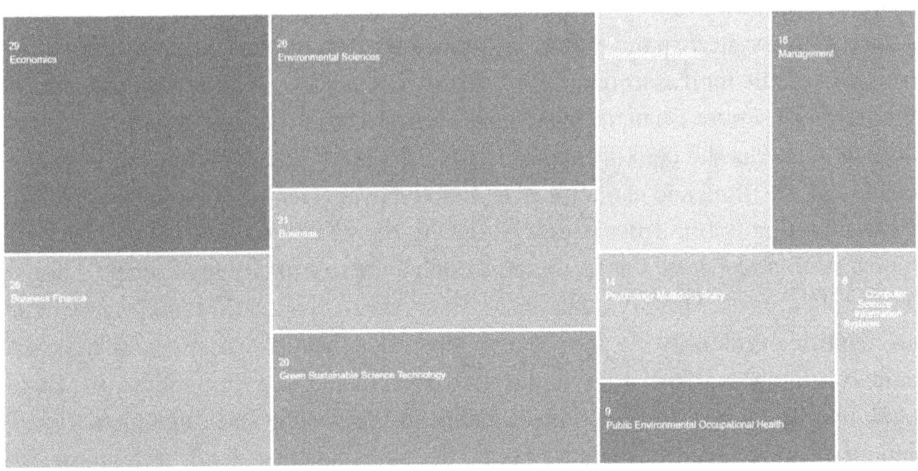


Figure 2 shows the web of science categories with the highest co-occurrence among Environmental Sciences, Psychology, Multidisciplinary, Management, Hospitality, Sport, Tourism, Green Sustainable, Science, Technology, Environmental Studies, Psychology, Applied Business, Engineering, Industrial Relations, Labor, Operations Research, Management Science, Psychology, Clinical Psychology, Experimental Social Sciences, Interdisciplinary Computer Science, Cybernetics,

Economics, Health Care Sciences, Services, Health Policy, Information Science, Library Science, and Psychology Developmental.

Figure 3 shows the web of science categories with the highest co-occurrence among Business Finance, Environmental Studies, Environmental Sciences, Business Management, Green Sustainable, and Science & Technology.

## COVID-19 AND BANKING

The COVID-19 pandemic has resulted in devastating human and economic consequences, causing millions of deaths and physical suffering, as well as significant economic damage that has led to recessions (Berger & Demirgüç-Kunt, 2021). The COVID-19 pandemic caused a global economic shock that affected both developed and developing nations, resulting in recessions including the sharpest economic descent in India's history. However, the Indian government responded quickly with trillions of rupees in stimulus packages, which led to two favorable outcomes - the shortest recession ever and the prevention of any financial crisis. These policies and outcomes occurred before the introduction of COVID-19 vaccinations.

The banking sector has an important role to play in supporting the real sector during times of economic downturn, but this can have consequences for the resilience of the banking system in the future. One concern is that as banks use up their buffers to provide credit, their asset quality may decline, which could ultimately threaten the stability of the entire financial system. It is unclear how these policy measures will ultimately impact the banking sector as the COVID-19 crisis continues, even after lockdowns are lifted and economies begin to recover (Demirgüç-Kunt et al., 2021).

Maintaining public trust is crucial during the COVID-19 pandemic, and it is important to understand the factors that contribute to trust in government's ability to control the virus. The Organization for Economic Co-operation and Development has identified reliability, responsiveness, openness, better regulation, fairness, and inclusive policy making as key areas for governments to gain public trust. Better regulation and organization of government in the design and implementation of responsive measures can increase public support and trust. Lack of transparency and timely communication from the government has been identified as a major factor contributing to the decline of trust in government during the pandemic. Trust in government is also influenced by the performance of the national economy and citizens' evaluations of the economy. Finally, the perception of fairness, including being treated equally as other people in society, can also affect trust in government, particularly during crises (Han et al., 2023).

This study acknowledge the abundance of research conducted on the economic and financial impacts of the COVID-19 crisis, particularly the effect of banking reactions and policy choices on Gig workers. However, it is impossible to cover all of the research comprehensively, and instead, this study in its first section aim to provide a summary of the existing research from the first year of the pandemic. Its main focus is on identifying how future banking research on the COVID-19 crisis can be improved for Gig workers.

## COVID-19 AND JOB INSECURITY

The global outbreak of COVID-19 has resulted in a state of emergency and has had a significant impact on the financial health of individuals and nations worldwide. The International Monetary Fund's World Economic Outlook report projected a sharp contraction of the global economy by three percentage points in 2020 due to the pandemic. The predicted economic downturn was expected to be even worse than the 2008 financial crisis and the most severe since the Great Depression (Bhowmik et al., 2022).

Research and survey reports indicate that lockdowns and social distancing measures during the COVID-19 pandemic led businesses to operate at only 50% or less capacity. This resulted in remote work, downsizing, and layoffs, which contributed to job insecurity among employees. In the United States, 41 million workers filed for unemployment between February and May 2020 due to the pandemic, while employment in the service sector dropped by 50%, and over 100 million workers worldwide lost their jobs in the hospitality industry. In countries facing political and economic insecurities, the impact of the pandemic on job security may be even worse. These situations can affect employees' employment status and working conditions, potentially exacerbating their sense of job insecurity (Farroukh et al., 2023).

The pandemic has caused economic instability, which has negatively impacted revenue growth in many sectors. A study based on qualitative research on gig workers in India shows that job insecurity is a common experience among the participants, regardless of whether they have a "fine work" or a "not satisfied with work." The study found that workers responded to this insecurity by evaluating their compatibility, increasing their skill sets to become more valuable, and engaging in spiritual practices. These findings highlight the complex nature of job insecurity in the gig economy and have implications for both scholars studying workers' experiences and the tech industry (Joo & Shawl, 2021).

The gig economy, in particular, has experienced significant growth since 2010. The global wave of digitalization and technological advancements has contributed to a rise in the gig economy, resulting in increased participation. Gig economy also involves digital platforms that connect workers or service providers with consumers to fulfill their needs. While these digital platforms are considered disruptive during uncertain events, they do not create an entirely new system of work or entirely upend existing employment relations. While several studies have examined the effects of the pandemic on stock markets and economies, very few have investigated whether the Indian gig economy - with its substantial potential - has been significantly impacted. This is despite the fact that there has been an increase in demand for online gig work in India during the pandemic.

## DEVELOPMENT OF CONCEPTUAL MODEL

The gig economy is considered to be a significant economic development of the past decade, and its growth rate has accelerated tremendously since the start of the COVID-19 pandemic. The pandemic-induced lockdown has had a significant impact on the global labor market, with an increasing trend towards short-term and temporary gig jobs. However, despite its potential, there has been limited research on the gig economy, particularly in the context of the ongoing pandemic. Given the significant potential of the gig economy in India, this study aims to investigate the impact of the pandemic on the Indian gig economy.

Studies have highlighted that job insecurity has led to increased levels of stress among workers, affecting not only their health but also their overall well-being. Financial stress is also a significant concern for employees who feel insecure about their jobs. In the wake of the COVID-19 outbreak, mental health issues have emerged as a major concern in Asian countries like India, according to previous literature. The pandemic has exacerbated job insecurity and created additional stressors for workers, further compounding mental health issues.

In the development of a conceptual model linking COVID-19 with job insecurity among employees, researchers and experts such as Alsharif et al. (2021), and, Xie et al. (2022) made significant contributions. Previous studies, including those by Nemteanu et al. (2021) and Camilleri (2021), supported such models and were also discussed in the current study. Based on a review of the literature, a hypothetical model was developed based on seminal works in the field of job insecurity among gig workers, linking uncertain events with job insecurity, such as those by Maas and Chanana (2021) and He et al. (2021). This model is presented in Figure 4.

The COVID-19 pandemic and the increase in banking activities have led to the emergence of contactless technologies that are expected to provide commercial opportunities to gig workers during and after the pandemic. In order to maintain social distancing while ensuring the continuity of daily activities such as shopping and payment transactions, mobile payment contactless technologies have become an

*Figure 4. A hypothetical model for showing job insecurity as a link between Covid and gig workers behavior*

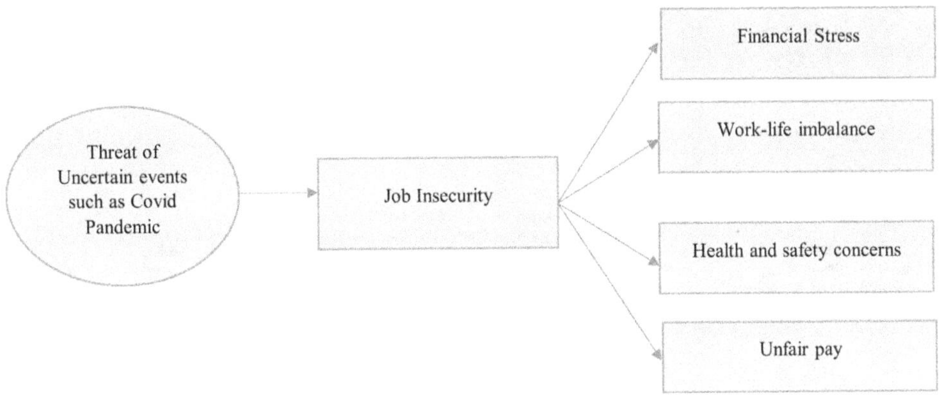


important option. These technologies offer benefits beyond the pandemic, particularly for those who find them affordable and valuable.

The researchers developed an integrated model to analyze the continued use of banking by gig workers during and after the COVID-19 pandemic. The model takes into account both micro and macro factors that may influence banking behavior and is extended to include gig workers' banking behavior (See Figure 5).

## EXPERT MINING

The conceptual model describing the impact of gig workers' exposure to COVID-19 on their job insecurity and banking behavior was evaluated using a rigorous expert mining approach. Twenty experts participated in the study, including five independent organization managers, three GIG consultants, two economics expert academics, and two policymakers. This study adopted the approach of previous research in the field of gig economics by using a five-point Likert scale to assess the awareness and depth of respondents' understanding of the Indian gig economy. The relevance of the COVID-19 related event was measured on a Likert scale from 1 to 5, with 5 indicating strong agreement and 1 indicating full disagreement. To verify the found variables in the COVID-19 associated experiences, expert mining was performed, and it was suggested to exclude variables with mean scores below 3.0. Yet, not a single known factor was ignored. It's obvious that there do not even appear to be a large number of experts, but that's consistent with comparable expert mining research done in the past (Singh & Misra, 2021). Factors related to 51 gig workers' experiences with COVID-19 were examined.

*Figure 5. A hypothetical model for showing decision making process as a link between external influence and gig workers banking behavior*

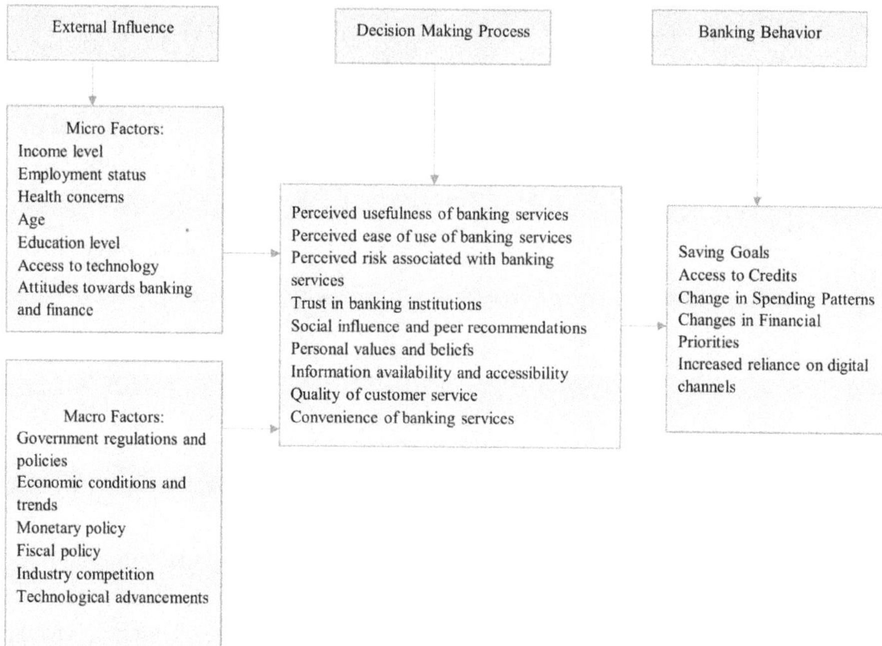


## DISCUSSION

This research is one of the first efforts to examine the micro and macro enhancers of gig workers' behavior in relation to job instability and banking practices. Understanding gig workers' banking and job-security habits has become more important in light of the recent expansion of the gig economy. The authors conclude that gig workers' confidence in their own ability to keep their jobs during the COVID-19 epidemic is crucial. Sustainability issues including economic volatility, industry decline, and organizational change all have a role in the subjective experience of job insecurity among gig workers. This view is based on an individual's subjective assessment of the risks to their job security. The widespread layoffs during the COVID-19 outbreak have shown how critical it's been to pay attention to the worries of gig workers about the future of their careers in light of the pandemic.

Because of the unusual and unexpected nature of the COVID-19 epidemic, gig workers often report feeling unprepared for the crisis at work due to the absence of defined policies or processes to guide their actions. To lessen the pandemic's influence on gig workers' job security and work behavior, it is crucial to communicate with and guide them clearly and effectively.

*Table 1. Expert mean score for identified enablers*

| S.No | Enablers | Expert Mean Score |
|---|---|---|
| Job Insecurity | | |
| 1 | Threat of Uncertain events such as Covid Pandemic | 3.30 |
| 2 | Financial Stress | 4.60 |
| 3 | Work-life imbalance | 3.15 |
| 4 | Health and safety concerns | 4.15 |
| 5 | Unfair pay | 3.05 |
| Banking Behavior | | |
| 1 | Income level | 3.25 |
| 2 | Employment status | 4.10 |
| 3 | Health concerns | 3.12 |
| 4 | Age | 3.20 |
| 5 | Education level | 4.15 |
| 6 | Access to technology | 3.10 |
| 7 | Attitudes towards banking and finance | 3.30 |
| 8 | Government regulations and policies | 4.02 |
| 9 | Economic conditions and trends | 3.15 |
| 10 | Monetary policy | 4.20 |
| 11 | Fiscal policy | 3.25 |
| 12 | Industry competition | 3.00 |
| 13 | Technological advancements | 4.10 |
| 14 | Perceived usefulness of banking services | 3.15 |
| 15 | Perceived ease of use of banking services | 3.30 |
| 16 | Perceived risk associated with banking services | 3.05 |
| 17 | Trust in banking institutions | 4.05 |
| 18 | Social influence and peer recommendations | 3.00 |
| 19 | Personal values and beliefs | 3.10 |
| 20 | Information availability and accessibility | 3.10 |
| 21 | Quality of customer service | 3.25 |
| 22 | Convenience of banking services | 4.85 |
| 23 | Saving Goals | 3.30 |
| 24 | Access to Credits | 3.30 |
| 25 | Change in Spending Patterns | 4.05 |
| 26 | Changes in Financial Priorities | 3.10 |
| 27 | Increased reliance on digital channels | 3.40 |

As seen from the other side, the financial industry has been particularly impacted by the COVID-19 pandemic's disruption of global capital markets. Bank values have fallen in most nations as a result of the epidemic, demonstrating the devastating effect on the financial industry. Banking practices of individuals, particularly gig workers, have been impacted by the heightened uncertainty and risk in the financial sector as a result of this instability and volatility.

Banks have made substantial modifications to their operations in response to the COVID-19 lockout. Indian financial institutions have adopted new policies that will likely alter the ways in which freelancers interact with financial institutions. Banks have taken steps to lessen the pandemic's effect by, among other things, introducing digital banking solutions and contactless payment methods, putting more emphasis on customer care and support, and creating new financial products and services to match the evolving demands of gig workers. It is anticipated that these measures will have a lasting effect on the banking behaviors of individuals, particularly gig workers, as they adjust to the new financial environment.

Low-income nations have encouraged the use of digital channels in the payment sector, according to a World Bank review of financial sector support measures implemented in response to the COVID-19 epidemic. To promote the use of digital payment systems, steps including fee waivers and streamlined digital identification processes are being taken. The goal of these reforms is to increase the usage of contactless payment technologies and decrease the prevalence of cash transactions. By encouraging the use of digital channels, low-income countries are not only helping themselves in their fight against the pandemic, but they are also helping those who may not have access to traditional banking services, such as gig workers, improve their financial literacy and their banking habits.

The spread of the COVID-19 epidemic has had a major effect on the employment security of gig workers. As a result of the uncertainty brought on by the epidemic, many gig workers have been obliged to make sacrifices and cut down on their short-term consumption, such as spending on livelihoods. As a result of their uncertain employment situations, gig workers also find it less likely to invest in longer-term goals like travelling.

The psychological stress brought on by the uncertainty and unpredictability of the epidemic is likely to be responsible for the harmful effects of job instability on the behaviors of gig workers. Gig workers might fear about their future financial security since they believe they have little influence in their job position. This might lead them to make decisions that put their immediate financial needs above those of the future.

The research eventually found, however, that gig workers' attitudes towards internet and mobile banking use increased during periods of COVID uncertainty. This means that during the epidemic, gig workers who have a favorable view of internet and mobile banking will be more likely to use these tools, thereby helping to lessen the financial effect of job instability.

Access to banking services through the internet and mobile devices can help freelancers have access to funds they would not have had otherwise. To prepare for the future despite the economic uncertainties brought on by the epidemic, individuals could have access to internet savings accounts or investing platforms, for example. They may also find that internet banking systems provide access to financial guidance and services that can aid them in managing their money during uncertain period.

## CONCLUSION

The study has found that job insecurity has a negative impact on the behavior of gig workers, who are more likely to sacrifice short-term consumption and perceive long-term life endeavors as unattainable. However, the study also reveals a strong association between attitude towards the internet and mobile banking usage among gig workers during COVID uncertainty. The study highlights the necessity of providing gig workers with clear and effective guidance and communication in order to mitigate the impact of the pandemic on their job security and job engagement. In addition, the study suggests that the implementation of digital banking solutions and contactless payment methods can help improve the banking behavior of individuals, such as gig workers with limited access to traditional banking services.

This study focuses primarily on the behavior of gig workers in India during the COVID-19 pandemic, which is one of its limitations. Consequently, the results might not be applicable to other nations or industries. In addition, the study employed only qualitative methods and collected no quantitative data, limiting the ability to draw statistical inferences and establish causal relationships between variables. Future research might resolve these limitations by employing a mixed method approach to examine the behavior of gig workers in various countries and industries during such economic crises. This could provide a greater understanding of how employment insecurity affects various categories of employees and how they react to changes in employees finance behavior.

## REFERENCES

Alsharif, H. Z. H., Shu, T., Obrenovic, B., Godinic, D., Alhujailli, A., & Abdullaev, A. M. (2021). Impact of entrepreneurial leadership and bricolage on job security and sustainable economic performance: An empirical study of Croatian companies during COVID-19 pandemic. *Sustainability*, *13*(21), 11958. doi:10.3390u132111958

Berger, A. N., & Demirgüç-Kunt, A. (2021). Banking research in the time of COVID-19. *Journal of Financial Stability*, *57*, 100939. doi:10.1016/j.jfs.2021.100939

Bhowmik, P., Padhi, M., & Pattnaik, S. (2022). Does financial anxiety affect job insecurity? Exploring the relationship and moderation by gender, tenure and income in the Indian context during COVID-19. *Benchmarking: An International Journal.*

Camilleri, M. A. (2021). The employees' state of mind during COVID-19: A self-determination theory perspective. *Sustainability*, *13*(7), 3634. doi:10.3390u13073634

Chanana, N., & Sangeeta. (2021). Employee engagement practices during COVID-19 lockdown. *Journal of Public Affairs*, *21*(4), e2508. doi:10.1002/pa.2508 PMID:33041656

Chirumbolo, A., Callea, A., & Urbini, F. (2021). The effect of job insecurity and life uncertainty on everyday consumptions and broader life projects during COVID-19 pandemic. *International Journal of Environmental Research and Public Health*, *18*(10), 5363. doi:10.3390/ijerph18105363 PMID:34069918

Demirgüç-Kunt, A., Pedraza, A., & Ruiz-Ortega, C. (2021). Banking sector performance during the COVID-19 crisis. *Journal of Banking & Finance*, *133*, 106305. doi:10.1016/j.jbankfin.2021.106305 PMID:34548747

Farroukh, N., Canaan Messarra, L., & Yunis, M. (2023). The perception of job insecurity and organizational citizenship behavior during COVID-19: the moderating roles of positive psychological capital and grit. *Journal of Asia Business Studies.* doi:10.1108/JABS-05-2022-0176

Han, Q., Zheng, B., Cristea, M., Agostini, M., Bélanger, J. J., Gützkow, B., Kreienkamp, J., & Leander, N. P. (2023). Trust in government regarding COVID-19 and its associations with preventive health behaviour and prosocial behaviour during the pandemic: A cross-sectional and longitudinal study. *Psychological Medicine*, *53*(1), 149–159. doi:10.1017/S0033291721001306 PMID:33769242

He, J., Mao, Y., Morrison, A. M., & Coca-Stefaniak, J. A. (2021). On being warm and friendly: The effect of socially responsible human resource management on employee fears of the threats of COVID-19. *International Journal of Contemporary Hospitality Management*, *33*(1), 346–366. doi:10.1108/IJCHM-04-2020-0300

Joo, B. A., & Shawl, S. (2021). COVID-19 pandemic and the rising gig economy: An emerging perspective. *Global Economics Science*, 16-23.

Keogh-Brown, M. R., Jensen, H. T., Edmunds, W. J., & Smith, R. D. (2020). The impact of Covid-19, associated behaviours and policies on the UK economy: A computable general equilibrium model. *SSM - Population Health*, *12*, 100651. doi:10.1016/j.ssmph.2020.100651 PMID:33072839

Nemteanu, M. S., Dinu, V., & Dabija, D. C. (2021). Job insecurity, job instability, and job satisfaction in the context of the COVID-19 pandemic. *Journal of Competitiveness*, *13*(2), 65–82. doi:10.7441/joc.2021.02.04

Singh, K., & Misra, M. (2022). The evolving path of CSR: Toward business and society relationship. *Journal of Economic and Administrative Sciences*, *38*(2), 304–332. doi:10.1108/JEAS-04-2020-0052

Xie, J., Ifie, K., & Gruber, T. (2022). The dual threat of COVID-19 to health and job security–Exploring the role of mindfulness in sustaining frontline employee-related outcomes. *Journal of Business Research*, *146*, 216–227. doi:10.1016/j.jbusres.2022.03.030 PMID:35340762

# Chapter 10
# FinTech Paving the Way for Sustainable Social Entrepreneurship:
## India's Journey Towards SDG Achievement

**Madhava Priya Dananjayan**
*Loyola Institute of Business Administration, India*

**Sridevi Gopakumar**
https://orcid.org/0000-0001-6704-6183
*Loyola Institute of Business Administration, India*

**Parthasarathi N.**
https://orcid.org/0000-0003-3586-3466
*Loyola Institute of Business Administration, India*

## ABSTRACT

*The potential of financial technology to foster sustainable social entrepreneurship in India and contribute to the attainment of the United Nations' sustainable development goals (SDGs) has become increasingly apparent with the technological advances of the past few decades revolutionizing the way we live, work, and communicate. India, despite its rapid economic growth, encounters notable obstacles in realising the SDGs, such as poverty, inequality, and environmental deterioration. Conventional financial institutions have not effectively addressed these concerns. This chapter analyses the influence of financial technology (FinTech) on financial inclusion, the emergence of digital payments, blockchain technology, and their potential to facilitate social entrepreneurship that can lead to favourable social and environmental outcomes. The chapter delineates the challenges and opportunities that the FinTech industry offers to social entrepreneurship in India.*

DOI: 10.4018/979-8-3693-0008-4.ch010

## INTRODUCTION

In recent times, there's been a marked rise in the Financial Technology (FinTech) sector's influence, acting as a pivotal force propelling sustainable social entrepreneurship. This is especially noticeable in India's scenario (Asif et al., 2023; Goswami et al., 2022; Masiero & Ravishankar, 2019). Despite being home to over 1.3 billion inhabitants and standing as one of the globe's rapidly expanding economic hubs, India grapples with pressing challenges in its journey toward achieving the UN's Sustainable Development Goals (SDGs). Beyond the evident issues of poverty and inequality, the nation wrestles with limited access to basic amenities, environmental deterioration, and the looming threat of climate change. Pioneering strategies from the FinTech domain are reshaping the modus operandi of social ventures, serving as a bridge connecting conventional financial bodies and marginalized sections of society (Salampasis & Mention, 2018).

Established financial entities have often come up short in addressing these prevailing challenges. Their typical focus on profitability often overshadows the larger purpose of societal impact, leading to the continued marginalization of vulnerable communities. However, the ground-breaking solutions pioneered by FinTech are ushering in a transformative era for social ventures, effectively narrowing the gap between these traditional financial powerhouses and the less privileged sections of society.

Anticipated developments in India's FinTech sector suggest a strong upward trend, with expected growth rates set at a Compound Annual Growth Rate (CAGR) of 22.7% spanning from 2020 to 2025, denoting a notable surge in momentum (Financial Services Sector in India I Fintech Industry in India, 2023). The national thrust towards digitization and encompassing financial inclusivity has played a pivotal role in fuelling this surge. Notably, since its rollout in 2014, the nation's cornerstone initiative, the Jan Dhan Yojana, with its ambitious aim to universalize banking access, has spearheaded the establishment of over 430 million bank accounts (Pradhan Mantri Jan-Dhan Yojana I Department of Financial Services I Ministry of Finance, n.d.). Several interlinked elements have driven the impressive growth of the FinTech industry (Maiti & Ghosh, 2023; León, 2021; Vaganova, 2021). These include the increasing prevalence of online financial exchanges, the broad reach of mobile internet users, and the innovative incorporation of blockchain methodologies. Capitalizing on these advancements, FinTech establishments have been adept at rolling out avant-garde financial solutions that are not only accessible and cost-effective but are also meticulously crafted to cater to the nuanced needs of previously underserved segments.

At its core, sustainable social entrepreneurship seeks to address environmental and societal challenges while simultaneously promoting economic progression. By melding entrepreneurial principles with a commitment to sustainable frameworks, this model offers innovative solutions to persistent issues such as poverty, stark inequalities, and the looming climate crisis. Integrating social and environmental objectives, sustainable social entrepreneurs not only contribute to community and environmental well-being but also play a crucial role in the broader societal fabric. They often target marginalized groups, providing essential products and services, generating jobs, and empowering through education and skills training. Moreover, by challenging traditional business paradigms and fostering stakeholder collaboration, they instigate systemic change. The eco-conscious practices adopted by these businesses, from renewable energy usage to sustainable sourcing, are instrumental in conserving natural resources and combating climate change repercussions.

Fintech presents a myriad of tools and platforms tailored for entrepreneurs driven by a sustainability ethos (Tripathy et al., 2022). Features like online payment solutions, mobile banking, and crowdfunding platforms empower these enterprises, allowing them to mobilize funds, optimize financial processes, and access a diverse pool of investors and philanthropists. Such technological leverage not only democratizes financial access but also strengthens the scalability and outreach of social enterprises. For instance, blockchain technology offers a transparent and robust mechanism for verifying and documenting impact metrics, enhancing both accountability and stakeholder trust (Spanò et al., 2022).

This chapter delves deep into the influence of Fintech on sustainable social entrepreneurship in India, examining its role in navigating the nation towards the SDGs. It emphasizes the application of Fintech innovations by Indian social enterprises, their strategies to overcome socio-environmental challenges, and potential avenues for expanding their influence. By shedding light on Fintech's transformative capabilities in endorsing sustainable entrepreneurship, we aim to provide policymakers, industry experts, and stakeholders with a strategic roadmap, guiding them towards harnessing Fintech's potential for a comprehensive sustainable development vision.

## REVIEW OF LITERATURE

The recent timeline has witnessed a pronounced evolution in India's Fintech domain, ushering in an era of rejuvenation within the financial services sector and championing the ethos of financial democratization. Scholarly endeavors have consistently highlighted the meteoric rise of Fintech ventures and the digital transaction landscape in the Indian milieu (Abhijith & Antony Joseph K., 2023; Joy

& Thomas, 2023; Bhasin & Rajesh, 2021; Rasiwala & Kohli, 2021). The proliferation of mobile banking, digital wallets, and online payment platforms has enabled enhanced accessibility to financial services, particularly for individuals who lack access to traditional banking services or have limited access to them (Shankar et al., 2023). The Indian government has been instrumental in promoting digital financial inclusion through various initiatives, including the Unified Payments Interface (UPI) and the Jan Dhan Yojana (Transforming India's Digital Payment Landscape, n.d.).

Lending, insurance, wealth management, and remittances are just a few of the industries where the Indian Fintech business has seen substantial innovation (Migozzi et al., 2023; Savitha et al., 2022; Fang et al., 2021). The emergence of peer-to-peer lending platforms, robo-advisory services, and insurtech solutions has disrupted traditional financial structures by offering accessible and cost-effective alternatives. (Barroso & Laborda, 2022). The Indian Fintech sector does, however, also confront some significant difficulties. Data privacy, cybersecurity, and legal frameworks are issues that have come to light (Sinha et al., 2018). Policymakers and business stakeholders still have a crucial job to do: strike a balance between innovation and consumer protection.

## The Current Landscape of Fintech in India

The emergence of fintech in the Indian economy has been a transformative force, inducing significant changes in the financial sector and promoting economic growth. The promotion of financial inclusion stands out as a significant effect of Fintech in India. The emergence of fintech advancements, including digital payment systems, mobile banking, and microfinance platforms, has facilitated the provision of financial services to populations that were previously underserved (Gichuru & Namada, 2022; Srivastava, 2022; Goel, 2020). Fintech has facilitated accessible and cost-effective financial transactions, thereby empowering individuals and small enterprises, and augmenting their involvement in the formal economy. India's budding Fintech sector has fostered new career opportunities, playing a pivotal role in boosting employment rates. Start-ups and companies in the Fintech ecosystem have generated employment across various sectors, including technology, marketing, customer support, and data analysis (Hendrikse et al., 2019; Leong et al., 2017). The rapid expansion of digital technology has not only resulted in a surge of employment prospects but has also aided the advancement of skill development and entrepreneurial endeavors within the digital economy.

India has exceeded the worldwide fintech adoption rate as a result of diverse government and private sector endeavours aimed at advancing financial inclusion through technological means. It is anticipated that the fintech industry in India will experience substantial growth in the forthcoming years, encompassing diverse segments and reaching a market size of multiple billion U.S. dollars by 2022 as seen in Figure 1. The upsurge in this phenomenon can be attributed to a confluence of factors, namely the proliferation of smartphones, the escalation in internet usage, and the mounting need for digital financial services among the expansive and heterogeneous populace of the nation (Fintech in India | Statista, 2023). In general, the prospects for fintech in India appear promising, with abundant possibilities for advancement and expansion in the foreseeable future.

*Figure 1. Fintech market size in India in 2022: Segment-wise breakdown in billions of U.S. dollars*
*Notes: Inc42, Statista*

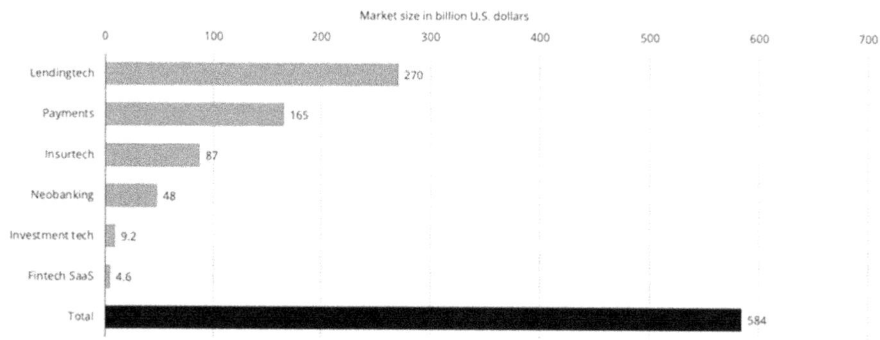


The ramifications of Fintech on the Indian economy transcend the domains of financial inclusion and employment generation. The implementation of this technology has made a significant contribution to the advancement of the economy through the enhancement of efficiency, innovation, and competition in the financial sector. The implementation of fintech solutions has resulted in enhanced efficiency and precision in financial transactions, decreased operational expenses, and amplified availability of credit for both individuals and enterprises. Because of technological advancements and shifting consumer preferences, the Indian Fintech industry has experienced accelerated growth and evolution. The structure of the industry incorporates numerous sectors that are transforming the financial landscape as seen below in Table 1.

*Table 1. Overview of the Indian Fintech industry structure*

| Sector | Description |
|---|---|
| **Payment Services** | Companies providing digital payment solutions, mobile wallets, payment gateways, and online transaction facilitation. |
| **Peer-to-Peer Lending** | Platforms connecting borrowers and lenders directly, eliminating the need for traditional financial intermediaries. |
| **Digital Banking** | Online banking services offered by fintech companies, providing seamless and convenient banking experiences. |
| **Insurance Tech** | Insurtech companies leveraging technology to offer innovative insurance products and streamline insurance processes. |
| **Personal Finance** | Platforms offering financial planning, budgeting, savings, investment advice, and wealth management services. |
| **Blockchain** | Companies exploring distributed ledger technology for secure transactions, smart contracts, and decentralized finance. |
| **Robo-Advisory** | Automated investment advisory platforms using algorithms and AI to provide personalized investment recommendations. |
| **Risk Assessment** | Fintech firms utilizing data analytics and AI to assess creditworthiness, fraud detection, and risk management. |
| **RegTech** | Regulatory technology companies helping financial institutions comply with regulations and reporting requirements. |
| **Wealth Management** | Digital platforms providing wealth management solutions, portfolio management, and investment advisory services. |

*Note:* Developed for the Study

## The Intersection of Fintech and Social Entrepreneurship

The convergence of financial technology and social entrepreneurship has given rise to a dynamic terrain wherein inventive financial technologies are utilised to tackle urgent social and environmental predicaments (Muganyi et al., 2021). The utilisation of fintech, a collection of digital tools and platforms designed for financial services, is progressively being adopted by social entrepreneurs to augment their impact and facilitate financial inclusion. Social entrepreneurs have demonstrated a longstanding dedication to effecting constructive social transformation, frequently with a focus on serving underprivileged communities and marginalised demographics. Fintech equips individuals with a potent array of instruments to attain their objectives with greater efficiency and efficacy. Mobile banking and digital payment systems have significantly transformed financial accessibility for individuals who are either unbanked or underbanked. This has enabled them to securely save, borrow, and transact. This phenomenon not only confers economic empowerment to individuals, but also fosters wider social development.

Furthermore, the funding landscape has been democratised by crowdfunding platforms and peer-to-peer lending, which have facilitated social entrepreneurs' direct access to capital from like-minded individuals who share their vision. The utilisation of alternative financing channels has resulted in a decreased reliance on conventional funding streams such as bank loans and grant programmes, while simultaneously creating novel opportunities for financial backing (Nguyen & Wald, 2022). The growth of the fintech industry has enabled the quantification and disclosure of social impact, a crucial factor in attracting financial backers and benefactors. By utilising blockchain technology, smart contracts, and data analytics, social entrepreneurs are able to effectively monitor the results and evaluate the influence of their initiatives in a transparent manner (Taherdoost, 2023). This approach enhances the reliability and credibility of their efforts.

In some communities, the digital divide, limited technology infrastructure, and lack of digital literacy can hinder the adoption of fintech solutions. Moreover, to safeguard vulnerable populations, ethical considerations such as data privacy and security must be meticulously addressed. Despite these obstacles, the intersection of fintech and social entrepreneurship possesses enormous potential for fostering sustainable development and establishing a more inclusive financial ecosystem. By leveraging the force of technology and entrepreneurship, this convergence can accelerate progress towards accomplishing the United Nations Sustainable Development Goals and bring about enduring positive change in communities around the globe.

## The Importance of Sustainable Social Entrepreneurship in Achieving the SDGs

Combining business innovation and social impact, sustainable social entrepreneurship plays a crucial role in attaining the Sustainable Development Goals (Ramadani et al., 2022). It offers a novel approach to addressing social and environmental issues, while also promoting economic expansion and inclusiveness. Here are several reasons why sustainable social entrepreneurship is crucial to attaining the SDGs.

- Sustainable social entrepreneurship combines business innovation and social impact to address complex societal challenges and contribute to the achievement of the SDGs.
- It fosters innovation and creativity by developing new business models, products, and services that are aligned with the SDGs, leading to scalable and sustainable solutions.

- Sustainable social entrepreneurship promotes inclusivity and empowerment by working closely with marginalized communities, providing training, employment opportunities, and access to essential goods and services.
- Emphasis is laid on adopting responsible and green business methodologies, like utilizing sustainable tech, minimizing waste, and endorsing optimal resource use, aligning with SDG 12 (Focused on Responsible Consumption and Production) and SDG 13 (Geared towards Climate Action).

Advancing ideals of innovation, inclusiveness, ecological sustainability, and collective action via sustainable social entrepreneurship is central to achieving the benchmarks set by the Sustainable Development Goals (SDGs). These enterprises have the potential to drive transformative change, creating a more equitable and sustainable future for all.

This research's exploration into the Sustainable Development Goals (SDGs) is nested within the global commitment to address pressing societal, financial, and environmental challenges. Endorsed unanimously by the United Nations' member nations in 2015, the Sustainable Development Goals (SDGs) lay out an intricate blueprint with 17 distinct goals and 169 related targets, all centered on achieving holistic sustainability by 2030. These goals encapsulate a broad spectrum of priorities: from eradicating poverty and ensuring quality education to championing gender equality, curbing climate alterations, and fostering sustainable urban development, to name a few (THE 17 GOALS | Sustainable Development, n.d.). The Sustainable Development Goals (SDGs) function as a strategic guide for governments, institutions, and individuals to collaboratively pursue a future that is characterised by fairness, inclusivity, and sustainability. Comprehending this particular context is of utmost importance when analysing the impact of financial technology on promoting sustainable social entrepreneurship and aiding India in accomplishing its Sustainable Development Goals.

## METHODOLOGY

The research applies a qualitative research methodology to explore the integration of fintech in sustainable social entrepreneurship in India. Qualitative research is chosen as it allows for in-depth exploration and understanding of the experiences, perspectives, and strategies employed by social entrepreneurs and stakeholders in leveraging fintech for social impact (Khoa et al., 2023). The qualitative approach enables the capture of rich and nuanced data, providing insights into the complexities and contextual factors that shape the intersection of fintech and social entrepreneurship.

Deep-diving interviews are employed as the central data collection technique. These in-depth conversations involve stakeholders, comprising social business founders, fintech aficionados, policy shapers, and organizational insiders. This method delivers a thorough perspective on personal experiences, strategies, challenges, and outcomes related to fintech-driven social entrepreneurship in India. The discussion format is semi-structured, providing flexibility in navigating specific topics while granting participants the latitude to voice their personal perspectives.

We leverage purposive sampling to curate a diverse mix of social ventures, weighing criteria like size, operational domain, geographical spread, and degree of fintech integration. The intent is to include both seasoned entities and budding initiatives. Our selected set mirrors a broad spectrum, encapsulating profit-driven and philanthropic organizations spanning sectors like health, education, farming, and fiscal inclusion. The sample also strives for a balanced representation across India's varied territories. The profiles of the respondents as seen in Table 2 encompass significant stakeholders who possess the potential to offer valuable insights into the convergence of fintech and social entrepreneurship in India. The inclusion of multiple respondents in the interviews has contributed a range of perspectives and areas of expertise, thereby enhancing the richness of the investigation's findings and analysis.

*Table 2. Respondents' profile for the interviews*

| Respondent Role | Description |
|---|---|
| **Social Entrepreneur** | Individuals leading social enterprises in India that have integrated fintech solutions into their operations and business models. |
| **Fintech Expert** | Professionals with expertise and knowledge of the fintech industry in India, including those working in fintech companies, consulting firms, or research institutions. |
| **Policymaker** | Government officials or policymakers involved in shaping policies and regulations related to social entrepreneurship and fintech innovation in India. |
| **Organization Representative** | Representatives from organizations or networks that support or collaborate with social enterprises and fintech initiatives in India. |

*Note:* Developed for the Study

The interview inquiries encompass a diverse array of subject matters, comprising the impetuses underpinning the adoption of financial technology, the particular financial technology tools and platforms employed, the ramifications of financial technology on the operations and social influence of social enterprises, the obstacles encountered in assimilating financial technology solutions, and the prospects for expanding the scope of influence. The interviews are administered through various modalities, including face-to-face interactions, video conferencing, or telephonic conversations, contingent upon the participants' preferences and accessibility. The interviews are recorded in audio format, with the explicit cooperation of the participants, in order to assure accurate preservation of the material shared during the conversations. The process of transcribing interview recordings is conducted with utmost attention to preserving the anonymity and confidentiality of the participants' identities. Post the interview process, the amassed data undergoes thematic analysis. This procedure focuses on discerning recurring patterns, themes, and vital observations within the qualitative dataset. Our exploration targets to highlight predominant strategies, fresh paradigms, success indicators, and challenges faced by Indian social ventures boosted by fintech.

Conversational data is meticulously dissected to unveil pivotal motifs and revelations. This study harnesses a thematic modus operandi, marked by repetitive undertakings. Each conversation is transcribed verbatim to ensure authenticity. These transcripts are coded, where unique markers get affiliated with data chunks representing specific thematic elements. Code genesis melds both deductive tactics, directed by research directives, and inductive strategies, discerning emergent motifs. Upon coding completion, these markers are systematically aggregated into thematic conglomerates, thus aligning related markers under broader themes. Subsequently, the clusters are subjected to a process of evaluation and enhancement, with the aim of achieving logical consistency and comprehensively representing the scope and complexity of the information. The themes are expounded upon and elucidated through the utilisation of illustrative quotations and instances derived from the interview data. The process of analysis is executed through the utilisation of software for qualitative data analysis, which serves to aid in the structuring, retrieval, and examination of the data.

The current investigation employs qualitative data analysis software, namely NVivo, to facilitate the data analysis process. The NVivo software is a prevalent tool utilised for the purpose of organising, managing, and analysing qualitative data. The functionality of the tool facilitates proficient encoding, classification, and examination of interview transcripts, thereby augmenting the precision and meticulousness of the analysis (Alam, 2020).

The analysis of secondary data obtained from official reports, government databases, and pertinent publications will serve as a supplement to the primary data. The forthcoming analysis aims to furnish contextual information pertaining to the current state of fintech adoption, social entrepreneurship landscape, and progress towards achieving the Sustainable Development Goals (SDGs) in India.

The research investigation adheres to ethical guidelines with strict compliance. The process of obtaining informed consent is implemented to secure the voluntary participation of all participants while also ensuring the confidentiality of their responses. The research adheres to ethical guidelines concerning the safeguarding of data, preservation of anonymity, and protection of privacy. All personally identifiable information is anonymized and securely maintained throughout the entirety of the research procedure.

In order to boost the validity and reliability of the investigation, steps are implemented to guarantee rigour and trustworthiness in the research procedure. A rigorous record-keeping approach for the research design, data collection techniques, and analytical methods is paramount. Introducing multifaceted data collection, encompassing exhaustive discussions and triangulation with existing literature, reinforces research validity. Employing diverse information sources offers an enriched understanding of fintech's role in sustainable social entrepreneurship, minimizing biases. To bolster the study's integrity, we maintain a thorough research chronicle, capturing design nuances, data capture techniques, and analytical procedures. This record-keeping amplifies transparency and replicability, positioning other scholars to authenticate and reproduce the outcomes. Furthermore, participant validation, where respondents review and endorse analysis results, is activated, boosting credibility and result precision.

## RESULTS

The ensuing segment unveils themes and revelations stemming from the qualitative analysis, as detailed in Table 3. The findings underline fintech's transformative potential on sustainable social entrepreneurship in India, propelling the Sustainable Development Goals (SDGs) realization.

### Theme One: Integration of Fintech

The theme of integration of fintech focuses on the incorporation and utilization of fintech tools and platforms within social entrepreneurship ventures. We delve into the manner in which social ventures assimilate specific fintech instruments to optimize operations and further societal and ecological objectives.

A notable sub-theme, under fintech's integration umbrella, is the deliberate choice of fintech instruments by social innovators. This facet underscores the diverse digital modalities and solutions that social initiatives infuse into their daily operations, such as mobile payment gateways, crowd-funding platforms, blockchain infrastructures, and e-marketplaces. Discussions illuminate rationales behind tool choices, spotlighting efficiency elevation, expansive audience engagement, and transactional ease. An entrepreneurial voice emphasized a mobile payment adoption, elucidating, *"By integrating a mobile payment solution, we have made it easy for*

*Table 3. Identified themes and subthemes*

| Themes | Subthemes |
|---|---|
| **Integration of Fintech** | - Adoption of specific fintech tools and platforms<br>- Enhancement of business operations and efficiency<br>- Contribution to social and environmental goals |
| **Impact and Outcomes** | - Improved efficiency and scalability<br>- Financial inclusion and empowerment of underserved communities<br>- Positive social and environmental outcomes |
| **Challenges and Lessons** | - Limited internet connectivity in rural areas<br>- Regulatory complexities and compliance<br>- User readiness and adoption challenges |
| **Measurement of Social Impact** | - Use of metrics and evaluation methods<br>- Tracking beneficiaries reached and changes in their lives<br>- Surveys and interviews for feedback and impact assessment |
| **Collaboration and Partnerships** | - Partnerships with fintech companies and financial institutions<br>- Resource access and expertise sharing<br>- Navigating regulatory requirements |
| **Policy and Regulatory Considerations** | - Supportive policies and regulatory frameworks<br>- Streamlining KYC requirements<br>- Data privacy, security, and protection |
| **Role of Fintech in Achieving SDGs** | - Financial inclusion and access to essential services<br>- Sustainable business models and impact investing<br>- Addressing social and environmental challenges |
| **Future Outlook and Opportunities** | - Growth potential and innovation<br>- Sustainable finance and impact investing<br>- Integration of fintech with emerging technologies |

*Note:* Developed for the Study

*both our customers and benefactors to make financial transactions.*" This inclusion not only revolutionized operational aspects but also accentuated transparency and operational efficacy, magnifying their societal impact.

Another extracted sub-theme within fintech's embrace is the augmentation of operational prowess and agility. Social innovators highlighted fintech's role in refining their operations, amplifying process robustness, and curbing administrative overheads. Digital modalities and automation have simplified responsibilities such as client relations, inventory management, and fiscal documentation. By leveraging fintech, social enterprises are able to operate more efficiently, allocate resources effectively, and optimize their overall business performance. According to another entrepreneur,

*"Since we started using financial tools in our work, I've seen a big change for the better. Our inventory management has become much more organized, which*

*makes it easier and more accurate for us to keep track of how much stock we have."(Participant 9)*

The subtheme of contribution to social and environmental goals explores how the integration of fintech in social entrepreneurship enables the pursuit of social and environmental objectives. Social entrepreneurs discussed how fintech tools and platforms have enabled them to reach marginalized communities, provide access to financial services, and support sustainable practices. For instance, mobile banking solutions have improved financial inclusion, while digital marketplaces have created opportunities for artisans and rural producers. By integrating fintech, social enterprises are able to align their operations with broader social and environmental goals, making a positive impact on their target communities and ecosystems.

Overall, the theme of integration of fintech in sustainable social entrepreneurship highlights the adoption of specific fintech tools and platforms, the enhancement of business operations and efficiency, and the contribution to social and environmental goals. These subthemes collectively demonstrate the transformative potential of fintech in empowering social entrepreneurs, driving positive change, and promoting sustainable development.

## Theme Two: Impact and Outcomes

The assessment of the effects and results of fintech-enabled social entrepreneurship initiatives is centred on the theme of impact and outcomes. The research investigates the diverse manners in which the incorporation of financial technology tools enhances efficacy and expandability, promotes financial inclusion and empowerment of marginalized populations, and generates favourable social and environmental consequences.

Fintech integration has increased the efficacy and viability of social entrepreneurship ventures, which emerged as a subtheme of the theme of impact and outcomes. This subtheme examines how fintech tools expedite operations, automate processes, and enable social enterprises to increase their impact. Digital platforms and data analytics, for example, enhance the efficiency of resource allocation, customer relationship management, and operational decision-making. By leveraging fintech, social enterprises can increase their operational efficiency and expand their influence. The participant statements listed below illustrate the same.

*"The use of financial technology has revolutionized our non-profits. It has helped us much in increasing productivity and expanding our business" (Participant 7)*

*"With the help of data analytics and computer process automation, we can make better decisions about how to use our resources and help more people in need. Since we started using finance, we've been able to reach more people and do more good in the communities we serve.."(Participant 12)*

The financial inclusion and empowerment of marginalized communities is another subtheme identified within the impact and outcomes theme. Social entrepreneurship initiatives enabled by fintech have facilitated access to financial services for underserved populations, including low-income individuals, women entrepreneurs, and rural communities. Through mobile banking, digital payment systems, and microfinance platforms, marginalized communities gain access to formal financial services, thereby gaining economic empowerment and the ability to participate more fully in economic activities. According to a participant's statement, this subtheme highlights the transformative potential of fintech to combat financial exclusion and promote inclusive economic growth.

*"Remote residents can use our mobile banking technology safely and easily. It empowered them to save, invest, and participate in economic activity. It's rewarding to see these people's lives improve." (Participant 10)*

The subtheme of positive social and environmental outcomes explores the broader impact of fintech-enabled social entrepreneurship on society and the environment. Fintech tools and platforms have enabled social enterprises to address social challenges and contribute to sustainable development. For instance, through crowdfunding platforms, social enterprises can mobilize resources and support for impactful projects. Additionally, digital marketplaces and supply chain tracking technologies promote fair trade, ethical sourcing, and environmental sustainability. This subtheme highlights the role of fintech in driving positive social change and environmental stewardship as stated by a participant.

*"Our blockchain-enabled supply chain ensures fair salaries and ethical sourcing. This benefits our artists and producers, the environment, and sustainable practices." (Participant 2)*

The integration of fintech in sustainable social entrepreneurship has been found to yield improved efficiency and scalability, financial inclusion and empowerment, and positive social and environmental outcomes. These outcomes are underpinned by the overarching theme of impact and outcomes. The aforementioned subthemes serve as a demonstration of the capacity of fintech to bring about significant and enduring change, with positive outcomes for marginalized populations as well as the wider populace.

## Theme Three: Challenges and Lessons

The theme of challenges and lessons concentrates on the obstacles and realizations encountered during the incorporation of fintech into sustainable social entrepreneurship. It examines the various obstacles social enterprises face when implementing fintech tools and highlights the valuable lessons learned from these experiences.

A subtheme that surfaced under the theme of challenges and lessons pertains to the restricted availability of internet connectivity in rural regions. The aforementioned subtheme highlights the notable obstacle encountered by social enterprises that are situated in rural or isolated areas. The inadequate or untrustworthy internet connectivity poses a hindrance to the optimal utilization of fintech tools and platforms, thereby restricting the availability of digital financial services and impeding operational efficacy. The social entrepreneurs recounted their experiences in devising inventive solutions, such as applications that can function without an internet connection, to surmount connectivity obstacles and guarantee the uninterrupted provision of their services.

*"Our major issue is remote Internet connectivity, to reach individuals in remote areas, we had to create offline applications" (Participant 5)*

The regulatory complexities and compliance requirements associated with integrating fintech in social entrepreneurship constitute a second subtheme identified within the theme of obstacles and lessons. To ensure compliance, social enterprises emphasized the need to navigate complex regulatory frameworks, such as financial regulations and data privacy laws. These regulatory obstacles frequently necessitate additional resources, expertise, and time to navigate, posing significant obstacles for smaller social enterprises. However, social entrepreneurs stressed the significance of engaging with policymakers and advocating for supportive regulatory environments in order to cultivate innovation and maximize the potential of fintech-enabled social entrepreneurship. *"Managing all the rules has been our largest challenge. Fintech integration is hindered by financial and data protection restrictions" (Participant 13)*

The user preparedness and adoption problems subtheme highlights the significance of user acceptance and adoption of financial solutions. Social entrepreneurs discussed their experiences with prospective consumers who were resistant or hesitant, especially those who were less technologically minded or inexperienced with digital technologies. Overcoming these adoption barriers requires education, training, and the development of confidence in the dependability and security of fintech platforms. To bridge the digital gap and guarantee the inclusive adoption of financial solutions, social entrepreneurs underlined the need of user-centric design and customized assistance.

*"We've had to figure out how to get people to use banking products. Some people are hesitant to use digital tools because they don't know how to use them or don't trust them." (Participant 13)*

The theme of challenges and lessons underscores the obstacles encountered by social enterprises in the process of incorporating fintech tools and platforms. The subthemes pertaining to restricted internet accessibility in rural regions, intricate regulatory frameworks and adherence, and difficulties related to user preparedness and acceptance, provide insight into the particular hindrances encountered during the course of the process. The aforementioned insights offer significant implications for social entrepreneurs, policymakers, and stakeholders to effectively tackle these challenges and facilitate the successful assimilation of fintech in sustainable social entrepreneurship.

## Theme Four: Measurement of Social Impact

The theme of measurement of social impact focuses on the methods and approaches used to assess and measure the impact of fintech-enabled social entrepreneurship initiatives. It explores the various ways in which social enterprises track and evaluate their social impact to understand the effectiveness of their interventions and make informed decisions.

Utilization of metrics and evaluation techniques arises as a subtheme within the measurement of social impact. This subtheme emphasizes the significance of defining and selecting suitable metrics and indicators for evaluating the social impact of fintech-enabled social entrepreneurship. To evaluate outcomes and monitor progress towards their intended social objectives, social enterprises employ a variety of quantitative and qualitative metrics. The number of beneficiaries reached, the quantity of funds raised or invested, and changes in important social and environmental indicators are examples of commonly employed metrics. For instance, contributors mentioned:

*"By keeping track of key factors and collecting measurable data, we can figure out how well our actions are working and make decisions based on the data." (Participant 7)*

*"Metrics like the number of people helped, the amount of money raised, and the effects on the world help us figure out how much of an impact we have and where we can improve." (Participant 1)*

The monitoring of beneficiaries reached and changes in their lives is another subtheme identified within the measurement of social impact. The importance of comprehending the direct impact of their interventions on individuals and communities is acknowledged by social enterprises. Utilizing data collection techniques such as surveys, interviews, and case studies, they collect beneficiary feedback and document the changes that have occurred. This subtheme emphasizes the significance of documenting qualitative narratives and personal experiences in addition to quantitative data for a comprehensive understanding of the social impact achieved.

The subtheme of surveys and interviews for gathering feedback and assessing the impact of fintech-enabled social entrepreneurship initiatives examines the use of surveys and interviews as instruments for gathering feedback and assessing the impact of such initiatives. Through structured surveys and in-depth interviews, social enterprises solicit feedback from beneficiaries, stakeholders, and other relevant actors. These techniques enable a greater comprehension of the outcomes and efficacy of their interventions, as well as valuable insights for program enhancement. Social enterprises recognize the significance of continuous feedback cycles and stakeholder engagement in effectuating significant social change. *"When we try to figure out what effect we're having, we value feedback from our beneficiaries and other important people. We use surveys and conversations to check how well our programs are working." (Participant 12)*

Overall, the theme of measurement of social impact underscores the importance of systematically assessing and tracking the social impact of fintech-enabled social entrepreneurship initiatives. The subthemes of the use of metrics and evaluation methods, tracking beneficiaries reached and changes in their lives, and surveys and interviews for feedback and impact assessment highlight the various approaches and tools utilized by social enterprises to measure and understand their social impact. These methods enable social entrepreneurs to gauge their effectiveness, learn from their experiences, and continuously improve their interventions to maximize positive social outcomes.

## Theme Five: Collaboration and Partnerships

The theme of collaboration and partnerships explores the role of collaborative efforts in fostering the success of fintech-enabled social entrepreneurship initiatives. It highlights the importance of partnerships with various stakeholders, including fintech companies, financial institutions, and other organizations, to leverage resources, expertise, and navigate regulatory requirements effectively.

The formation of collaborations with fintech businesses and financial institutions is one subtheme under the cooperation and partnerships theme. Collaboration with fintech businesses provides social entrepreneurs with the opportunity to utilize their technical knowledge, get access to new tools and platforms, and acquire insights into industry best practices. Similarly, creating collaborations with financial institutions may give access to financial resources, networks, and experience, allowing social businesses to develop their operations and create sustainable business models. As an illustration, the individuals who provided input stated:

*"Our partnership with fintech companies and financial institutions has been instrumental in driving our social impact." (Participant 9)*

*"By working with fintech companies, we've gotten access to cutting-edge technology and new ideas that have helped us improve how we run our business." (Participant 10)*

*"Our relationships with banking institutions have given us the money and knowledge we need to make our projects bigger and help more people." (Participant 4)*

The subtheme of resource access and sharing of expertise emphasizes the significance of collaboration in gaining access to resources and exchanging knowledge. Partnerships play a crucial role in overcoming resource limitations faced by social enterprises, which are a common occurrence. Collaborations with stakeholders, such as corporate partners, foundations, and government agencies, can provide opportunities for financial support, network access, and knowledge sharing. These partnerships give social enterprises access to essential resources and the expertise of their collaborators, resulting in improved programmatic outcomes and sustainable growth. *"Through partnerships, we have gained access to critical resources such as funding, networks, and mentorship." (Participant 8)*

Understanding and managing regulatory standards acknowledges the difficulties and complexity of regulatory compliance. Social businesses may learn to comprehend and navigate the regulatory environment with the help of collaboration and partnerships with regulatory agencies, legislators, and legal professionals. Social businesses may actively participate in debates and push laws that encourage fintech-enabled social entrepreneurship by establishing cooperative ties. These alliances help people follow the law, deal with legal issues, and provide an atmosphere where creative solutions may flourish.

In summary, the collaboration and partnerships theme underscores the importance of forming strategic alliances with fintech companies, financial institutions, and other stakeholders. The subthemes of partnerships with fintech companies and financial institutions, resource access and expertise sharing, and navigating regulatory requirements demonstrate the various ways in which collaboration strengthens the ecosystem for fintech-enabled social entrepreneurship. By working together, social enterprises and their partners can leverage resources, share expertise, and overcome challenges, ultimately contributing to sustainable social impact.

## Theme Six: Policy and Regulatory Considerations

The theme of policy and regulatory considerations focuses on the importance of supportive policies and regulatory frameworks in facilitating the growth and success of fintech-enabled social entrepreneurship initiatives. It explores the various policy and regulatory factors that impact the operation, scalability, and impact of these initiatives.

The availability of supporting policies and regulatory frameworks is one subtheme under the policy and regulatory concerns theme. This subtheme emphasizes the importance of policies that promote innovation, social entrepreneurship, and the incorporation of fintech solutions. Tax breaks, subsidies, and laws that encourage the use and development of fintech-enabled social impact solutions are examples of supportive policies. Such regulations provide an atmosphere in which social entrepreneurs may flourish and contribute to long-term development.

*"Policies that reward projects that have a positive effect on society and encourage the use of fintech solutions can open up new ways for sustainable development to happen."(Participant 1)*

Streamlining know-your-customer (KYC) requirements focuses on the difficulties involved with KYC processes and the necessity for simplified procedures. Compliance with onerous KYC regulations may be problematic for social businesses, limiting their capacity to enroll beneficiaries and offer financial services. Streamlining KYC procedures using digital identity systems and risk-based techniques may improve accessibility, lower administrative constraints, and allow fintech-enabled social entrepreneurs to reach underprivileged groups more efficiently as expressed by few participants.

*"Digital solutions that make it easier to identify and verify people can improve access to financial services and help social companies better serve people who are on the fringes of society." (Participant 14)*

*"By cutting down on routine work, we can spend more time helping people and less time figuring out how to follow complicated rules."(Participant 7)*

The data privacy, security, and protection subtheme emphasizes the significance of protecting sensitive data in fintech-enabled social entrepreneurship efforts. To secure user information, social companies must traverse the intricacies of data privacy rules and implement comprehensive security measures. Adhering to data protection regulations, establishing secure data storage and transfer techniques, and gaining user permission are critical concerns in preserving trust, guaranteeing compliance, and safeguarding people' data privacy and security.

In summary, the policy and regulatory considerations theme emphasizes the role of supportive policies and regulatory frameworks in fostering the growth of fintech-enabled social entrepreneurship initiatives. The subthemes of supportive policies and regulatory frameworks, streamlining KYC requirements, and data privacy, security, and protection underscore the specific areas of policy and regulatory focus. By addressing these considerations, policymakers and regulators can create an enabling environment that supports the development and implementation of fintech solutions for social impact while ensuring data privacy and security.

## Theme Seven: Role of Fintech in Achieving SDGs

The theme of the role of fintech in achieving Sustainable Development Goals (SDGs) explores how fintech solutions can contribute to the advancement of SDGs. It highlights the transformative potential of fintech in addressing key challenges and driving sustainable development.

The subtheme of financial inclusion and access to critical services stresses how fintech may assist bridge the gap in financial access and deliver important services to underrepresented groups. Fintech technologies, such as mobile banking, digital wallets, and microfinance platforms, allow consumers and companies to access financial services in a simple and cost-effective manner. Fintech may enable people to manage their money, obtain loans, and participate in economic activities through fostering financial inclusion, eventually contributing to poverty reduction and economic prosperity.

*"Through digital banking and mobile payment options, we can make it easier and cheaper for people to get financial services, which will help them get involved in the economy and reduce poverty." (Participant 11)*

*"Fintech is a game-changer in breaking down barriers and ensuring that no one is left behind in the journey towards achieving the SDGs." (Participant 13)*

The importance of fintech in fostering sustainable business models and impact investing is highlighted by the discussion of sustainable business models and impact investing. Fintech facilitates the creation of innovative business models that incorporate social and environmental concerns into their operations. Fintech-enabled enterprises can optimize resource utilization, reduce environmental footprints, and generate positive social impact by leveraging technology. In addition, fintech facilitates impact investing, in which investors prioritize projects and businesses that generate measurable social and environmental outcomes in addition to financial returns. *"Fintech-powered platforms are attracting impact investors who recognize the potential to generate both financial and social returns. It is a win-win situation, where business growth goes hand in hand with addressing pressing global challenges." (Participant 5)*

Underscoring how fintech may help resolve urgent social and environmental problems is the subtheme of resolving social and environmental difficulties. Scalable and effective tools may be provided by fintech solutions to address issues including healthcare access, education, energy efficiency, reducing climate change, and sustainable agriculture. Fintech facilitates the creation and execution of cutting-edge solutions that spur positive change, improve social well-being, and safeguard the environment by harnessing data, analytics, and digital platforms. *"We can use data-driven insights and digital platforms to better healthcare, education, sustainable energy, and more..... fintech lets us create and scale life-changing solutions..... we can build a sustainable future where social and environmental issues are solved with technology." (Participant 8)*

The theme of the role of fintech in achieving SDGs highlights how fintech solutions can contribute to sustainable development. The subthemes of financial inclusion and access to essential services, sustainable business models and impact investing, and addressing social and environmental challenges demonstrate the multifaceted ways in which fintech can drive positive social, economic, and environmental outcomes. By leveraging technology and innovation, fintech plays a transformative role in advancing the SDGs and creating a more inclusive and sustainable future.

## Theme Eight: Future Outlook and Opportunities

The theme of future outlook and opportunities explores the potential growth and prospects for fintech in the context of sustainable social entrepreneurship. It examines the emerging trends, opportunities, and challenges that lie ahead, shaping the future landscape of fintech-enabled social entrepreneurship.

The emphasis of the subtheme on growth potential and innovation is on the growing possibilities for social entrepreneurship supported by fintech. Due to growing internet connection, technical developments, and changing customer needs, the fintech industry has enormous growth potential. This subtheme investigates the cutting-edge business models, goods, and services that fintech can provide to help social entrepreneurs expand their influence, penetrate new markets, and more successfully affect positive change.

The subtheme of sustainable finance and impact investing concentrates on the changing landscape of sustainable social entrepreneurship financing. Fintech facilitates impact investing, which emphasizes both financial returns and quantifiable social and environmental outcomes. This subtheme investigates the integration of fintech with sustainable financing mechanisms, including green bonds, social impact bonds, and crowdfunding platforms. It emphasizes the opportunities for social enterprises to access capital, mobilize resources, and attract impact investors who prioritize investments aligned with their values and the SDGs.

The fusion of fintech with pioneering tech paradigms like blockchain, artificial intelligence (AI), the Internet of Things (IoT), and expansive data analytics exemplifies the intersection of fintech with modern tech. This amalgamation holds promise in heralding novel avenues and refining the proficiency, safeguarding, and resonance of social entrepreneurship infused with fintech. This subtheme delves into the potential benefits and impediments that come with integrating these forefront technologies, underscoring the imperative of ethical governance, data safeguarding, and conscientious innovation.

The motif of prospective trajectories casts a spotlight on the invigorating horizon of fintech-augmented social entrepreneurship. The underlying subthemes - envisioning growth and inventive flair, eco-conscious financing and effect-driven investing, and the synthesis of fintech with cutting-edge tech trends - illuminate the transforming terrain and prospective avenues for social ventures to harness fintech in championing sustainable progress. By embracing innovation, collaboration, and responsible practices, fintech-enabled social entrepreneurship can contribute significantly to achieving the SDGs and shaping a more sustainable and inclusive future.

## DISCUSSION

The convergence of financial technology and sustainable social entrepreneurship has garnered considerable interest in contemporary times. The field of financial technology, commonly known as fintech, is distinguished by its technological advancements within the financial industry. Fintech has the capacity to generate favourable social and environmental consequences, aid in the attainment of the Sustainable Development Goals (SDGs), and influence the trajectory of social entrepreneurship. The present discourse endeavours to examine the principal discoveries of an investigation that investigates the function of financial technology in promoting sustainable social entrepreneurship and its consequences for diverse stakeholders.

## Key Findings

The results highlight the significant role of fintech in driving positive social and environmental outcomes, contributing to the achievement of the Sustainable Development Goals (SDGs), and shaping the future of social entrepreneurship.

The primary outcomes of the research provide insight into the assimilation of financial technology tools and platforms within social enterprises, leading to improved business functionality and efficacy. The implementation of distinct financial technology solutions, such as mobile banking and digital payment systems, has facilitated operational efficiency and enhanced financial inclusivity. The aforementioned results emphasize the possibility of fintech to transform the operational procedures of social enterprises, facilitating their expansion of influence and efficient penetration into novel markets.

Additionally, the research demonstrates the favourable influence of financial technology on the enhancement of financial inclusion and empowerment of marginalized populations. Digital financial services facilitate access to crucial financial products and services for disadvantaged communities, thereby promoting economic engagement and mitigating poverty. This statement underscores the significant impact of financial technology (fintech) in advancing equitable economic expansion and mitigating structural hindrances to access to financial services.

Notwithstanding these encouraging results, the investigation also reveals noteworthy obstacles encountered by social enterprises in harnessing financial technology. The significant hindrance posed by restricted internet connectivity in rural regions underscores the necessity for the establishment of infrastructure and digital literacy initiatives. Social enterprises encounter challenges in navigating complex legal frameworks due to regulatory complexities and compliance requirements. The resolution of these obstacles is of utmost importance in fully utilizing the potential of financial technology in promoting sustainable social entrepreneurship.

This research highlights the significance of assessing the social impact within the realm of social enterprises facilitated by fintech. The assessment of the effectiveness and outcomes of social entrepreneurship initiatives is heavily reliant on metrics and evaluation methods. In order to effectively evaluate the impact of a given intervention, it is imperative to utilize resilient assessment frameworks and integrate input from beneficiaries through methods such as surveys and interviews.

Collaboration and partnerships are also highlighted as significant factors in maximizing the potential of fintech-enabled social entrepreneurship. Collaborative arrangements with fintech firms and financial institutions afford social enterprises with access to valuable resources, specialized knowledge, and assistance. It is imperative to engage in cooperation with regulatory entities to establish a favourable milieu for the advancement and implementation of fintech. The discussion also emphasizes the significance of enabling policies and regulatory frameworks. Policies that simplify Know Your Customer (KYC) requirements while prioritizing data privacy, security, and protection are critical for building trust and accelerating the development of fintech-enabled social companies.

The investigation's outcomes add to the expanding pool of information regarding the convergence of fintech and sustainable social entrepreneurship. The discourse underscores the prospects, obstacles, and acquired knowledge, underscoring the necessity for cooperation, regulatory backing, and inventive methodologies to exploit financial technology for the sake of sustainable advancement. The study's practical implications offer feasible and effective insights for individuals and organizations engaged in fintech-enabled social entrepreneurship, including social entrepreneurs, fintech companies, policymakers, investors, and NGOs. By integrating these perspectives into their approaches and endeavours, stakeholders can leverage the revolutionary potential of financial technology to facilitate favourable societal and ecological outcomes, thereby advancing the attainment of the Sustainable Development Goals.

## Contributions to the Existing Literature

This research significantly adds to the body of knowledge on the relationship between fintech and social entrepreneurship in a number of ways. First, it offers data and analysis on the use of fintech platforms and tools by social companies, emphasizing the effects on productivity and business processes. This research advances knowledge of how fintech may transform the operations of social businesses by demonstrating how certain fintech solutions, such as mobile banking and digital payment systems, expedite procedures and increase financial access.

Second, this research adds to the body of knowledge on the benefits of social entrepreneurship facilitated by fintech. It offers empirical proof of the transformational potential of fintech in tackling societal concerns by looking at the results and consequences of fintech adoption, notably in terms of financial inclusion, empowerment of underprivileged populations, and beneficial social and environmental outcomes. This adds to the amount of information on the potential for fintech to promote sustainable development and aid in the accomplishment of the SDGs that is constantly rising.

In addition, this research adds to a better understanding of the problems and lessons learnt in harnessing fintech for social entrepreneurship. It underlines the constraints that must be overcome to fully realize the promise of fintech by identifying and addressing difficulties such as low internet availability in rural regions, regulatory complications, and user readiness and adoption challenges. This adds to a better understanding of the difficulties and subtleties of incorporating fintech into social entrepreneurship efforts.

This research also adds to the body of knowledge about the measurement and assessment of social effect in the context of fintech-enabled social entrepreneurship. It offers insights into how impact assessment may be carried out successfully in this field by highlighting the significance of measurements, evaluation techniques, and beneficiary feedback. This advances our knowledge of how to quantify and convey the social and environmental impacts of fintech-enabled social entrepreneurship and helps to establish comprehensive impact assessment frameworks.

As a whole, this research advances our knowledge of how fintech influences sustainable social entrepreneurship by adding insightful empirical data, concerns, and insights to the current literature. It adds to the current discussion on using fintech for social impact by addressing important research gaps and offering relevant practical consequences. This information will help guide future research, policy development, and practice in this area.

## Practical Implications

For many players engaging in fintech-enabled social entrepreneurship in India, the study's practical implications provide useful insights. These implications provide light on the possible advantages and difficulties of using fintech for sustainable development, assisting in decision-making and influencing plans for next projects.

1. Social Entrepreneurs: The research's conclusions have applications for social entrepreneurs integrating fintech into their business strategies. They may increase their operational effectiveness, expand their impact, and improve financial access by using the fintech tools and platforms that have been identified. Social entrepreneurs may develop solutions to get beyond these obstacles and realize the full potential of fintech by being aware of the difficulties and lessons learnt, such as the limitations of internet access and the complexity of regulatory frameworks.
2. Fintech Businesses: By using the information from this research, fintech businesses may modify their products to better meet the demands of social enterprises. Fintech businesses may provide novel solutions that efficiently meet these objectives by comprehending the particular difficulties experienced by social entrepreneurs and the intended results. Through collaborations, resource sharing, and information exchange, working with social enterprises

and financial institutions may develop a collaborative environment that fosters long-term social entrepreneurship.

3. Policymakers and Regulators: The results of the research provide policymakers and regulators important information on the policy and regulatory factors necessary to advance the development of fintech-enabled social entrepreneurship. They may make use of the results to design helpful policies, reduce compliance procedures, and streamline laws to make it easier to incorporate fintech into social entrepreneurship. To guarantee that everyone in society benefits from fintech, policymakers may also use the study's suggestions to close the digital divide, increase internet connection in rural regions, and boost digital literacy.
4. Investors and Impact Funds: The research shows how fintech-enabled social entrepreneurship produces favourable social and environmental benefits. These insights may be used by investors and impact funds to find possibilities to invest in social entrepreneurs that employ fintech to solve urgent problems. Investors may be guided by the study's focus on sustainable finance and impact investing to connect their financial aims with social and environmental objectives and support businesses that have both financial success and good social effect.
5. Non-Governmental Organizations (NGOs) and Development Organizations: NGOs and development organizations may utilize the implications of this research to guide their efforts to assist and improve the capacity of social entrepreneurs. They are able to provide specialized training, coaching, and tools to enable social entrepreneurs in efficiently using fintech by understanding the difficulties and possibilities connected with fintech adoption. NGOs and development organizations may also promote laws that foster an environment favourable to social entrepreneurship supported by fintech.

Overall, the research's practical implications provide insightful advice for NGOs, fintech businesses, politicians, investors, and social entrepreneurs working in the field of sustainable social entrepreneurship. Stakeholders may embrace the transformational potential of fintech to spur good social and environmental change and help achieve the Sustainable Development Goals by integrating these insights into their strategy and actions.

## CONCLUSION

The current research examines the convergence of financial technology (fintech) and social entrepreneurship in India, and its potential contribution towards the attainment of the Sustainable Development Goals (SDGs). The results of the analysis have illuminated a range of themes and subthemes, offering significant insights into the incorporation of fintech within the context of sustainable social entrepreneurship. The results have practical ramifications for social entrepreneurs, fintech firms, policymakers, investors, and non-governmental organizations, providing direction for their tactics and undertakings. Despite the presence of constraints, potential avenues for future research have been delineated. These avenues have the potential to augment our comprehension of the domain and provide guidance for the creation of efficacious social entrepreneurship tactics, policies, and interventions. Through the utilization of fintech, stakeholders can strive towards the attainment of the Sustainable Development Goals and the establishment of a future that is characterized by inclusivity and sustainability.

## Limitations and Future Research Directions

It is important to recognize the investigation's many limitations. The study's initial emphasis on a specific context—namely, the nexus of fintech and social entrepreneurship in India—may have limited the results' application to other areas or nations with different socioeconomic and legal settings. Second, biases may have been introduced by the sample size and selection process, and certain stakeholders' views may not have been adequately represented. Thirdly, there is a potential of social desirability bias, or respondents giving positive or socially acceptable answers, when using self-reported data, such as interviews and surveys. Last but not least, temporal restrictions could have restricted the breadth and scope of data gathering and analysis, ignoring emerging patterns and changes over time.

To overcome these constraints and get a wider view on the integration of fintech and social entrepreneurship, future study should look at comparative studies across other nations or regions. Longitudinal studies might be used to follow the development and long-term effects of fintech-enabled social entrepreneurship activities. Quantitative analysis combined with qualitative data would also provide statistical evidence of these programs' effects. Additional study might be done on these subjects as well as user adoption and behavior, ethical and social ramifications, and the integration of emerging technologies with fintech-enabled social entrepreneurship. The creation of successful social entrepreneurship strategies, policies, and interventions would be aided by these potential future study paths, which would improve our understanding of the subject.

## REFERENCES

Abhijith, P. S., & Antony Joseph, K.Antony Joseph K. (2023, January 6). Reverse FinTech Socialisation. *International Journal of E-Business Research*, *18*(1), 1–17. doi:10.4018/IJEBR.316146

Alam, M. K. (2020, August 20). A systematic qualitative case study: Questions, data collection, NVivo analysis and saturation. *Qualitative Research in Organizations and Management*, *16*(1), 1–31. doi:10.1108/QROM-09-2019-1825

Asif, M., Khan, M. N., Tiwari, S., Wani, S. K., & Alam, F. (2023, February 15). The Impact of Fintech and Digital Financial Services on Financial Inclusion in India. *Journal of Risk and Financial Management*, *16*(2), 122. doi:10.3390/jrfm16020122

Barroso, M., & Laborda, J. (2022). Digital transformation and the emergence of the Fintech sector: Systematic literature review. *Digital Business*, *2*(2), 100028. doi:10.1016/j.digbus.2022.100028

Bhasin, N. K., & Rajesh, A. (2021, January 1). Impact of E-Collaboration Between Indian Banks and Fintech Companies for Digital Banking and New Emerging Technologies. *International Journal of e-Collaboration*, *17*(1), 15–35. doi:10.4018/IJeC.2021010102

Fang, H., Chung, C. P., Lu, Y. C., Lee, Y. H., & Wang, W. H. (2021, October). The impacts of investors' sentiments on stock returns using fintech approaches. *International Review of Financial Analysis*, *77*, 101858. doi:10.1016/j.irfa.2021.101858

*Fintech in India* (2023, January 1). Statista. https://www.statista.com/study/68286/fintech-in-india/

Gichuru, L., & Namada, J. M. (2022, April 20). Regulatory Requirements and Financial Inclusion in FinTech Companies. *International Journal of Applied Management Theory and Research*, *4*(1), 1–13. doi:10.4018/IJAMTR.300345

Goel, A. (2020, October). Financial Inclusion. *International Journal of Applied Behavioral Economics*, *9*(4), 33–57. doi:10.4018/IJABE.2020100103

Goswami, S., Sharma, R. B., & Chouhan, V. (2022, March). Impact of Financial Technology (Fintech) on Financial Inclusion(FI) in Rural India. *Universal Journal of Accounting and Finance*, *10*(2), 483–497. doi:10.13189/ujaf.2022.100213

Hendrikse, R., van Meeteren, M., & Bassens, D. (2019, November 11). Strategic coupling between finance, technology and the state: Cultivating a Fintech ecosystem for incumbent finance. *Environment and Planning A. Economy and Space*, *52*(8), 1516–1538. doi:10.1177/0308518x19887967

Joy, B., & Thomas, A. E. (2023, January 13). The Ecosystem of FinTech Companies in India. *International Journal of E-Business Research, 18*(1), 1–16. doi:10.4018/IJEBR.316148

Khoa, B. T., Hung, B. P., & Brahmi, M. H. (2023). Qualitative research in social sciences: Data collection, data analysis and report writing. *International Journal of Public Sector Performance Management, 12*(1/2), 187–209. doi:10.1504/IJPSPM.2023.132247

León, C. (2021, December). The adoption of a mobile payment system: The user perspective. *Latin American Journal of Central Banking, 2*(4), 100042. doi:10.1016/j.latcb.2021.100042

Maiti, M., & Ghosh, U. (2023, February 1). Next-Generation Internet of Things in Fintech Ecosystem. *IEEE Internet of Things Journal, 10*(3), 2104–2111. doi:10.1109/JIOT.2021.3063494

Masiero, S., & Ravishankar, M. N. (2019). Exploring Hybridity in Digital Social Entrepreneurship. *IFIP Advances in Information and Communication Technology, 551*, 295–306. doi:10.1007/978-3-030-18400-1_24

Migozzi, J., Urban, M., & Wójcik, D. (2023, March). "You should do what India does": FinTech ecosystems in India reshaping the geography of finance. *Geoforum, 103720*, 103720. doi:10.1016/j.geoforum.2023.103720

Muganyi, T., Yan, L., & Sun, H. P. (2021, July). Green finance, fintech and environmental protection: Evidence from China. *Environmental Science and Ecotechnology, 7*, 100107. doi:10.1016/j.ese.2021.100107 PMID:36160697

Nguyen, C., & Wald, J. K. (2022, May 16). Debt maturity and the choice between bank loans and public bonds. *Review of Quantitative Finance and Accounting, 59*(1), 239–272. doi:10.100711156-022-01067-7

Ramadani, V., Agarwal, S., Caputo, A., Agrawal, V., & Dixit, J. K. (2022, April 18). Sustainable competencies of social entrepreneurship for sustainable development: Exploratory analysis from a developing economy. *Business Strategy and the Environment, 31*(7), 3437–3453. doi:10.1002/bse.3093

Rasiwala, F. S., & Kohli, B. (2021, January). Artificial Intelligence in FinTech. *International Journal of Business Intelligence Research, 12*(1), 48–65. doi:10.4018/IJBIR.20210101.oa3

Salampasis, D., & Mention, A. L. (2018). *FinTech: Harnessing Innovation for Financial Inclusion. Handbook of Blockchain* (Vol. 2). Digital Finance, and Inclusion. doi:10.1016/b978-0-12-812282-2.00018-8

Savitha, B., Hawaldar, I. T., & Kumar, K. N. (2022, November). Continuance intentions to use FinTech peer-to-peer payments apps in India. *Heliyon*, *8*(11), e11654. doi:10.1016/j.heliyon.2022.e11654 PMID:36411928

Sinha, S., Pandey, K. R., & Madan, N. (2018, March). Fintech and the demand side challenge in financial inclusion. *Enterprise Development & Microfinance*, *29*(1), 94–98. doi:10.3362/1755-1986.17-00016

Srivastava, A. (2022, July 8). Digital Financial Inclusion. *International Journal of Innovation in the Digital Economy*, *13*(1), 1–12. doi:10.4018/IJIDE.303611

Taherdoost, H. (2023, February 13). Smart Contracts in Blockchain Technology: A Critical Review. *Information*, *14*(2), 117. doi:10.3390/info14020117

*Transforming India's Digital Payment Landscape*. (n.d.). Press Information Bureau. https://pib.gov.in/FeaturesDeatils.aspx?NoteId=151163

Tripathy, K. K., Paliwal, M., & Singh, A. (2022, May 8). Women's social entrepreneurship and livelihood innovation: An exploratory study from India. *Service Business*, *16*(4), 863–881. doi:10.100711628-022-00493-w

UN. (n.d.). *THE 17 GOALS*. UN. https://sdgs.un.org/goals

Vaganova, O. (2021, March 8). Growth Points Of Fintech Industry In The Perception Of Financial Market Transformation. *European Proceedings of Social and Behavioural Sciences*. doi:10.15405/epsbs.2021.03.54

# Chapter 11
# Russia-Ukraine War:
## A Study on the Network of Green and Dirty Cryptocurrencies

**Gaurav Kumar**
https://orcid.org/0000-0001-9067-4161
*Dr. B.R. Ambedkar National Institute of Technology, Jalandhar, India*

**Brahmadev Panda**
https://orcid.org/0000-0003-0391-1523
*Rajagiri Business School, Kochi, India*

## ABSTRACT

*This chapter examines the network dynamics of green and dirty crypto currencies around Russia-Ukraine war of 2022. The war is acting as a catalyst for the growth and popularity of crypto currency market across the globe. The study uses price data of crypto currencies from the years 2021 to 2022. Based on the minimum spanning tree (MST), the study finds that network for the green and dirty crypto currencies is different before the war and during the war period. Furthermore, using the MST diagram, the study finds some key crypto currencies which play a significant role in the crypto networks. The study also makes use of dendrogram, to identify the clusters in the green and dirty crypto currency markets. This work has practical implications for crypto portfolio diversification during the war period.*

DOI: 10.4018/979-8-3693-0008-4.ch011

# 1. INTRODUCTION

Cryptocurrencies and other digital assets are being used by more and more businesses throughout the world for a variety of transactional, operational, and investment needs. Since its launch in 2009, cryptocurrency trading has swept the financial industry by storm. Economies all around the world have seen an increase in the use of cryptocurrencies in recent years. The adoption has been driven by economic dynamics like inflation and has varied across businesses, from gaming to banking. However, issues have been brought up regarding the amount of energy used in cryptocurrency mining. This motivates fresh measures to raise the environmental credentials of this digital asset. These include increasing the use of renewable energy sources, implementing more energy-efficient processes, and offsetting carbon emissions. The Crypto Climate Accord, which aims to decarbonize the industry and achieve net-zero emissions from the electricity consumption connected with cryptocurrencies by 2030, has also attracted the support of more than 45 businesses and individuals from the cryptocurrency, banking, energy, and technology sectors.[1] Understanding the dynamics of green crypto currencies and how they compare to dirty crypto currencies is crucial in this context.

Since Russia's invasion of Ukraine, cryptocurrencies have been frequently in the news, with the increased demand for the cryptocurrencies.[2] These currencies have had a big impact on the conflict between Russia and Ukraine. This war is one of the most extensively documented military operations in history and the first significant cyberwar between two nations. The war has also featured widespread use of crypto. Various war activities have reportedly been funded with cryptocurrency, according to Ukrainian officials and government fundraising websites.[3] The products bought vary from helmets and protective vests to drones and demining tools. Cryptocurrency donations have gone towards purchasing radios and medical supplies as well as infrastructure. The greater use of crypto currencies during war is attributed to its decentralised nature. Crypto currencies may be transferred swiftly due to their decentralised structure, which makes them a handy tool for transferring money into conflict and catastrophe areas.

A strong and effective method for describing links between individual stocks is network structure. It also shows how contagion effects can spread across financial markets. Based on the network structure methodology, this study has constructed Minimum Spanning Tree (MST) and conducted hierarchical analysis using dendrogram around the Russia-Ukraine war. Given that Russia is a major centre for cryptocurrency mining, such an analysis is worthwhile of investigation. Both visualizations are obtained using Pearson correlations between daily returns. This methodology helps to clearly visualise complex and challenging crypto market linkages. The generated network graph and dendrograms shows the respective positions of the clean and dirty crypto currencies. The study adds to the growing body of knowledge about the impact of the Russia-Ukraine war on the financial market by presenting the empirical investigation of the impact of the Russia-Ukraine war on the networks of green and dirty cryptocurrency market. This study is useful for global investors optimizing their investment by understanding the systemic risk in the crypto currency market.

The chapter is structured as follows: Section 2 briefly explains the current state of research on cryptocurrencies market, contagion, and the application of minimum spanning tree in the financial market's context. Section 3 describes the data and methodological set up. Section 4 presents and discusses the findings. Section 4 concludes by summarizing the study, discusses some limitations and future extension of the study.

## 2. LITERATURE REVIEW

The understanding of cryptocurrency investment is still in its infancy, with most of the attention paid to Bitcoin's price trends. Numerous research shows that, investing in cryptocurrencies can be quite lucrative. However, high level of volatility is associated with this asset class (Bouri et al., 2019; Youssef, 2020). Therefore, an investor may be able to diversify away Bitcoin-specific risk by examining other crypto currencies in the portfolio (Canh et al., 2019). Canh et al. (2019) detects structural break in the cryptocurrencies indicating the integration in the market. A highly integrated market limits the benefits of the diversification. This study investigates the efficiency of seven largest cryptocurrencies by examining the structural breaks and volatility spill over among these cryptos.

Based on the energy usage and efficiency, Ren and Lucy (2022) classify the cryptocurrencies as green and dirty crypto currencies. The study then investigates the herding behaviour of these two distinctive types of cryptocurrencies. The study reported strong evidence on the herding behaviour of the dirty cryptos. On other side, this behaviour is not exhibited by clean cryptos. Recently, many studies investigate the link between geo-political risk and financial markets (Kumari et al., 2023; Appiah-Otoo, 2023). According to the study by Ahmed et al. (2022), the Russia-Ukraine war las led to considerable variation across industries, firm size and markets across Europe. Motivated by the crypto bifurcation and the fearful environment of the war, Patel et al. (2023) investigates the interactions between Green-Dirty cryptocurrencies and socially responsible investing (SRI's) during the conflict. The degree of interconnectedness before and during the war situations shows considerable changes. Ethereum is consistently identified as a key crypto in transmitting return and volatility shocks. One of the interesting findings of the study that both SRIs and green cryptocurrencies assume the alternating role of risk transmitter and receiver.

Although various research articles have offered various techniques in the literature on financial contagion, there is no single accepted methodology for recognising contagion. Some studies applied network analysis to visualize the complex dynamics of the network of the financial markets (Sun et al., 2015; Chi et al., 2010; Smith, 2009). Using daily prices, Francés et al. (2018) visualizes the relationship between cryptocurrencies. This study employs minimum spanning tree (MST) and dendrogram to analyse the integrated behaviour of the crypto market and identifying the key crypto currency. Interestingly, this study reported that Bitcoin is not the key crypto currency but the Ethereum is. Similarly, Rešovský (2013) applied minimum spanning tree to visualize the complex networks in the foreign exchange market. The graph structure obtained is supported by the geographic couplings. The Central European region is found to be very dependent on Polish currency. Similarly, Ashwani (2017) looks at the network dynamics of 14 Asian Stock Markets (ASMs) before, during, and after the 2008 financial crisis. According to obtained network statistics, the study finds that the ASMs network is more connected during a crisis than it is before and after one. The stock markets of Hong Kong, Japan, Korea, and India play a vital role in these networks and any shock to these markets might result in contagion. The study further reported that the main drivers of the inter-links between markets are trade and the interest rate differential. Also, there are studies that analysis the impact of COVID-19 pandemic on the connections between banks and other financial markets. A study by Tabak et al. (2022) offer information about the systemic integration of banking markets across developed and emerging economies, during the pandemic. The study reported that developed economies typically transmit shocks more effectively than emerging economies, except Japan and the United States.

On the methodological side, Millington and Niranjan (2021) argues the majority of the research on application of MST in financial markets uses the Pearson correlation coefficient. This type of correlation is unsuitable for the study of returns since it is based on the assumption of normality and is susceptible to the presence of outliers. The study makes use of MSTs generated from daily financial returns in the US, the UK, and Germany utilising Pearson and two rank correlation approaches, Spearman and Kendall's. The study finds the correlation matrices produced using the rank correlations are more robust, and stable.

Overall, the literature summarizes that MST has been used in the finance contagion literature in order to study the inter-connections between financial assets. The literature also highlights that compared to dirty cryptocurrencies, green cryptocurrencies consume less energy and resources. Due to changes in the underlying factors such as war and pandemic, the crypto markets' integration may change. This changing network may have a repercussion on the portfolio diversification strategies. This calls for the need to study the network dynamics of the clean and dirty cryptocurrencies in the context of the ongoing war between Russia and Ukraine.

To this end, the primary research question is whether Russia-Ukraine war (global exogenous shock) has changed the connectedness across green and dirty crypto currencies. The objective is to analyse the market of both types of cryptocurrencies and its dependencies using two different techniques. Making the MST graph whose nodes are cryptocurrencies and whose linkages are built from the correlation matrix, is the first step. This method analyses the degree of connectedness between the cryptocurrencies and determines the ones that have the biggest impact on price changes and market volatility. The second method involves creating a dendrogram and analysing the network's hierarchical structure by clustering the currencies according to their behaviour in the market.

## 3. DATA AND METHODOLOGY

### 3.1 Sample

The war between Russia and Ukraine began on 24 February 2022. However, following Ahmed et al. (2022), the study chooses 21 February 2022 as the date of Russia-Ukraine war. On this date, Russia declared the Donetsk and Luhansk regions of Ukraine to be independent states and deployed Russian troops there. The study examines the network among Green crypto currencies and Dirty cryptocurrencies. For the study, daily closing prices at the end of trading have been taken from 04 May, 2021 to 12 December, 2022, which involves a total of 587 observations for each of the cryptocurrencies. The dataset is split into two periods: Pre-war period (04-05-2021 to 20-02-2022) and during-war period (21-02-2022 to 12-12-2022). The data-set is limited by the earliest available data on a particular date. The data for the active crypto currencies is sourced from the online platform www.coinmarketcap.com. The study follows Ren & Lucey (2022a) and some web-portals such as iberdrola.com, and thetimes.co.uk etc. for the recent bifurcation between environmental-friendly and non-friendly cryptocurrencies. This bifurcation is based on proof-of-work and proof-of-stake technology. Clean cryptocurrencies are built on a variety of energy-efficient consensus algorithms, such as Proof-of-Stake (PoS), Ripple Protocol, Stellar Protocol, and some other alternatives. On other hand, dirty cryptocurrencies are all built on PoW algorithms for consensus, which results in significant energy usage for mining and transactions. The former is associated with dirty crypto such as Bitcoin and the later one is associated with clean cryptos such as Stellar. Table 1 tabulates the list of green and dirty cryptocurrencies. Cryptocurrency ID, symbol and date of commencement of trading is extracted from coinmarketcap.com website.

*Table 1. List of cryptocurrencies included in the sample*

| # | Name | ID | Symbol | Date-start |
|---|---|---|---|---|
| **Green Cryptocurrencies** | | | | |
| 1 | Solar coin | 4279 | SXP | 26-08-2019 |
| 2 | Hedera | 4642 | HBAR | 17-09-2019 |
| 3 | Cardano | 2010 | ADA | 01-10-2017 |
| 4 | Iota | 1720 | MIOTA | 13-06-2017 |
| 5 | Chia | 9258 | XCH | 03-05-2021 |
| 6 | Stellar Lumens | 512 | XLM | 05-08-2014 |
| 7 | Algorand | 4030 | ALGO | 21-06-2019 |
| 8 | Bitcoin Green | 2604 | BITG | 22-03-2018 |
| **Dirty Cryptocurrencies** | | | | |
| 1 | Bitcoin | 1 | BTC | 13-07-2010 |
| 2 | Ethereum | 1027 | ETH | 07-08-2015 |
| 3 | Bitcoin Cash | 1831 | BCH | 23-07-2017 |
| 4 | Ethereum Classic | 1321 | ETC | 24-07-2016 |
| 5 | Litecoin | 2 | LTC | 28-04-2013 |
| 6 | Monera | 328 | XMR | 21-05-2014 |

**Source**: Compiled from coinmarketcap.com

The study computed daily log returns of the crypto currencies based on the following formulae:

$$R_{it} = \ln\left(P_{it}\right) - \ln\left(P_{i(t-1)}\right)$$

Where $P_{it}$ and $P_{i(t-1)}$ are the prices of the cryptocurrencies at day "t" and day "t – 1." The descriptive stats of the crypto returns are summarised in Tables 2-3. BITG is reported to be the only crypto having mean positive return in the green crypto sample. Given standard deviation, BITG seems to be highly volatile. Among, the dirty crypto sample ETH, ETC and XMR possess nearly "Zero" mean returns and the rest possess negative mean returns.

The correlation matrix between crypto returns is presented in Tables 4-5. Among the green cryptos, the highest and lowest correlation is found between ADA-XLM pair and XCH-BITG pair respectively. Among the dirty cryptos, the highest and lowest correlation is found between BTC-ETH pair and XMR-ETC pair respectively. Overall, the dirty cryptos seems to correlated with each other to a higher degree in comparison to the green cryptos. Also, the correlation among all crypto pairs is found to be positive. The observations made can be used in risk diversification strategies between green and dirty crypto currencies. The systemic risk mapping of the crypto currencies can be improved by understanding the channels from where it experiences the greatest spillover effects.

## 3.2 Methodology

### 3.2.1 Minimum Spanning Tree (MST)

The market dynamics and the constantly shifting behaviours can be better understood through network analysis. In order to analyse complicated networks such as that of crypto currencies, a graph technique such as Minimum Spanning Tree (MST) is a useful tool (Mantegna, 1999).

*Table 2. Summary statistics of green crypto currencies*

| | Median | Mean | Stdev | Skewness | Kurtosis |
|---|---|---|---|---|---|
| **BITG** | -0.002 | 0.011 | 0.248 | 10.763 | 175.83 |
| **ALGO** | 0.002 | -0.001 | 0.062 | 0.703 | 9.633 |
| **XLM** | 0.000 | -0.002 | 0.049 | -0.512 | 4.335 |
| **XCH** | -0.006 | -0.003 | 0.066 | 3.444 | 30.031 |
| **MIOTA** | 0.001 | -0.002 | 0.061 | -0.046 | 6.226 |
| **ADA** | -0.002 | -0.001 | 0.055 | 0.339 | 2.809 |
| **HBAR** | 0.001 | -0.001 | 0.059 | 0.382 | 6.104 |
| **SXP** | 0.002 | -0.003 | 0.064 | -0.935 | 8.47 |

**Source**: Authors computation. The symbols of the crypto currencies are described in Table 1.

*Table 3. Summary statistics of dirty crypto currencies*

| | Median | Mean | Stdev | Skewness | Kurtosis |
|---|---|---|---|---|---|
| **BTC** | -0.001 | -0.001 | 0.037 | -0.227 | 2.499 |
| **ETH** | -0.001 | 0.000 | 0.05 | -0.116 | 3.503 |
| **BCH** | 0.000 | -0.002 | 0.056 | 1.244 | 18.988 |
| **ETC** | -0.003 | 0.000 | 0.068 | 1.361 | 9.026 |
| **LTC** | 0.000 | -0.001 | 0.053 | -0.441 | 5.929 |
| **XMR** | 0.003 | 0.000 | 0.054 | -0.113 | 12.58 |

**Source**: Authors computation. The symbols of the crypto currencies are described in Table 1.

*Table 4. Correlation matrix of green cryptocurrencies*

| | BITG | ALGO | XLM | XCH | MIOTA | ADA | HBAR | SXP |
|---|---|---|---|---|---|---|---|---|
| **BITG** | 1 | 0.047 | 0.099 | 0.002 | 0.084 | 0.163 | 0.225 | 0.079 |
| **ALGO** | 0.047 | 1 | 0.7 | 0.357 | 0.619 | 0.684 | 0.695 | 0.697 |
| **XLM** | 0.099 | 0.7 | 1 | 0.391 | 0.731 | 0.806 | 0.7 | 0.766 |
| **XCH** | 0.002 | 0.357 | 0.391 | 1 | 0.358 | 0.366 | 0.35 | 0.416 |
| **MIOTA** | 0.084 | 0.619 | 0.731 | 0.358 | 1 | 0.724 | 0.69 | 0.734 |
| **ADA** | 0.163 | 0.684 | 0.806 | 0.366 | 0.724 | 1 | 0.71 | 0.744 |
| **HBAR** | 0.225 | 0.695 | 0.7 | 0.35 | 0.69 | 0.71 | 1 | 0.715 |
| **SXP** | 0.079 | 0.697 | 0.766 | 0.416 | 0.734 | 0.744 | 0.715 | 1 |

**Source**: Authors computation. The symbols of the crypto currencies are described in Table 1.

*Table 5. Correlation matrix of dirty cryptocurrencies*

| | BTC | ETH | BCH | ETC | LTC | XMR |
|---|---|---|---|---|---|---|
| **BTC** | 1 | 0.861 | 0.778 | 0.705 | 0.816 | 0.729 |
| **ETH** | 0.861 | 1 | 0.782 | 0.773 | 0.83 | 0.717 |
| **BCH** | 0.778 | 0.782 | 1 | 0.813 | 0.85 | 0.684 |
| **ETC** | 0.705 | 0.773 | 0.813 | 1 | 0.754 | 0.619 |
| **LTC** | 0.816 | 0.83 | 0.85 | 0.754 | 1 | 0.708 |
| **XMR** | 0.729 | 0.717 | 0.684 | 0.619 | 0.708 | 1 |

**Source**: Authors computation. The symbols of the crypto currencies are described in Table 1.

A graph is made up of two sets, V and E, each of which represents a set of vertices and an edge generated by a pair of vertices or nodes. A spanning tree is a subset of an undirected graph in which all of the vertices are connected by the fewest possible edges. A graph will have at least one spanning tree if all of its vertices are linked together. There may be more than one spanning tree in a graph. A subset of edges in a connected weighted undirected graph that joins all the vertices with the least amount of edge weight is known as a Minimum Spanning Tree (MST). This study has employed Prim's algorithm to find MST.

Before moving on understanding the Prim's algorithm, it is important to compute the distances between the vertices or nodes. This involves two steps:

**Step I:** Computing the Pearson's correlation between the returns of the two crypto currencies i and j as:

$$C_{ij} = \frac{n(\sum r_i r_j) - (\sum r_i)(\sum r_j)}{\sqrt{\left[n\sum r_i^2 - (\sum r_i)^2\right]\left[n\sum r_j^2 - (\sum r_j)^2\right]}}$$

$$-1 \leq C_{ij} \leq 1$$

**Step II:** Based on the correlations obtained in Step I, a square correlation matrix (K × K) is constructed. Here, K is number of crypto currencies. This symmetrical matrix has *ij* entry as the correlation between two cryptos.

**Step III:** Following Mantegna (1999), the elements of the correlation matrix obtained in Step II are converted in to distance matrix as:

$$d_{ij} = \sqrt{2(1 - C_{ij})}$$

$$0 \leq d_{ij} \leq 2$$

If the distance between two nodes is short, it implies high degree of correlation and vice-versa.

Prim's algorithm is a greedy algorithm that determines the undirected graph's smallest spanning tree from any graph vertex. The spanning tree used by the technique is empty at first. Maintaining two sets of vertices is the goal. Vertices that have previously been included in the MST are in the first set, while those that have not yet been included are in the second set. It selects the minimum weight edge from among all the edges that join the two sets at each stage. After selecting the edge, it then adds the opposite endpoint to the set containing MST. The study makes use of "*igraph*" package in R to draw the MST network diagrams.

### 3.2.2 Dendrogram

The study makes use of dendrograms to understand the hierarchical relationship between crypto currencies. It helps to understand the cluster of crypto currencies. The dendrogram is made up of stacked branches (referred to as clades) that further divide into even more compact branches. Crypto currencies will be at the lowest level, and they will be organised into clusters based on qualities, with fewer and fewer clusters on higher levels. The information is located at the leaves of each clade.

## 4. RESULTS AND DISCUSSION

This section analysis the effect of Russia-Ukraine war on the MST and dendrogram of the green and dirty crypto currencies.

### 4.1 MST Network Diagram

Table 6 shows the comparative summary of the MST (Figures 1-2) between green crypto currencies for the two time periods. In the pre-war period, it is observed that the most central currency is SXP (Solar coin), with more connections than any other and acting as a connector between the other green crypto currencies. A larger goal of promoting the use of clean energy underpins Solar coin. SXP is found to be directly connected with HBAR, XCH, ADA and MIOTA. Its dominance however, reduces during the war period as shown by its reduced degree. During war period, SXP connection with the MIOTA is retained and a new connection with BITG is established. Interestingly, MIOTA degree increases during the war period with three nodes (SXP, ADA and HBAR) directly connecting with it. This model, centralized in MIOTA, can be explained by the growth of Internet of Things (IoT). This technology is now a reality, and its effects in the future will have a significant impact on how people go about their daily lives. BITG and ALGO are found to be farthest distant vertices during pre-war. On other hand, BITG and XCH are found to be farthest distant vertices during war period. The spread of the MST as shown by the diameter appears to be reduced during war time. The degree of six green cryptos out of eight

*Table 6. Degree of the green crypto nodes during pre-war and during-war time periods*

| Crypto | Pre-war | During-war |
|---|---|---|
| BITG | 1 | 1 |
| ALGO | 1 | 1 |
| XLM | 1 | 1 |
| XCH | 1 | 1 |
| MIOTA | 1 | 3 |
| ADA | 3 | 3 |
| HBAR | 2 | 2 |
| SXP | 4 | 2 |
| Diameter | 2.305 | 2.075 |
| Farthest Vertices | BITG-ALGO | XCH-BITG |

**Source**: Authors computation. The symbols of the crypto currencies are described in Table 1.

green cryptos does not change in both the time period. It means the degree of 75% of the sample of green cryptos remain unchanged during both time periods.

*Figure 1. MST of the green crypto currencies in the pre-war period*
*Notes: This figure shows the pre-war MST between the studied green cryptocurrencies. The symbols of the crypto currencies are described in Table 1.*

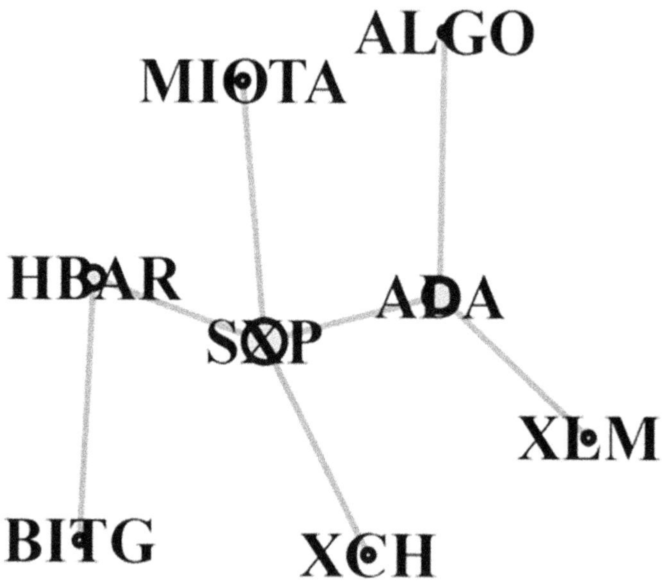


Table 7 is based the summary of the MST (Figures 3-4), presents a differentiated network between dirty crypto currencies for the two time periods. In the pre-war period, it is observed that the most central currencies are BCH (Bitcoin Cash) and LTC (Litecoin), with more connections than any other and acting as a connector between the other dirty crypto currencies. BCH is found to be directly connected with LTC, XMR and ETC. Bitcoin cash is considered as the fork of Bitcoin. Compared to Bitcoin, it permits more transactions per block, which result in to reduced fees and faster execution of transactions. Litecoin also offers quick, inexpensive payments to anyone in the world. It enjoys significant industry backing, trading volume, and liquidity. LTC is found to be directly connected with ETH, BTC and BCH. The dominance of both dirty cryptos, however, reduced during the war period as shown by their reduced degree. During war period, LTC connection with BCH and ETH is retained and the connection with other dirty cryptos is lost. On other hand, during the same period, BCH is able to maintain the connection only with LTC.

*Figure 2. MST of the green crypto currencies in the during-war period*
*Notes: This figure shows the during-war MST between the studied green cryptocurrencies. The symbols of the crypto currencies are described in Table 1.*

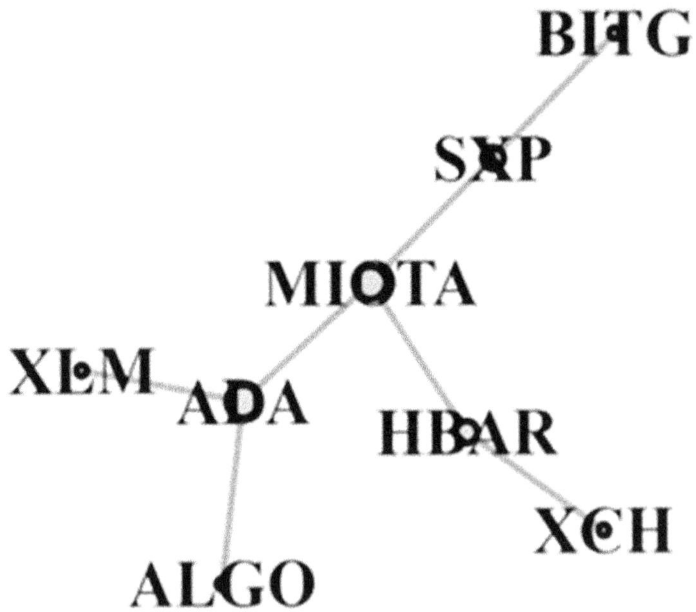


Interestingly, ETH degree increases during the war period with three nodes (ETC, BTC and LTC) directly connecting with it. Following the study of Francés et al. (2018), BTC (Bitcoin) which is the most popular cryptocurrency, did not appear as a central node in the both time periods. The MST network, centralized in ETH, can be explained by the fact that dozens of games and financial apps running on top of the its blockchain. Since it is so well-liked, even other cryptocurrency coins run on the network. BTC and XMR are found to be farthest distant vertices during pre-war. On other hand, XMR and BCH are found to be farthest distant vertices during war period. The spread of the MST as shown by the diameter appears to be increased during war time. The degree of two dirty cryptos out of six does not change in both the time periods. It means the degree of more than 50% of the sample changed during both time periods.

*Table 7. Degree of the dirty crypto nodes during pre-war and during-war time periods*

| Crypto | Pre-war | During-war |
|---|---|---|
| BTC | 1 | 2 |
| ETH | 1 | 3 |
| BCH | 3 | 1 |
| ETC | 1 | 1 |
| LTC | 3 | 2 |
| XMR | 1 | 1 |
| Diameter | 1.034 | 1.534 |
| Farthest Vertices | BTC-XMR | XMR-BCH |

**Source**: Authors computation. The symbols of the crypto currencies are described in Table 1.

*Figure 3. MST of the dirty crypto currencies in the pre-war period*
*Notes: This figure shows the pre-war MST between the studied dirty cryptocurrencies. The symbols of the crypto currencies are described in Table 1.*

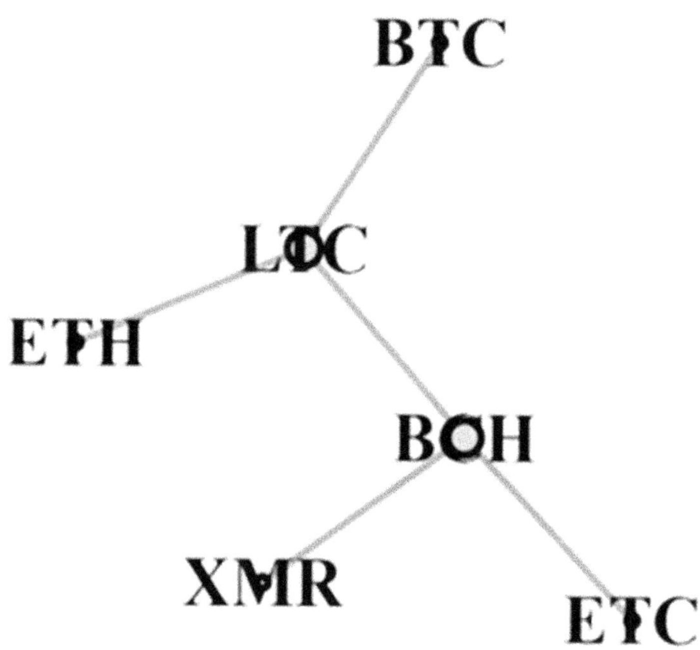

*Figure 4. MST of the dirty crypto currencies in the during-war period*
*Notes: This figure shows the during-war MST between the studied dirty cryptocurrencies. The symbols of the crypto currencies are described in Table 1.*

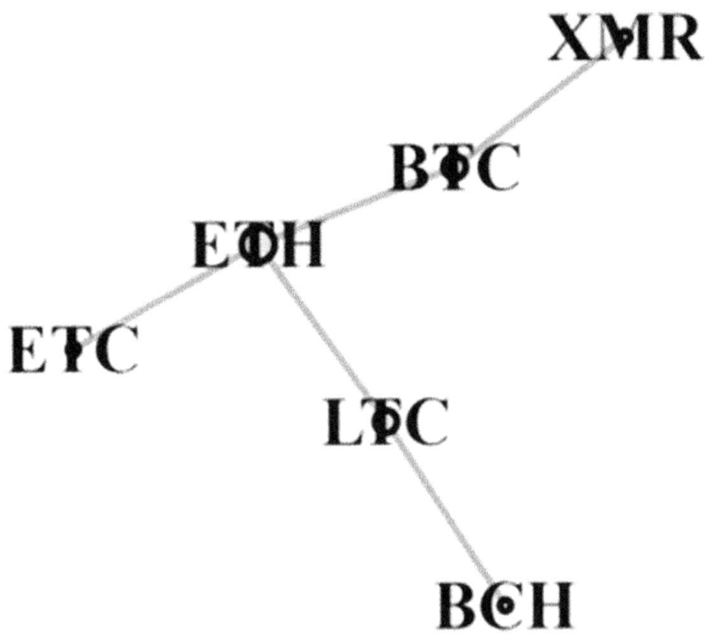


## 4.1 Dendrogram

This study makes use of hierarchical clustering to analyse the joint behaviour of the green and dirty cryptocurrencies during the two time periods. Figures 6-9 show the dendrograms that demonstrates hierarchical clustering, or the connections between related groups of crypto currencies.

As per Figure 5, during Pre-war time period, XLM and ADA clades are at same height. This implies that these two cryptos are similar two each other and forms a cluster. The difference in the height of this cluster and BITG is very high. This shows the high degree of dissimilarity between the clusters. At height level of 20, three separate clusters are observed. Cluster 1 comprises of BITG, cluster 2 comprises XCH and a large cluster 3 comprising of the remaining crypto currencies such as ALGO, MIOTA, HBAR, SXP, XLM and ADA. The difference in height of these remaining cryptos is found to be less in comparison with BITG and XCH.

Figure 6 shows that the dendrogram of the green crypto currencies undergone a structural change during the war period. At height level of 20, four distinctive clusters are observed. Cluster 1 comprises of BITG, cluster 2 comprises of XCH, cluster 3 comprises of ALGO, XLM, and ADA; and cluster 4 comprises of SXP, MIOTA and HBAR. Similar to the pre-war dendrogram, cluster 3 is quite different from cluster 1 as a greater difference in height of the two clusters is observed. MIOTA and HBAR are found to be most similar during the war period. In both time-periods, the behaviour of BITG appear to be different than other green cryptos. Similarly, the behaviour of XMR is different from others dirty cryptos.

*Figure 5. Pre-war dendrogram of green crypto-currencies*

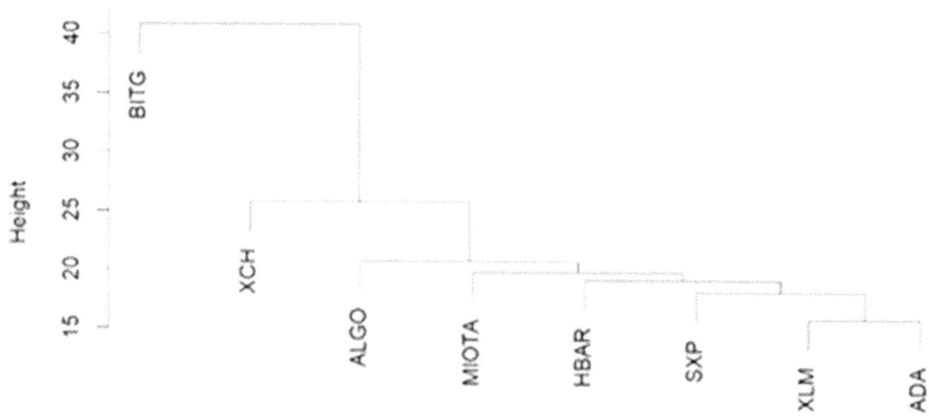


*Figure 6. During-war dendrogram of green crypto-currencies*

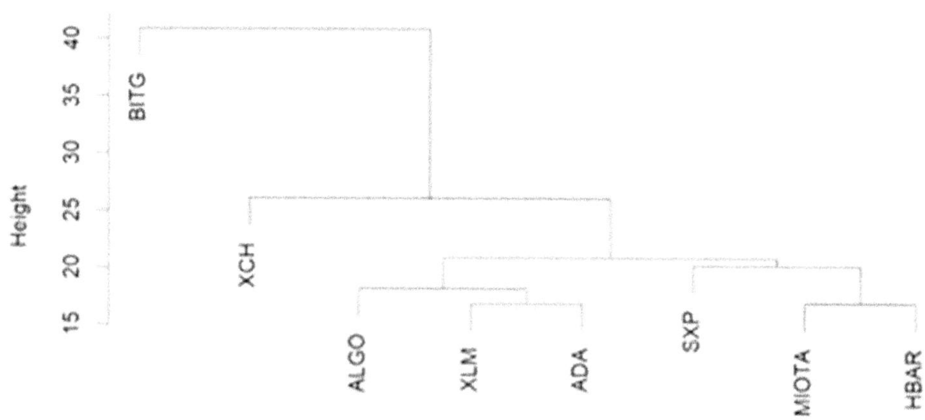

As per Figure 7, during Pre-war time period, the dirty crypto currencies such as BTC, ETH; and BCH, LTC forms clades at same height. This implies that BTC is similar to ETH and BCH is similar to LTC. These two pairs of cryptos form two clusters. At height level of 20, five separate clusters are observed. Cluster 1 comprises of XMR, cluster 2 comprises ETC and cluster 3 comprises of pair of BCH and LTC and cluster 4 comprises of BTC and cluster 5 comprises of ETH. The difference in the height of cluster 1 and clusters 2,3,4 and 5 seems to be very high. This shows the high degree of dissimilarity between cluster 1 and the other clusters.

Figure 8 shows that the dendrogram of the dirty crypto currencies undergone a structural change during the war period. At height level of 20, five distinctive clusters are observed. Cluster 1 comprises of XMR, cluster 2 comprises of ETC, cluster 3 comprises of the pair of BTC and ETH; and cluster 4 comprises of BCH and cluster 5 comprises of LTC. The pair of BTC and ETH; and BCH and LTC are found to be most similar during the war period.

In both time-periods, XMR appear as *simplicifolious*, meaning that the behaviour of this crypto currency is completely different from all the others cryptos in the studied sample.

*Figure 7. Pre-war dendrogram of dirty crypto-currencies*

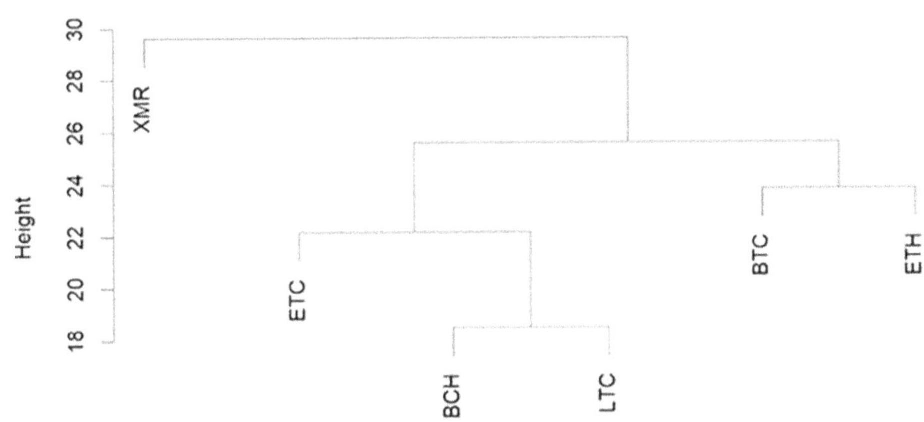


Based on the MST network diagram and dendrograms, the study reports that the relationships between green and dirty crypto currencies is heterogeneous in the pre-war and during-war period. Furthermore, using the Minimum Spanning Tree (MST) diagram, the study finds that SXP and; MIOTA and ADA plays a significant role in green crypto networks during pre-war and during-war time respectively.

Similarly, BCH and LTC; and ETH plays a significant role in dirty crypto networks during pre-war and during-war time respectively. The shock to these key cryptos can lead to the contagion effect in the green and dirty crypto market. In addition, the cluster analysis through the construction of the dendrogram places BITG and XMR in a different cluster than from the one obtained with other green and dirty cryptocurrencies, respectively.

*Figure 8. During-war dendrogram of dirty crypto-currencies*

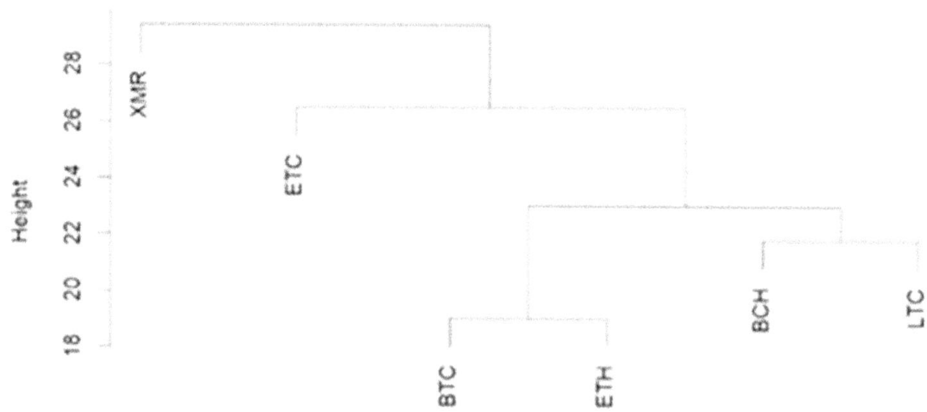


## 5. CONCLUSION

The Russia-Ukraine war not only led to social unrest but also impacted almost all major economies of the world. Since Russia's invasion of Ukraine, cryptocurrencies have been frequently in the news, with demand for the cryptos such as bitcoin in both Russia and other countries. Therefore, the spillover effect fell upon cryptocurrencies as well. This chapter examines the impact of the Russia-Ukraine war on the green and dirty cryptocurrency market. The study makes use of Minimum Spanning Tree (MST) to understand the systemic relationship among cryptocurrencies. The network obtained is a useful tool to understand the interrelationships among green and dirty cryptocurrencies. The network of both type of cryptocurrencies is found to be different in the two time periods. The study identifies SXP, MIOTA and ADA as systemically important cryptos among green crypto market. Similarly, BCH, LTC and ETH are identified as systemically important cryptos among dirty cryptos market. Additionally, the results of hierarchical clustering are presented with the help of dendrograms. As per the dendrograms, BITG appears to exhibit anomalous behaviour among green cryptocurrencies. XMR appears to exhibit anomalous behaviour among dirty cryptocurrencies.

This study adds to the body of knowledge on crypto market contagion and portfolio optimization. In future studies, network position of the cryptos can be utilized to construct the portfolios and containing risks in extreme events. The current study is limited to selected crypto currencies. Future studies should use a large and diverse sample of cryptocurrencies to re-estimate these associations. Exploring causal association between the extreme events such as war and crypto currency returns and trading volume can also be an area of future research.

## REFERENCES

Ahmed, S., Hasan, M. M., & Kamal, M. R. (2022). Russia–Ukraine crisis: The effects on the European stock market. *European Financial Management*, eufm.12386. doi:10.1111/eufm.12386

Appiah-Otoo, I. (2023). *The Impact of the Russia-Ukraine War on the Cryptocurrency Market. Asian Economics Letters, 4*. Early View.

Aswani, J. (2017). Impact of global financial crisis on network of Asian stock markets. *Algorithmic Finance*, *6*(3-4), 79–91. doi:10.3233/AF-170192

Bouri, E., Gupta, R., & Roubaud, D. (2019). Herding behaviour in cryptocurrencies. *Finance Research Letters*, *29*, 216–221. doi:10.1016/j.frl.2018.07.008

Canh, N. P., Wongchoti, U., Thanh, S. D., & Thong, N. T. (2019). Systematic risk in cryptocurrency market: Evidence from DCC-MGARCH model. *Finance Research Letters*, *29*, 90–100. doi:10.1016/j.frl.2019.03.011

Chi, K. T., Liu, J., & Lau, F. C. (2010). A network perspective of the stock market. *Journal of Empirical Finance*, *17*(4), 659–667. doi:10.1016/j.jempfin.2010.04.008

Francés, C. J., Carles, P. G., & Arellano, D. J. (2018). The cryptocurrency market: A network analysis. *Esic Market Economics and Business Journal*, *49*(3), 569–583. doi:10.7200/esicm.161.0493.4

Kumari, V., Kumar, G., & Pandey, D. K. (2023). Are the European Union stock markets vulnerable to the Russia–Ukraine war? *Journal of Behavioral and Experimental Finance*, *37*, 100793. doi:10.1016/j.jbef.2023.100793

Mantegna, R. N. (1999). Hierarchical structure in financial markets. *European Physical Journal. B, Condensed Matter and Complex Systems*, *11*(1), 193–197. doi:10.1007100510050929

Millington, T., & Niranjan, M. (2021). Construction of minimum spanning trees from financial returns using rank correlation. *Physica A*, *566*, 125605. doi:10.1016/j.physa.2020.125605

Patel, R., Kumar, S., Bouri, E., & Iqbal, N. (2023). Spillovers between green-and dirty cryptocurrencies and socially responsible investments around the war in Ukraine. *International Review of Economics & Finance*, *87*, 143–162. doi:10.1016/j.iref.2023.04.013

Ren, B., & Lucey, B. (2022). A clean, green haven?—Examining the relationship between clean energy, clean and dirty cryptocurrencies. *Energy Economics*, *109*, 105951. doi:10.1016/j.eneco.2022.105951

Ren, B., & Lucey, B. (2022). Do clean and dirty cryptocurrency markets herd differently? *Finance Research Letters*, *47*, 102795. doi:10.1016/j.frl.2022.102795

Rešovský, M., Horváth, D., Gazda, V., & Siničáková, M. (2013). Minimum spanning tree application in the currency market. *Biatec*, *21*(7), 21–23.

Smith, R. D. (2009). *The spread of the credit crisis: view from a stock correlation network.* arXiv preprint arXiv:0901.1392.

Sun, W., Tian, C., & Yang, G. (2015). *Network analysis of the stock market.*

Tabak, B. M., Silva, I. B. D. R., & Silva, T. C. (2022). Analysis of connectivity between the world's banking markets: The COVID-19 global pandemic shock. *The Quarterly Review of Economics and Finance*, *84*, 324–336. doi:10.1016/j.qref.2022.03.002 PMID:35310015

Youssef, M. (2022). What drives herding behavior in the cryptocurrency market?q. *Journal of Behavioral Finance*, *23*(2), 230–239. doi:10.1080/15427560.2020.1867142

## ENDNOTES

1 https://www.businessinsider.in/cryptocurrency/news/what-is-the-crypto-climate-accord/articleshow/83946286.cms

2 https://www.weforum.org/agenda/2023/03/the-role-cryptocurrency-crypto-huge-in-ukraine-war-russia/

3 https://cointelegraph.com/app/public/index.php/news/what-the-russia-ukraine-conflict-has-revealed-about-crypto/amp

# Chapter 12
# FinTech in India:
## A Systematic Literature Review

**Gowtham Ramkumar**
https://orcid.org/0000-0001-7885-9171
*Department of Commerce, School of Commerce, Finance and Accountancy, CHRIST University (Deemed), Bangalore, India*

## ABSTRACT

*India is the second-most populous country in the world, with a rapidly growing economy. Its population is highly tech-savvy and has a high level of adoption of digital technologies. The Indian government has taken several initiatives to promote digital transactions and financial inclusion. These initiatives have been instrumental in the growth of fintech in India. Fintech, or financial technology, is transforming the financial sector worldwide. Fintech solutions have led to the creation of new business models, streamlined operations, and enhanced customer experience. India is no exception to this trend, as it has witnessed a significant growth in fintech in recent years. The fintech ecosystem in India is highly diverse, consisting of startups, technology companies, banks, and non-banking financial companies (NBFCs). There are various challenges faced by fintech companies in India, such as lack of access to capital, regulatory hurdles, and competition from established players. This chapter proposal aims to provide a basic literature review on the development of fintech in India.*

DOI: 10.4018/979-8-3693-0008-4.ch012

## 1. INTRODUCTION

The term "FinTech" was first used in 1972 by a banker in New York. Foreign exchange, e-commerce lending, Payment methods, mobile applications, financing and money transfers, distributed databases, digital currency, robots and AI in finance, crowd-sourced funding, insurance, and financial management are just a few of the services provided by fintech firms. Different people define FinTech differently. As a result, the financial services industry has been significantly impacted by new technical advancements that enable innovation. Nine more technologies or technology-enabled trends were discovered in a recent Ernst & Young report titled Capital Markets: Innovations and the FinTech Landscape that have the potential to, individually or together, improve both present and future FinTech innovations:

- Digital Transformation
- Artificial Intelligence (AI)
- Cloud technology
- Smart Contracts
- Blockchain
- Internet of Things
- Process and service externalisation
- Robotic Process Automation (RPA)
- Advanced Analytics

The global use of fintech, or new financial technology, has skyrocketed (Vijai et al., 2020). When someone uses the term "FinTech" or "financial technology," they are referring to a business that uses the most recent technical developments to offer better financial solutions to their clients via digital payments and transactions (Varga, D. 2017). Numerous firms have recently joined the Indian fintech sector. With each new company, the sector has grown tremendously and is becoming more well-known worldwide. These 20 Indian fintech companies are among the 250 most promising ones worldwide. According to the most recent CB Insights study, startups (Rajeswari et al.; C., 2021) plus many other services available on a similar basis, like BHIM, digital banks, and many others. Which demonstrates the significance of both money and technology in our modern lives? (Pal et. al. 2018)

- **Fintech's first decade (1867–1967)**

Coins and paper money were among the earliest financial instruments used in analogue technology. Fintech is commonly regarded as having origins in the 1867 installation of the transatlantic cable linking London, Paris, and New York to exchange telegraphic messages. Later, London was connected to Shanghai and Hong Kong and then to all other markets worldwide. To connect individuals, media, authorities, organisations, and financial markets worldwide, a sizable infrastructure was also being established at this time (Arner et al., 2016).

- **Finance 2.0 (1967–2008)**

Texas Instruments introduced the first handheld calculator in 1967, the same year Barclay's Bank installed the first ATM in London. They were both significant developments that ushered in the second fintech age. During this period of digitisation, the use of calculators, computers, and ATMs marked the beginning of the shift from the analogue world of paper to the digital one. Payment systems like SWIFT developed between 1960 and 1970, laying the groundwork for extensive online transactions. With the launch of the initial electronic stock exchange, NASDAQ, the stock market strived towards digitisation in 1971. The majority of banks in wealthy nations switched from manual to computerised systems around the beginning of the 1980s. The evolution of internet technology from email to online commerce services (Arner et al., 2017). There were three noteworthy market crashes between those two occurrences: the Black Monday stock market disaster in 1987 and the 2000 implosion of the dot-com boom. Due to defaults on subprime real estate financing, the dot com bubble burst in 1999, and the global financial system collapsed in 2008, SIDTM Journal Volume 13 Issue 1 September 2020 Telecom Business Review. Every time a catastrophe like this occurred, new laws and regulations were implemented.

- **Fintech 3.0 (since 2008)**

After the 2008 market meltdown, several regulatory adjustments raised compliance costs and reduced profitability. Many workers who lost employment started working for fintech businesses providing cutting-edge financial solutions. These firms provided financial solutions but were not really "banks" in the traditional sense. The 20th century saw the widespread use of cryptocurrencies, mobile payment systems, crowdfunding, initial coin offerings, cutting-edge peer-to-peer lending models, and data-driven finance (F. Giglo, 2022).

## 1.1 India's Fintech Challenges

Despite the many opportunities, fintech still has problems. The following is a list of potential barriers facing fintech companies:

- The Indian market is challenging to enter and operate in due to the strict regulatory framework established to combat scams. For recruits, it acts as a considerable barrier. Before they may start working, several conditions must be met.
- People without bank accounts, unreliable Internet, and poor literacy rates are some of the additional obstacles. In India, 48% of people still lack the bank accounts required for online transactions. Even though most people have bank accounts, transaction times are prolonged by slow internet connectivity. As a result, people typically prefer cash transactions over internet ones. Despite the advantages of having a bank account and internet connection, most Indians still lack the financial literacy required to use these opportunities.
- It is tough to Changing the traditional thinking of companies and customers that do daily cash transactions is extremely difficult. It could be not easy to abruptly alter their habits and introduce them to new options when they are older because most seniors have long done these transactions with cash.
- The diversity of scams that cause money loss in online transactions is a bitter pill for the clients to chew. For fintech businesses, the exploitation of technology by thieves to steal peoples' money is a severe problem. As a result, companies must work very hard to modernise their infrastructure and cater to customers.
- The absence of government incentives and support for safeguarding its interests hurts India's fintech industry. Fundamentally speaking, this demotivates business owners. They were not provided the correct direction and assistance to get started, even though it would help the country's economy.
- The Fintech sector is now having difficulty attracting investors, just like in every other business. The inability to get the necessary seed money and additional investments would severely impact operations.
- E KYC, UPI, and BHIM reorganised the Indian banking system by integrating with the Aadhaar card. After the ban on the 500 and 1000 notes, sources claim that digital transactions in India soared by much to 22%. There was a 435% rise in website and app traffic for fintech businesses like PayTM. Various FinTech start-ups emerged in India due to the various growth opportunities.
- Numerous government regulations for new businesses have helped digital banking enterprises. The Reserve Bank of India recently authorised a simple process for establishing a FinTech company. Customers started using the virtual currency for both personal and professional transactions.
- Due to several economic disruptions, Indian banks and financial institutions were forced to change their internal financial systems and mandate the usage of digital wallets for payment transfers.

- Digital currencies such as Bitcoins have become more valuable due to the confluence of IT and finance. The use of cryptocurrencies and the blockchain architecture has sped up the processing of digital payments.
- The Government of India (GOI) is pushing for aggressive steps to foster the establishment of a cashless digital economy with a robust fintech ecosystem in India at the policy and financial levels.
- The lack of transparency in legislation and employment practises is one of the main issues plaguing the Indian FinTech sector. The following list includes the significant efforts that the GOI has carried out in collaboration with other regulatory institutions, including the Reserve Bank of India and the Exchange Board of India.

*Figure 1. Government initiatives*

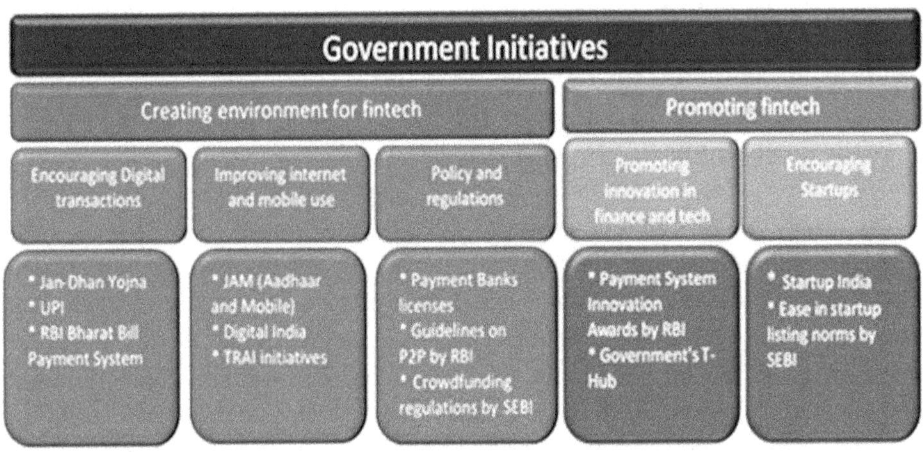


*Source: Televisory's Research*

## 1.2 Research Objective

The current study examines India's fintech adoption and its challenges and opportunities. The study's specific goals are as follows within this more extensive framework:

**RO 1:** To ascertain the factors influencing the adoption of fintech.
**RO 2:** To investigate the problems that FinTech consumers are experiencing.
**RO3:** To look into the precautions users have taken to lower the risk of using fintech.
**RO 4:** To formulate sensible policy suggestions for promoting FinTech uptake.

## 1.3 Fintech Trends

In the financial services sector, new technological developments will emerge in 2020. For financial institutions to continue growing, it will be essential that they can influence the sharing economy, collect client data, and work with cutting-edge technology like blockchain, robotics, artificial intelligence (AI), and others.

- **Fintech and artificial intelligence**

Artificial intelligence has revolutionised the financial sector (Rajeswari et al.; C., 2021). Before the creation of AI and FinTech, just a few industry titans in our modern, technologically savvy culture had the power to engage with the planet's intrinsic quantitative nature. These AI implementations show how the FinTech industry has developed (Buttice, C., 2020). Fintech companies and financial institutions leverage AI and machine learning to boost productivity. They offer consumers more pertinent, reasonably priced, user-friendly financial services and products to fulfil their banking demands (Darcy Tyrrell, 2020).

- **Bitcoin and Fintech**

Organisations concentrating on blockchain development will have a clear edge going forward as fintech confronts the banking system (Shah, P., 2019). The importance of blockchain was emphasised, focusing on four uses of blockchain in fintech, in a study recently published by the steering committee on fintech-related issues of the government of India (Jacob, C., 2020). Blockchain technology is fundamentally altering the financial sector through several methods, including removing intermediaries, reducing costs and operational time, enhancing identity verification, etc. (Srivastav, S, 2020).

- **Fintech Cloud Computing**

According to Vajid, A., and Farooqi, A. W. 2022, FinTech businesses can scale up and down entirely while maintaining regulatory compliance thanks to cloud infrastructure. Cloud technology is enabling FinTech to grow rapidly and persistently. FinTech improves service portfolio and customer experience while lowering CAPEX and OPEX expenses (Ray, T., 2020).

- **Using NLP, chatbots**

By leveraging cutting-edge Conversational User Interface (CUI) and NLP-based chatbots, PwC India claims that Fintech will transform mobile banking. The customer experience will be improved by these chatbots' ability to respond in real time to client inquiries and offer helpful solutions.

## 2. LITERATURE REVIEW

### 2.1. Fintech

The creative delivery of financial services utilising modern technologies is called fintech. Schueffel (2016) asserts, "Fintech is a novel financial sector which employs technology to improve financial activities." According to Schindler (2017), "FinTech" refers to financial innovation that is technologically enabled and may lead to new businesses, programmes, products, or services that fundamentally transform the financial system, institutions, and the way financial services are provided. This definition is thorough and emphasises innovation that improves business operations and makes a significant difference. The phrase "FinTech," a neologism that combines the terms "financial" and "technology," refers broadly to the interplay between modern technologies, mainly those related to the Internet, and long-standing business practices in the financial services industry (Gomber, 2017).

### 2.2. Banks

Banks generally served as a pass-through gateway for fintech companies and missed the early stages of the revolution. Banks must implement targeted internal programmes, organisational reforms, and cultural changes to foster innovation, advance transformation projects, and engage in fintech enterprises and businesses. Banks and fintech companies may coexist and support one another in the future. Larger fintech companies may eventually overtake smaller ones to become the dominant financial institutions, leaving banks mainly responsible for overseeing wholesale funding. According to Adrian et al. (2019), banks may have a limited role before transitioning to fractional banks. Due to the preference of internet-age consumers for online transactions, most banks now have websites. For decision-making, banks must utilise data-driven analytics. Money laundering, SIM swaps, vishing, and phishing are a few of the frequent frauds that affect banking consumers. Programmes that increase customer knowledge have proven effective in preventing these frauds and should be maintained.

## 2.3 Central Bank and Regulator

Maintaining interbank operability is the central bank's top priority; however, if digital money companies adopt interbank operability and maintain reserves comparable to the central bank, this responsibility may be challenged in the future. This might result in a monopoly of powerful e-money suppliers, which would be dangerous for the system. In order to ensure stringent governance and compliance, central banks might act as the licencing authority for e-money service providers (Adrian et al., 2019). Central banks are establishing regulatory sandbox settings for fintech to assess regulatory compliance. Before releasing their products, fintech companies have occasionally only partially complied with central bank procedures, such as the Know Your Customer (KYC) procedure. A fintech company's long-term objectives do not coincide with those of the pertinent authorities (Philippon, 2016). Fintech companies may provide regulators with insights into altering consumer behavioural data that they can use to design consumer-friendly policies, so working together can benefit both sides (Romnova et al., 2016). For the regulatory framework, enforcement, and compliance in the USA, it would be essential to research human behavioural imitation using machine language, artificial intelligence, and big data (Bauguess, 2017).

## 2.4. Online Payments

With online payments, cash transfers, and other financial services, Internet customers know about and use digital money, e-money, and mobile wallets. M-Pesa, one of the first mobile digital currency options, was launched in Africa in March 2007 and immediately gained popularity among a sizeable unbanked community.

## 2.5. Cross-Border Transactions

Cross-border payments are the International Monitoring Fund's (IMF) main area of interest for fintech innovation leveraging blockchain, an accessible distributed ledger technology. This approach can resolve concerns about money laundering and terrorism financing by establishing trust between intermediaries (He et al., 2017). This might lower expenses and raise service standards. Whether financial market developments will be gradual and evolutionary or possibly disruptive is a significant area of uncertainty.

## 2.6. Blockchain

The introduction of the first cryptocurrency, Bitcoin, signalled a significant turning point for blockchain technology. Without a central bank and using open-source distributed ledger technology, participants on a reliable and secure network engage transparently to handle Bitcoin and other cryptocurrencies (Nakamoto, 2019). Modern financial technology includes the internet of trustworthy data, distributed internet reliable authorities, reliable digital identification, wide availability and distributed safe computation (Pentland et al., 2016).

## 2.7. Niche Technologies

Some key technologies that fintech companies utilise to create their products include blockchain, machine learning, data analytics, artificial intelligence, robots, and cloud computing. According to an empirical study (Chen et al., 2019), the Internet of Things (IoT), robo-advising, and blockchain are the developments that will benefit the financial sector the most. Unmanned drones can be used in the banking, underwriting, and insurance industries to collect sensor data and wirelessly transmit it for reviewing insurance claims (Luciani et al., 2016). Mobile wallets, the expansion of online neobanks, and new millennial-generation customers with close ties to internet giants like Amazon and Google are some of the rising trends. These businesses utilise blockchain for peer-to-peer lending and contract administration, artificial intelligence for investment advice, machine learning, data analytics for customer service, etc. Augmented reality (AR) can increase customer engagement and substantially distinguish a service. Thanks to augmented reality (AR), customers can view content in a concise, immersive, and engaging manner (Dubey, 2019).

## 2.8. Research Topics in Fintech

With the development and maturation of newer technologies, fintech, which is in the growth stage, can further innovate and revolutionise corporate products, services, and processes. Fintech offers several research opportunities, particularly in developing fields like digital insurance, electronic invoicing, electronic factoring or leasing, crowdsourcing, robot investing advice, and knowledge of cryptocurrencies other than bitcoins and their connections (Gomber, 2017).

## 3. Fintech in India

With 87% of fintech acceptance of digital payments among digitally active users, India is one of the areas for fintech innovations that are expanding the fastest. The additional global leader in this field is China. Similar to this, 99.5% of Indians who use the internet frequently are aware that fintech services exist for sending and receiving money online. The Indian government announced in 2017 that it would reduce the utilisation of paper money in open commerce, which led to this information (Global FinTech adoption. 2019). A few of the cutting-edge fintech products that government organisations have successfully introduced include the Immediate Payments Service (IMPS), the Unified Payments Interface (UPI), the Bharat Interface for Money, the Aadhaar-enabled Payments System (AePS) and the Bharat Bill Pay System (BBPS). These tools or interfaces are used by banks as well as fintech companies. Financial inclusion, Supertech (information technology for supporting regulatory, supervisory role), regtech (technology for regulatory function) and sandbox infrastructures for fintech innovators are some of the topics on which the Reserve Bank of India, a central bank, has concentrated (Pant et al., 2020). The social sector in India has seen the emergence of fintech use cases as well, with companies like Milaap assisting with online fundraising (Jutla et al., 2016). More excellent data analytics, the need for increased stakeholder collaboration, tailored solutions, and data democratisation were listed by NASSCOM as the major fintech themes for India in 2020. (Fintech Lending - Unlocking Untapped Potential, 2019) They advise the regulator to use digital KYC, streamline the KYC process, and establish a default reporting platform.

With a 64% global adoption rate (Figure 2), FinTech is unquestionably becoming more widely used in all markets evaluated. The adoption rates from this data show a consistent upward trend over the preceding five years compared to those from earlier surveys taken in 2015 and 2017. In the six markets under study, adoption rates rose by about 100% every two years, from 16% in 2015 to 31% in 2017 to 60% in 2019 (Hwa, M. 2019).

New benchmarks for the country's financial services are being set by India's FinTech enterprises (Mathur P. et al., 2022). The implementation of UPI, Jan Dhan Yojana, and other government initiatives that improve financial inclusion in India are driving the fintech industry in that nation, and FinTech adoption is highest among people aged 25 to 44, at about 94%, while globally, this age group adopts FinTech at a rate of about 73%. In terms of demographics, male and female use of FinTech apps was 88% and 84%, respectively. In the world of FinTech, India has one of the quickest growth rates. China and India are the two countries with the most significant fintech adoption rates worldwide. The $65 billion digital payment value is expected to increase at a CAGR of 20% up to 2023. The fintech market shares several traits with other markets. With its challenges and potential, India stands out as a unique market for FinTech, particularly in the payments sector (Rajeswari et al.; C., 2021).

*Figure 2. Global consumers have adopted FinTech*

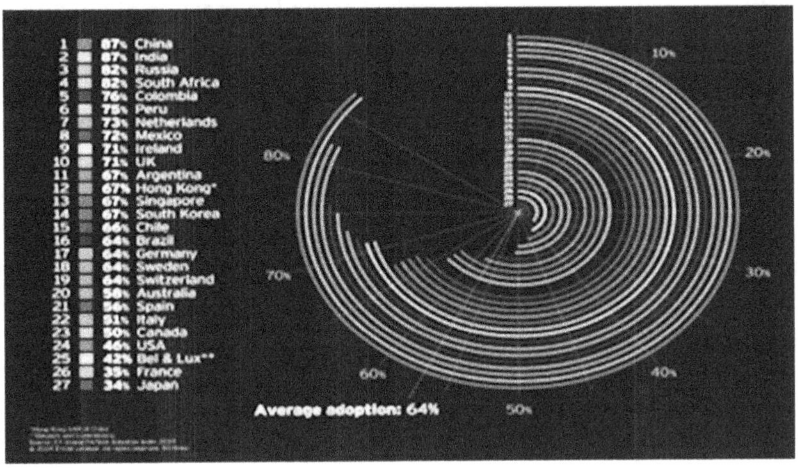


*Figure 3. Indian Fintech industry structure*

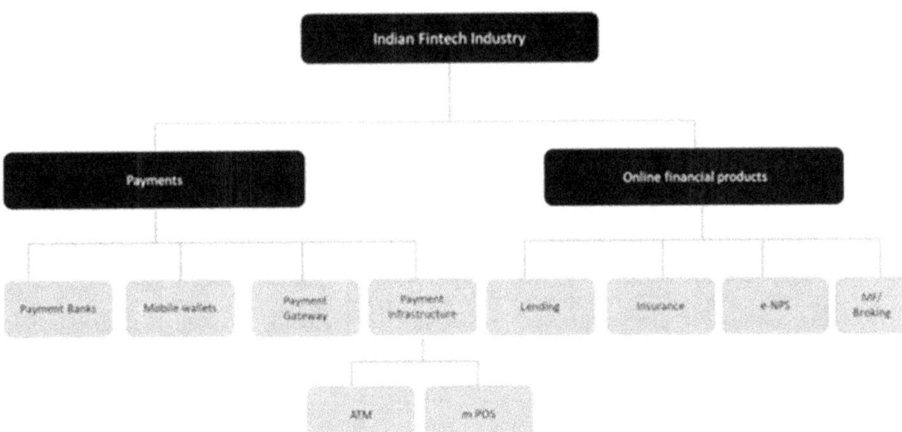

## 3.1 Fintech Adoption in India

Fintech companies are helping to change the Indian financial services sector. India now uses fintech services more than China, according to a study (EY Fintech Usage Index 2017) (A.L. 2019). Unexpectedly, India has a strong fintech acceptance rate. Indian customers have quickly embraced mobile payments in their daily activities thanks to mobile wallets and various other cutting-edge technologies, like the Unified Payment Interface platform. To compare prices, customers hurry to the bank websites. In India, the use of fintech has significantly increased during the previous two years. In addition, India ranked second internationally in terms of its fintech acceptance rate in 2017 according to the EY Fintech Acceptance Index, which examined 20 economies. Each of the five service categories showed this to be the case. Adoption rates among digitally active Indian consumers were between 50% and 100% higher than the worldwide norm, which served as evidence of this.

According to EY's FinTech Acceptance Index 2017, India has joined a market with the second-highest FinTech acceptance rate (51%) among 20 economies worldwide. Fintech usage has grown significantly during the past two years in India. For all five service categories, digitally active Indian consumers adopt services at rates that are 50% to 100% greater than the global average.

## 3.2 Coverage of the Indian Fintech Ecosystem

The government plays a significant role in whether fintech succeeds or fails in the heavily regulated banking sector (Vijai, C. 2019). According to a 2016 KPMG study on fintech in India, the Indian government and organisations like SEBI and the RBI actively encourage the Indian economy's goal to establish a robust fintech ecosystem and go digital.

*Figure 4. Financial technology adoption among online users*

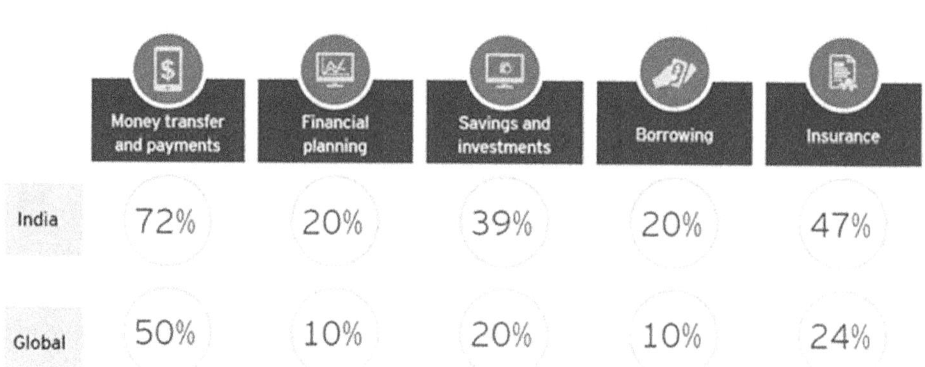

*Figure 5. Fintech investments in India by sector*

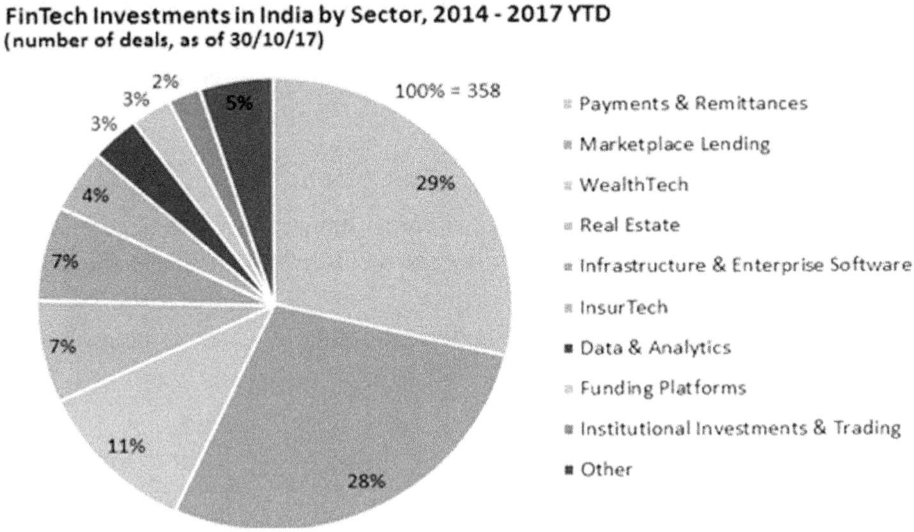


A multi-pronged approach has been utilised to help institutional and general people gain access to financial systems that are digitally enabled:

## 1. Finances support

- A USD 1.5 billion fund for businesses is part of the Indian government's Start-Up India programme, revealed in January 2016.

## 2. Enabling and promoting financial inclusion

- The Jan Dhan Yojana, the provident fund, and Aadhar have all been enlarged.
- Thanks to the Jan Dhan Yojana, more than 200 million formerly unbanked people now have accounts.

## 3. Relief from surcharge and tax

A few noteworthy programmes on this front include:

- Tax credits for businesses that process more than 50% of their transactions online.
- For start-ups, there are 80 per cent discounts on patent costs.
- A three-year income tax exemption for new businesses.

- A capital gains tax exemption for holding investments in unlisted companies for more than 24 months (instead of the previous requirement of 36 months).
- The Ministry of Finance has recommended eliminating the surcharge for using a credit card or the Internet to pay for government services.

## 4. Infrastructure support

- The Digital India and Smart Cities programmes have been created to encourage digital infrastructure development in the nation and attract international investment.
- Thegovernmentrecentlylaunchedadedicatedportaltoprovideeaseinregistration tostart-ups.

## 5. Support for IP facilitation

- The government will fund startups to help defray the cost of facilitators for their patents, trademarks, and other types of design work.

*Figure 6. The five elements of the Fintech ecosystem*

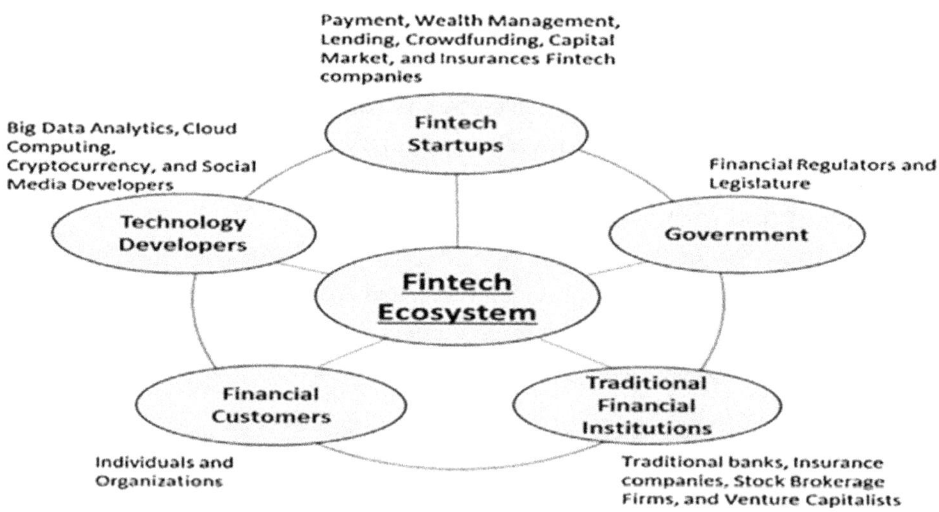

## 4. FINTECH INDUSTRY SEGMENTS

The word "fintech" refers to the innovative procedures and goods currently offered by the financial sector thanks to advances in digital technology. According to the Financial Stability Board, "financial innovation enabled by technology" (fintech) is defined as "financial innovation that may give rise to new business models, applications, processes, or products with a corresponding material impact on financial markets and institutions and the provision of financial services."

The Fintech industry, according to Dortfleitner et al. 2017, is made up of a variety of elements that may be broadly divided into four main categories: "financing," "asset management," "payments," and "other Fintechs." The four major components are depicted in Figure 7, along with their minor parts.

*Figure 7. Fintech segments and components*

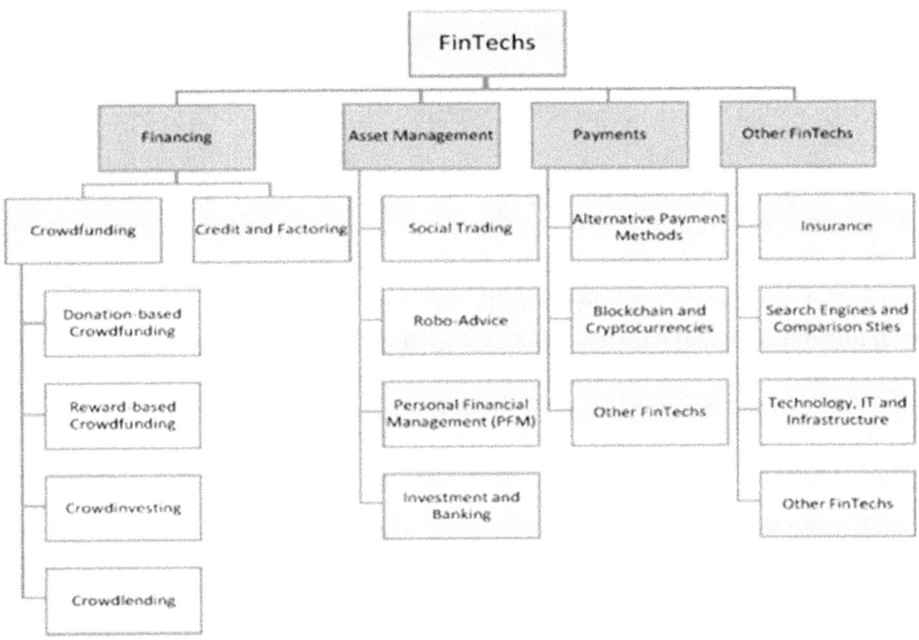

## 4.1. Financing

Fintech enterprises are transforming the loan or financing process. People are no longer needed to obtain a bank loan. Many fintech businesses increasingly provide customers with loans directly (Alt et al., 2018). They may apply for loans online, and they will be authorised right away. Businesses quickly automate the underwriting process after evaluating the borrowers' creditworthiness. There are two ways to obtain money: crowdsourcing and credit and factoring.

### 1. Crowdfunding

Various forms of crowdsourcing funding exist. For investors and companies, each has unique advantages (Ma et al., D. 2017). Based on their needs, the consumer must choose one of these.

- **Crowdfunding based on donations**

Donations made through crowdsourcing are utilised to support charities or causes. Donations are made here with nothing except satisfaction as the only goal.

- **Incentive-based crowdsourcing**

It is a particular kind of financial source for small enterprises. This is used in the majority of creative projects. As a result, investors can donate funds to the project other than for financial gain (Martinazzi, S. 2017). It looks like an old machine. The award (which might be event tickets, gift cards, freebies, etc.) will rise according to the amount of his donation. It will not cost much to deliver the offered incentive. The firm will benefit from this.

- **Crowd investing**

The phrase is used when many individuals or businesses invest in one another's internet ventures. Loan and equity contributions are also included in crowdsourcing. The collective of investors is not required to be acquainted before investing. They may receive interest or shares in return for their investment (Wonglimpiyarat, J. 2018).

- **Public lending**

Businesses and regular people can obtain general public loans through crowdfinance. It offers a place for both borrowers and lenders. Lending and borrowing money is a powerful and effective strategy for bringing together investors and borrowers (Yuniarti et al., A. 2020). The lender will get a certain amount as interest for the money lent. This platform completes several tasks for banks.

### 2. Credit and Factoring

As a result, factoring has gone online, much like lending. Fintech businesses offer online applications that may be accessed with a single mouse click. Small business owners now have a new option for obtaining operating capital (Branzoli et al., 2020). By pushing a single button, businesses may swiftly and conveniently sell their accounts receivable and deposit the money into their bank accounts. A seller who uses factoring can obtain a loan on his receivables.

## 4.2 Payments

Payments are the other popular subcategory of the financial technology industry. These businesses let people transfer money to each other without utilising banks. Peer-to-peer transfers are a straightforward payment method, yet banks charge exorbitant fees for them. Fintech companies make it possible for customers to send money quickly and cheaply. Thanks to blockchain technology, firms can now handle transactions more affordably than banks (Mehrotra et al., 2021).

- **Additional payment options**

If we need to pay, we typically log into the bank account and take care of it there. Since then, Fintech companies have developed several payment options for user convenience. Most customers do not need to register with their bank accounts in order for them to enable payments (Omarini et al., 2018). Customers can now pay at many establishments using their social media accounts, including Facebook Messenger and Twitter. The customer can sign in to the bank's app without leaving their current app.

- **Bitcoin and blockchain technology**

Fintech startups employed blockchain technology to upend the banking and finance industry. Blockchain is being utilised to better track the flow of one's assets and record activities in a shared digital ledger (Fosso Wamba et al., 2020). Case studies in the supply chain and a thorough review of bitcoin, blockchain, and fintech. The data cannot be stolen because it is dispersed through a network, including private devices. The security issue, now the biggest challenge, is being fixed. It encourages prompt payments and is more affordable. Like banks, they do not use intermediaries.

## 4.3. Asset Management

Highly net-worth individuals obtain financial and investment advisory services as part of asset management (Kato, Y. 2020). People can speak with wealth managers directly to make arrangements for their monetary requirements, such as insurance, retirement, and portfolio management. They do not have to turn to several people or organisations for assistance.

- **Social trading**

Social trading, a young idea, is predicated on the fundamental tenet that the collective knowledge of many traders is more insightful than that of a single trader. Social trading hubs connect international traders (Kern, A. 2017).

- **Robot counsel**

A brand-new type of software has been created to help you manage your finances. Algorithms are used to automate the majority of investing advice (Muthaiyah et al., T. O. K. 2020). It performs brilliantly as a financial counsellor for people who do not want to use one or cannot afford it due to cost or lack of funds. Robo advisers diversify customers' portfolios.

- **PMF**

Personal financial management (PFM) is the term used to describe the software that assists people in managing their finances (Lee et al., 2019). Said, the phrase refers to technology-based budgeting. Budgeting is made more accessible by adding accounts from numerous organisations. It helps users keep track of their income and outgoing costs, create a budget, and stay out of debt.

- **Investment and banking**

Like any other business, the financial sector is being significantly impacted by investing and banking automation. Fintech is now ready to take on the present investment banking models with platforms for no-fee finance and financial planning (Romnova et al., 2016). Important investment banks' business plans started to come under attack and intrusion from the firms. They started researching private investing, asset management, and lending to small businesses.

## 4.4. Other Fintech's

Fintech businesses provide extra services, such as payments, asset management, and finance, besides those provided by traditional banks. It comprises technology, IT and infrastructure, search engines and comparison websites, and insurance.

- **Insurance**

Financial technology firms also had sway over the insurance market. Most businesses in this sector concentrate on marketing (Yan et al., 2018). These businesses work to connect with their customers through a variety of apps.

They are significantly more flexible than traditional insurance. Due to the strict rules and regulations of the insurance sector, businesses strive to cooperate with traditional insurance providers. These Fintech companies are referred to as InsurTech companies.

- **Comparison websites and search engines**

In this sub-segment, search engines compare financial products and services various service providers provide (Priya et al., 2019).

- **Technology, IT, and Infrastructure**

Fintech businesses that provide the technological solutions needed by various financial services providers make up the sub-segment of technology, IT, and infrastructure (Pant et al., 2020).

# 5. METHODOLOGY

Various financial services and products offered by different service providers are compared in this sub-segment using search engines (Priya et al., 2019). The International Monetary Fund website and Google Scholar's most highly cited research publications were the basis for the selection criteria. The websites of top market research firms provided some of the most critical information and trends for upcoming fintech developments.

## 6. DISCUSSION

The definition of fintech, current developments in fintech, its effects on financial institutions, risks associated with fintech breakthroughs, and potential future applications are all examined in the paper. Using more recent technologies, fintech is revolutionising the financial sector more quickly than ever. Key conclusions from the review of the literature include the following:

- According to key findings from the 2019 fintech consumer survey, 64% of consumers globally have adopted fintech, Digital payment services are known to 96% of people, 68% of individuals want non-banking organisations to provide financial services, and 45% are willing to give the non-banking organisation access to their banking information. (Adoption of fintech worldwide, 2019) Globally, 56% of customers employ banking payment fintech services, and 46% use fintech financial services, with a 25% adoption rate for the SME sector.
- India and China are the world leaders in digital payment usage and awareness. It now serves as the foundation for non-financial sectors, including insurance (comparison, purchase), Travel (bookings, payments, offers), FMCG (point of sale), Transportation, Telecom & Utility (bill payments, recharges), Hospitality (booking, payments) and Entertainment (content purchases), travel (booking, payments), etc. (Chaffey, D et al., 2019). Even the governments of many nations, like India, use direct financial transfers for purchases and subsidies to decrease transaction costs and eradicate corruption. The essential fintech services of digital payments will remain unchanged while being progressively innovated.
- Banks spearhead initiatives to encourage innovation in the fintech sector, but they must solve problems with organisational culture, personnel, and workflow. Neo-banks are upending traditional banks by selling cutting-edge products at lower prices.
- By creating sandbox environments and adjusting licencing and governance policies, regulatory agencies and central banks promote fintech development (M Taylor et al., 2020). The regulator must use advances in fintech for its governance and oversight duties and be more proactive by utilising cutting-edge tools.
- Blockchain technology has enormous potential to change industries, save prices, and increase trust and openness (Saha et al., 2021). Examples of compelling use cases for blockchain's ability to track purchases from source to target with dependable intermediaries include tracking organic farming from farmer to market, tracking diamond stones from mine to retail store,

sharing secure patient medical records, tracking organic farming from farmer to market, and maintaining a transparent history of ownership of land titles (Patki et al., 2020).

- Blockchain, AI, cognitive learning, big data, robots, augmented reality, machine learning, IoT, and drones are just a few examples of the cutting-edge technologies used by fintech organisations (Allen et al., 2020).
- The IMF, a major international financial organisation, thinks blockchain distributed ledger technology might enhance the efficiency of cross-border payments, lower transaction costs, and increase transparency (Hashemi Joo et al., 2020).
- More recent study concentrates on links between cryptocurrencies besides bitcoin, crowd investing, digital invoicing, electronic leasing, electronic factoring and digital insurance.
- Robotic financial advice can potentially upend the investment consulting industry (Xiao et al.; T. A., 2021). A hybrid approach that includes a human face and a robo-advisor can be used to provide investing advice to customers who still desire human-to-human interaction. These robo-advisors can provide superior, informed advice at a reduced cost while meeting the customer's expectations for trust and openness.

## 7. CONCLUSION

With the help of technology and creativity, fintech has transformed the banking industry and is expanding more quickly than ever. The future of business is one where digital money serves as the foundation. Due to this, fintech companies must actively address worries about online business dangers. Fintech was created in response to the 2008 financial crisis and has since developed. The coronavirus epidemic has significantly raised the hurdles facing fintech companies this year. However, the current environment also allows them to profit from growing digital transactions and rising demand for telemedicine and insurance goods. As many businesses are compelled to cut costs and eliminate redundancy, fresh investments in fintech have almost wholly ceased. Online and digital commerce will continue to exist, and fintech firms may continue to draw lessons from the current financial crisis and succeed in the 2020 report by coming up with innovative solutions. Across India, Fin Techs are proliferating across all areas of financial services. Financial innovations are developing quickly, demonstrating India's tremendous entrepreneurial potential. In the two years before this one, 1,500 FinTech startups in India were founded, accounting for over half of the total. The fintech industry requires excellent financial and technological grooming. The most significant proportion of profitable startups is in the payments industry, and this trend is anticipated to extend to other financial sectors as well. The government and other regulatory agencies must take additional action to support the fintech industry.

## REFERENCES

Adrian, M. T., & Griffoli, M. T. M. (2019). *The rise of digital money*. International Monetary Fund.

Allen, S. J. (2020). On the cutting edge of the chopping block? Fostering a digital mindset and tech literacy in business management education. *Journal of Management Education*, *44*(3), 362–393. doi:10.1177/1052562920903077

Alt, R., Beck, R., & Smits, M. T. (2018). FinTech and the transformation of the financial industry. *Electronic Markets*, *28*(3), 235–243. doi:10.100712525-018-0310-9

Arner, D. W., Barberis, J., & Buckley, R. P. (2016). One hundred fifty years of Fintech: An evolutionary analysis. *JASSA The Finsia Journal of Applied Finance*, (3), 22.

Arner, D. W., Barberis, J., & Buckley, R. P. (2017). *FinTech and RegTech in a Nutshell, and the Future in a Sandbox*. CFA Institute Research Foundation. doi:10.2139srn.3088303

Bauguess, S. W. (2017). *The role of big data, machine learning, and AI in assessing risks: A regulatory perspective*. U.S. Securities and Exchange Commission.

Branzoli, N., & Supino, I. (2020). Fintech credit: A critical review of empirical research literature. *Bank of Italy Occasional Paper*, (549).

Buttice, C. (2020). [AI Use Cases: Artificial Intelligence in FinTech. AltaML-Techopedia.]. *Top (Madrid)*, 12.

Chaffey, D., Edmundson-Bird, D., & Hemphill, T. (2019). *Digital business and e-commerce management*.

Chen, M. A., Wu, Q., & Yang, B. (2019). How valuable is FinTech innovation? *Review of Financial Studies*, *32*(5), 2062–2106. doi:10.1093/rfs/hhy130

Dorfleitner, G., Hornuf, L., Schmitt, M., Weber, M., Dorfleitner, G., Hornuf, L., & Weber, M. (2017). Definition of FinTech and description of the FinTech industry. *FinTech in Germany*, 5-10.

Dubey, V. (2019). FinTech innovations in the digital banking. [IJERT]. *International Journal of Engineering Research & Technology (Ahmedabad)*, *8*(10).

Ernst & Young. (2016): *German FinTech landscape: an opportunity for Rhein-Main-Neckar*. Ernst & Young.

Giglio, F. (2022). Fintech: A literature review. *International Business Research*, *15*(1), 80–85. doi:10.5539/ibr.v15n1p80

Global Fintech Adoption. (2019). *Index*. EY. https:// www.ey.com/en_gl/ey-global-fintech-adoption-index

Gomber, P., Koch, J. A., & Siering, M. (2017). Digital finance and FinTech: Current research and future research directions. *Journal of Business Economics*, *87*(5), 537–580. doi:10.100711573-017-0852-x

Hashemi Joo, M., Nishikawa, Y., & Dandapani, K. (2020). Cryptocurrency a successful application of blockchain technology. *Managerial Finance*, *46*(6), 715–733. doi:10.1108/MF-09-2018-0451

He, M. D., Leckow, M. R. B., Haksar, M. V., Griffoli, M. T. M., Jenkinson, N., Kashima, M. M., & Tourpe, H. (2017). *Fintech and financial services: Initial considerations*. International Monetary Fund.

Hwa, G. (2019). Eight ways FinTech adoption remains on the rise. *Vers*, *1*, 2019.

Jutla, S., & Sundararajan, N. (2016). India's FinTech ecosystem. *The FinTech Book: The Financial Technology Handbook for Investors, Entrepreneurs and Visionaries*, 56-57.

Kato, Y. (2020). AI/FinTech and asset management businesses. *Public Policy Review*, *16*(4), 1–28.

Kern, A. (2017). *Wikifolio: Social Trading*. Springer Fachmedien Wiesbaden.

Lee, S. K. (2019). *Fintech nudges: Overspending messages and personal finance management*. NYU Stern School of Business.

Luciani, T. C., Distasio, B. A., Bungert, J., Sumner, M., & Bozzo, T. L. (2016). U.S. Patent Application No. 14/843,455.

Ma, Y., & Liu, D. (2017). Introduction to the special issue on Crowdfunding and FinTech. *Financial Innovation*, *3*(1), 1–4. doi:10.118640854-017-0058-9

Martinazzi, S. (2017). *The age of fintech: providing a liquid and efficient secondary market for security-based crowdfunding with distributed ledger technologies*.

Mathur, P., Gupta, N., & Agarwal, M. (2022). *Are banking & andfinancial institutions ready for the transformation? An analysis of FinTech adoption challenges using DEMATEL.*

Mehrotra, A., & Menon, S. (2021, January). The second round of FinTech trends and challenges. In *2021 2nd International Conference on Computation, Automation and Knowledge Management (ICCAKM)* (pp.–243–248). IEEE. 10.1109/ICCAKM50778.2021.9357759

Mention, A. L. (2019). The future of fintech. *Research Technology Management, 62*(4), 59–63. doi:10.1080/08956308.2019.1613123

Muthaiyah, S., & Zaw, T. O. K. (2020). Digital know-how and FinTech readiness. In *Understanding Digital Industry* (pp. 1–4). Routledge. doi:10.1201/9780367814557-01

Nakamoto, S. (2019). *Bitcoin: A peer-to-peer electronic cash system.* Manubot.

Omarini, A. E. (2018). Fintech and the future of the payment landscape: The mobile wallet ecosystem. A challenge for retail banks? *International Journal of Financial Research, 9*(4), 97–116. doi:10.5430/ijfr.v9n4p97

Pal, J., Chandra, P., Kameswaran, V., Parameshwar, A., Joshi, S., & Johri, A. (2018, April). Digital payment and its discontents: Street shops and the Indian government's push for cashless transactions. In *Proceedings of the 2018 CHI Conference on Human Factors in Computing Systems* (pp. 1–13). IEEE. 10.1145/3173574.3173803

Pant, S. K. (2020). Fintech: Emerging Trends. *Telecom Business Review, 13*(1).

Patki, A., & Sople, V. (2020). Indian banking sector: Blockchain implementation, challenges and way forward. *Journal of Banking and Financial Technology, 4*(1), 65–73. doi:10.100742786-020-00019-w

Pentland, A., & Shrier, D. L. (Eds.). (2016). *Frontiers of financial technology: Expeditions in future commerce, from blockchain and digital banking to prediction markets and beyond.* VisionaryFuture.

Philippon, T. (2016). *The fintech opportunity (No. w22476).* National Bureau of Economic Research. doi:10.3386/w22476

Priya, P. K., & Anusha, K. (2019). Fintech issues and challenges in India. *International Journal of Recent Technology and Engineering, 8*(3), 904–908.

Rajeswari, P., & Vijai, C. (2021). Fintech industry in India: the revolutionised finance sector. *Eur. J. Mol. Clin. Med, 8*(11).

Rajeswari, P., & Vijai, C. (2021). Fintech industry in India: the revolutionised finance sector. *Eur. J. Mol. Clin. Med, 8*(11).

Rajeswari, P., & Vijai, C. (2021). Fintech industry in India: the revolutionised finance sector. Eur. J. Mol. Clin. Med, 8(11).

Ray, T. (2020). *Scopes and Impact of Cloud Computing on Banking & FinTech.*

Romānova, I., & Kudinska, M. (2016). Banking and Fintech: A challenge or opportunity? In *Contemporary Issues in Finance: Current Challenges from across Europe*. Emerald Group Publishing Limited. doi:10.1108/S1569-375920160000098002

Romānova, I., & Kudinska, M. (2016). Banking and fintech: A challenge or opportunity? In Contemporary issues in finance: Current challenges from across *Europe*, *98*, 21–35.

Saha, A. K., Barua, S., & Nath, S. D. (2021). Blockchain for financial technology: Challenges and opportunities for India. The Impact of Artificial Intelligence on Governance. *Economics and Finance*, *1*, 247–261.

Schindler, J. W. (2017). *FinTech and financial innovation: Drivers and depth.*

Schueffel, P. (2016). Taming the Beast: A scientific definition of fintech. *Journal of Innovation Management*, *4*(4), 32–54. doi:10.24840/2183-0606_004.004_0004

Shah, P. (2019). *How fintech is revolutionising with blockchain technology.*

Srivastav, S. (2020). *Blockchain in Fintech: A Catalyst for Disruption in Finance World.*

Taylor, M. C. R., Wilson, C., Holttinen, E., & Morozova, A. (2020). *Institutional arrangements for Fintech regulation and supervision*. International Monetary Fund. doi:10.5089/9781513520308.063

Vajid, A., & Farooqi, A. W. (2022). ISSUES AND CHALLENGES TO THE FINTECH INDUSTRY IN INDIA. [JEBR]. *EPRA International Journal of Economic and Business Review*, *10*(12), 16–22. doi:10.36713/epra12006

Varga, D. (2017). Fintech is the new era of financial services. *Vezetéstudomány-Budapest Management Review*, *48*(11), 22–32. doi:10.14267/VEZTUD.2017.11.03

Vijai, C. (2019). *FinTech in India–opportunities and challenges. SAARJ Journal on Banking & Insurance Research* (Vol. 8). SJBIR.

Wonglimpiyarat, J. (2018). Challenges and dynamics of FinTech crowd funding: An innovation system approach. *The Journal of High Technology Management Research*, *29*(1), 98–108. doi:10.1016/j.hitech.2018.04.009

Xiao, S., & Adekola, T. A. (2021). Investment Robo-Advisors: Some Reflections on China's Regulatory Experience. *Banking & Finance Law Review*, *37*(1), 127–148.

Yan, T. C., Schulte, P., & Chuen, D. L. K. (2018). *InsurTech and FinTech: banking and insurance enablement. Handbook of Blockchain* (Vol. 1). Digital Finance, and Inclusion.

Yuniarti, S., & Rasyid, A. (2020, March). Consumer Protection in Lending Fintech Transaction in Indonesia: Opportunities and Challenges. In Journal of Physics: Conference Series, 1477(5), 052016. IOP Publishing.

# Chapter 13
# Financial Inclusion and Sustainable Development of Rug Weavers Through Innovative Traditional Practices of MANCHAHA Programme

**Nisha Kumari**
https://orcid.org/0000-0002-1998-9467
*Department of Entrepreneurship, GITAM School of Business, GITAM University (Deemed), Visakhapatnam, India*

**Mukesh Kondala**
https://orcid.org/0000-0002-1965-5088
*Department of Operations, GITAM School of Business, GITAM University (Deemed), Visakhapatnam, India*

## ABSTRACT

*The Indian carpet industry, one of the country's most important sources of foreign exchange, is also well-known worldwide for its rich art and tradition. However, there is concern about innovation, financial inclusion, and sustainability. The current study explores the MANCHAHA initiative, a step taken by the Jaipur Rugs carpet industry toward sustainability, as well as its relevance and significance for other hand-craft or carpet industries. It also examines how it affects the financial inclusion of rug weavers. The single-case study method has been used in conjunction with the descriptive research design to conduct the study. The idea of innovation utilizing conventional methods is somewhat obsolete and underappreciated, but the company's MANCHAHA project disproved this preconceived notion.*

DOI: 10.4018/979-8-3693-0008-4.ch013

## 1. INTRODUCTION

The Indian carpet industry, one of the country's most important sources of foreign exchange, is also well-known worldwide for its rich art and tradition (Kumar et al., 2020). It has a long history and tradition of production in India, even though it is still regarded as a cottage industry (Bano, 2016).

According to IBEF (2022), in terms of value and volume, India now holds the highest place in manufacturing and exporting handmade carpets and other floor coverings. The nation is the world's top exporter of carpets, exporting around 85% to 90% of the entire amount it produces. Regarding handmade carpet exports, India is responsible for about 40% of the total. In 2021–2022, India's exports of handmade carpets and other floor coverings increased by 19.5% to reach US$ 2.23 billion.

However, there needs to be more concern about innovation, financial inclusion, and sustainability. At the same time, innovation is needed to address the worldwide sustainability challenge (Luqmani et al., 2017). Despite the fact that the rug sector might need to be given more consideration at green summits, it is estimated that it wastes billions of dollars worth of yarn annually, with the extra being burned or disposed of in landfills (Kumar R., 2022). Carpets comprise 1-2 percent of all solid wastes globally, making them one of the biggest waste products (Mohammadhosseini & Awal, 2013). To achieve sustainability, a transformative approach that seeks systemic transformation in the consumption and production systems should be encouraged (Ahmadifard & Farhadian, 2023).

In this regard, Jaipur Rugs launched the MANCHAHA initiative, in which leftover yarn from the manufacturing process is used to improve weavers' ability to make a sustainable livelihood through traditional practices and contribute to overall sustainable development. The current study explores the MANCHAHA initiative, a step taken by the Jaipur Rugs carpet industry in the production system toward sustainability, as well as its relevance and significance for other hand-craft or carpet industries. It also examines how it affects the financial inclusion of rug weavers.

Further, in the second section, the related literature has been covered to understand the status of the carpet industry, its contribution to waste and the economy, and the role of innovation in sustainability and financial inclusion. Then, the methodology has been discussed under which the study area and the method used for sampling, data collection, and analysis have been covered. This is followed by the findings and discussion in which the collected data has been analyzed and interpreted. Finally, the study's implications and summary of the findings have been covered in the conclusion, followed by the limitations and the scope of future studies.

## 2. LITERATURE

Industrialization is any country's primary driver of economic growth (Kondala et al., 2023), and the handmade carpet business stands out among the various cottage industries (Bano, 2015). The handcrafted Indian carpet's distinctive weaving has demonstrated its ability to compete worldwide. The steadily increasing growth in export value indicates this firm's high sustainability potential in the coming years (Bano, 2016). The handmade carpet business is predominantly a labor-intensive, export-focused market. The basic purpose of this industry is to employ people to undertake specialized jobs such as dyeing, designing, weaving carpets, finishing, and so on. It is a skill-based domain-specific enterprise (Mishra & Ray, 2018). However, decision-makers and authorities must safeguard the sector's viability because, over time, the living standard in the handmade carpet (HC) industry has declined as a result of the introduction of machine-made carpets, low wages, etc. (Pourmoradian et al., 2021). In order to improve the quality of life in the handmade carpet industry, policymakers need to implement the policies without detaching the culture and traditional practices (Ahmadifard & Farhadian, 2023).To be at the top of the market, the Indian carpet business needs to learn new skills, work harder, use fewer resources, and ensure production is done ethically (Kumar et al., 2020). As a means of addressing issues related to sustainable economic development, innovation is gaining more and more attention from policymakers (Lamprinopoulou et al., 2014). Sustainability is a global challenge that necessitates new approaches (Nudurupati et al., 2022). There is still a behavior gap, and despite many organizations' stated commitments to drive innovation for environmental, societal, and economic sustainability, there remains a behavior gap (Luqmani et al., 2017). Hansen et al. (2009) referred to innovation that leads to greater sustainability as "sustainability-oriented innovation" (SOI). Many of the world's most successful companies have readily adopted such a perspective and promise in their annual reports to advance goals like sustainable development, well-being, and social inclusion through their core business operations with the support of their shareholders (Kondala et al.,2023).

Using industrial waste carpet fiber has the added benefit of reducing waste and conserving resources (Mohammadhosseini & Awal, 2013). However, there are numerous studies on generating eco-friendly carpets and recycling discarded carpets (Ghanbarzadeh-Shams et al., 2022; Luqmani et al., 2017; Thiry, 2004), but few on recycling waste generated during carpet manufacturing while also increasing the company's productivity and the innovativeness of the artisans.

## 3. METHODOLOGY

The current research is a qualitative study in which descriptive analysis was utilized to achieve the study's goals of exploring the MANCHAHA initiative and its application to other handcraft industries and its significance in the financial inclusion of rug weavers. Under the descriptive analysis approach, the inductive single-case study method was used to conduct the study. Using the purposive-convenience sampling, 35 weavers and 11 company executives were selected. Further, the data has been collected using Focussed Group Discussions (FGDs) and semi-structured interviews. The research was carried out at Jaipur Rugs' headquarters, warehouse, finishing center, and Aspura hamlet in Rajasthan's Sikar district.

The research coordinator supervised semi-structured interviews and focus groups. Following consent from the participants, notes from the conversation were taken and recorded using a recorder. In order to better understand the situation and the themes, the narrative analysis method was utilized to organize the notes from the information obtained. No tool or technical software was used throughout the manual narrative analysis. The co-author verifies the codes and themes. A description of each FGD and interview was given for validation, even if member-checking was impossible. This made it possible to ensure that the focus groups and interviews accurately reflected the participants' perspectives.

## 4. FINDINGS AND DISCUSSION

### 4.1. MANCHAHA Process

The company took the MANCHAHA initiative in 2018, but it was boosted during the COVID period. The meaning of MANCHAHA is "made from the heart". The separate department was formed apart from research and development, i.e., the design and development department. The MANCHAHA initiative gave a new meaning to sustainability. Through the initiative, Jaipur Rugs contributes to sustainability in various ways, such as sustaining artisan's skills, sustaining yarn, sustaining innovation, sustaining culture, etc. (Figure 1).

The company allowed workers to weave whatever design they wanted as part of this program. There is no map design provided to weave the rug. At the initial stage, the unused or excess yarn after completing one rug allowed weavers to create the rug according to their thoughts and ideas. The process at the initial stage is illustrated in Figure 2.

*Figure 1. MANCHAHA's contribution in sustainability*
*Source: The author(s)*

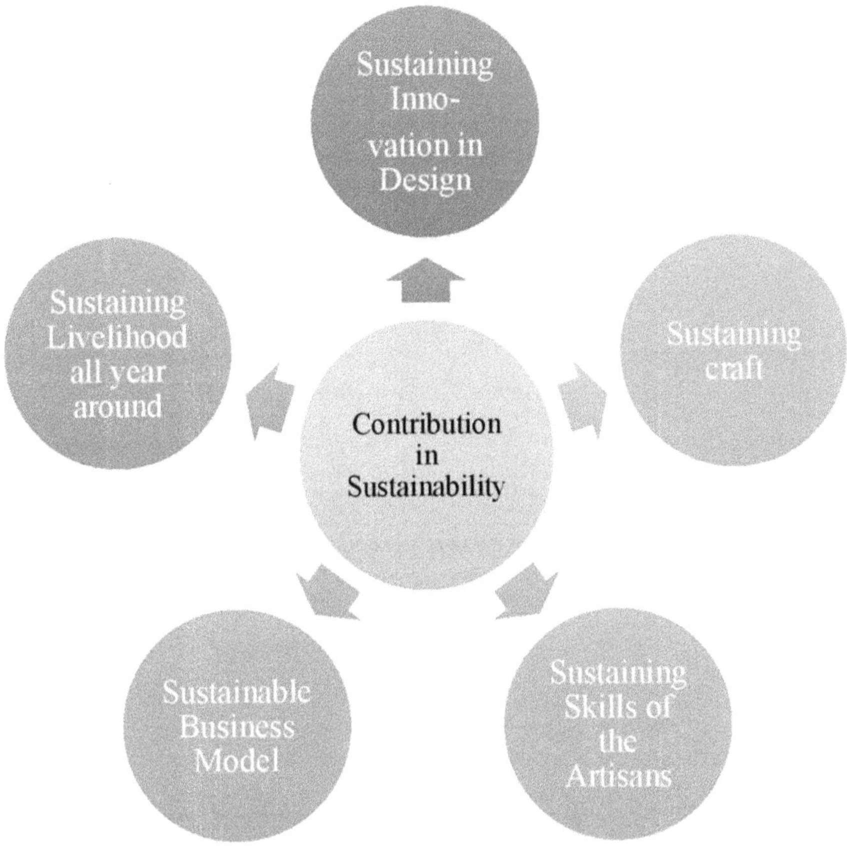


Later, the company modified the process, and rather than just utilizing the excess yarn, they started performing all the steps of rug manufacturing. They divide residual yarn into three categories: unused, to-be-processed, and entirely wasted yarn. The unused yarn is combined with fresh and unused yarn for use in new carpets and MANCHAHA designs. The unprocessed yarn was shipped to be carded, spun, and spooled before being used in MANCHAHA productions. They sell entirely wasted yarn to waste retailers. The modified procedure is depicted in Figure 3

The MANCHAHA was not for existing or rural weavers only, and it went out to convicts in Dausa, Bikaner, and Jaipur. It taps into the exotic fashion in rural India by nurturing their creative potential and transforming a community from exploitation to empowerment. Each rug is hand-knotted with over 200,000 knots and recounts the story of its maker, complete with emotions, culture, goals, and personality.

*Figure 2. MANCHAHA process (at initial stage)*
*Source: The author(s)*

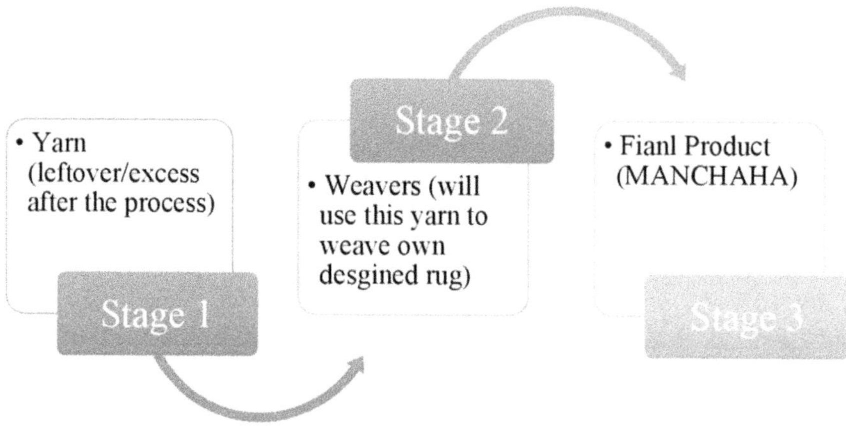


*Figure 3. Advanced model of MANCHAHA process*
*Source: The author(s)*

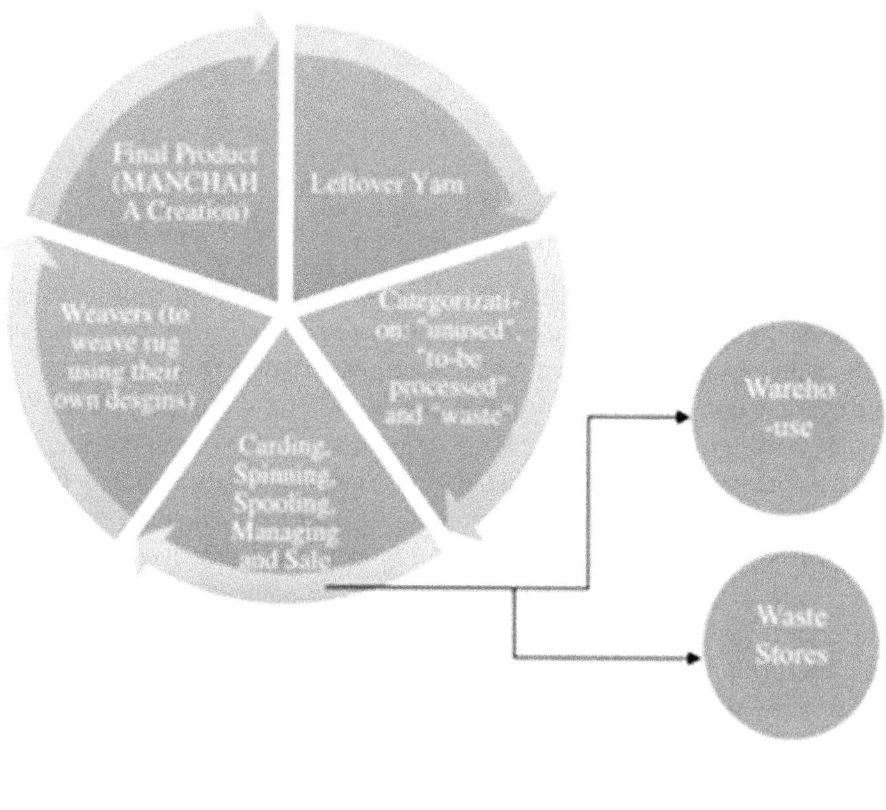

## 4.2. Skill Development, Financial Inclusion, and Sustainability

The Jaipur Rugs company uses traditional and hand tools in all 18 stages it follows for rug manufacturing. Those 18 stages are measurement, knot counting, pile height checking, raffu-repairing, thukai-knot beating, kachi kainchi-first shear, sua birai-design correction, back-burning, back-burn cleaning, dipping, washing, khinchai-stretching, cutting, binding, pucci kainchi-final shearing, kalam birai-detailing, chinte nikalna-snipping visible cotton, carving & embossing.

In the beginning, every weaver got one-month training, and during the training period, the weavers got ₹100 per day, and after completion of training, they got wages based on their work completion, i.e., ₹20 per line. Usually, they got a map design for weaving the rug, but under the MANCHAHA initiative, no map design was provided; it reflects their own thought, ideas, culture, and story. At the initial stage, weavers were hesitant, but once they started work, their opinions got changed. Later, 86 percent of weavers from the studied sample wanted to work for MANCHAHA creation. In comparison, around 14 percent of weavers still preferred map designing (Figure 4) as, according to them, rather than putting their thoughts using weaving, it is better to use the design they got from the company.

*Figure 4. Weaver's interest in participation in MANCHAHA*
*Source: The author(s)*

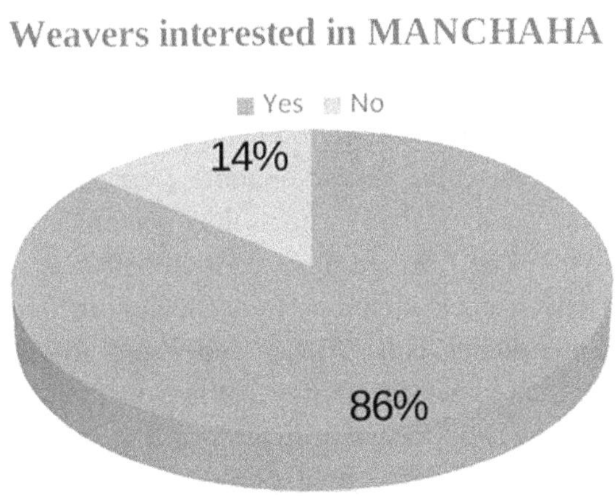


This innovative initiative does not only enhance the skill of the artisans, their thought process, and idea generation.

*"At first, I was terrified and confused, but I eventually reasoned that if the company was implying it, I should at least try. And I made some bizarre patterns out of a variety of colourful yarns. My first MANCHAHA rug had mountains, birds, arbitrary lines, and tea cups sized to resemble the figures of my kids by envisioning how they ask me for tea every morning."-Weaver.*

*"Celebrations were in full swing at the time, and we were making a lot of sweets for our numerous festivals. Weaving random lines to make patterns resembling mountains, forests, and other arbitrary shapes takes place in between weaving the Rajasthani sweets (ghewar, ladoo, sakarpara, and kaju katali). When we initially started weaving the rug, we were afraid. Still, as soon as the cheerful thoughts started to come to us, we were able to weave in a fun way by combining a variety of surprising ideas."- Group of weavers.*

*"Even though the three of us were used to working together using the map. It was our first time working without a predetermined layout, so we were immediately scared. Because of this, our minds were not in sync when we first began weaving, and the patterns we produced made no sense. However, as time passed, we better understood one another's perspectives, which made the patterns we developed through time more coherent." -Another group of weavers.*

*"The MANCHAHA allowed me to create the rug of my dreams because I've always appreciated vibrant colours. I felt ecstatic that other people now preferred my option."- another weaver.*

Likewise, each series of MANCHAHA rugs has a rich history. When given a chance to express themselves, the weavers include a variety of components from their own cultures and environments, as well as their personal experiences, into the weaving of their carpets. The finished pieces are vibrant masterpieces that draw inspiration from various sources, including food and colour, flowers and animals, objects and musical equipment, close friends and family members, dreams, and experiences. Also, the weavers got recognition at the global as well as national level for their creations. Manju Devi received three awards for single design- Dezeen Awards, Future Design Awards, Kyoorius Design Awards, Bimla Devi and Kavita Chaudhary (Design Director) won the German Design Award.

The initiative was not limited to skill enhancement but also contributed to financial inclusion and sustainability. The initiative's goal was to help weavers grow and stay in business using their traditional methods. The recognition and display of weaver's work gave them exposure at the global level, which can provide them with many opportunities for sustainable livelihood. In addition to enhancing skills and exposure to a sustainable livelihood, the company gave financial increments to the weavers, contributing to the weaver's financial inclusion. The company not only provides the wage for their work but also gives a share in the profit they make through the sale of weaver's MANCHAHA creations. As a thank you, the company gave the weavers presents or products of their choice. According to the profit they made from the production, weavers asked for various things, such as blankets, mixer grinders, refrigerators, silver or gold ornaments, etc. The business claims that they made this choice because they thought that if they distributed cash, it would not be used correctly and that if someone came from a dysfunctional or abusive household, they would extort from the weavers.

Through the initiative, rural residents with, at most, the most elementary education have stunned the world with creative designs that are on par with those of top-tier professionals worldwide. This social innovation has successfully saved the disappearing old craft of hand-knotting by resurrecting the joy of weaving via uninhibited expression. It seeks to change the economy by promoting self-assurance and a sustainable livelihood.

Although the initial concepts and designs weavers created were recognized nationally and worldwide, the company continued without any breaks. The business works with organizations and art schools to professionalize the thoughts, ideas, and weaving designs. The corporation chose a limited group of weavers for the partnership who were eager to learn and whose patterns had more polish. Recently, the business worked with Central Saint Martin College, University of the Arts, London, on a similar project. Weavers learn about the cognitive processes of professionals and students pursuing professional degrees during this process. Conversely, university students are taught the value of intrinsic artistic abilities. Additionally, the company works with many charities to provide corporate training through collaboration.

Apart from weavers, company, culture, and tradition sustainability, this initiative contributes directly or indirectly to the Sustainable Development Goals (SDGs). These are Responsible Consumption and Production (SDG 12), Gender Equality (SDG 5), No Poverty (SDG 1), Partnership to achieve the Goal (SDG 17), Decent Work and Economic Growth (SDG 8), Zero Hunger (SDG 2) and Reduced Inequality (SDG 10).

## 5. IMPLICATIONS

### 5.1. Managerial Implications

The procedures used in MANCHAHA may assist other carpet and handcraft-based industries in empowering their artisans and improving their abilities. It will also be helpful to comprehend the procedure for using leftover material effectively rather than putting more waste in landfills. Additionally, what other ways besides CSR activities they can make a difference in sustainable development

## 5.2. Policy Implications

This study will offer the theoretical underpinnings and comprehension of sustainable practices using traditional methods, which may aid government and policymakers in formulating programs and policies supporting weavers or other artisans without displacing culture and conventional practices. Furthermore, it will benefit policymakers or Self-Help Groups (SHGs) to enlighten rural Indian artisans about financial technology, its significance for growth, and how they can use it to boost their income through investments.

## 5.3. Theoretical Implications

Although studies on artisans or weavers have been conducted, there are few studies on rug weavers and enhancing their skills without detaching the culture and traditional practices. This study will add to existing literature and aid researchers in exploring novel ideas and methods that may impact the productivity and development of artisans and entire industries.

# 6. CONCLUSION

Working one-on-one with poor weavers and artisans in isolated communities to give them access to the global market is a particular feature of Jaipur Rugs' business strategy. The Jaipur Rugs strives to build and empower disadvantaged people in addition to advocating for the overall sustainable development of society. Jaipur Rugs began a fresh business by hand-spinning and weaving unused yarn batches into carpets with unique patterns. The "MANCHAHA" collection is how they referred to it. They are moving closer to fulfilling their major goal of empowering their artisans, and one of the initiatives that help them do so is MANCHAHA. This project helps the business achieve its primary goal and redefines what sustainability means. However, the company can provide more benefits or increase the contribution to weaver's financial inclusion by including financial technology, like how they can save or invest their profits and take one more step towards financial growth or giving extra knowledge class of fintech.

## 6.1. Limitations of the Study

The Jaipur Rugs operate in 600 distant villages, but the current study covers one village, which limits the scope of the study. Given that there is only one village, depicting the knowledge and viewpoint of all weavers must be challenging.

## 6.2. Scope for Future Research

The researchers can cover more villages to comprehensively understand the initiative. Also, the current study has been done using qualitative methods. The researchers can also employ the mixed method to get that static impact in the future. Further, the researchers can study such initiatives taken by other handcraft industries to compare and provide new knowledge to handcraft industries, policymakers, and other institutions.

## REFERENCES

Ahmadifard, E., & Farhadian, H. (2023). An Analysis of Transformation Institutions in the Knowledge and Innovation System of the Handmade Carpet Industry. *Journal of Agricultural Science and Technology*, *25*(2), 285–300. https://jast.modares.ac.ir/files/jast/user_files_749497/h_farhadian-A-10-45013-8-85afdb4.pdf. doi:10.52547/jast.25.2.285

Bano, R. (2015). GROWTH PERFORMANCE AND GLOBAL PERSPECTIVE OF INDIAN HAND. *Asia Pacific Journal of Research, I*(XXIV). https://d1wqtxts1xzle7.cloudfront.net/51378759/230220152-with-cover-page-v2.pdf?Expires=1656527924&Signature=hClrHq80aWFSs

Bano, R. (2016). Role of Handicrafts in Economic Development: A Case Study of Carpet Industry of India. *IRA-International Journal of Management & Social Sciences, 04*(03), 512-525. https://d1wqtxts1xzle7.cloudfront.net/58663209/Role_of_Handicrafts_in_Economic_Developm-libre.pdf?1553090395=&response-content-disposition=inline%3B+filename%3DPg_no_512_525_Industry_of_India.pdf&Expires=1683444310&Signature=IQoIVaSgZ91aj6qCtb-mZB1KIie1i4

Bano, R. (2016). Role of Handicrafts in Economic Development:A Case Study of Carpet Industry of India. *IRA-International Journal of Management &Social Sciences*, *04*(03), 512–525. doi:10.21013/jmss.v4.n3.p1

Ghanbarzadeh-Shams, M., Yaghin, R. G., & Sadeghi, A. H. (2022). A hybrid fuzzy multi-objective model for carpet production planning with reverse logistics under uncertainty. *Socio-Economic Planning Sciences, 83*, 101344. doi:10.1016/j.seps.2022.101344

Hansen, E., Grosse-Dunker, F., & Reichwald, R. (2009). Sustainability innovation cube—A framework to evaluate sustainability-oriented innovations. *International Journal of Innovation Management, 13*(04), 683–713. doi:10.1142/S1363919609002479

IBEF. (2022, November). *Carpet Industry and Exports*. India: IBEF India Brand Equity Foundation. https://www.ibef.org/exports/carpet-industry-in-india

Kondala, M., Nudurupati, S. S., & Pappu, R. P. (2023). (Article in press). The challenges in adoption of circular economy in SMEs–a research agenda and way forward. *Benchmarking*. doi:10.1108/BIJ-04-2023-0272

Kondala, M., Nudurupati, S. S., Riwayadi, E., Chavan, A., Asif, S. R., & Gupta, N. (2023). Original Research Article Moving towards a sustainable world with the circular economy prac-tices concerning the SMEs in Visakhapatnam's ice-cream industry. *Journal of Autonomous Intelligence, 6*(1). Advance online publication. doi:10.32629/jai.v6i1.676

Kumar, V., Kumar, P., & Mishra, K. (2020). Managing Sustainable Development of Indian Carpet Industry. *Journal of Seybold Report, 15*(8), 1193–1201. https://d1wqtxts1xzle7.cloudfront.net/64181686/Managing_Sustainable_Development_Of_Indian_Carpet_Industry-libre.pdf?1597421334=&response-content-disposition=inline%3B+filename%3DManaging_Sustainable_Development_of_Indi.pdf&Expires=1683189558&Signature=ZY8

Kumar, V. R. (2022, April 03). Weaving sustainable designer rugs in the hinterland. India. *The Hindu Businessline*. https://www.thehindubusinessline.com/specials/clean-tech/weaving-sustainable-designer-rugs-in-the-hinterland/article65281543.ece

Lamprinopoulou, C., Renwick, A., Klerkx, L., Hermans, F., & Roep, D. (2014). Application of an integrated systemic framework for analysing agricultural innovation systems and informing innovation policies: Comparing the Dutch and Scottish agrifood sectors. *Agricultural Systems, 129*, 40–54. doi:10.1016/j.agsy.2014.05.001

Luqmani, A., Leach, M., & Jesson, D. (2017, September). Factors behind sustainable business innovation: The case of a global carpet manufacturing company. *Environmental Innovation and Societal Transitions, 24*, 94–105. doi:10.1016/j.eist.2016.10.007

Luqmani, A., Leach, M., & Jesson, D. (2017). Factors behind sustainable business innovation: The case of a global carpet manufacturing company. *Environmental Innovation and Societal Transitions, 24*, 94–105. doi:10.1016/j.eist.2016.10.007

Mishra, A., & Ray, B. (2018). Need of skill development in hand made carpet industry: A socio- economic perspective. *Journal of the Textile Association, 79*(1), 24–27.

Mohammadhosseini, H., & Awal, A. A. (2013). PHYSICAL AND MECHANICAL PROPERTIES OF CONCRETE CONTAINING FIBERS FROM INDUSTRIAL CARPET WASTE. *IJRET: International Journal of Research in Engineering and Technology, 2*(12), 464-468. https://citeseerx.ist.psu.edu/document?repid=rep1&type=pdf&doi=696db3c274267eff4b37a07641ffb5b63f0c4fb5

Nudurupati, S. S., Budhwar, P., Pappu, R. P., Chowdhury, S., Kondala, M., Chakraborty, A., & Ghosh, S. K. (2022). Transforming sustainability of Indian small and medium-sized enterprises through circular economy adoption. *Journal of Business Research, 149*, 250–269. doi:10.1016/j.jbusres.2022.05.036

Pourmoradian, S., Shoari, A. V., Omarzadeh, D., Sharifi, A. N. S., & Hosseini, S. S. (2021). An Integrated Approach to Assess Potential and Sustainability of Handmade Carpet Production in Different Areas of the East Azerbaijan Province of Iran. *Sustainability (Switzerland), 13*(4), 1–21. doi:10.3390u13042251

Thiry, M. C. (2004). A carpet of green. *AATCC Review, 4*(7), 9–13.

Yadav, U. S., Tripathi, R., & Tripathi, M. A. (2022). Digital Analysis of theTransformation of Institutions in theKnowledge and Innovation Systemof the Handmade Carpet Industry. *SEDME (Small Enterprises Development,Management & Extension Journal), 49*(1). doi:10.1177/0970846422109690

# Chapter 14
# A Decade of Sustainable FinTech Research:
## Bibliometric Analysis, Current Research Status, and Future Research Directions

**Sunil Kumar**
*GITAM University (Deemed), India*

**V. V. Devi Prasad Kotni**
https://orcid.org/0000-0002-2951-2160
*GITAM University (Deemed), India*

**Sujit Kumar Patra**
https://orcid.org/0000-0001-9623-9777
*GITAM University (Deemed), India*

## ABSTRACT

*Financial service firms are increasingly using financial technologies in order to offer bundle of financial services to the customers. In this process, the firms started adopting emerging technologies like AI, blockchain, bigdata, cloud computing, in their financial transactions and operations. The objective of this research is to provide bibliometrics such as top journals, top articles, most cited articles, most cited authors, top keywords, and so on related to sustainable finance research in order to provide future research directions to potential researchers. The appropriate articles, book chapters, conference papers, and reviews were identified from available sources using the search term "sustainable fintech" in the Scopus database, where 339 articles (as of 24-04-2023) from the years 2014 to 2023 were considered for bibliometric analysis using Vosviewer software. The study's future research paths will motivate researchers to conduct further research in the field of sustainable fintech.*

DOI: 10.4018/979-8-3693-0008-4.ch014

## 1. INTRODUCTION

The word Fintech comes as an amalgamation of two words that is finance and technology. Technology helps finance industry to enhance their scope, function, acceptance and awareness among the consumers (Schueffel, 2016). As per the Industry report by KPMG, the estimated value of the global Fintech market in 2022 was at USD 194.1 billion, and it is anticipated to augment between 2023 and 2028 at a CAGR of 16.8% to arrive at USD 492.81 billion (KPMG, 2022). Finance and technology has seen its convergence with an era called Fintech 1.0 (1886-1967), technology involved was telegraph and maritime, followed by Fintech 2.0 (1967-2008) marked by a shift from analog to digital, the current age in the history of Fintech is known as "Fintech 3.0," which began in 2008 and lasted till 2014, which was dominated by the global crisis and financial instability, when trust in the banking system was lost, followed by Fintech 4.0, which is based on block-chain technology (Leong & Song, 2018). Fintech is one of the instruments of Financial Inclusion, which leads to the route to sustainable finance and sustainable Fintech, where in the basic argument of financial inclusion is access of financial services to all adults of a nation. The global financial inclusion average is less than 50.0% of adults having access to financial services. The problem is worse in developing and emerging nations, therefore achieving a higher level of financial inclusion has become a global task and Fintech can help in achieving the goals of financial inclusion (Ardic et al., 2011). Looking into the definition of "Financial technology" it is an advanced innovation process, which is used in smooth, transparent and responsible delivery of financial instruments and its services, keeping technology like Internet of things, artificial intelligence and machine learning at the backend (Olowookere, 2019). Some authors defined Fintech as "any new ideas that enhance financial service operations by offering technological solutions that take into account various business requirements" (Leong& Sung, 2018). As a new sector with features distinct from the conventional financial sector, Fintech is also seen as a driving force behind sustainable economic growth. Global Fintech investments have expanded dramatically as a result of the high expectations for the industry's expansion (KPMG, 2022). Fintech refers to new financial services applications, processes, products, and business models that consist of one or more financial services, mostly or entirely provided over the World Wide Web (Kabulova&Stankevičienė, 2020). Fintech may be integrated into new sectors and social organizations, creating an innovative economic paradigm that has the potential to boost economic growth and to create a sustainable eco system for financial growth of all individuals (Deng, 2019). The Society, economy and the ecological concerns are important dimensions of sustainable development, which looks in perpetual growth of the planet without disturbing the balance. However, the critical concern of the study is to see whether Fintech is contributing towards sustainable development or not. There are not many researches which talks about relation between Fintech and sustainable development, therefore a number of research question like relationship between financial inclusion, Fintech and sustainable development is the need of the hour. The economy, society, and the environment are all critical components of long-term development. The question is whether Fintech has an impact on long-term development. Direct research on how Fintech affects sustainable development and its specific direction of action is lacking. As a result, a number of research questions have yet to be thoroughly examined and evaluated.

## 2. LITERATURE REVIEW

Fintech is an innovative technology to overcome financial exclusion, which is considered to be the biggest challenge for under developed and developing countries. Financial exclusion is experienced by the poor citizens of underdeveloped nation but it is not limited to developing and under developed countries like in Europe, the percentage of adults who do not have bank passbook is astounding: Italy has 22.4 percent, Greece has 17.9 percent, Ireland has 16.8 percent, Portugal has 16.7 percent, Austria has 13.5 percent, and the United Kingdom has 10.5 percent. In terms of the repercussions of financial exclusion, the researchers discovered that, while the problem of financial exclusion is not new, its ramifications are growing increasingly severe (Carbo et al, 2007). Financial inclusion and exclusion are cyclical in nature with changes in the economic cycle, Financial inclusion is affected and influenced by the extent of financial innovation, poverty, financial sector stability, the status of the economy, financial literacy, and regulatory frameworks that differ across nations (Ozili, 2021). Financial inclusion has various advantages for low-income households and positively impacts in reducing poverty of a nation. It can be one policy solution for levelling income distribution because it can give low-income people with income-generating business alternatives (Khan et al, 2022). Before looking into the definitions of Fintech, it is crucial to examine the historical evolution of financial technologies in order to create the groundwork for understanding the relationship between Fintech and financial inclusion. The term "Fintech" is derived from the words "financial" and "technology" and refers to the integration of modern Internet technologies with commercial activities created in the banking industry. Some experts define Fintech as activities in the financial sector that use technology to disrupt conventional roles, business structures, and service offerings (Gomber et al., 2017). Fintech refers to innovative ideas that develop financial service operations by offering technology solutions based on diverse business situations, as well as concepts that build models or even entire enterprises. In its simplest form, it refers to the process of creating opportunities through lowering the costs of delivering financial services in order to enhance financial inclusion (leong and sung, 2018). Fintech companies help bank to aware and distribute their financial products to the consumer and is supported by disruptive innovation theory and consumer behaviour theory (Phan et al., 2020). According to consumer theory, a new service can function as a substitute if it can replace the previous service by meeting the same customer needs in a better way and customer convenience and trust is considered (Aaker and Keller, 1990). According to the disruptive innovation concept, new entrants to a market who use cutting-edge technology to provide more accessible and cost-effective goods and services may create competition in that industry (Christensen, 2013). Fintech contributes to sustainable finance through cutting transaction costs and increasing capital efficiency, reducing information gaps, improving risk management, and making green finance more accessible (Cen et al, 2018). Fintech is also seen as a driver of long-term sustainable economic growth. In-depth analysis of Fintech sustainability intentions is essential to achieve long-term development and growth. Despite the fact that the Fintech business is booming and has a rising client base, research on consumer satisfaction with Fintech services are still in its infancy and needs attention (Campanella et al, 2021). Customers are increasing their pressure on their financial institutions to provide transparent information about the environmental and social effects of their operations and goods. Users regard firms as socially responsible in this manner, and shows loyalty to continue using their services as a result (Alwi et al., 2019). Sustainable finance and Fintech have many characteristics, and Fintech can help financial organizations become more sustainable overall by encouraging green finance (Chueca Vergara, 2021). Fintech is a critical driver of "financial development, inclusion, social stability, and integrity, as well as consequential sustainable development, by constructing an infrastructure for an innovative digital financial ecosystem." (Zang et al, 2020). Fintech provides new ways of doing business in financial markets through platform implementation, due to "technological implementation, related to digital business models, and bundled services from various areas," delivering "offerings beyond the traditional banking boundaries." (Hommel,2020) One thing is certain: Fintech is rapidly expanding. And Fintech innovation is permeating more and more sectors of the digital economy and it is reaching to the masses, therefore sustainability is an important dimension to look into for its long survival.

# 3. SCOPE AND DATA SOURCE

## 3.1 Data Collection and Scope of the Research

The data for this study has been sourced from the Scopus database. Scopus is a leading, high-quality and popular database used by millions of researchers (Montoya et al., 2018; Moed, et al., 2018; Singh et al., 2021).TITLE-ABS-KEY ("sustainable Fintech" OR" sustainable-fintech" OR" sustainable financial technology") was searched in the TOPIC tab of the Scopus database; the search was not limited to only the '*Business and Economics*' area listed in Scopus '*refine*' key. Scopus is the only database that combines a comprehensive, highly managed abstract and citation database with enriched data and connected scholarly literature from multiple fields. Scopus quickly locates specialists, relevant and reputable research, as well as trustworthy data, measurements, and analytical tools. Possess the assurance to advance research, teaching, or other priorities with the help of a single database and subscription. Around 25,000 active titles and 7,000 publishers have material indexed by Scopus, all of which have undergone comprehensive verification and selection by an independent review board. The data was collected from the above mentioned index. A total of 273 articles were shortlisted, and the bibliographic information was exported and analyzed in the VOSviewer and R Studios' Biblioshiny application. The date of downloading the bibliometric file from the Scopus database is the 25$^{th}$ April 2023, with the earliest and the latest paper from the year 1990 and 2022 respectively. The data file was exported in the text format, covering bibliographic information such as title, authors, abstract, keywords, affiliation, bibliography and citations.

Section 2 and 3 report the results of the analysis. Section 2 discusses the key features based on the influential publications and productivity popularly known as "foundational features" (Alshater, Atayah, & Khan, 2022; Arslan, et al., 2022). These features are based on bibliometric characteristics such as total publications, citations of publications, average citation per paper, average citation per year. These characteristics can be measured for articles, authors, countries, and institutions. Section 3 provides the visual representations of the various critical bibliometric indicators.

# 4. FOUNDATIONAL CHARACTERISTICS OF LITERATURE RELATED TO *SUSTAINABLE FINTECH*

This section presents the analysis based on the foundational bibliographic attributes of the research paper on slow sustainable Fintech. These attributes include *article types* (such as journal articles of research conference proceedings); *research direction,* i.e., critical sub-areas of research; *total annual publications*; and the *productivity of countries, institutions, and journals*. The ranking is based on *"Total Articles," "Total citations," and "Average citations per article."*.

## 4.1 Types of Publications

Figure 1 presents the breakup of the types of publications on the topic of "sustainable finance" in the Scopus database. The most frequent category of *article type* is 'article' (published articles), with 151 counts. The next, most frequent category of *document type* is conference paper (n=46) followed by book chapter (n=43), books (n=14), review (n=10), conference review (n=7), editorial survey (n=1), and short survey (n=1). The other categories of article types like 'Erratum', and 'Retracted'have not appeared even once.

*Figure 1. Types of documents*

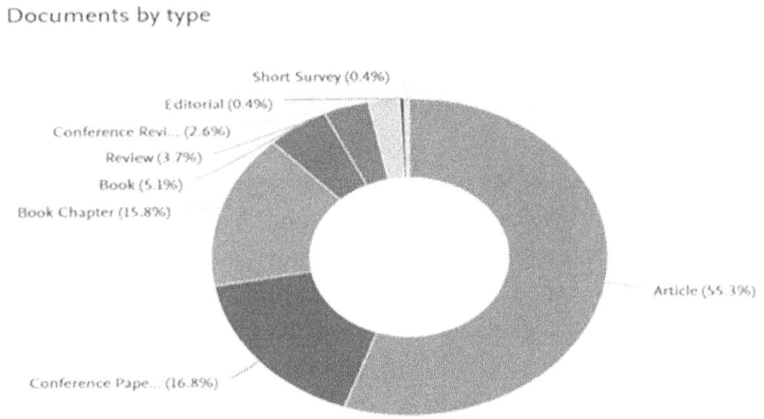


## 4.2 Publications Journey

Figure 2 shows the trends in the number of publications on in the area of *"sustainable Fintech"* in including*all* area from the Scopus database. The first appearance of the word *sustainable Fintech* in the collection of articles in the present sample is from 2014, which gradually increases year after year. We can observe five different peaks from the trend line plotted for the number of articles published each year. These peaks are for the following years 2017(n=2), 2018 (n=12), 2019 (n=19), 2020 (n=53), 2021 (n=64), and 2022 (n=84). Till the collection of data in the month 28$^{th}$ April, year 2023 (n=37). It is evident from the result of then data that in oneyear (e.g.2015) none of the articles are published on sustainable Finch. One possible reason for less publication in the area was late emergence financial technologyin the field finance. It is also evident from the data that since 2017 onwards pace of publication on sustainable finance has increased significantly.

*Figure 2. Documents year-wise*

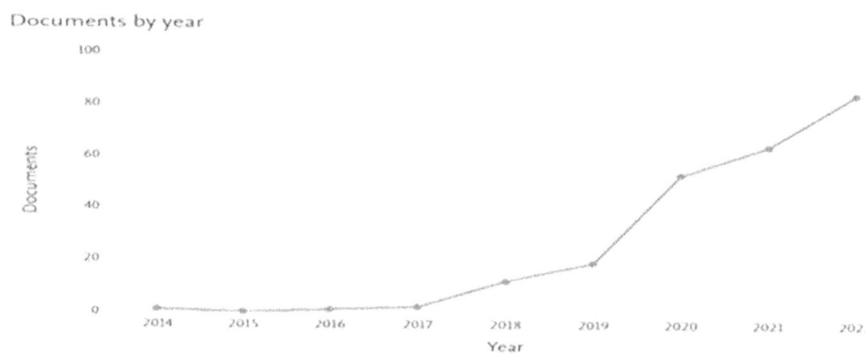


## 4.3 Popular Research Directions

Figure 3 shows the top 16 most popular research directions ("*Scopus*" database). Among the top areas, Business, Management and Accounting (n=107), Social Sciences (n=105), Economics, Econometrics and Finance (n=100), Computer Science (n=82), Environmental Science (n=59), Engineering (n=58), Energy (n=51), decision Sciences (n=28), mathematics (n=16), Earth and Planetary Sciences (n=8), Medicine (n=6), Psychology (n=6), Agricultural and Biological Sciences (n=5), Multidisciplinary (n=4), Biochemistry, Genetics and Molecular Biology (n=3), Materials Science (n=3), Pharmacology, Toxicology and Pharmaceutics (n=3), Physics and Astronomy (n=3), Arts and Humanities (n=2) and Chemical Engineering (n=2). It is also evident from the result of the study that business management and accounting, engineering, social sciences Economics, Econometrics and Finance, computer sciences, environmental sciences, engineering and energy has more contribution on sustainable Fintech than rest of the areas.

## 4.4 Most Productive Country

Table 1 exhibits the most productive countries in the world. The table shows the ten most productive countries based on the number of total documents (TD) published, total citations (TC) and average citation (AC) per article for each country are also shown in the table. The top five most productive countries are the China (TD=125),

*Figure 3. Sustainable Fintech research directions*

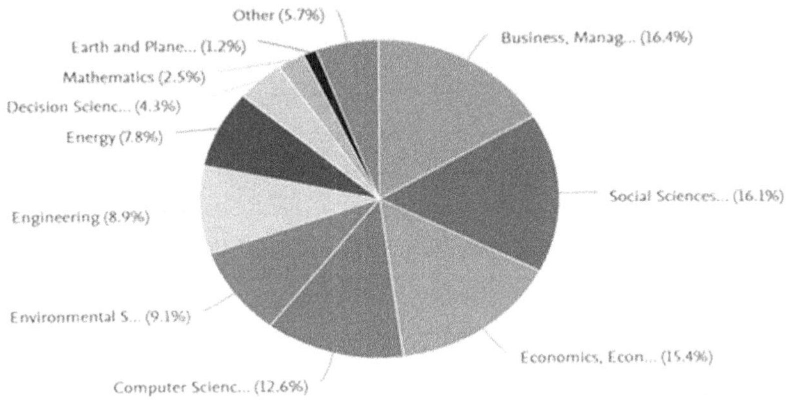


the India (TD=66), MALAYSIA(TD=44), USA (TD=32), and UK (TD=30). It is observable that the top five countries have a minimum of 30 articles on the topic of *sustainable Fintech.*

The top five countries in terms of total citations are China (TC=358), UK (TC=260), Korea(TC=161), Spain (TC=111), and Hong Kong (TC=104). Regarding the ratio of average citations per article, LITHUANIA (AC=41) has performed exceptionally well, despite having fewer articles. The remaining top four countries with the highest average citations per article are Canada, Hong Kong, USA, and UK having average citations per article as 34, 26, 26, and 25.9 respectively in the area of sustainable Fintech.

The China has emerged as the most productive country in terms of the number of articles by publishing 125 articles on the topic of *sustainable Fintch.* India is the only country in the sample with more than 66 publications. These 66 articles published in the India have garnered only 17 citations, with an average 1.9 citations per article. It shows Indian researchers could not research the topics in good way. We have produced 66 articles but could not get decent number of citations. The third most productive country in the sample is MALAYSIA, with 44 papers and 61 citations and average citation is 6.1 only. USA is the fourth most productive country in the number of articles published (32). The average citation of the countries like LITHUANIA and Canada is 41 and 34 respectively. Which shows that it is not the total publication which is important but how frequently a research is cited is also equally important.

*Table 1. Most productive country*

| Region | No. of Documents | TC | Average Article Citations |
|---|---|---|---|
| China | 125 | 358 | 9.7 |
| India | 66 | 17 | 1.9 |
| Malaysia | 44 | 61 | 6.1 |
| USA | 32 | 104 | 26 |
| UK | 30 | 207 | 25.9 |
| Bahrain | 28 | 30 | 15 |
| Indonesia | 28 | 61 | 7.6 |
| Italy | 28 | 53 | 7.6 |
| South Korea | 27 | 161 | 16.1 |
| Spain | 27 | 111 | 13.9 |

## 4.5 Most Productive Institutions

Institutions plays a significant role in research quality and productivity of the researchers. Figure 4 shows the top ten most productive institutions. Universiti Brunei Darussalam (9), Computational Social Science (6), Shanghai (6), Xi'an Jiaotong University (6), Guangdong University of Foreign Studies (5), Jeju National University (5), Lahore School of Economics (5), Market Economy Institute (5), Al-Farabi Kazakh National University (4) and Anhui University (4). We can say that most of the high impact literature on sustainable Fintech comes from institutions from mixed countries. This may also be due to the major concern on sustainable Fintech all across the world.

## 4.6 Most Cited Reference

Table 2 highlighted the list of most cited references where respective references are listed with citations. The first reference "applied energy" discussed about sustainability in details. The second Reference "Fintech and Sustainable Development: Evidence from China Based On P2p Data" Discussed The Empirical Findings Indicate the Existence of a U-Shaped Relationship Between Fintech and sustainable development, which is mostly determined by the pattern of broad economic expansion. Furthermore, heterogeneity analysis shows that there are significant regional differences in its impact on sustainable development, with the impact being significant in China's eastern and central regions but insignificant in the western region; additionally, the impact on the central region is significantly greater than

*Figure 4. Most production institutions*

that on the eastern region. The third reference "digital marketplace and Fintech to support agriculture sustainability" highlights a digital marketplace powered by Fintech could make agriculture's business processes more sustainable in terms of funding and distribution. Fintech provides farmers with convenient ways to obtain finance through crowdsourcing and digital payment systems. as a result, the digital marketplace can serve as a platform for Fintech to integrate innovative financial solutions into the larger agricultural ecosystem. fourth reference "the global index database 2017: measuring financial inclusion and the Fintech revolution" explore financial services can assist in driving development. they assist people in escaping poverty by making investments in their health, education, and enterprises possible. they also make it easier to deal with financial calamities, such as job loss or crop failure, which can lead to family destitution. fifth reference "the Fintech revolution: interpreting the forces of innovation, disruption, and transformation in financial services" highlights the long-standing dominance of leading corporations unable to adequately connect with the "Fintech revolution" is at threat. we introduce a novel Fintech innovation mapping approach that allows us to measure the extent to which changes and transformations are occurring in four domains of financial services. the sixth reference "blockchain: blueprint for a new economy" talks about role of blockchain in economic development. seventh reference "business models, investment decisions, and challenges, business horizons"Fintech ushers in a new paradigm in which information technology drives financial industry innovation. fintech is hailed as a game-changing, disruptive invention that has the potential to upend established financial markets. eight reference "do Fintech trigger renewable energy use? evidence from OECD countries" the importance of financial technologies ("Fintech") as a factor influencing renewable energy consumption in organization for economic cooperation and development (OECD) nations is highlighted. reduced carbon dioxide emissions, increased energy security concerns, and oil price volatility are driving renewable energy growth. Fintech influences renewable energy use, savings, and investment decisions. ninth reference and second reference are same. tenth reference "the emergence of the global Fintech market: economic and technological determinants"investigate the economic and technological factors that motivate entrepreneurs to start businesses with the goal of redefining financial technology (Fintech). it discovers that when a country's economy is well-developed and venture capital is readily available, more Fintech startups are formed. furthermore, the number of secure internet servers, mobile phone subscriptions, and available labor force all help to drive the growth of this new market segment. finally, the greater the difficulty for businesses to obtain loans, the greater the number of Fintech startups in a country. overall, the research demonstrates that the establishment of Fintech startups should not be left to chance, but that active policy can affect the emergence of this new sector.

*Table 2. Most cited reference*

| Sr. No. | Most Cited References | Citations |
|---|---|---|
| 1. | Applied Energy, (2018) | 18 |
| 2. | Deng et al., (2019) | 11 |
| 3. | Anshari et al., (2019) | 10 |
| 4. | Demirguc-Kunt et al., (2018) | 9 |
| 5. | Gomber et al., (2018) | 8 |
| 6. | Swan (2015) | 8 |
| 7. | Lee et al., (2018) | 7 |
| 8. | Croutzet & Dabbous (2021) | 6 |
| 9. | Haddad & Hornuf (2019) | 6 |

## 4.7 Thematic Evolution

Figure 5 shows the three stages of thematic development of author's keywords (2014-2018, 2019-2019, and 2020-2023. During 2014 to 2018 one word was used extensively e.g. Fintech. Other important keywords include "sustainability", "banking", "financial market", "sustainable development", "financial sectors" during 2019 mainly. It appears in other stages, whereas “sustainability”, sustainable development, financial services, decision making and human only appears in the last stage as well. It is evident from the result of the study that sustainability, sustainable development and financial services are the common keywords during these timeframes. Sustainability andfinancial services are major themes at this level of research. Figure 5 demonstrates that stage one (2019-2019) and stage three (2020–2023) have strong connections because they share two keywords whichdemonstrate how closely related these keywords over a period of time.

*Figure 5. Thematic Evolution of Sustainable Fintech*

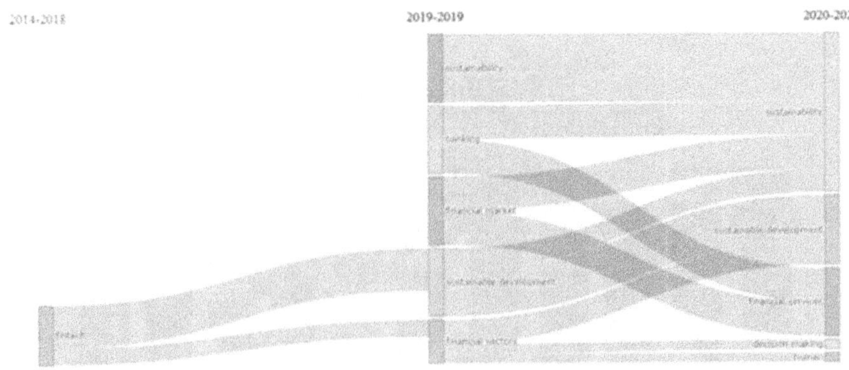


## 4.8 Word Cloud

A ‘word cloud’ is a graphical depiction of the frequency of words in written text.The larger the word appears in the image generated, the more frequently it appears in the section being evaluated. This offers visitors with a summary of the main concepts found in the text. Word clouds are increasingly being utilized as a method to detect the focus of written material in the public and business sectors.Figure 6 indicates the word cloud analysis where it is indicative that Fintech has appeared 125 times, the main keywords are Blockchain, sustainable development, financial inclusion, sustainability, financial technology, sustainable development goals, sustainable finance, artificial intelligence, covid-19, green finance, technology, innovation, banks, climate change, entrepreneurship, green digital finance, machine learning, digitalization, financial sector, banking, big data, financial services, governance, corporate social responsibility etc. are the main keywords.It is a visual representation which reflects the frequency of words used in various research articles. Maximum frequency of the word gets reflected by size of the words in the word cloud. Top ten keywords appeared 24, 22, 21, 17, 15, 12, 10, 9, 8 times minimum.It was evident from the result of the study has shown that impressive growth was seen and visible in the study since 2014 onwards. It can be inferring from the result of the study that it has various antecedent and consequences. Most of them dealt with impact of Fintech on sustainability etc. The bigrams of word cloud indicate few major variables which are financial inclusion, financial technology, sustainable development, artificial intelligence, machine learning, financial sector and financialtechnology. The trigrams include words such as sustainable development goals, corporate social responsibility etc.

*Figure 6. Word cloud: Sustainable Fintech*

## 4.9 Co-Authorship With Countries

In this section, an attempt has been to explore the co-authorship of authors of other countries which means the collaboration of one country with other country while planning and executing "sustainable fintech" research. From the Table 3, it can be noticed that China is executing more research Total Documents (TD)=38 in Scopus, Total Citations (TC)=339 and Average Citations (AC)=8.92, citations per document and Total Link Strength (TLS)=13, followed by India with TD=27, TC=118, AC=4.37 and TSL=14. Following these two countries, UK (TD=23, TC=512, AC=22.26, TLS=11), Malaysia (TD=22, TC=159, AC=7.23, TLS=14), USA (TD=19, TC=282, AC=14.84, TLS=14), Australia (TD=16, TC=193, AC=12.06, TLS=9), Indonesia (TD=13, TC=108, AC=8.31, TSL=5), Italy (TD=13, TC=142, AC=10.92, TLS=4), Pakistan (TD=11, TC=27, AC=2.45, TLS=6), Russia (TD=11, TC=31, AC=2.82, TLS=4) and Spain (TD=11, TC=164, AC=14.91, TLS=4) are other countries in top 10 list of countries which are collaborating with each other to perform research in "sustainable fintech" research. Based on the link strength, TD, TC and AC together, it can be concluded that the advanced economies like UK, USA, Spain, Italy and Australia are the top nations involved in "sustainable fintech" research. But based on number of documents, emerging economies like China and India are found to be top countries.

*Table 3. Collaboration network of countries (top ten countries)*

| Sr.No. | Country | Documents (TD) | Citations (TC) | Total Link Strength (TLS) |
|---|---|---|---|---|
| 1 | China | 38 | 339 | 13 |
| 2 | India | 27 | 118 | 14 |
| 3 | United Kingdom | 23 | 512 | 11 |
| 4 | Malaysia | 22 | 159 | 14 |
| 5 | United States | 19 | 282 | 14 |
| 6 | Australia | 16 | 193 | 9 |
| 7 | Indonesia | 13 | 108 | 5 |
| 8 | Italy | 13 | 142 | 4 |
| 9 | Pakistan | 11 | 27 | 6 |
| 10 | Russian Federation | 11 | 31 | 4 |
| 11 | Spain | 11 | 164 | 4 |
| Source: Scopus database | | | | |

*Figure 7. Co-Author network*

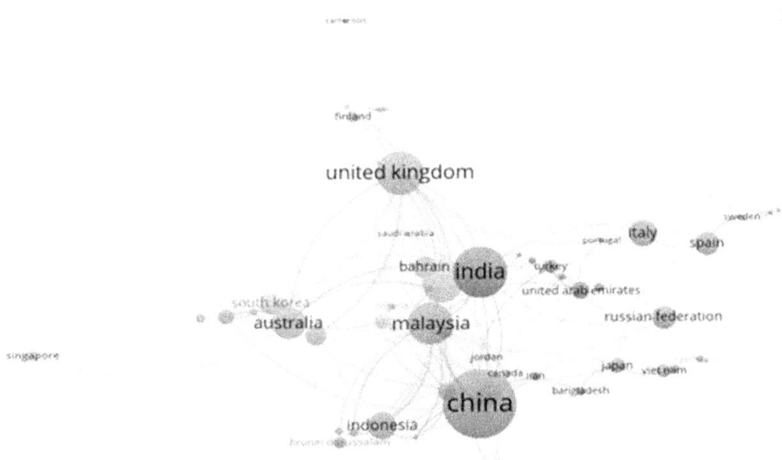

## 4.10 Co-Authorship With Organization

In this section an attempt has been made to explore top universities in the world which are engaged in the research of "Sustainable Fintech" research. It can be identified from the figure 8and table 4 that there are ten universities at the top level. They are University of New Orleansla, United States (Total Documents(TD)=3, Total Citations(TC)=15, Average Citations(AC)=5 per document and Total Link Strength (TLS)=7), followed by Kingdom University, Bahrain(TD=3, TC=65, AC=21.67, TLS=8), University of Bahrain, Bahrain(TD=2, TC=59, AC=29.50, TLS=5), University College of Bahrain, Bahrain(TD=2, TC=15, AC=7.50, TLS=7), Faculty of Economics and Business, Perbanas institute, Indonesia (TD=2, TC=2, AC=1, TLS=4), Faculty of Information Technology, Perbanas institute, Jakarta, Indonesia (TD=2, TC=2, AC=2, TLS=4), University of Sharjah, UAE (TD=2, TC=16, AC=8.00, TLS=0),Perbanas Institute, Indonesia(TD=2, TC=2, AC=1.00, TLS=0),Scientific Research Council, Bahrain(TD=2, TC=15, AC=7.50, TLS=7) and Shanghai University, China(TD=2, TC=3, AC=1.50, TLS=4).It can be concluded that University of New Orleansla, United States and Kingdom University, Bahrain are universities engaged in the "Sustainable Fintech" research. Further it can be explored that finance and economics schools, Information Technology schools, science schools are involved more in "Sustainable Fintech" research as per the documents in the scopus database.

*Figure 8. Network of institutions*

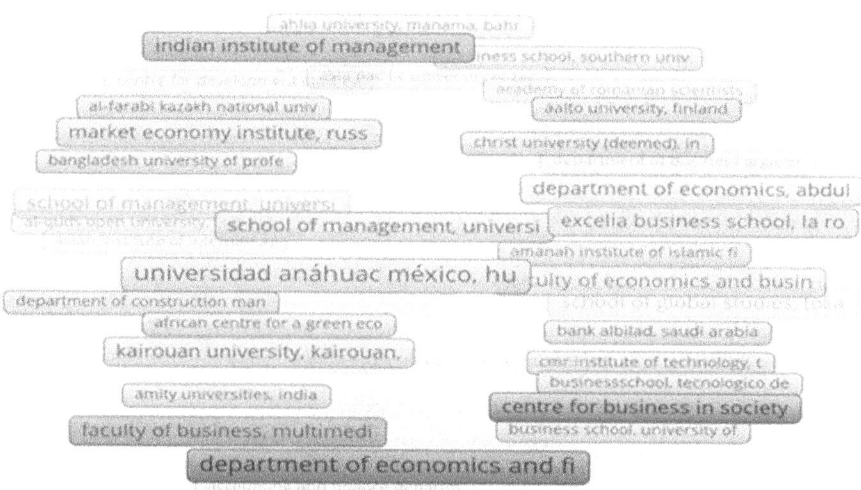

*Table 4. Co-authorship and countries*

| Sr.No. | Organization | Documents (TD) | Citations (TC) | Total Link Strength (TLS) |
|---|---|---|---|---|
| 1 | University of New Orleansla, (Department of Economics and Finance), United States | 3 | 15 | 7 |
| 2 | Kingdom University, (Department of Finance and Accounting), Bahrain | 3 | 65 | 8 |
| 3 | University of Bahrain, (College of Business Administration), Bahrain | 2 | 59 | 5 |
| 4 | University College of Bahrain, (Department of Information Technology), Bahrain | 2 | 15 | 7 |
| 5 | Perbanas institute, (Faculty of Economics and Business), Jakarta, Indonesia | 2 | 2 | 4 |
| 6 | Perbanas institute, (Faculty of Information Technology), Jakarta, Indonesia | 2 | 2 | 4 |
| 7 | University of Sharjah (Finance and Economics), United Arab Emirates | 2 | 16 | 0 |
| 8 | Perbanas Institute (Postgraduate School), Jakarta, Indonesia | 2 | 2 | 0 |
| 9 | Scientific Research Council, Bahrain | 2 | 15 | 7 |
| 10 | Australian Studies Centre, Shanghai University, China | 2 | 3 | 4 |

## 4.11 Co-Occurrence- Author Keywords

Figure 9 and table 5 indicates that this section, an attempt has been made to identify the keywords associated with the research of "Sustainable Fintech". There are nine top keywords identified which are closely associated with the research of "Sustainable Fintech". They are Fintech(Total Occurrences (TO)=144 and Total Link Strength (TLS)=151) followed by Sustainable Development (TO=67 and TLS=115), Sustainability (TO=31 and TLS=59), Blockchain (TO=28 and TLS=35), Financial Inclusion (TO=21 and TLS=30), Banking (TO=18 and TLS=37), Finance (TO=18 and TLS=43), china (TO=17 and TLS=41), Innovation (TO=17 and TLS=42) and Financial Technology (TO=16 and TLS=27). It can be concluded that, out of all keywords, the keyword "Fintech" and "Sustainable Development" generating highest link strength in vosviewer, followed by "Sustainability "and "Blockchain".

Table 5. Co-occurrences and author keywords

*Table 5.*

| S.No | Keyword | Occurrences (TO) | Total Link Strength (TLS) |
|---|---|---|---|
| 1 | Fintech | 144 | 151 |
| 2 | Sustainable Development | 67 | 115 |
| 3 | Sustainability | 31 | 59 |
| 4 | Blockchain | 28 | 35 |
| 5 | Financial Inclusion | 21 | 30 |
| 6 | Banking | 18 | 37 |
| 7 | Finance | 18 | 43 |
| 8 | China | 17 | 41 |
| 9 | Innovation | 17 | 42 |
| Source: Scopus file | | | |

*Figure 9. Author keywords: Co-Occurrence*

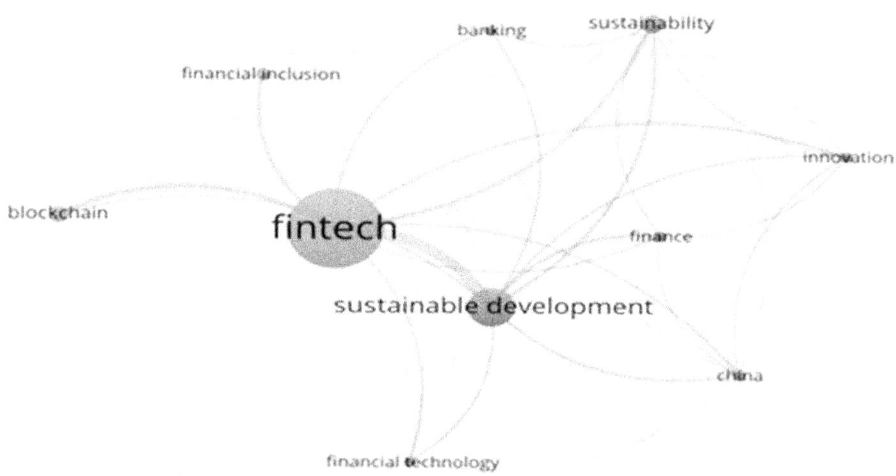

## 4.12 Citation With Author

In this section an attempt has been made to explore the top authors in the research domain of "Sustainable Fintech" research from the documents indexed in the Scopus database. The top ten researchers identified as Rabbani M.R. (with Total Documents (TD)=6, Total Citations (TC)=118, Average Citations (AC)=19.67 per document, Total Link Strength (TLS)=5), followed by Hassan M.K.(TD=5, TC=78, AC=15.60 and TLS=5), Anshari M.(TD=3, TC=71, AC=23.67 and TLS=3), Arner D.W. (TD=3, TC=103, AC=34.33 and TLS=3), Buckley R.P. (TD=3, TC=103, AC=34.33 and TLS=3), Khan S (TD=3, TC=29, AC=9.67 and TLS=4), Legowo M.B. (TD=3, TC=9, AC=3.00 and TLS=2), Reyes-Mercado P (TD=3, TC=0, AC=0.00 and TLS=0) and Subanija S. (TD=3, TC=9, AC=3.00 and TLS=2) and Zetzsche D.A.(TD=3, TC=98, AC=32.67 and TLS=3).It can be concluded that based on total number of documents (TD) and total number of citations (TC), Rabbani M.R.is identified as a top author. Based on average number of citations per document (AC), Arner D.W. and Buckley R.P.is identified as top authors. Based on total link strength (TLS) Rabbani M.R.andHassan M.K.are identified as top authors in "Sustainable Fintech" research (see table 6 and figure10).

*Table 6. Authors and citations*

| S.No | Author | Documents | Citations | Total Link Strength |
|---|---|---|---|---|
| 1 | Rabbani M.R. | 6 | 118 | 5 |
| 2 | Hassan M.K. | 5 | 78 | 5 |
| 3 | Anshari M. | 3 | 71 | 3 |
| 4 | Arner D.W. | 3 | 103 | 3 |
| 5 | Buckley R.P. | 3 | 103 | 3 |
| 6 | Khan S. | 3 | 29 | 4 |
| 7 | Legowo M.B. | 3 | 9 | 2 |
| 8 | Reyes-Mercado P. | 3 | 0 | 0 |
| 9 | Subanidja S. | 3 | 9 | 2 |
| 10 | Zetzsche D.A. | 3 | 98 | 3 |
| Source: Scopus database | | | | |

*Figure 10. Authors and citations*

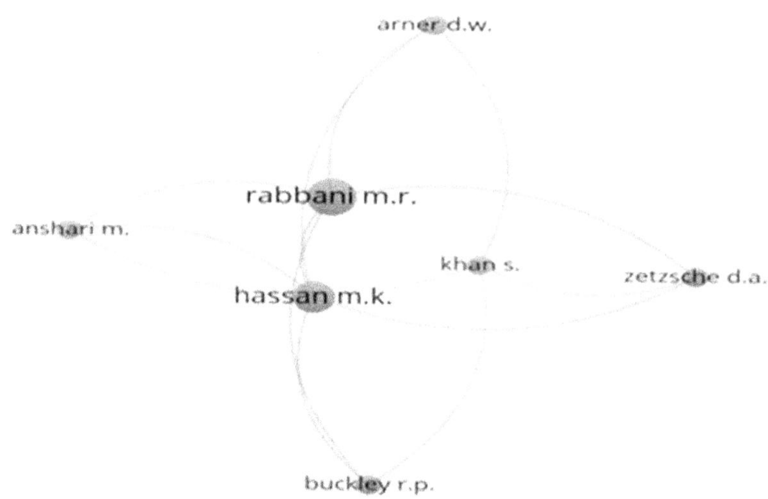


## 4.13 Citation With Organization

In this section an attempt has been made to explore top universities in the world with highest number of citations in "Sustainable Fintech" research. It can be identified from the figure 11 that the top ten universities with highest number of citations are found to be, Singapore University of Social Sciences, Singapore (Total Documents=2, Total Citations=23 and Average Citations=11.50 per document), followed by Scientific Research council, Bahrain (TD=2, TC=15, AC=7.50), School of Management, University of Science and Technology of China (USTC), China (TD=2, TC=12, AC=6.00), Soochow University, Australian Studies Centre, Shanghai University, China (TD=2, TC=3, AC=3.50), Faculty of Economics and Business, Perbanas Institute, Jakarta, Indonesia (TD=2, TC=2, AC=1.00), Faculty of Information Technology, Perbanas Institute, Jakarta, Indonesia (TD=2, TC=2, AC=1.00), Postgraduate School, Perbanas Institute, Jakarta, Indonesia (TD=2, TC=2, AC=1.00), Tokai Research Institute for Environment and Sustainability (TRIES), Tokai University, Japan (TD=2, TC=1, AC=0.50), University of Ghana Business School, Accra, Ghana (TD=2, TC=1, AC=0.50) and University of Hong Kong, Hong Kong (TD=2, TC=1, AC=0.50). It can be concluded that Singapore University of Social Sciences, Singapore is the top university engaged in the "Sustainable Fintech" research with highest number of citations (see table 7).

*Figure 11. Institutions and citations*

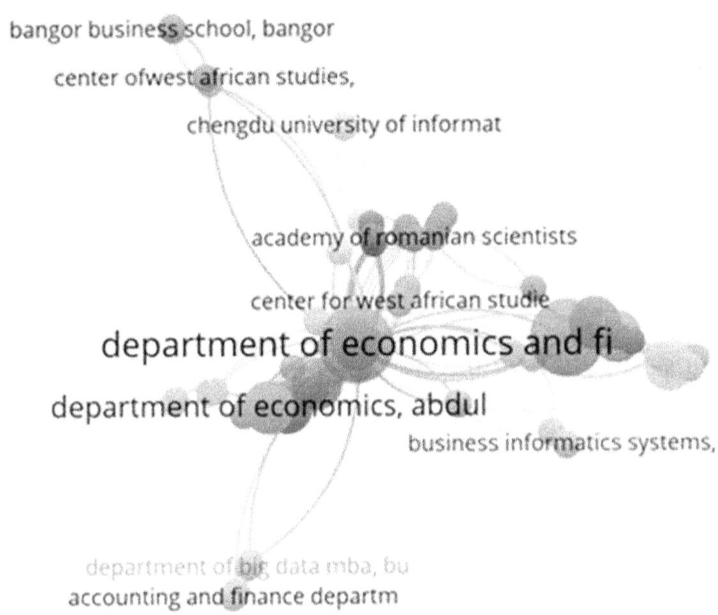


*Table 7. Most cited institutions*

| Sr. No. | Organization | Documents (TD) | Citations (TC) | Average Citations (AC) |
|---|---|---|---|---|
| 1 | Singapore University of Social sciences, Singapore | 2 | 23 | 11.50 |
| 2 | Scientific Research council, Bahrain | 2 | 15 | 7.50 |
| 3 | University of Science and Technology of China (USTC) (School of Management), China | 2 | 12 | 6.00 |
| 4 | Australian Studies Centre, Shanghai University, China | 2 | 3 | 1.50 |
| 5 | Perbanas Institute (Faculty of Economics and Business), Jakarta, Indonesia | 2 | 2 | 1.00 |
| 6 | Perbanas Institute (Faculty of Information Technology), Jakarta, Indonesia | 2 | 2 | 1.00 |
| 7 | Perbanas Institute (Postgraduate School), Jakarta, Indonesia | 2 | 2 | 1.00 |
| 8 | TRIES (Tokai Research Institute for Environment and Sustainability), Tokai University, Kanagawa, Hiratsuka, Japan | 2 | 1 | 0.50 |
| 9 | University of Ghana Business School, Accra, Ghana | 2 | 1 | 0.50 |
| 10 | University of Hong Kong, Hong Kong | 2 | 1 | 0.50 |

## 4.14 Citation With Countries

In this section an attempt has been to identify the top countries with highest number of citations in "Sustainable Fintech" research. From the Table 8, it can be noticed that the UK is having highest number of citations with Total Documents (TD)=23 in Scopus, Total Citations (TC)=512, Average Citations (AC)=22.26 citations per document and Total Link Strength (TLS)=25 followed by China (TD=38, TC=339, AC=22.26, TLS=25), USA (TD=19, TC=282, AC=14.84, TLS=8), Australia (TD=16, TC=193, AC=12.06, TLS=17), Spain (TD=11, TC=164, AC=14.91, TLS=23), Malaysia (TD=22, TC=159, AC=7.23, TLS=12), Italy (TD=13, TC=142, AC=10.92, TLS=21), India (TD=27, TC=118, AC=4.37, TLS=9), Indonesia (TD=13, TC=108, AC=8.31, TLS=6) and Pakistan (TD=11, TC=27, AC=2.45, TLS=12). It can be concluded that based on the highest number of citations and also average number of citations, UK is the top country supplying "Sustainable Fintech" research.

*Figure 12. Countries and citations*

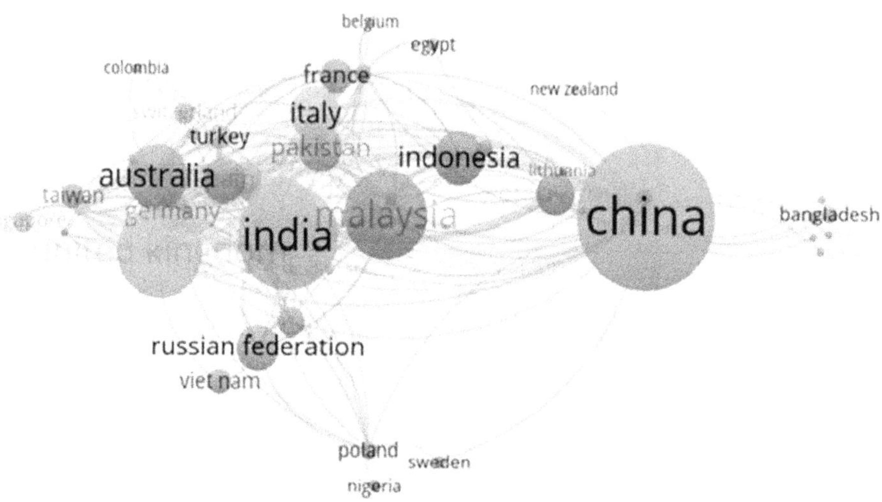

*Table 8. Countries and citations*

| S.No. | Country | Documents (TD) | Citations (TC) | Total Link Strength (TSL) |
|---|---|---|---|---|
| 1 | United Kingdom | 23 | 512 | 25 |
| 2 | China | 38 | 339 | 21 |
| 3 | United States | 19 | 282 | 8 |
| 4 | Australia | 16 | 193 | 17 |
| 5 | Spain | 11 | 164 | 23 |
| 6 | Malaysia | 22 | 159 | 12 |
| 7 | Italy | 13 | 142 | 21 |
| 8 | India | 27 | 118 | 9 |
| 9 | Indonesia | 13 | 108 | 6 |
| 10 | Pakistan | 11 | 27 | 12 |

## 4.15 Co-Citation: Cited Authors

In this section an attempt has been made to identify the top 10 authors with highest number of citations in "Sustainable Fintech" research. From the table 9, it can be seen that Buckley, R.P. (Total Citations=95 and Total Link Strength=1191) is the top author with highest number of citations followed by Arner, D.W. (TC=86 and TLS=1084), Rabbani, M.R. (TC=73 and TLS=1008), Hassan, M.K. (TC=67 and TLS=1031), Gomber, P. (TC=57 and TLS=111), Zetzsche, D.A. (TC=53 and TLS=885), Khan, S. (TC=52 and TLS=747), Klapper, L. (TC=50 and TLS=376), Demirguc-Kunt, A. (TC=49 and TLS=287) and Hockett, R. (TC=47 and TLS=0). It can be concluded that, based on number of citations and also based on total link strength, Buckley, R.P. is found to be top author in "Sustainable Fintech" research.

## 4.16 Bibliographic Coupling Authors

In this section an attempt has been made to identify the bibliometric coupling between the authors' documents in slow fashion research. In this analysis, from the table 10, there are six authors identified as top authors in bibliometric coupling i.e. Rabbani M.R. (Total Documents=6, Total Citations=118, Average Citations=19.67, and Total Link Strength (TSL)=338), followed by Hassan M.K.(TD=5, TC=78, AC=15.60, TLS=498), Abdulla Y.(TD=3, TC=16, AC=5.33, TLS=96), Anshari M. (TD=3, TC=71, AC=23.67, TLS=3), Arner D.W.(TD=3, TC=103, AC=34.33, TLS=691), Buckley R.P. (TD=3, TC=103, AC=34.33, TLS=691), Khan S. (TD=3, TC=29, AC=9.67, TLS=268), Legowo M.B. (TD=3, TC=9, AC=3.00, TLS=188),

Subanidja S. (TD=3, TC=9, AC=3.00, TLS=188) and Zetzsche D.A. (TD=3, TC=98, AC=32.67, TLS=698). It can be concluded that basing on documents and citations Rabbani M.R., Arner D.W. and BuckleyR.P.are identified as top authors in bibliometric coupling.

*Table 9. Co-citation and cited authors*

| S.No. | Author | Citations (TC) | Total Link Strength (TLS) |
|---|---|---|---|
| 1 | Buckley, R.P. | 95 | 1191 |
| 2 | Arner, D.W. | 86 | 1084 |
| 3 | Rabbani, M.R. | 73 | 1008 |
| 4 | Hassan, M.K. | 67 | 1031 |
| 5 | Gomber, P. | 57 | 111 |
| 6 | Zetzsche, D.A. | 53 | 885 |
| 7 | Khan, S. | 52 | 747 |
| 8 | Klapper, L. | 50 | 376 |
| 9 | Demirguc-Kunt, A. | 49 | 287 |
| 10 | Hockett, R. | 47 | 0 |

*Figure 13. Co-citation and cited authors*

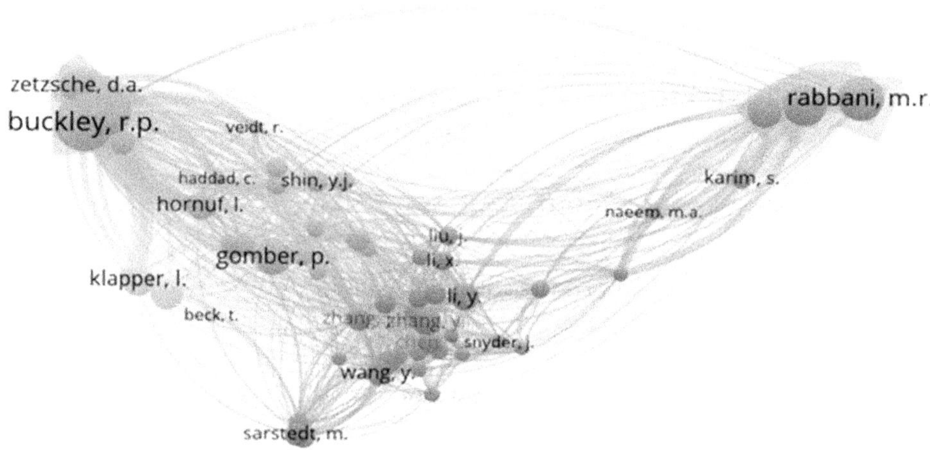

*Figure 14. Bibliometric coupling of authors*

*Table 10. Bibliometric coupling and authors*

| S.No. | Author | Documents (TD) | Citations (TC) | Total Link Strength (TSL) |
|---|---|---|---|---|
| 1 | Rabbani M.R. | 6 | 118 | 338 |
| 2 | Hassan M.K. | 5 | 78 | 249 |
| 3 | Abdulla Y. | 3 | 16 | 96 |
| 4 | Anshari M. | 3 | 71 | 3 |
| 5 | Arner D.W. | 3 | 103 | 691 |
| 6 | Buckley R.P. | 3 | 103 | 691 |
| 7 | Khan S. | 3 | 29 | 268 |
| 8 | Legowo M.B. | 3 | 9 | 188 |
| 9 | Subanidja S. | 3 | 9 | 188 |
| 10 | Zetzsche D.A. | 3 | 98 | 698 |

## 5. CONCLUSION

We presented a complete analysis and extremely general assessment of articles on the issue of sustainable Fintech up to April 2023 in this study. The first document was published in 2014. On average, 26.6 papers are published per year. Because there were few papers published during the early days of technological advancement, the value is high. This study item has been quoted in most studies that discuss rapid and slow trends and their elements or applications. It also pushes us to investigate the impact of sustainable Fintech on financial inclusion.

The results of this study are outlined below: It has been found that there are six years' publications, which happened in 2017, 2018, 2019, 2020, 2021 and 2022, respectively. The phenomenon explains why consumers are rethinking their stance on sustainable Fintech.Re-evaluation and change in sustainable Fintech are assessed by analysing opportunities and obstacles. The study of Sustainable Fintech has been enriched by a variety of research strands, including business economics, social sciences, and psychology. These research topics and keywords primarily address blockchain, sustainable development, financial inclusion, sustainability, financial technology, sustainable development goals, sustainable finance, artificial intelligence, covid-19, green finance, technology, innovation, etc.These studies involve all over the world, the China dominates, followed by India, Malaysia, USA, UK, Bahrain and Indonesia. For the citations, the China has the greatest number (358) followed by UK (207), etc. Next, From The Top Influential Institutions, Such as University Brunei Darussalam (9), Computational Social Science (6), Shanghai (6), Xi'an Jiaotong University (6), Guangdong University of Foreign Studies (5), And Jeju National University (5). The main research themes, such as sustainable Fintech and financial services are clear. It was also discovered that studies published in various institutions and journals all highlight current research hotspots in this field.

On the other hand, this research shows that network is still another important factor influencing the outcomes of successes in this domain. Learning new information from specialists in many professions leads to the improvement of several industries. Overall, the findings of this paper will be useful to future academics interested in sustainable Fintech. However, the material may need to be improved in the future because the data presented in this study is limited to the Scopus database and the searching phrase may not be sufficient. New discoveries will be introduced into Sustainable Fintech on a regular basis to remedy its shortcomings and weaknesses. We'll collect the products and focus more on the reform.

## 6. LIMITATIONS

A variety of factors limit the ability to generalize from this study. Initially, it was restricted to the Scopus database. As discussed in the methodology section, there are numerous benefits to doing so, including exceptional breadth and quality considerations. Nonetheless, even when the journal is covered, certain journals and some journal publications are not included in the Scopus database. To enhance the number of seminal works and mitigate the effects of this constraint, we employed Google Scholar to conduct completeness checks. Nonetheless, we did not include them in the analysis in any other way to aid replication of the study.

A second constraint is the search's specific parameters. Our goal was to assemble a collection of studies on Sustainable Fintech that has been published in peer-reviewed journals. To do this, we employed the search phrases "Sustainable" and "Fintech" in the titles, abstracts, or keywords of the papers. The Scopus search engine was quite accurate, returning just a small number of conference papers, book chapters, non-English articles, and off-topic publications that were readily removed. This will also hide a few publications made before the word "sustainable Fintech" became the preferred name for these types of studies. Although we chose to be specific in learning what is already known about sustainable Fintech, researchers interested in related topics may wish to expand our research.

## REFERENCES


Aaker, D., & Keller, K. (1990). Consumer evaluations of brand extensions. *Journal of Marketing*, *54*(1), 27–41. doi:10.1177/002224299005400102

Alshater, M. M., Atayah, O. F., & Khan, A. (2022). What do we know about business and economics research during COVID-19: A bibliometric review? *Economic Research-EkonomskaIstraživanja*, *35*(1), 1884–1912. doi:10.1080/1331677X.2021.1927786

Alwi, S., Alpandi, R. M., Salleh, M. N. M., & Najihah, I. (2019). An empirical study on the customers' satisfaction on Fintech mobile payment services in Malaysia. *International Journal of Advanced Science and Technology*, *28*(16), 390–400.

Ardic, O. P., Heimann, M., & Mylenko, N. (2011). Access to financial services and the financial inclusion agenda around the world: a cross-country analysis with a new data set. *Policy Research working paper; no. WPS 5537*. World Bank. https://openknowledge. worldbank.org/bitstream/handle/10986/3310/WPS5537.pdf?sequence51&isAllowed5y

Arslan, H. M., Chengang, Y., Siddique, M., & Yahya, Y. (2022). Influence of senior executive's characteristics on corporate environmental disclosures: A bibliometric analysis. *Journal of Risk and Financial Management*, *15*(3), 136. doi:10.3390/jrfm15030136

Campanella, F., Serino, L., Crisci, A., & D'Ambra, A. (2021). The role of corporate governance in environmental policy disclosure and sustainable development. Generalized estimating equations in longitudinal count data analysis. *Corporate Social Responsibility and Environmental Management*, *28*(1), 474–484. doi:10.1002/csr.2062

Cen, T., & He, R. (2018). Fintech, green finance and sustainable development. In *Proceedings of the 2018 International Conference on Management, Economics, Education, Arts and Humanities (MEEAH 2018)*. Atlantis Press.

Christensen, C. (2013). *The Innovator's Dilemma: When New Technologies Cause Great Firms to Fail*. Harvard Business Review Press.

Chueca Vergara, C., & Ferruz Agudo, L. (2021). Fintech and sustainability: Do they affect each other? *Sustainability*, *13*(13), 7012. doi:10.3390u13137012

Deng, X., Huang, Z., & Cheng, X. (2019). FinTech and sustainable development: Evidence from China based on P2P data. *Sustainability*, *11*(22), 6434. doi:10.3390u11226434

Gomber, P., Koch, J. A., & Siering, M. (2017). Digital Finance and Fintech: Current research and future research directions. *Journal of Business Economics*, *87*(5), 537–550. doi:10.100711573-017-0852-x

Hommel, K., & Bican, P. M. (2020). Digital entrepreneurship in finance: Fintechs and funding decision criteria. *Sustainability*, *12*(19), 8035. doi:10.3390u12198035

Kabulova, J., & Stankevičienė, J. (2020). Valuation of fintech innovation based on patent applications. *Sustainability*, *12*(23), 10158. doi:10.3390u122310158

Khan, I., Khan, I., Sayal, A. U., & Khan, M. Z. (2022). Does financial inclusion induce poverty, income inequality, and financial stability: Empirical evidence from the 54 African countries? *Journal of Economic Studies (Glasgow, Scotland)*, *49*(2), 303–314. doi:10.1108/JES-07-2020-0317

KPMG. (2022). *The Pulse of Fintech 2022*. KPMG. https://assets.kpmg/content/dam/kpmg/xx/ pdf/2018/07/h1--2018-pulse-of-fintech.pdf (accessed on 26 Aprilr 2023).

Leong, K., & Sung, A. (2018). Fintech (financial technology): What is it and how to use technologies to create business value in fintech way? *International Journal of Innovation, Management and Technology*, *9*(2), 74–78. doi:10.18178/ijimt.2018.9.2.791

Moed, H. F., Markusova, V., & Akoev, M. (2018). Trends in Russian research output indexed in Scopus and Web of Science. *Scientometrics*, *116*(2), 1153–1180. doi:10.100711192-018-2769-8

Montoya, F. G., Alcayde, A., Baños, R., & Manzano-Agugliaro, F. (2018). A fast method for identifying worldwide scientific collaborations using the Scopus database. *Telematics and Informatics*, *35*(1), 168–185. doi:10.1016/j.tele.2017.10.010

Olowookere, D. (2019). Role of fintech in accelerating financial inclusion in Nigeria. *Business Post Nigeria*. https://businesspost.ng/featureoped/role-of-fintech-in-acceleratingfinancial-inclusion-in-nigeria/

Ozili, P. K. (2021). Financial inclusion research around the world: A review. *The Forum for Social Economics*, *50*(4), 457–479. doi:10.1080/07360932.2020.1715238

Phan, D. H. B., Narayan, P. K., Rahman, R. E., & Hutabarat, A. R. (2020). Do financial technology firms influence bank performance? *Pacific-Basin Finance Journal*, *20*, 1–13. doi:10.1016/j.pacfin.2019.101210

Schueffel, P. (2016). Taming the beast: A scientific definition of fintech. *Journal of Innovation Management*, *4*(4), 32–54. doi:10.24840/2183-0606_004.004_0004

Singh, V. K., Singh, P., Karmakar, M., Leta, J., & Mayr, P. (2021). The journal coverage of Web of Science, Scopus and Dimensions: A comparative analysis. *Scientometrics*, *126*(6), 5113–5142. doi:10.100711192-021-03948-5

Zhang-Zhang, Y., Rohlfer, S., & Rajasekera, J. (2020). An eco-systematic view of cross-sector fintech: The case of Alibaba and Tencent. *Sustainability*, *12*(21), 8907. doi:10.3390u12218907

# Chapter 15
# Exploring the Interconnection of FinTech and Climate Sustainability:
## Scoping Through a Qualitative Methodology

**Sreelekshmi G.**
https://orcid.org/0000-0002-0114-1951
*University of Kerala, India*

**Biju A. V.**
https://orcid.org/0000-0001-5583-6495
*University of Kerala, India*

## ABSTRACT

*The escalating climate catastrophe has made climate-sustainable development indispensable, the success of which relies on the sustainable adoption of innovative ideas and technologies. Against this backdrop, the FinTech industry saw the emergence of a novel FinTech model with a climate action motive, known as climate FinTech or green FinTech. This chapter contributes to the scanty climate FinTech literature by providing insights on the state of the art using an inductive qualitative methodology comprising a literature review, case research on Indian climate FinTech, and sentiment analysis of climate FinTech tweets. The chapter puts forward suggestions for the growth of the market, and the future implications. The results suggest that the climate FinTech landscape is made up of a multitude of business types and activities and this innovative yet impactful FinTech model is a promising proposition for countering climate catastrophe, especially using blockchain technology.*

DOI: 10.4018/979-8-3693-0008-4.ch015

## 1. INTRODUCTION

Sustainability has become our prime focus ever since the adoption of the 2030 agenda by the United Nations (UN) in 2015, which seeks to achieve sustainable development in its three dimensions, namely, economic, social, and environmental, in a balanced and integrated manner (United Nations, 2015). Decision-making should take into account the interdependencies and trade-offs of all three pillars to ensure that the development pathways adopted guarantee a sustainable future (Mensah, 2019). In the last few years, the rapidly growing climate emergency has risked environmental health, raising apprehensions over sustainability in the long run. Both human and planetary well-being is in peril (IPCC, 2022a), leading to escalated risks, uncertainty, and costs, reduced productivity, and resulting in rising sea levels and carbon pricing, brutally affecting the food and energy sector, the realty sector, and many others (Hong et al., 2020). The reckoning is at hand and any further delay in action may cause irreversible and collateral damage to the people and society.

Nordhaus (2018) says that the 2°C targets of the 2015 Paris Climate Accord need the support of significant policy initiatives—extensive planning and institutional frameworks aid in combating climate change (Fuso Nerini et al., 2019). However, the funding bottleneck could stymie climate action. There is a growing gap in the current global financial flows and there is a high chance that the adverse climate crisis impedes national economic development, further increasing the financial constraints for adaptation, especially in developing and least-developed countries (IPCC, 2023). Thus, it is crucial that we seek alternative modes of climate finance for a just transition, and technology could be a driver in this feat.

The application of technology to finance, popularly called FinTech, has brought drastic transformation, with segments such as digital investment solutions, payment and lending solutions, blockchain, cryptocurrencies, RegTech, InsurTech, etc. A vast majority of these FinTech market segments have risen in prominence globally, with double-digit growth rates in many countries (Stolbov & Shchepeleva, 2023). The Green Digital Finance Alliance (GDFA) and the Swiss Green FinTech Network, with the support of the Swiss State Secretariat for International Finance (SIF), in their green FinTech taxonomy released in 2022, which is the first of its kind in the world talks about three stages of FinTech evolution. Digitised versions of already prevalent financial products like digital payment, wealth management, and lending solutions led the first wave. In contrast, innovations like programmable utility tokens or security token offerings led to the second one. The third wave saw the onset of solutions that leverage FinTech for environmental good (GDFA, 2022). They are known as green FinTech, a portmanteau of green finance and FinTech. They could be alternatively called climate FinTech as the climate crisis has become the cardinal green concern. In sum, green FinTech or climate FinTech is a FinTech solution based on data analytics, artificial intelligence (AI), Internet of Things (IoT), blockchain, etc., with novel business models that aid in environmental conservation.

Climate FinTech may include platforms for green investments, green bonds, crowdfunding, emissions trading, carbon footprint reduction, ESG (Environmental, Social, and Governance) data provision, planting plants and trees and forests, wooden smartcards, etc. Doconomy, Ant Forest, Paygreen, and FNZ are some of the top climate FinTech solutions (GDFA, 2022). Though climate FinTech solutions are rising in number, the research is yet to gain scholarly attention. To bridge this gap, this chapter is an attempt to examine the progress and the prospects of the concept and applications of climate FinTech, using a qualitative methodology. This is expected to aid in the awareness of innovative opportunities for environment enthusiasts and climate activists, aid investors in comparison with peers, and identify alternative business opportunities and investment options for profit-oriented investors.

This research follows an inductive qualitative approach based on a step-by-step design for qualitative research by Merriam (1998): beginning with a literature review, then constructing a theoretical framework, problem identification, the definition of the research questions, and sample selection by purposive sampling. The authors explore the climate FinTech concept using the literature, case analysis on climate FinTech solutions, and sentiment analysis. This chapter presents an overall view of climate FinTech in theory and practice focusing on India, an emerging country with an emerging climate FinTech market. Although global markets show enhanced progress, the state-of-the-art remains nascent in India. In essence, this chapter contributes to the existing knowledge on climate FinTech by synthesising the relevant literature and examining the practical applications and public response to the field.

To provide a holistic view of climate FinTech, the chapter is structured as follows. Section 2 provides an account of the literature on climate FinTech by thoroughly examining the factors that make up the concept. The methodology of the study is briefed in Section 3. Section 4 comprises the results and discussion. Section 5 presents the conclusion and final remarks of the chapter.

## 2. LITERATURE REVIEW

### 2.1. Finance for Sustainability

Sustainable development demands an efficient, sustainable finance model leveraging the public and private financial systems that interpenetrate and complement each other (Ziolo et al., 2020). Migliorelli (2021) opines that sustainable finance is synonymous with "finance for sustainability" and is defined as "finance to support sectors or activities that contribute to achieving or improving at least one of the relevant sustainability dimensions". It promotes both ecological and social well-being (Pástor et al., 2021). The most significant subsets within the ambit of sustainability include SDG finance, green finance, and climate finance (Migliorelli, 2021). Green finance is the financial flows aimed at accomplishing environment and climate-related SDGs. In contrast, climate finance is a component of green finance concentrating on climate action or reducing greenhouse gas emissions (Lindenberg, 2014). The critical conundrum brought by climate change and global warming makes climate finance significant for sustainable development. However, financing the huge climate action gap continues to challenge world governments (Fankhauser et al., 2016).

In 2009, the $100 billion goal a year for climate action, to be mobilised from developed countries, was adopted at the 15th Conference of Parties (COP 15) of the United Nations Framework Convention on Climate Change (UNFCCC). The 2015 Paris Agreement also required its signatories to provide "finance flows consistent with a pathway toward low greenhouse gas emissions and climate-resilient development." The COP 27 of 2022 witnessed another significant stride toward climate justice with the agreement to set up a loss and damage compensation fund. India also unveiled a Long-Term Low Emission Development Strategy at COP 27. It is argued that these conventional financing initiatives would compensate the island nations and developing countries that have been disproportionately hit by the climate disaster, in line with the argument of moral responsibility of the Global North to the Global South. In the context of the Global South, aspirational views of climate finance as a justice tool and game changer are severely questioned (Anantharajah & Setyowati, 2022).

Despite an upward trend in globally tracked climate finance, a vast majority of funding that primarily comes from public sources is utilised for mitigation, whereas adaptation financing is meagre (IPCC, 2023). Climate-resilient development is largely financed by intergovernmental and philanthropic contributions (Schalatek, 2012). The Organisation for Economic Co-operation and Development (OECD) report on climate finance shows that developed nations' $100 billion commitment still needs to be met (OECD, 2022). The scale of the crisis makes it difficult for the public sector to meet the enormous financial pre-requisite. Wüstenhagen and Menichetti (2012) found private capital outlay to be indispensable for climate action earlier. Bhandary et al. (2021) say that climate finance policies should have environmental and economic advantages and capital mobilisation adequacy. Feed-in tariffs, tax credits, loan guarantees, and national development banks have effectively mobilised private capital. In contrast, national climate funds, green bonds, and targeted lending and disclosure policies could have been more effective (Bhandary et al., 2021). In essence, the role of existing arrangements is praiseworthy but needs to be improved.

Aside from the numerous scientific studies that have been conducted, social science research may enable us to use economic and political systems for climate action (Nordhaus, 2011). Stroebel and Wurgler (2021) find that as the climate emergency escalates, so does climate finance research. Long et al. (2022) found a significant increase in publications in recent years, with the peak of interest in the topic occurring after 2017 due to the Paris Climate Accord. Climate finance research in the future is critical to channelling finances toward action against global warming, the ever-increasing sea levels, and the disrupted natural flow of our systems.

## 2.2. Leveraging FinTech for Climate Action

The conventional financial system saw a radical revolution with technology adoption (Lee & Shin, 2018). The use of technology in trading and risk management surged following the 2008 global financial crisis, and technologies like Artificial Intelligence (AI), blockchain, cloud computing, and big data have become the "ABCD" of FinTech (Lai et al., 2020). Gomber et al. (2018) found the growth of FinTech to have drastically transformed the functioning of financial systems, resulting in efficient, informed, and customer-oriented businesses. The global FinTech industry is booming with innovative solutions resulting from better network connectivity and ease of use.

A major chunk of literature speaks about the sustainability aspects of FinTech, which leverage agile technologies to deliver efficient financial services. FinTech can contribute to sustainability by improved financial inclusion (Arner et al., 2020; Goldstein et al., 2019), reduced emissions, environmental threats, and a greener economy (Awais et al., 2023). When technology is leveraged for sustainable finance, it is known as sustainable FinTech. The potentiality of this interlinkage is vital for the developed and developing alike (Abad-Segura et al., 2020). This impactful interlinkage of FinTech and sustainability has opened wide doors for attaining sustainability in all three dimensions: environmental, social, and economic. The nexus between environmental sustainability and FinTech lays the foundation for climate FinTech.

The financial sector is widely considered more environmentally sustainable (Mumtaz & Yoshino, 2021); hence, the FinTech sector would rank even higher in terms of environmental sustainability when compared to its conventional counterparts. The potential of leveraging FinTech for climate action presents an innovative opportunity for effective climate action. It contributes to emissions reductions (Muganyi et al., 2021) and the green energy sector (Chiu et al., 2021). Nassiry (2018) presents a nexus between FinTech and green finance, including the decentralisation of energy markets, carbon credits, and innovative financial instruments for climate finance. The blockchain application could facilitate transparent, standardised transactions, improvements in monitoring and accreditation processes, coordination of stakeholders, and impact assessment (Schulz & Feist, 2021). It sheds light on the need to dive deeper into the nexus between FinTech and green finance and what constitutes green FinTech.

In the case of India, the FinTech market has been booming with the onset of enhanced internet connectivity, a tech-savvy population, and a surge in digital adoption driven by the pandemic (EY, 2022). The JAM (Jan Dhan Yojana, Aadhaar, and Mobile) trio fuelled India's exploding FinTech industry even further. Migozzi et al. (2023) suggest the development of FinTech as a state-supported, tech-driven "Tech-Fin-State" ecosystem has been enabled and moulded by the export-oriented information and communication technology (ICT) sector, the implementation of large-scale, open digital public infrastructures (DPI), and enabling regulatory frameworks. Nenavath (2022) finds that India's green financing policies and development of FinTech lead to significant emissions reduction, urging the policymakers to support FinTech for environmental quality protection ingenuity and promote green consumption.

## 2.3. From FinTech to Climate FinTech

With new, possibly disruptive technologies and practices, climate-driven innovation in industry and finance can help adapt to and limit global warming to 1.5 °C (IPCC, 2018). In this respect, the possibility of a novel FinTech model with a climate action motive, known as climate FinTech or green FinTech, garnered entrepreneurial attention. The sole difference between climate FinTech and FinTech is this greener end goal. The means are more or less similar as they also leverage advanced technologies like AI, IoT, machine learning (ML), blockchain, data analytics, etc., for their functioning. The literature exclusively on green FinTech is small but emerging. Most of the studies have researched isolated aspects; thus, a comprehensive outlook on the concept is yet to be made (Puschmann et al., 2020).

Macchiavello and Siri (2020) outlined the potential interconnections between FinTech and sustainable finance, which include the detection and prevention of greenwashing, green crowdfunding, applications of distributed ledger technology (DLT) like blockchain, integration of blockchain with smart contracts and big data, integration of DLT with AI for disclosure and benchmarking in the climate finance market, etc. As per Taghizadeh-Hesary and Yoshino (2019), DLTs increase confidence and reduce risk, by increasing transparency, traceability, and auditability, encouraging private sector involvement in green finance and investment. Despite finding applications for green FinTech, Macchiavello and Siri share concerns about high energy consumption, hardware and software product requirements, systemic and cyber risks, data security, accessibility, portability, interoperability, granular segmentation, financial exclusion, and inaccurate algorithms leading to wrongful assessments. Pee and Pan (2022) opine that FinTech, as the digital economy's powerhouse, has a plethora of climate-related applications that enable responsible investing and financing. Besides, for decision-making in climate FinTech, the role of information researchers in augmented intelligence is significant.

Start-ups are largely dominating in the climate FinTech area. They have been at the forefront rather than the incumbents, focusing on tech-enabled innovations. In contrast, incumbents such as banks and other financial institutions have concentrated their efforts on investing in similar startups and projects (Puschmann et al., 2020). Puschmann et al. identify robo-advisors for sustainable investments, payment tokens for peer-to-peer energy networks, and blockchain solutions for sustainable supply chains as green FinTech solutions and provides a concept map of green FinTech. They opine that the concept needs to be defined, and a framework for a multi-case study setting is yet to be developed. Kabaklarlı (2022) studied cryptocurrencies specifically as an area within the field of green FinTech. Green FinTech has the potential to manage many people using technologies like extensive data analysis, IoT, and ML without charging additional costs. However, they share concerns about the energy requirements like Macchiavello and Siri (2020). The crypto miners rely on unsustainable energies such as coal, which leads to high carbon dioxide and other greenhouse gas emissions, highlighting the need to transition to sustainable alternatives like solar, wind, and geothermal.

Many FinTech definitions and classifications have been developed. The world's first green FinTech classification, launched by GDFA, was formulated considering the various FinTech classifications, including the FinTech classification by the Bank of International Settlements and other FinTech reports. It proposes eight green FinTech categories, which include green digital payment and account solutions, green digital investment solutions, digital ESG-data and -analytics solutions, green digital crowdfunding, and syndication platforms, green digital risk analysis and insure-tech solutions, green digital deposit and lending solutions, green digital asset solutions, and green RegTech solutions (GDFA, 2022). This chapter primarily focuses on the two climate FinTech categories in the case study: green digital investment solutions, and digital ESG data and analytics solutions.

Green digital investment solutions are FinTech solutions that aid investing in eco-friendly projects. The concept in its traditional form is mainly in the form of sustainability investing, ESG investing, impact investing, etc. It assists non-profit organizations in achieving their financial goals and profit organizations in ensuring socially responsible behaviour (Wilburn & Wilburn, 2014). However, the role of technology in such financial services still needs to be studied. Green digital investments combine technology with such conventional concepts. In contrast, digital ESG data and analytics solutions are ESG data providers that enable entities to achieve sustainability compliance. They aid in sustainability and impact investing. Although they show promising prospects, greenwashing remains a concern for impact investing, whether digital or not. Chueca Vergara and Ferruz Agudo (2021) suggest standardisation to eliminate greenwashing. Coordination, scrutiny, cross-listing, and, most importantly, the initiative among ESG data providers and improved stock exchange guidelines all have critical roles to play (Kotsantonis & Serafeim, 2019; Yu et al., 2020). The lack of adequate standards hampers data uniformity and reliability (Amir & Serafeim, 2018; Siew, 2015), which further impacts the adoption of ESG in decision-making (Huang et al., 2021). Although Papoutsi and Sodhi (2020) found sustainability reports to be a true depiction of actual sustainability performance, greenwashing is a concern as the sustainability reports are not audited (Yu et al., 2020).

Although scholarly interest in this area has grown, relevant studies still need more rigour. This knowledge gap in the interconnection of FinTech and green finance warrants future research (Wang et al., 2021), which this study addresses. Based on these theoretical underpinnings discussed, this chapter attempts to better comprehend the concept of climate FinTech and its possibilities for sustainable development. The authors have specifically focused on green digital investment, digital ESG data and analytics solutions, and the overall implications of climate FinTech.

## 3. METHODOLOGY

### 3.1. Case Design

A case study typically adopts a triangulation approach using multiple sources of evidence and can be exploratory, explanatory, or descriptive (Yin, 2009). The present study has centred on an explorative method focusing on theory building. An exploratory case study with multiple cases of climate FinTech in India was undertaken to draw insights into the concept of climate FinTech and its progress in India. Although case study design widely differs (Yazan, 2015) as per the research questions and objectives, it typically comprises an intensive study of the nature, background, physical setting, and other institutional and political factors. It is a study in depth rather than breadth. Moreover, the presentation should invite the reader to join in case discovery (Ebneyamini & Sadeghi Moghadam, 2018).

#### 3.1.1. Selection Criteria and Rationale

Yin (1994) suggests that a case study can be used to investigate situations in which the intervention being evaluated does not have a clear set of outcomes. The preliminary analysis reveals green FinTech as a growing area globally, still, the field is in nascency in India. As any novel model would certainly involve associated uncertainties, case study research at this juncture could be beneficial. It is widely used in social entrepreneurship and impact investing research. The lack of a formal dataset on climate FinTech motivated the authors to resort to the purposive sampling technique.

The study by Puschmann et al. (2020) used the following criteria to select green FinTech solutions for analysis, which included (1) it facilitates a customer's interaction with a financial institution or a non-financial institution, (2) it is linked to a customer process in financial services (advisory, payments, investments, financing, non-life insurance, underwriting, claims management, and cross-processes) and/or has an indirect connection to financial services while being part of another industry's ecosystem (e.g., peer-to-peer (P2P) payment in energy networks), (3) it is enabled by information technology, and (4) it has an influence on one of the climate-related Sustainable Development Goals (SDGs), more notably SDGs 7, 11, 12, 13, 14, 15, and 17. In this study, the green FinTech classification by GDFA, released in 2022, has been leveraged to further refine the selection criteria for the case research. The previous literature insights were also used to frame the sample case selection criteria, as shown in Table 1.

*Table 1. Criteria used for selecting entities for case analysis*

| Sl. No. | Case Selection Criteria | Criteria Yes/No |
|---|---|---|
| (1) | the entity must be a tech-based financial sector enterprise working for environmental or climate action | Yes |
| (2) | it must be an Indian entity operational in India | Yes |
| (3) | it must be a green FinTech as per the green FinTech categories in the GDFA's taxonomy | Yes |

Those entities that fulfilled the criteria and were assessable under the study were included in the sample and thus covered three climate FinTech: Pyse and Climate Angels, two green digital investment solutions, and a digital ESG data and analytics solution, ESGDS.

### 3.1.2. Data and Analysis

Secondary data has been used for case analysis, accessed from the official documentation of the climate FinTech firms, other information, and resources provided on their websites, newsletters, social media activities and interactions, and news articles. Approaches include data reduction, display, explanation building, content analysis, cross-case analysis, etc. Yin (1994) has prescribed the tactics that could be employed to secure reliability and validity in case study research, some of which were resorted to. First, a case study protocol with multiple cases was followed. All possible data sources and chains of evidence were examined at the data collection point and an explanation-building approach was used in the data analysis phase.

### 3.2. Twitter Sentiments Analysis

For analysing public sentiments in the area, sentiment analysis, a text-mining technique whereby subjective knowledge is extracted from text using natural language processing (NLP) and text analytics (Hussein, 2018; Medhat et al., 2014) was employed, which helped validate the literature and the case study outcomes. Social media is significant in unveiling public sentiments (Drus & Khalid, 2019), which cannot be fetched from conventional quantitative data. Among the many platforms, the data from Twitter was used as it allows for analysing sentiments across time and space, as geotagged tweets include timestamps and geographic coordinates. The tweets were retrieved using the keywords “climate finance” and “climate FinTech”, and the analysis has been done with MaxQDA, a popular software tool for qualitative analysis.

## 4. RESULTS

### 4.1. Case Study Findings

The case study results imply that the characteristics of FinTech apply to climate FinTech as well. It is difficult to draw a differentiation between both as many of the FinTech solutions are found to be environmentally sustainable, irrespective of their prime goal. Furthermore, the climate FinTech landscape is made up of a variety of business models that involve a variety of activities. The case study results show that they all differ in terms of the means to achieve their goals, but the end goal is climate sustainability. They may range from digital investment, data provision, and analytics to crowdfunding, digital lending, and so on.

The key characteristics of the three climate FinTech solutions assessed are briefed in Table 2.

Most of the investor-customers of these digital investment platforms are climate activists, showing their positive sentiments towards climate FinTech. Pyse makes sustainable investing accessible to the ordinary public by reducing investment ticket sizes, which were confined to an expensive niche segment. Climate Angels, on the other hand, brings ease to investing by providing opportunities to invest along with the experienced. Both contribute to hassle-free sustainability adherence and carbon footprint reduction, leading to the democratization of impact investing and climate action. This further leads to the confidence and empowerment of people in their contribution to environmental health. Furthermore, the possibility of enhanced individual involvement by digitalising green investments heightens this. The analysis of ESGDS suggests that ESG data and reporting have excellent prospects in mainstreaming sustainable investments by the prevention and detection

*Table 2. Climate FinTech in India studied using the case study approach*

| Climate FinTech | Category | Case Description | Key Features | Key Outcome |
|---|---|---|---|---|
| **Pyse** | Green Digital Investment Solutions | Pyse FinTech Private Limited is a for-profit, private company working to bridge the gap between green projects needing financing and investors looking to deliver impact with returns. They provide a sustainable digital investment platform where users access verified deals through a simple, hassle-free mechanism, ensuring returns and liquidity. | ● profit-centric impact investment platform<br>● Smaller ticket sizes and fractional investments<br>● Assures returns from sustainability investing<br>● Risk reduction and liquidity provisions are guaranteed | Inclusiveness in impact investing |
| **Climate Angels** | Green Digital Investment Solutions | Climate Angels is a VC fund promoting promising climate tech start-ups at their pre-revenue stage needing access to finance. They do not charge fees on startups. Investors can invest along with experienced and angel investors. As they manage legal compliance, vet the deals before they are listed, and provide quarterly updates to investors, they offer frictionless investment. | ● Cleantech VC fund<br>● Impact investing along with the experienced<br>● Friction-free investment<br>● Startup-friendly business model<br>● Focus on Climate tech | Hassle-free impact investment |
| **ESGDS** | Digital ESG-Data and Analytics Solutions | ESGDS provides tools for creating custom assessments that are aligned with organizational use cases. It offers ESG data and analytical tools, assessment models, and a SaaS platform for interpreting and integrating ESG in risk assessments, scrip selection, performance monitoring, and issuer engagement. Their platform, designed specifically for ESG analytics, is built on a glass box model, allowing for complete customization via the front end. It acts as an ESG database for institutional investors, asset managers, and investment banks and helps in custom corporate and portfolio assessments. | ● Provision of ESG data in compliance with multiple regulations<br>● Greater data provenance and transparency using 'click to source' option<br>● Based on a glass box model where every aspect of the model could be customised using the front end<br>● Monitoring corporate and project performance<br>● Portfolio management platform | Combat green washing |

of greenwashing using technology. The bottlenecks include a need for more standardisation and continuous monitoring and innovation to tackle innovative ways of greenwashing.

The case research highlights the strengths of climate FinTech which include transparency, inclusiveness, reduced costs, and risks, a large market size, and knowledge sharing without the limitations of geography. In contrast, their limitations include greenwashing, data quality concerns, and a lack of regulation. In India, the focus has been on making green FinTech inclusive. The findings indicate that the climate FinTech landscape is on the verge of becoming a goldmine consequent to increased sustainability adherence. Besides, the tensions from fossil fuel depletion and climate extremes have made the market grow.

## 4.2. Insights from Sentiment Analysis

The overall sentiment analysis results show climate finance and climate FinTech as promising areas, as per the opinions of Twitter users, as shown in Figures 1 and 2.

The analysis of sentiments projects that the overall public views are highly positive, which could be evidence of the high prospects of both concepts in the future. In Figure 1, the first diagram shows the sentiments on "climate finance", which are 9% positive, 30% slightly positive, the majority, i.e., 38% neutral, 21% slightly negative, and only 2% have negative sentiments towards "climate finance". The second graph shows that 12% are positive, the majority, i.e., 49%, are slightly positive, 28% are neutral, and only 8% and 2% have slightly negative and negative sentiments towards 'climate FinTech'. Thus, there has been a largely positive sentiment among the public regarding climate finance and FinTech, with climate FinTech garnering more promising public attention.

Figure 2 provides a glimpse of the public discussions with the frequency of hashtags used. This shows the topics most discussed by the public on social media about the given keywords. The most frequently used hashtag related to climate finance is #climatecrisis followed by #cop27, whereas those related to climate FinTech are #FinTech and #ai. Thus, most tweets discussed the climate crisis and FinTech. This demonstrates the significance that the public has placed on climate catastrophe. The share of #FinTech in the climate FinTech graph shows that the public has been interested in linking FinTech with the climate.

*Figure 1. Sentiments towards 'climate finance' and 'climate FinTech'*

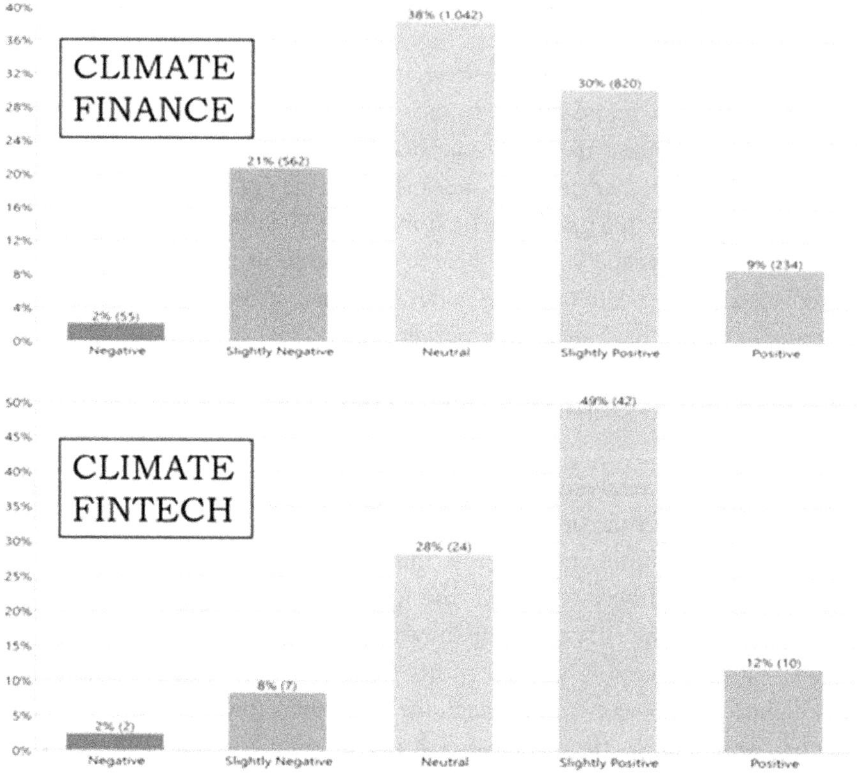


*Figure 2. Most frequently used hashtags on 'climate finance' and 'climate FinTech'*

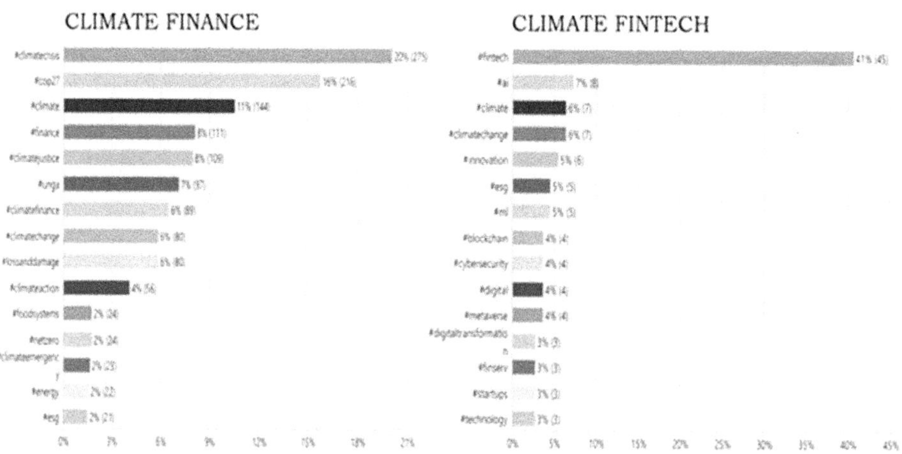

## 5. CONCLUSION

This study aimed to understand the application of FinTech for climate action. The literature review provided insights into the concept in general, whereas the case analysis presented the Indian context. The sentiment analysis indicates positive public sentiments on the same. Thus, the study finds the climate FinTech model as an effective climate crisis solution in the making. Hinson et al. (2019) opine that it will aid inclusive business. The global climate FinTech markets have been showing promising prospects. Unlike the European and Western markets, the field is only at its initial stages in India. India's recent sustainability developments bring a ray of hope for the climate FinTech market. The market in India is about to emerge as a significant segment in the FinTech landscape for environmentally conscious users. In sum, it is conclusive that the FinTech sector boom will continue and that climate FinTech will undoubtedly have a share in the market. Future research could focus on the other green FinTech categories excluded from the study, or replication can be made in other countries with nascent climate FinTech markets.

### 5.1. Suggestions

This article concludes that the climate FinTech model is a highly promising proposition for countering climate catastrophe. The area will advance in the future provided adequate policy support is taken. Climate FinTech, as a category among various business models, needs to be appropriately marketed. Business incubation programmes can help such start-ups by providing the necessary support for their advancement. The role of government in promoting novel business ideas needs to be understood and utilised. Moreover, joint efforts by academics, industry, and the government would benefit in creating a knowledge base on the topic. Above all, the responsibility for climate action should never be confined to the government alone. It is equally the responsibility of the enlightened public.

### 5.2. Limitations of the Study

The study is limited to an exploratory design. A qualitative methodology was adopted because a quantitative approach was infeasible. The case study could include only two categories of green FinTech. The dependency on the sentimental analysis results is also limited due to the fewer tweets on the topic and the limited time frame (Saura et al., 2019). All these may have hindered a comprehensive confirmatory study, which marks future research opportunities as the field progresses.

## 5.3. Final Remarks

This chapter suggests the potentiality of green FinTech in financial inclusion and enhancing transparency more efficiently than conventional green financial systems and institutions. The climate FinTech concept contributes to carbon neutrality and sustainable development. Despite its great capabilities, the scalability of the concept is an area of concern. As per IPCC (2022b), leveraging digital technology for decarbonisation must be appropriately governed. Thus, the implementation and regulatory aspects need to be enhanced. In sum, the concept's scholarly interest, regulatory aspects, and adoption rate must improve.

The Indian climate FinTech arena remains promising as the global inclination towards ESG adoption and rising demand for purpose-driven business is evident in the Indian markets too. The Jan Dhan Yojana, the India Stack, the rollout of Central Bank Digital Currency (CBDC), and other significant policy improvements and trends are expected to boost the industry further. Against the backdrop of India's G-20 presidency until November 2023, and the chairmanship of the Shanghai Cooperation Organisation (SCO) until September 2023, the agenda of sustainable development assumes greater importance for the country. This opportunity for both the host and all members could be used to rethink the global development path. The results suggest that the climate FinTech idea has excellent potential to contribute to the same meaningfully.

## REFERENCES

Abad-Segura, E., González-Zamar, M. D., López-Meneses, E., & Vázquez-Cano, E. (2020). Financial Technology: Review of trends, approaches and management. *Mathematics*, *8*(6), 951. doi:10.3390/math8060951

Amir, A. Z., & Serafeim, G. (2018). Why and how investors use ESG information: Evidence from a global survey. *Financial Analysts Journal*, *74*(3). doi:10.2469/faj.v74.n3.2

Anantharajah, K., & Setyowati, A. B. (2022). Beyond promises: Realities of climate finance justice and energy transitions in Asia and the Pacific. *Energy Research & Social Science*, *89*, 102550. doi:10.1016/j.erss.2022.102550

Arner, D. W., Buckley, R. P., Zetzsche, D. A., & Veidt, R. (2020). Sustainability, FinTech and Financial Inclusion. *European Business Organization Law Review*, *21*(1), 7–35. doi:10.100740804-020-00183-y

Bhandary, R. R., Gallagher, K. S., & Zhang, F. (2021). Climate finance policy in practice: A review of the evidence. *Climate Policy*, *21*(4), 529–545. doi:10.1080/14693062.2020.1871313

Chiu, W.-H., Lin, W. C., & Liang, C.-J. (2021). The Role of Green Finance in Community Renewable Energy Projects of main Region and Taiwan. *Lex Localis - Journal of Local Self-Government, 19*(3), 503–519. doi:10.4335/19.3.503-519(2021)

Chueca Vergara, C., & Ferruz Agudo, L. (2021). FinTech and Sustainability: Do They Affect Each Other? *Sustainability*, *13*(13), 7012. doi:10.3390u13137012

Drus, Z., & Khalid, H. (2019). Sentiment analysis in social media and its application: Systematic literature review. *Procedia Computer Science*, *161*, 707–714. doi:10.1016/j.procs.2019.11.174

Ebneyamini, S., & Sadeghi Moghadam, M. R. (2018). Toward Developing a Framework for Conducting Case Study Research. *International Journal of Qualitative Methods*, *17*(1). doi:10.1177/1609406918817954

EY. (2022). *The winds of change Trends shaping India's FinTech Sector: edition II*. EY.

Fankhauser, S., Sahni, A., Savvas, A., & Ward, J. (2016). Where are the gaps in climate finance? *Climate and Development*, *8*(3), 203–206. doi:10.1080/17565529.2015.1064811

Fuso Nerini, F., Sovacool, B., Hughes, N., Cozzi, L., Cosgrave, E., Howells, M., Tavoni, M., Tomei, J., Zerriffi, H., & Milligan, B. (2019). Connecting climate action with other Sustainable Development Goals. In Nature Sustainability, 2(8). doi:10.103841893-019-0334-y

GDFA. (2022). *Green FinTech Classification*. GDFA. https://www.greendigitalfinancealliance.org/initiatives/green-FinTech-classification

Goldstein, I., Jiang, W., & Karolyi, G. A. (2019). To FinTech and Beyond. *Review of Financial Studies*, *32*(5), 1647–1661. doi:10.1093/rfs/hhz025

Gomber, P., Kauffman, R. J., Parker, C., & Weber, B. W. (2018). On the FinTech Revolution: Interpreting the Forces of Innovation, Disruption, and Transformation in Financial Services. *Journal of Management Information Systems*, *35*(1), 220–265. doi:10.1080/07421222.2018.1440766

Hinson, R., Lensink, R., & Mueller, A. (2019). Transforming agribusiness in developing countries: SDGs and the role of FinTech. In *Current Opinion in Environmental Sustainability* (Vol. 41, pp. 1–9). Elsevier B.V. doi:10.1016/j.cosust.2019.07.002

Hong, H., Karolyi, G. A., & Scheinkman, J. A. (2020). Climate Finance. *Review of Financial Studies*, *33*(3), 1011–1023. doi:10.1093/rfs/hhz146

Huang, W. S., Karolyi, G. A., & Kwan, A. (2021). Paying Attention to ESG : Evidence from Big Data Analytics. *AFA, 607.*

Hussein, D. M. E.-D. M. (2018). A survey on sentiment analysis challenges. *Journal of King Saud University -. Engineering and Science*, *30*(4), 330–338. doi:10.1016/j.jksues.2016.04.002

IPCC. (2018). IPCC, 2018: Global Warming of 1.5°C. An IPCC Special Report. In In Press, 2.

IPCC. (2022a). Impacts, Adaptation and Vulnerability Working Group II Contribution to the Sixth Assessment Report of the Intergovernmental Panel on Climate Change. *Climatic Change.*

IPCC. (2022b). [Mitigation of Climate Change Working Group III Contribution to the Sixth Assessment Report of the Intergovernmental Panel on Climate Change.]. *Climatic Change*, •••, 2022.

IPCC. (2023). *Synthesis Report of The IPCC Sixth Assessment Report (AR6).* IPCC.

Kabaklarlı, E. (2022). Green FinTech: sustainability of Bitcoin. *Digital Finance, 4*(4), 265–273. 10.1007/S42521-022-00053-X

Kotsantonis, S., & Serafeim, G. (2019). Four Things No One Will Tell You About ESG Data. *Journal of Applied Corporate Finance*, *31*(2), 50–58. doi:10.1111/jacf.12346

Lai, T. L., Liao, S.-W., Wong, S. P. S., & Xu, H. (2020). Statistical models and stochastic optimization in financial technology and investment science. *Annals of Mathematical Sciences and Applications*, *5*(2), 317–345. doi:10.4310/AMSA.2020.v5.n2.a5

Lee, I., & Shin, Y. J. (2018). FinTech: Ecosystem, business models, investment decisions, and challenges. *Business Horizons*, *61*(1), 35–46. doi:10.1016/j.bushor.2017.09.003

Lindenberg, N. (2014). *Definition of green finance.*

Long, S., Lucey, B., Kumar, S., Zhang, D., & Zhang, Z. (2022). Climate finance: What we know and what we should know? *Journal of Climate Finance*, *1*, 100005. doi:10.1016/j.jclimf.2023.100005

Macchiavello, E., & Siri, M. (2020). *Sustainable Finance and FinTech: Can Technology Contribute to Achieving Environmental Goals? A Preliminary Assessment of 'Green FinTech.* SSRN Electronic Journal. doi:10.2139srn.3672989

Medhat, W., Hassan, A., & Korashy, H. (2014). Sentiment analysis algorithms and applications: A survey. *Ain Shams Engineering Journal*, *5*(4), 1093–1113. doi:10.1016/j.asej.2014.04.011

Mensah, J. (2019). Sustainable development: Meaning, history, principles, pillars, and implications for human action. *Literature review*, *5*(1). 10.1080/23311886.2019.1653531

Merriam, S. B. (1998). Merriam S 1998 S1.pdf. In Qualitative Research and Case Study Applications in Education.

Migliorelli, M. (2021). What Do We Mean by Sustainable Finance? Assessing Existing Frameworks and Policy Risks. *Sustainability*, *13*(2), 975. doi:10.3390u13020975

Migozzi, J., Urban, M., & Wójcik, D. (2023). "You should do what India does": FinTech ecosystems in India reshaping the geography of finance. *Geoforum*, *103720*, 103720. doi:10.1016/j.geoforum.2023.103720

Muganyi, T., Yan, L., & Sun, H. (2021). Green finance, FinTech and environmental protection: Evidence from China. *Environmental Science and Ecotechnology*, *7*, 100107. doi:10.1016/j.ese.2021.100107 PMID:36160697

Mumtaz, M. Z., & Yoshino, N. (2021). Greenness index: IPO performance and portfolio allocation. *Research in International Business and Finance*, *57*, 101398. doi:10.1016/j.ribaf.2021.101398

Nassiry, D. (2018). *The role of FinTech in unlocking green finance: Policy insights for developing countries*. Econstor. https://www.econstor.eu/handle/10419/190304

Nenavath, S. (2022). Impact of FinTech and green finance on environmental quality protection in India: By applying the semi-parametric difference-in-differences (SDID). *Renewable Energy*, *193*, 913–919. doi:10.1016/j.renene.2022.05.020

Nordhaus, W. D. (2011). The architecture of climate economics: Designing a global agreement on global warming. *Bulletin of the Atomic Scientists*, *67*(1), 9–18. doi:10.1177/0096340210392964

Nordhaus, W. D. (2018). Projections and Uncertainties about Climate Change in an Era of Minimal Climate Policies †. *American Economic Journal. Economic Policy*, *10*(3), 333–360. doi:10.1257/pol.20170046

OECD. (2022). *Aggregate Trends of Climate Finance Provided and Mobilised by Developed Countries in 2013-2020*. OECD. https://www.oecd.org/climate-change/finance-usd-100-billion-goal/aggregate-trends-of-climate-finance-provided-and-mobilised-by-developed-countries-in-2013-2020.pdf

Papoutsi, A., & Sodhi, M. M. S. (2020). Does disclosure in sustainability reports indicate actual sustainability performance? *Journal of Cleaner Production, 260*, 121049. doi:10.1016/j.jclepro.2020.121049

Pástor, Ľ., Stambaugh, R. F., & Taylor, L. A. (2021). Sustainable investing in equilibrium. *Journal of Financial Economics, 142*(2), 550–571. doi:10.1016/j.jfineco.2020.12.011

Pee, L. G., & Pan, S. L. (2022). Climate-intelligent cities and resilient urbanisation: Challenges and opportunities for information research. *International Journal of Information Management, 63*, 102446. doi:10.1016/j.ijinfomgt.2021.102446

Puschmann, T., Hoffmann, C. H., & Khmarskyi, V. (2020). How Green FinTech Can Alleviate the Impact of Climate Change-The Case of Switzerland. *Sustainability, 12*(24), 10691. doi:10.3390u122410691

Saura, J. R., Palos-Sanchez, P., & Grilo, A. (2019). Detecting Indicators for Startup Business Success: Sentiment Analysis Using Text Data Mining. *Sustainability, 11*(3). 917. doi:10.3390/SU11030917

Schalatek, L. (2012). Democratizing climate finance governance and the public funding of climate action. *Democratization, 19*(5), 951–973. doi:10.1080/13510347.2012.709690

Schulz, K., & Feist, M. (2021). Leveraging blockchain technology for innovative climate finance under the Green Climate Fund. *Earth System Governance, 7*, 100084. doi:10.1016/j.esg.2020.100084

Siew, R. Y. J. (2015). A review of corporate sustainability reporting tools (SRTs). *Journal of Environmental Management, 164*, 180–195. doi:10.1016/j.jenvman.2015.09.010 PMID:26379255

Stolbov, M., & Shchepeleva, M. (2023). Does one size fit all? Comparing the determinants of the FinTech market segments expansion. *The Journal of Finance and Data Science, 9*, 100095. doi:10.1016/j.jfds.2023.01.002

Stroebel, J., & Wurgler, J. (2021). What do you think about climate finance? *Journal of Financial Economics, 142*(2), 487–498. doi:10.1016/j.jfineco.2021.08.004

Taghizadeh-Hesary, F., & Yoshino, N. (2019). The way to induce private participation in green finance and investment. *Finance Research Letters*, *31*, 98–103. doi:10.1016/j.frl.2019.04.016

United Nations. (2015). *Transforming our world: the 2030 Agenda for Sustainable Development*. UN.

Wang, M., Li, X., & Wang, S. (2021). Discovering research trends and opportunities of green finance and energy policy: A data-driven scientometric analysis. *Energy Policy*, *154*, 112295. doi:10.1016/j.enpol.2021.112295

Wilburn, K., & Wilburn, R. (2014). The double bottom line: Profit and social benefit. *Business Horizons*, *57*(1), 11–20. doi:10.1016/j.bushor.2013.10.001

Wüstenhagen, R., & Menichetti, E. (2012). Strategic choices for renewable energy investment: Conceptual framework and opportunities for further research. *Energy Policy*, *40*(1), 1–10. doi:10.1016/j.enpol.2011.06.050

Yazan, B. (2015). Three Approaches to Case Study Methods in Education: Yin, Merriam, and Stake. *Qualitative Report*, *20*(2), 134–152. doi:10.46743/2160-3715/2015.2102

Yin, R. K. (1994). Discovering the future of the case study method in evaluation research. *Evaluation Practice*, *15*(3), 283–290. doi:10.1016/0886-1633(94)90023-X

Yin, R. K. (2009). *Case study research: Design and methods*. Sage.

Yu, E. P., Van Luu, B., & Chen, C. H. (2020). Greenwashing in environmental, social and governance disclosures. *Research in International Business and Finance*, *52*, 101192. doi:10.1016/j.ribaf.2020.101192

Ziolo, M., Bak, I., & Cheba, K. (2020). The Role of Sustainable Finance in Achieving Sustainable Development Goals: Does It Work? *Technological and Economic Development of Economy*, *27*(1), 45–70. doi:10.3846/tede.2020.13863

# Compilation of References

Aaker, D., & Keller, K. (1990). Consumer evaluations of brand extensions. *Journal of Marketing*, *54*(1), 27–41. doi:10.1177/002224299005400102

Abad-Segura, E., González-Zamar, M. D., López-Meneses, E., & Vázquez-Cano, E. (2020). Financial Technology: Review of trends, approaches and management. *Mathematics*, *8*(6), 951. doi:10.3390/math8060951

Abhijith, P. S., & Antony Joseph, K.Antony Joseph K. (2023, January 6). Reverse FinTech Socialisation. *International Journal of E-Business Research*, *18*(1), 1–17. doi:10.4018/IJEBR.316146

Accenture. (n.d.). *Let there be change*. 360° Value Report. https://www.accenture.com/content/dam/accenture/final/corporate/corporate-initiatives/sustainability/document/360-Value-Report-2022.pdf

Adams, C. A., & Frost, G. R. (2008). Integrating sustainability reporting into management practices. *Accounting Forum*, *32*(4), 288–302. doi:10.1016/j.accfor.2008.05.002

Adrian, M. T., & Griffoli, M. T. M. (2019). *The rise of digital money*. International Monetary Fund.

Aggrawal, S. (2023). How green finance is paving the way for India's sustainable future. *Times of India Blog*. https://timesofindia.indiatimes.com/blogs/voices/how-green-finance-is-paving-the-way-for-indias-sustainable-future/

Agrawal, A. K., Kumar, D., & Rahman, Z. (2017). An ISM approach for modelling the enablers of sustainability in market-oriented firms. *International Journal of Business Excellence*, *12*(1), 23. doi:10.1504/IJBEX.2017.083331

Ahamed, M. M., & Mallick, S. K. (2019). Is financial inclusion good for bank stability? International evidence. *Journal of Economic Behavior & Organization*, *157*, 403–427. doi:10.1016/j.jebo.2017.07.027

Ahmadifard, E., & Farhadian, H. (2023). An Analysis of Transformation Institutions in the Knowledge and Innovation System of the Handmade Carpet Industry. *Journal of Agricultural Science and Technology*, *25*(2), 285–300. https://jast.modares.ac.ir/files/jast/user_files_749497/h_farhadian-A-10-45013-8-85afdb4.pdf. doi:10.52547/jast.25.2.285

Ahmed, S., Hasan, M. M., & Kamal, M. R. (2022). Russia–Ukraine crisis: The effects on the European stock market. *European Financial Management*, eufm.12386. doi:10.1111/eufm.12386

Ajigini, O. A., & Chinamasa, T. J. W. (2023). Modelling Digital Transformation Within the Financial Sector: A South African Perspective. [IRMJ]. *Information Resources Management Journal, 36*(1), 1–20. doi:10.4018/irmj.320642

Aker, J. C., & Mbiti, I. M. (2010). Mobile phones and economic development in Africa. *The Journal of Economic Perspectives, 24*(3), 207–232. doi:10.1257/jep.24.3.207

Alam, M. K. (2020, August 20). A systematic qualitative case study: Questions, data collection, NVivo analysis and saturation. *Qualitative Research in Organizations and Management, 16*(1), 1–31. doi:10.1108/QROM-09-2019-1825

Ali, O., Ally, M., & Dwivedi, Y. (2020). The state of play of blockchain technology in the financial services sector: A systematic literature review. *International Journal of Information Management, 54*, 102199. doi:10.1016/j.ijinfomgt.2020.102199

Allen, S. J. (2020). On the cutting edge of the chopping block? Fostering a digital mindset and tech literacy in business management education. *Journal of Management Education, 44*(3), 362–393. doi:10.1177/1052562920903077

Al-Sabaawi, M. Y. M., Alshaher, A. A., & Alsalem, M. A. (2023). User trends of electronic payment systems adoption in developing countries: An empirical analysis. *Journal of Science and Technology Policy Management, 14*(2), 246–270. doi:10.1108/JSTPM-11-2020-0162

Alsharif, H. Z. H., Shu, T., Obrenovic, B., Godinic, D., Alhujailli, A., & Abdullaev, A. M. (2021). Impact of entrepreneurial leadership and bricolage on job security and sustainable economic performance: An empirical study of Croatian companies during COVID-19 pandemic. *Sustainability, 13*(21), 11958. doi:10.3390u132111958

Alshater, M. M., Atayah, O. F., & Khan, A. (2022). What do we know about business and economics research during COVID-19: A bibliometric review? *Economic Research-EkonomskaIstraživanja, 35*(1), 1884–1912. doi:10.1080/1331677X.2021.1927786

Alt, R., Beck, R., & Smits, M. T. (2018). FinTech and the transformation of the financial industry. *Electronic Markets, 28*(3), 235–243. doi:10.100712525-018-0310-9

Alwi, S., Alpandi, R. M., Salleh, M. N. M., & Najihah, I. (2019). An empirical study on the customers' satisfaction on Fintech mobile payment services in Malaysia. *International Journal of Advanced Science and Technology, 28*(16), 390–400.

Ameer, R., & Othman, R. (2012). Sustainability practices and corporate financial performance: A study based on the top global corporations. *Journal of Business Ethics, 108*(1), 61–79. doi:10.100710551-011-1063-y

American Economic Review. (2013). Why Don't the Poor Save More? Evidence from Health Savings Experiments. *The American Economic Review, 103*(4), 1138-71.

Amir, A. Z., & Serafeim, G. (2018). Why and how investors use ESG information: Evidence from a global survey. *Financial Analysts Journal, 74*(3). doi:10.2469/faj.v74.n3.2

Anantharajah, K., & Setyowati, A. B. (2022). Beyond promises: Realities of climate finance justice and energy transitions in Asia and the Pacific. *Energy Research & Social Science, 89*, 102550. doi:10.1016/j.erss.2022.102550

Anderson, K. (2023). *The UK's Green Finance Strategy: principles, objectives and steps.* Greenly. https://greenly.earth/en-gb/blog/ecology-news/the-uks-green-finance-strategy-principles-objectives-and-steps

Appiah-Otoo, I. (2023). *The Impact of the Russia-Ukraine War on the Cryptocurrency Market. Asian Economics Letters, 4.* Early View.

Ardic, O. P., Heimann, M., & Mylenko, N. (2011). Access to financial services and the financial inclusion agenda around the world: a cross-country analysis with a new data set. *Policy Research working paper; no. WPS 5537.* World Bank. https://openknowledge. worldbank.org/bitstream/handle/10986/3310/WPS5537.pdf?sequence51&isAllowed5y

Aria, M., & Cuccurullo, C. (2017). bibliometrix: An R-tool for comprehensive science mapping analysis. *Journal of Informetrics, 11*(4), 959–975. doi:10.1016/j.joi.2017.08.007

Arner, D. W., Barberis, J., & Buckley, R. P. (2016). One hundred fifty years of Fintech: An evolutionary analysis. *JASSA The Finsia Journal of Applied Finance*, (3), 22.

Arner, D. W., Barberis, J., & Buckley, R. P. (2017). *FinTech and RegTech in a Nutshell, and the Future in a Sandbox.* CFA Institute Research Foundation. doi:10.2139srn.3088303

Arner, D. W., Buckley, R. P., Zetzsche, D. A., & Veidt, R. (2020). Sustainability, FinTech and Financial Inclusion. *European Business Organization Law Review, 21*(1), 7–35. doi:10.100740804-020-00183-y

Arslan, H. M., Chengang, Y., Siddique, M., & Yahya, Y. (2022). Influence of senior executive's characteristics on corporate environmental disclosures: A bibliometric analysis. *Journal of Risk and Financial Management, 15*(3), 136. doi:10.3390/jrfm15030136

Arun, T., & Kamath, R. (2015). Financial inclusion: Policies and practices. *IIMB Management Review, 27*(4), 267–287. doi:10.1016/j.iimb.2015.09.004

Asif, M., Khan, M. N., Tiwari, S., Wani, S. K., & Alam, F. (2023, February 15). The Impact of Fintech and Digital Financial Services on Financial Inclusion in India. *Journal of Risk and Financial Management, 16*(2), 122. doi:10.3390/jrfm16020122

Asli Demirguc-Kunt, L. K. (2014). *Global Financial Index Report.* World Bank. https://pubdocs.worldbank.org/: https://thedocs.worldbank.org/en/doc/681361466184854434-0050022016/original/2014GlobalFindexReportDKSV.pdf

Asli Demirgüç-Kunt, L. K. (2021). *The Global Findex Database- Financial Inclusion,Digital Payments and Resilience in the Age of Covid19.* World Bank Group.

Aswani, J. (2017). Impact of global financial crisis on network of Asian stock markets. *Algorithmic Finance, 6*(3-4), 79–91. doi:10.3233/AF-170192

Babu, G. R. (2005). *Financial services in India*. Concept Publishing Company.

Banerjee, A., & Newman, A. F. (1993). Occupational choice and the process of development. *Journal of Political Economy*, *101*(2), 274–298. doi:10.1086/261876

Banna, H., Kabir Hassan, M., & Rashid, M. (2021). Fintech-based financial inclusion and bank risk-taking: Evidence from OIC countries. *Journal of International Financial Markets, Institutions and Money*, *75*, 101447. doi:10.1016/j.intfin.2021.101447

Banna, H., Mia, M. A., Nourani, M., & Yarovaya, L. (2022). Fintech-based Financial Inclusion and Risk-taking of Microfinance Institutions (MFIs): Evidence from Sub-Saharan Africa. *Finance Research Letters*, *45*, 102149. doi:10.1016/j.frl.2021.102149

Bano, R. (2015). GROWTH PERFORMANCE AND GLOBAL PERSPECTIVE OF INDIAN HAND. *Asia Pacific Journal of Research*, *I*(XXIV). https://d1wqtxts1xzle7.cloudfront.net/51378759/230220152-with-cover-page-v2.pdf?Expires=1656527924&Signature=hClrHq80aWFSs

Bano, R. (2016). Role of Handicrafts in Economic Development: A Case Study of Carpet Industry of India. *IRA-International Journal of Management & Social Sciences*, *04*(03), 512-525. https://d1wqtxts1xzle7.cloudfront.net/58663209/Role_of_Handicrafts_in_Economic_Developm-libre.pdf?1553090395=&response-content-disposition=inline%3B+filename%3DPg_no_512_525_Industry_of_India.pdf&Expires=1683444310&Signature=IQoIVaSgZ91aj6qCtb-mZB1KIie1i4

Bano, R. (2016). Role of Handicrafts in Economic Development:A Case Study of Carpet Industry of India. *IRA-International Journal of Management &Social Sciences*, *04*(03), 512–525. doi:10.21013/jmss.v4.n3.p1

Bapat, D. (2022). Exploring the relationship between lifestyle, digital financial element and digital financial services experience. *International Journal of Bank Marketing*, *40*(2), 297–320. doi:10.1108/IJBM-12-2020-0575

Barik, R., & Sharma, P. (2019). Analyzing the progress and prospects of financial inclusion in India. *Journal of Public Affairs*, *19*(4). doi:10.1002/pa.1948

Barrachina, M. D., & Baporikar, N. (2022). (IGI Global publishing)). Comparative Analysis of Factors Influencing Informal Investors of Spain and the United States. *International Journal of Applied Behavioral Economics*, *11*(1), 1–14. doi:10.4018/IJABE.311051

Barroso, M., & Laborda, J. (2022). Digital transformation and the emergence of the Fintech sector: Systematic literature review. *Digital Business*, *2*(2), 100028. doi:10.1016/j.digbus.2022.100028

Bauguess, S. W. (2017). *The role of big data, machine learning, and AI in assessing risks: A regulatory perspective*. U.S. Securities and Exchange Commission.

Bayero, M. A. (2015). Effects of Cashless Economy Policy on Financial Inclusion in Nigeria: An Exploratory Study. *Procedia: Social and Behavioral Sciences*, *172*, 49–56. doi:10.1016/j.sbspro.2015.01.334

Beck, T. (2016). Financial Inclusion –measuring progress and progress in measuring. *Fourth IMF Statistical Forum "Lifting the Small Boats: Statistics for Inclusive Growth."* IMF.

Behl, A., Kumari, P. S. R., Makhija, H., & Sharma, D. (2022). Exploring the relationship of ESG score and firm value using cross-lagged panel analyses: Case of the Indian energy sector. *Annals of Operations Research, 313*(1), 231–256. doi:10.100710479-021-04189-8

Belghiti, S., Ochs, A., Lemoine, J. F., & Badot, O. (2017). The phygital shopping experience:An attempt at conceptualization and empirical investigation. In *Academy of Marketing Science World Marketing Congress* (pp. 61-74). Springer, Cham.

Bento, N., Gianfrate, G., & Thoni, M. H. (2019). Crowdfunding for sustainability ventures. *Journal of Cleaner Production, 237*, 117751. doi:10.1016/j.jclepro.2019.117751

Berger, A. N., & Demirgüç-Kunt, A. (2021). Banking research in the time of COVID-19. *Journal of Financial Stability, 57*, 100939. doi:10.1016/j.jfs.2021.100939

Bhandary, R. R., Gallagher, K. S., & Zhang, F. (2021). Climate finance policy in practice: A review of the evidence. *Climate Policy, 21*(4), 529–545. doi:10.1080/14693062.2020.1871313

Bhasin, N. K., & Rajesh, A. (2021, January 1). Impact of E-Collaboration Between Indian Banks and Fintech Companies for Digital Banking and New Emerging Technologies. *International Journal of e-Collaboration, 17*(1), 15–35. doi:10.4018/IJeC.2021010102

Bhat, J. R., AlQahtani, S. A., & Nekovee, M. (2023). FinTech enablers, use cases, and role of future internet of things. *Journal of King Saud University-Computer and Information Sciences, 35*(1), 87–101. doi:10.1016/j.jksuci.2022.08.033

Bhowmik, P., Padhi, M., & Pattnaik, S. (2022). Does financial anxiety affect job insecurity? Exploring the relationship and moderation by gender, tenure and income in the Indian context during COVID-19. *Benchmarking: An International Journal.*

Bouri, E., Gupta, R., & Roubaud, D. (2019). Herding behaviour in cryptocurrencies. *Finance Research Letters, 29*, 216–221. doi:10.1016/j.frl.2018.07.008

Branzoli, N., & Supino, I. (2020). Fintech credit: A critical review of empirical research literature. *Bank of Italy Occasional Paper*, (549).

Bravo, E., & Ostos, J. (2023). Rational or Emotional User: The Dual Processing Approach to Understanding Continuance Usage. *Information Resources Management Journal, 36*(1), 1–20. doi:10.4018/IRMJ.325241

Brunen, A.-C., & Laubach, O. (2022). Do sustainable consumers prefer socially responsible investments? A study among the users of robo advisors. *Journal of Banking & Finance, 136*, 106314. doi:10.1016/j.jbankfin.2021.106314

Buchner, B., Naran, B., Fernandes, P., Padmanabhi, R., Rosane, P., Solomon, M., Stout, S., Strinati, C., Tolentino, R., Wakaba, G., Zhu, Y., Meattle, C., & Guzmán, S. (2021). *Global Landscape of Climate Finance 2021*. Climate Policy Initiative.

Buttice, C. (2020). [AI Use Cases: Artificial Intelligence in FinTech. AltaML-Techopedia.]. *Top (Madrid)*, 12.

Bux, H., Zhang, Z., & Ahmad, N. (2020). Promoting sustainability through corporate social responsibility implementation in the manufacturing industry: An empirical analysis of barriers using the ISM-MICMAC approach. *Corporate Social Responsibility and Environmental Management*, *27*(4), 1729–1748. doi:10.1002/csr.1920

Camilleri, M. A. (2021). The employees' state of mind during COVID-19: A self-determination theory perspective. *Sustainability*, *13*(7), 3634. doi:10.3390u13073634

Campanella, F., Serino, L., Crisci, A., & D'Ambra, A. (2021). The role of corporate governance in environmental policy disclosure and sustainable development. Generalized estimating equations in longitudinal count data analysis. *Corporate Social Responsibility and Environmental Management*, *28*(1), 474–484. doi:10.1002/csr.2062

Campbell-Verduyn, M., & Lenglet, M. (2022). Imaginary failure: RegTech in finance. *New Political Economy*, 1–15.

Canh, N. P., Wongchoti, U., Thanh, S. D., & Thong, N. T. (2019). Systematic risk in cryptocurrency market: Evidence from DCC-MGARCH model. *Finance Research Letters*, *29*, 90–100. doi:10.1016/j.frl.2019.03.011

Cao, L. (2022). Ai in finance: Challenges, techniques, and opportunities. [CSUR]. *ACM Computing Surveys*, *55*(3), 1–38. doi:10.1145/3502289

Cavaliere, L. P. L., Dhaliwal, S., Dutta, M., & Ahamed, F. (2022). A Pathway towards Green India: Green Funds and Green Investment. *Journal of Positive School Psychology*, *6*(2), 4151–4156.

CBI. (2022). *Sustainable debt global state of the market 2022*. Green Finance Platform. https://www.greenfinanceplatform.org/sites/default/files/downloads/resource/cbi_sotm_2022_03b.pdf

Cen, T., & He, R. (2018). Fintech, green finance and sustainable development. In *Proceedings of the 2018 International Conference on Management, Economics, Education, Arts and Humanities (MEEAH 2018)*. Atlantis Press.

Chaffey, D., Edmundson-Bird, D., & Hemphill, T. (2019). *Digital business and e-commerce management*.

Chagwesha, M. (2022). Intergenerational Leadership Practices in African Family Firms: A Bibliometric Analysis. *International Journal of Applied Management Sciences and Engineering* *9*(1), 1-13. doi:10.4018/IJAMSE.312850.

Chanana, N., & Sangeeta. (2021). Employee engagement practices during COVID-19 lockdown. *Journal of Public Affairs*, *21*(4), e2508. doi:10.1002/pa.2508 PMID:33041656

Chang, V., Baudier, P., Zhang, H., Xu, Q., Zhang, J., & Arami, M. (2020). How Blockchain can impact financial services–The overview, challenges and recommendations from expert interviewees. *Technological Forecasting and Social Change*, *158*, 120166. doi:10.1016/j.techfore.2020.120166 PMID:32834134

Chen, M. A., Wu, Q., & Yang, B. (2019). How valuable is FinTech innovation? *Review of Financial Studies*, *32*(5), 2062–2106. doi:10.1093/rfs/hhy130

Chen, W., & Yuan, X. (2021). Financial inclusion in China: An overview. *Frontiers of Business Research in China*, *15*(1), 4. doi:10.118611782-021-00098-6

Chi, K. T., Liu, J., & Lau, F. C. (2010). A network perspective of the stock market. *Journal of Empirical Finance*, *17*(4), 659–667. doi:10.1016/j.jempfin.2010.04.008

Chirumbolo, A., Callea, A., & Urbini, F. (2021). The effect of job insecurity and life uncertainty on everyday consumptions and broader life projects during COVID-19 pandemic. *International Journal of Environmental Research and Public Health*, *18*(10), 5363. doi:10.3390/ijerph18105363 PMID:34069918

Chiţimiea, A., Minciu, M., Manta, A. M., Ciocoiu, C. N., & Veith, C. (2021). The Drivers of green investment: A bibliometric and systematic review. *Sustainability*, *13*(6), 3507. doi:10.3390u13063507

Chiu, W.-H., Lin, W. C., & Liang, C.-J. (2021). The Role of Green Finance in Community Renewable Energy Projects of main Region and Taiwan. *Lex Localis - Journal of Local Self-Government, 19*(3), 503–519. doi:10.4335/19.3.503-519(2021)

Christensen, C. (2013). *The Innovator's Dilemma: When New Technologies Cause Great Firms to Fail*. Harvard Business Review Press.

Chueca Vergara, C., & Ferruz Agudo, L. (2021). Fintech and sustainability: Do they affect each other? *Sustainability*, *13*(13), 7012. doi:10.3390u13137012

Collins, T. (2015). Library evolution, trends and the road ahead from the EBSCO lens. *Information Services & Use*, *35*(1-2), 99–107. doi:10.3233/ISU-150771

Contreras, G., Bos, J. W. B., & Kleimeier, S. (2019). Self-regulation in sustainable finance: The adoption of the Equator Principles. *World Development*, *122*, 306–324. doi:10.1016/j.worlddev.2019.05.030

Corsini, F., & Frey, M. (2023). Exploring the development of environmentally sustainable products through reward-based crowdfunding. *Electronic Commerce Research*, *23*(2), 1183–1207. doi:10.100710660-021-09509-5

Crona, B., Folke, C., & Galaz, V. (2021). The Anthropocene reality of financial risk. *One Earth*, *4*(5), 618–628. doi:10.1016/j.oneear.2021.04.016

Cross, C. (2022). Using artificial intelligence (AI) and deepfakes to deceive victims: The need to rethink current romance fraud prevention messaging. *Crime Prevention and Community Safety*, *24*(1), 30–41. doi:10.105741300-021-00134-w

Cui, Y., Geobey, S., Weber, O., & Lin, H. (2018). The Impact of Green Lending on Credit Risk in China. *Sustainability, 10*(6). doi:10.3390/SU10062008

Das, S. R. (2019). The future of Fintech. *Financial Management, 48*(4), 981–1007. doi:10.1111/fima.12297

Deepankar, R. & Amarendra, S. (2016). Payment Systems in India: Opportunities and Challenges. *Journal of Internet Banking and Commerce, 21*(2).

Delhi, P. (2021). *Press Release.* PIB. https://pib.gov.in/: https://pib.gov.in/PressReleaseIframePage.aspx?PRID=1778084

Deloitte. (2018). *Rise of Phygital Banking.* Deloitte. https://www2.deloitte.com/content/dam/Deloitte/in/Documents/financial-services/in-fs-phygital-banking-noexp.pdf

Demetriades, S. H., & Hook Law, S. (2006). Finance, Institutions and Economic Development. *International Journal of Finance & Economics, 11*(3), 245–260. doi:10.1002/ijfe.296

Demir, A., Pesqué-Cela, V., Altunbas, Y., & Murinde, V. (2022). Fintech, financial inclusion and income inequality: A quantile regression approach. *European Journal of Finance, 28*(1), 86–107. doi:10.1080/1351847X.2020.1772335

Demirguc-Kunt, A., Klapper, L., Singer, D., & Ansar, S. (2018). The Global Findex Database 2017: Measuring Financial Inclusion and the Fintech Revolution. World Bank Publications. 10.1596/978-1-4648-1259-0

Demirgüç-Kunt, A., & Klapper, L. F. (2012). Financial inclusion in Africa: An overview. *World Bank Policy Research Working Paper*, 6088.

Demirgüç-Kunt, A., Pedraza, A., & Ruiz-Ortega, C. (2021). Banking sector performance during the COVID-19 crisis. *Journal of Banking & Finance, 133*, 106305. doi:10.1016/j.jbankfin.2021.106305 PMID:34548747

Deng, X., Huang, Z., & Cheng, X. (2019). FinTech and sustainable development: Evidence from China based on P2P data. *Sustainability, 11*(22), 6434. doi:10.3390u11226434

Dennissen, M., Benschop, Y., & van den Brink, M. (2019). Diversity Networks: Networking for Equality? *British Journal of Management, 30*(4), 966–980. doi:10.1111/1467-8551.12321

Department for Environment, Food, and Rural Affairs. (2023). *Green Finance Boost for Nature in the UK.* GOV.UK. https://www.gov.uk/government/news/green-finance-boost-for-nature-in-uk#:~:text=The%20 government%20has%20 set%20a,to%20 achieving%20our%20 Environment%20 Targets.

Dethe, A. (2019). *Not just Google, the world is watching India's UPI.* BFSI. https://bfsi.economictimes.indiatimes.com/news/editors-view/not-just-google-the-world-is-watching-indias-upi/

Ding, Q., Huang, J., & Chen, J. (2023). Does digital finance matter for corporate green investment? Evidence from heavily polluting industries in China. *Energy Economics, 117*, 106476. doi:10.1016/j.eneco.2022.106476

Dorfleitner, G., Hornuf, L., Schmitt, M., Weber, M., Dorfleitner, G., Hornuf, L., & Weber, M. (2017). Definition of FinTech and description of the FinTech industry. *FinTech in Germany*, 5-10.

Dos Santos, S., Singh, J., Thulasiram, R. K., Kamali, S., Sirico, L., & Loud, L. (2022, June). A new era of blockchain-powered decentralized finance (DeFi)-a review. In *2022 IEEE 46th Annual Computers, Software, and Applications Conference (COMPSAC)* (pp. 1286-1292). IEEE.

Drus, Z., & Khalid, H. (2019). Sentiment analysis in social media and its application: Systematic literature review. *Procedia Computer Science*, *161*, 707–714. doi:10.1016/j.procs.2019.11.174

Dubey, V. (2019). FinTech innovations in the digital banking. [IJERT]. *International Journal of Engineering Research & Technology (Ahmedabad)*, *8*(10).

Duhan, P., & Singh, A. (2019). *M-commerce: Experiencing the Phygital Retail*. Apple Academic Press. doi:10.1201/9780429487736

Ebneyamini, S., & Sadeghi Moghadam, M. R. (2018). Toward Developing a Framework for Conducting Case Study Research. *International Journal of Qualitative Methods*, *17*(1). doi:10.1177/1609406918817954

Economic Times (24, Nov, 2021). *World of phygital banking will be way forward: Bankers.* accessed on 6 July 2023

Elimam, H. (2023). Opportunities and Constraints Confronting Transformation Towards a Green Economy in the Developing Countries. *Economics and Business Quarterly Reviews, 6*(1).

Ernst & Young (2021), *Why digital, ecosystem-enabled banking transformation is the way forward* accessed on 21 June, 2023

Ernst & Young. (2016): *German FinTech landscape: an opportunity for Rhein-Main-Neckar*. Ernst & Young.

EY. (2022). *The winds of change Trends shaping India's FinTech Sector: edition II*. EY.

Eyraud, LClements, BWane, A. (2013). Green investment: Trends and determinants. Energy Policy, 60, 852-865.

Fang, H., Chung, C. P., Lu, Y. C., Lee, Y. H., & Wang, W. H. (2021, October). The impacts of investors' sentiments on stock returns using fintech approaches. *International Review of Financial Analysis*, *77*, 101858. doi:10.1016/j.irfa.2021.101858

Fankhauser, S., Sahni, A., Savvas, A., & Ward, J. (2016). Where are the gaps in climate finance? *Climate and Development*, *8*(3), 203–206. doi:10.1080/17565529.2015.1064811

Fan, L. (2022). Mobile investment technology adoption among investors. *International Journal of Bank Marketing*, *40*(1), 50–67. doi:10.1108/IJBM-11-2020-0551

Farahani, M. S., Esfahani, A., Moghaddam, M. N. F., & Ramezani, A. (2022). The impact of Fintech and artificial intelligence on COVID 19 and sustainable development goals. *International Journal of Innovation in Management. Economics and Social Sciences*, *2*(3), 14–31.

Farroukh, N., Canaan Messarra, L., & Yunis, M. (2023). The perception of job insecurity and organizational citizenship behavior during COVID-19: the moderating roles of positive psychological capital and grit. *Journal of Asia Business Studies*. doi:10.1108/JABS-05-2022-0176

Fedorova, E. P. (2020). Role of the State in the Resolution of Green Finance Development Issues. *Finansovyj Žhurnal — Financial Journal, 12*(4), 37–51. doi:10.31107/2075-1990-2020-4-37-51

*Fintech in India* (2023, January 1). Statista. https://www.statista.com/study/68286/fintech-in-india/

FinTech Mmagazine (2020), *The Phygital touch: fusing digital and physical in finance*. accessed on 12 June 2023

Forbes (2022), *How Banks can compete in the Post –Neobank Era* accessed on 14 July 2023

Francés, C. J., Carles, P. G., & Arellano, D. J. (2018). The cryptocurrency market: A network analysis. *Esic Market Economics and Business Journal, 49*(3), 569–583. doi:10.7200/esicm.161.0493.4

Fuso Nerini, F., Sovacool, B., Hughes, N., Cozzi, L., Cosgrave, E., Howells, M., Tavoni, M., Tomei, J., Zerriffi, H., & Milligan, B. (2019). Connecting climate action with other Sustainable Development Goals. In Nature Sustainability, 2(8). doi:10.103841893-019-0334-y

G20 Argentina. (2018). *Sustainable finance synthesis report.* UN. https://unepinquiry.org/wp-content/uploads/2018/11/G20_Sustainable_Finance_Synthesis_Report_2018.pdf?showiframe=true

G20. (2023). India's G20 Halfway Milestone. *G20 Secretariat NEWSLETTER*. G20. https://www.g20.org/content/dam/gtwenty/gtwenty_new/document/G20_Newsletter%20English_May%20 2023_D8.pdf

Gai, K., Qiu, M., & Sun, X. (2018). A survey on FinTech. *Journal of Network and Computer Applications, 103*, 262–273. doi:10.1016/j.jnca.2017.10.011

Gangopadhayay, S. (2009). How Can Technology Facilitate Financial Inclusion in India? A Discussion Paper. *Review of Market Integration, 1*(2). doi:10.1177/097492920900100206

Garz, S., Giné, X., Karlan, D., Mazer, R., Sanford, C., & Zinman, J. (2021). Consumer protection for financial inclusion in low-and middle-income countries: Bridging regulator and academic perspectives. *Annual Review of Financial Economics, 13*(1), 219–246. doi:10.1146/annurev-financial-071020-012008

GDFA. (2022). *A Green Fintech Taxonomy and Data Landscaping.* Interim Report. https://www.greenfinanceplatform.org/sites/default/files/downloads/resource/GreenFintechTaxonomyDataLandscaping-v5%20.pdf

GDFA. (2022). *Green FinTech Classification*. GDFA. https://www.greendigitalfinancealliance.org/initiatives/green-FinTech-classification

Gernego, I., Urvantseva, S., & Sandulskyi, R. (2022). Green investment opportunities for sustainable agriculture. *Management Theory and Studies for Rural Business and Infrastructure Development, 44*(2), 185–194. doi:10.15544/mts.2022.19

Ghanbarzadeh-Shams, M., Yaghin, R. G., & Sadeghi, A. H. (2022). A hybrid fuzzy multi-objective model for carpet production planning with reverse logistics under uncertainty. *Socio-Economic Planning Sciences*, *83*, 101344. doi:10.1016/j.seps.2022.101344

Ghodoosi, B. T.-S., Torrisi-Steele, G., West, T., & Li, Q. (2023). (IGI Global Publishing)). An Exploration of the Definition of Data Literacy in the Academic and Public Domains. *International Journal of Adult Education and Technology*, *14*(1), 1–16. doi:10.4018/IJAET.325218

Ghosh, K. (2022). Green Finance Initiatives in India. *IUP Journal of Accounting Research & Audit Practices, 21*(2).

Gichuru, L., & Namada, J. M. (2022, April 20). Regulatory Requirements and Financial Inclusion in FinTech Companies. *International Journal of Applied Management Theory and Research*, *4*(1), 1–13. doi:10.4018/IJAMTR.300345

Giglio, F. (2022). Fintech: A literature review. *International Business Research*, *15*(1), 80–85. doi:10.5539/ibr.v15n1p80

Gilchrist, D., Yu, J., & Zhong, R. (2021). The Limits of Green Finance: A Survey of Literature in the Context of Green Bonds and Green Loans. *Sustainability, 13*(2), 478. doi:10.3390/SU13020478

Global Fintech Adoption. (2019). *Index.* EY. https:// www.ey.com/en_gl/ey-global-fintech-adoption-index

Goecks, L. S., Korzenowski, A. L., Gonçalves Terra Neto, P., de Souza, D. L., & Mareth, T. (2022). Anti-money laundering and financial fraud detection: A systematic literature review. *Intelligent Systems in Accounting, Finance & Management*, *29*(2), 71–85. doi:10.1002/isaf.1509

Goel, A. (2020, October). Financial Inclusion. *International Journal of Applied Behavioral Economics*, *9*(4), 33–57. doi:10.4018/IJABE.2020100103

Goldstein, I., Jiang, W., & Karolyi, G. A. (2019). To FinTech and Beyond. *Review of Financial Studies*, *32*(5), 1647–1661. doi:10.1093/rfs/hhz025

Gomber, P., Kauffman, R. J., Parker, C., & Weber, B. W. (2018). On the fintech revolution: Interpreting the forces of innovation, disruption, and transformation in financial services. *Journal of Management Information Systems*, *35*(1), 220–265. doi:10.1080/07421222.2018.1440766

Gomber, P., Koch, J. A., & Siering, M. (2017). Digital finance and FinTech: Current research and future research directions. *Journal of Business Economics*, *87*(5), 537–580. doi:10.100711573-017-0852-x

Gordon, M. (2018). Regulatory reporting: Success is found in a solid foundation. *Journal of Securities Operations & Custody*, *10*(1), 57–66.

Gosain, S., & Agrawal, N. (2021). Factors Affecting the Financial Success of Crowdfunding Campaigns: A Systematic Literature Review. *South Asian Journal of Management*, *28*(3).

Goswami, S., Sharma, R. B., & Chouhan, V. (2022, March). Impact of Financial Technology (Fintech) on Financial Inclusion(FI) in Rural India. *Universal Journal of Accounting and Finance, 10*(2), 483–497. doi:10.13189/ujaf.2022.100213

Gupta, P., Gupta, P., & Indoriya, N. (2020). New trends of Indian banking industry. *Studies in Indian Place Names, 40*(1), 311-319.

Gupta, S. K., Tiwari, S., Hassan, A., & Gupta, P. (2023). Moderating Effect of Technologies into Behavioural Intensions of Tourists toward Use of Mobile Wallets for Digital Payments: TAM Model Perspective. *International Journal of Hospitality & Tourism Systems, 16*(1).

Gupta, R., Kaur, H., & Kaur, M. (2023). Evolution of Fintech Ensuring Sustainability in Financial Markets: A Bibliometric Analysis. *International Management Review.*

Gupta, S., & Prusty, S. (2023). Does consumer empowerment influence e-payment systems adoption? A digital consumer-centric perspective. *Journal of Financial Services Marketing.* doi:10.105741264-023-00238-4

Haddad, C., & Hornuf, L. (2019). The emergence of the global fintech market: Economic and technological determinants. *Small Business Economics, 53*(1), 81–105. doi:10.100711187-018-9991-x

Hafner, S., Jones, A., Anger-Kraavi, A., & Pohl, J. (2020). Closing the green finance gap – A systems perspective. *Environmental Innovation and Societal Transitions, 34*, 26–60. doi:10.1016/j.eist.2019.11.007

Han, Q., Zheng, B., Cristea, M., Agostini, M., Bélanger, J. J., Gützkow, B., Kreienkamp, J., & Leander, N. P. (2023). Trust in government regarding COVID-19 and its associations with preventive health behaviour and prosocial behaviour during the pandemic: A cross-sectional and longitudinal study. *Psychological Medicine, 53*(1), 149–159. doi:10.1017/S0033291721001306 PMID:33769242

Hansen, E., Grosse-Dunker, F., & Reichwald, R. (2009). Sustainability innovation cube—A framework to evaluate sustainability-oriented innovations. *International Journal of Innovation Management, 13*(04), 683–713. doi:10.1142/S1363919609002479

Hashemi Joo, M., Nishikawa, Y., & Dandapani, K. (2020). Cryptocurrency a successful application of blockchain technology. *Managerial Finance, 46*(6), 715–733. doi:10.1108/MF-09-2018-0451

He, J., Mao, Y., Morrison, A. M., & Coca-Stefaniak, J. A. (2021). On being warm and friendly: The effect of socially responsible human resource management on employee fears of the threats of COVID-19. *International Journal of Contemporary Hospitality Management, 33*(1), 346–366. doi:10.1108/IJCHM-04-2020-0300

He, M. D., Leckow, M. R. B., Haksar, M. V., Griffoli, M. T. M., Jenkinson, N., Kashima, M. M., & Tourpe, H. (2017). *Fintech and financial services: Initial considerations.* International Monetary Fund.

Hendrikse, R., van Meeteren, M., & Bassens, D. (2019, November 11). Strategic coupling between finance, technology and the state: Cultivating a Fintech ecosystem for incumbent finance. *Environment and Planning A. Economy and Space*, *52*(8), 1516–1538. doi:10.1177/0308518x19887967

Henisz, W. J., Dorobantu, S., & Nartey, L. J. (2014). Spinning gold: The financial returns to stakeholder engagement. *Strategic Management Journal*, *35*(12), 1727–1748. doi:10.1002mj.2180

He, Z., Cao, C., & Feng, C. (2022). Media attention, environmental information disclosure and corporate green technology innovations in China's heavily polluting industries. *Emerging Markets Finance & Trade*, *58*(14), 3939–3952. doi:10.1080/1540496X.2022.2075259

He, Z., Liu, Z., Wu, H., Gu, X., Zhao, Y., & Yue, X. (2020). Research on the Impact of Green Finance and Fintech in Smart City (2020) Complexity, 2020, art. no. 6673386. *DOI*, *10*, 6673386.

Hinson, R., Lensink, R., & Mueller, A. (2019). Transforming agribusiness in developing countries: SDGs and the role of FinTech. In *Current Opinion in Environmental Sustainability* (Vol. 41, pp. 1–9). Elsevier B.V. doi:10.1016/j.cosust.2019.07.002

HM. (2023). *A Green Future: Our 25 Year Plan to Improve the Environment*. HM Government. https://assets.publishing.service.gov.uk/government/uploads/system/uploads/attachment_data/file/693158/25-year-environment-plan.pdf

Hoang, T. G., Nguyen, G. N. T., & Le, D. A. (2022). Developments in financial technologies for achieving the Sustainable Development Goals (SDGs): FinTech and SDGs. In *Disruptive technologies and eco-innovation for sustainable development* (pp. 1–19). IGI Global. doi:10.4018/978-1-7998-8900-7.ch001

*Home*. (n.d.). IFRS. https://www.ifrs.org/issued-standards/sasb-standards/

Hommel, K., & Bican, P. M. (2020). Digital entrepreneurship in finance: Fintechs and funding decision criteria. *Sustainability*, *12*(19), 8035. doi:10.3390u12198035

Hong, H., Karolyi, G. A., & Scheinkman, J. A. (2020). Climate Finance. *Review of Financial Studies*, *33*(3), 1011–1023. doi:10.1093/rfs/hhz146

Hu, A. S., Parlour, C. A., & Rajan, U. (2019). Cryptocurrencies: Stylized facts on a new investible instrument. *Financial Management*, *48*(4), 1049–1068. doi:10.1111/fima.12300

Huang, W. S., Karolyi, G. A., & Kwan, A. (2021). Paying Attention to ESG : Evidence from Big Data Analytics. *AFA, 607*.

Hussain, F. & Dill, H. (2023). *India incorporates green bonds into its climate finance strategy*. World Bank Blogs. https://blogs.worldbank.org/climatechange/india-incorporates-green-bonds-its-climate-finance-strategy

Hussein, D. M. E.-D. M. (2018). A survey on sentiment analysis challenges. *Journal of King Saud University -. Engineering and Science*, *30*(4), 330–338. doi:10.1016/j.jksues.2016.04.002

Hwa, G. (2019). Eight ways FinTech adoption remains on the rise. *Vers, 1*, 2019.

IBEF(2023), *Digital Transformation Shaping the Future of the Finance Industry*, India Brand Equity Eoundation. Accessed On 22, June 2023).

IBEF. (2022, November). *Carpet Industry and Exports*. India: IBEF India Brand Equity Foundation. https://www.ibef.org/exports/carpet-industry-in-india

Investopedia. (2022). *Basics of what a credit bureau is and does, plus major ones*. Investopedia. https://www.investopedia.com/terms/c/creditbureau.asp

IPCC. (2018). IPCC, 2018: Global Warming of 1.5°C. An IPCC Special Report. In In Press, 2.

IPCC. (2022a). Impacts, Adaptation and Vulnerability Working Group II Contribution to the Sixth Assessment Report of the Intergovernmental Panel on Climate Change. *Climatic Change*.

IPCC. (2023). *Synthesis Report of The IPCC Sixth Assessment Report (AR6)*. IPCC.

Jabłonowska, A., Kuziemski, M., Nowak, A. M., Micklitz, H. W., Pałka, P., & Sartor, G. (2018). Consumer law and artificial intelligence: Challenges to the EU consumer law and policy stemming from the business' use of artificial intelligence-final report of the ARTSY project. *EUI Department of Law Research Paper*, (2018/11).

Jain, S. (2020). *Financing India's Green Transition*, 338. ORF. https://www.orfonline.org/wp-content/uploads/2020/01/ORF_IssueBrief_338_FinancingGreenTransition_NEW27Jan.pdf

Jain, S. (2023). A study on Digital Payment System and its Future Feasibility in India. *International Journal of International Institute of Management Studies, 2*(1).

Jarvis, R., & Han, H. (2021). Fintech Innovation: Review and Future Research Directions. *International Journal of Banking. Finance and Insurance Technologies*, *1*(1), 79–102.

Jeronen, E. (2020). Economic Sustainability. In S. Idowu, R. Schmidpeter, N. Capaldi, L. Zu, M. Del Baldo, & R. Abreu (Eds.), *Encyclopedia of Sustainable Management. Springer*. Online. doi:10.1007/978-3-030-02006-4_197-1

Joia, L. A., & Cordeiro, J. P. V. (2021). Unlocking the potential of fintechs for financial inclusion: A delphi-based approach. *Sustainability (Switzerland)*, *13*(21), 11675. doi:10.3390u132111675

Joo, B. A., & Shawl, S. (2021). COVID-19 pandemic and the rising gig economy: An emerging perspective. *Global Economics Science*, 16-23.

Jose, S. (2023). Impact of Demonetization and Pandemic on Digital Payments Usage. *International Journal of Science and Research, Volume 12*(3). https://ssrn.com/abstract=4383173

Joy, B., & Thomas, A. E. (2023, January 13). The Ecosystem of FinTech Companies in India. *International Journal of E-Business Research*, *18*(1), 1–16. doi:10.4018/IJEBR.316148

Jun, J., Cho, I., & Park, H. (2018). Factors influencing continued use of mobile easy payment service: An empirical investigation. *Total Quality Management & Business Excellence*, *29*(9-10), 1043–1057. doi:10.1080/14783363.2018.1486550

Jutla, S., & Sundararajan, N. (2016). India's FinTech ecosystem. *The FinTech Book: The Financial Technology Handbook for Investors, Entrepreneurs and Visionaries*, 56-57.

Kabaklarlı, E. (2022). Green FinTech: sustainability of Bitcoin. *Digital Finance, 4*(4), 265–273. 10.1007/S42521-022-00053-X

Kabulova, J., & Stankevičienė, J. (2020). Valuation of fintech innovation based on patent applications. *Sustainability, 12*(23), 10158. doi:10.3390u122310158

Kadyan, S., Bhasin, N. K., & Sharma, M. (2022). Fintech: Review of theoretical perspectives and exploring challenges to trust building and retention in improving online Digital Bank Marketing. *Transnational Marketing Journal, 10*(3), 579–592.

Kajol, K. Singh, R., & Paul, J. (2022). Adoption of digital financial transactions: A review of literature and future research agenda. *Technological Forecasting and Social Change, 184*. doi:10.1016/j.techfore.2022.121991

Kalia, C. (2020).*Green Finance is gaining traction for net zero transition in India*. EY US - Home. https://www.ey.com/en_in/climate-change-sustainability-services/green-finance-is-gaining-traction-for-net-zero-transition-in-india

Kanchi, S., Joglekar, S., & Manjare, R. (2023). Study of Technology Adoption and Perceived Usefulness of Digital Payment of the hawkers in Pune City. *Rabindra Bharati University Journal of Philosophy*.

Kanojia, P. & Lal, M. (2020). *Impact of Trust on Customer Adoption of Digital Payment Systems*. doi:. doi:10.4018/978-1-7998-2398-8.ch002

Kathari, S. (2019). Phygital banking: A game changer in Indian banking sector. *International Journal of Innovative Technology and Exploring Engineering*, *8*(9), 289–292. doi:10.35940/ijitee.H7283.078919

Kathial, K. (2018). Impact of Demonetization on Digital Transactions in India. *Asian Journal of Management*, *9*(1), 281–287. doi:10.5958/2321-5763.2018.00042.2

Kato, Y. (2020). AI/FinTech and asset management businesses. *Public Policy Review*, *16*(4), 1–28.

Kaur, H., & Mehta, R. (2023). A Study on the Adoption of Digital Payments by Indian Youth. In *ICASDMBW 2022: Proceedings of the International Conference on Application of AI and Statistical Decision Making for the Business World, ICASDMBW 2022*, (p. 247). European Alliance for Innovation. 10.4108/eai.16-12-2022.2326162

Kaur, S. & Walia, N. (2020). Impact of demonetization on digital payments in India – Event study methodology. *Pacific Business Review International, 13*(4).

Keogh-Brown, M. R., Jensen, H. T., Edmunds, W. J., & Smith, R. D. (2020). The impact of Covid-19, associated behaviours and policies on the UK economy: A computable general equilibrium model. *SSM - Population Health, 12*, 100651. doi:10.1016/j.ssmph.2020.100651 PMID:33072839

Kern, A. (2017). *Wikifolio: Social Trading*. Springer Fachmedien Wiesbaden.

Khando, K., Islam, M. S., & Gao, S. (2022). The Emerging Technologies of Digital Payments and Associated Challenges: A Systematic Literature Review. Future Internet, 15(1), 21. MDPI AG. doi:10.3390/fi15010021

Khan, I., Khan, I., Sayal, A. U., & Khan, M. Z. (2022). Does financial inclusion induce poverty, income inequality, and financial stability: Empirical evidence from the 54 African countries? *Journal of Economic Studies (Glasgow, Scotland)*, *49*(2), 303–314. doi:10.1108/JES-07-2020-0317

Khan, M. A., Riaz, H., Ahmed, M., & Saeed, A. (2022). Does green finance really deliver what is expected? An empirical perspective. *Borsa Istanbul Review*, *22*(3), 586–593. doi:10.1016/j.bir.2021.07.006

Khetwani, K., & Jain, S. (2022). *An analysis on the awareness & insight of cryptocurrency.*

Khoa, B. T., Hung, B. P., & Brahmi, M. H. (2023). Qualitative research in social sciences: Data collection, data analysis and report writing. *International Journal of Public Sector Performance Management*, *12*(1/2), 187–209. doi:10.1504/IJPSPM.2023.132247

Kitsios, F., Giatsidis, I., & Kamariotou, M. (2021). Digital transformation and strategy in the banking sector: Evaluating the acceptance rate of e-services. *Journal of Open Innovation*, *7*(3), 204. doi:10.3390/joitmc7030204

Klein, A., Widge, V., Bergedieck, L., & Maheshwari, A. (2019, November 1). *Green Finance : A Bottom-up Approach to Track Existing Flows (Vol. 2) : Full Report*. World Bank. https://documents.worldbank.org/en/publication/documents-reports/documentdetail/788041573021878350/full-report

Kling, G., Pesqué-Cela, V., Tian, L., & Luo, D. (2020). A theory of financial inclusion and income inequality. *European Journal of Finance*, doi:10.1080/1351847X.2020.1792960

Knaack P., & Gruin, J. (2017). *From Shadow Banking to Digital Financial Inclusion: Regulatory Framework Constestation between China and the FSB*. Academic Press.

Kondala, M., Nudurupati, S. S., & Pappu, R. P. (2023). (Article in press). The challenges in adoption of circular economy in SMEs–a research agenda and way forward. *Benchmarking*. doi:10.1108/BIJ-04-2023-0272

Kondala, M., Nudurupati, S. S., Riwayadi, E., Chavan, A., Asif, S. R., & Gupta, N. (2023). Original Research Article Moving towards a sustainable world with the circular economy practices concerning the SMEs in Visakhapatnam's ice-cream industry. *Journal of Autonomous Intelligence*, *6*(1). Advance online publication. doi:10.32629/jai.v6i1.676

Kotsantonis, S., & Serafeim, G. (2019). Four Things No One Will Tell You About ESG Data. *Journal of Applied Corporate Finance*, *31*(2), 50–58. doi:10.1111/jacf.12346

KPMG (2022), *Customer on boarding - a key tool in the fight against financial crime. The benefits of getting it right from the beginning*. accessed on 15 July, 2023

KPMG. (2016). *Fintech in India, A global growth story*. KPMG. https://assets.kpmg.com/content/dam/kpmg/pdf/2016/06/FinTech-new.pdf

KPMG. (2022). *Enabling tomorrow: The emergent ESG Fintech ecosystem*. KPMG. https://assets.kpmg.com/content/dam/kpmg/sg/pdf/2022/11/enabling-tomorrow-the-emergent-esg-fintech-ecosystem.pdf

KPMG. (2022). *The Pulse of Fintech 2022*. KPMG. https://assets.kpmg/content/dam/kpmg/xx/pdf/2018/07/h1--2018-pulse-of-fintech.pdf (accessed on 26 Aprilr 2023).

Krishna Priya, P., & Anusha, K. (2019). Fintech issues and challenges in India. *International Journal of Recent Technology and Engineering*, *8*(3). doi:10.35940/ijrte.C4087.098319

Kumar, K., & Prakash, A. (2019). Examination of sustainability reporting practices in Indian banking sector. *Asian Journal of Sustainability and Social Responsibility 2019*, *4*(1), 1–16. doi:10.1186/S41180-018-0022-2

Kumar, V. R. (2022, April 03). Weaving sustainable designer rugs in the hinterland. India. *The Hindu Businessline*. https://www.thehindubusinessline.com/specials/clean-tech/weaving-sustainable-designer-rugs-in-the-hinterland/article65281543.ece

Kumari, V., Kumar, G., & Pandey, D. K. (2023). Are the European Union stock markets vulnerable to the Russia–Ukraine war? *Journal of Behavioral and Experimental Finance*, *37*, 100793. doi:10.1016/j.jbef.2023.100793

Kumar, K., Kumari, R., Poonia, A., & Kumar, R. (2021). Factors influencing corporate sustainability disclosure practices: Empirical evidence from Indian National Stock Exchange. *Journal of Financial Reporting and Accounting*, *21*(2), 300–321. doi:10.1108/JFRA-01-2021-0023

Kumar, K., & Prakash, A. (2020). Managing sustainability in banking: Extent of sustainable banking adaptations of banking sector in India. *Environment, Development and Sustainability*, *22*(6), 5199–5217. doi:10.100710668-019-00421-5

Kumar, R., Singh, T., Mohanty, S. N., Goel, R., Gupta, D., Alharbi, M., & Khanna, R. (2023). Study on online payments and e-commerce with SOR model. *International Journal of Retail & Distribution Management*. doi:10.1108/IJRDM-03-2023-0137

Kumar, T., Vaidyanathan, S., Ananthapadmanabhan, H., Parthasarathy, S., & Ravindran, B. (2020). Hypergraph clustering by iteratively reweighted modularity maximization. *Applied Network Science*, *5*(1), 1–22. doi:10.100741109-020-00300-3

Kumar, V., Kumar, P., & Mishra, K. (2020). Managing Sustainable Development of Indian Carpet Industry. *Journal of Seybold Report*, *15*(8), 1193–1201. https://d1wqtxts1xzle7.cloudfront.net/64181686/Managing_Sustainable_Development_Of_Indian_Carpet_Industry-libre.pdf?1597421334=&response-content-disposition=inline%3B+filename%3DManaging_Sustainable_Development_of_Indi.pdf&Expires=1683189558&Signature=ZY8

Kurniasari, F., Gunardi, A., Putri, F. P., & Firmansyah, A. (2021). The role of financial technology to increase financial inclusion in Indonesia. *International Journal of Data and Network Science*, *5*(3), 391–400. doi:10.5267/j.ijdns.2021.5.004

Laing, K., & James, K. (2023). EBSCO and Summon Discovery Generator Tools: How Accurate Are They? *Journal of Academic Librarianship*, *49*(1), 102587. doi:10.1016/j.acalib.2022.102587

Lai, T. L., Liao, S.-W., Wong, S. P. S., & Xu, H. (2020). Statistical models and stochastic optimization in financial technology and investment science. *Annals of Mathematical Sciences and Applications*, *5*(2), 317–345. doi:10.4310/AMSA.2020.v5.n2.a5

Lamprinopoulou, C., Renwick, A., Klerkx, L., Hermans, F., & Roep, D. (2014). Application of an integrated systemic framework for analysing agricultural innovation systems and informing innovation policies: Comparing the Dutch and Scottish agrifood sectors. *Agricultural Systems*, *129*, 40–54. doi:10.1016/j.agsy.2014.05.001

Lee, C. C., Chen, P. F., & Chu, P.J. (2023). Green recovery through financial inclusion of mobile payment: A study of low- and middle-income Asian countries. *Economic Analysis and Policy*, *77*, 729-747. doi:10.1016/j.eap.2022.12.012

Lee, I. & Shin, Y. (2017). Fintech: Ecosystem, business models, investment decisions, and challenges. *Iran Arze*. https://iranarze.ir/wp-content/uploads/2019/01/E10696-IranArze.pdf

Lee, I., & Shin, Y. J. (2018). FinTech: Ecosystem, business models, investment decisions, and challenges. *Business Horizons*, *61*(1), 35–46. doi:10.1016/j.bushor.2017.09.003

Lee, S. K. (2019). *Fintech nudges: Overspending messages and personal finance management*. NYU Stern School of Business.

León, C. (2021, December). The adoption of a mobile payment system: The user perspective. *Latin American Journal of Central Banking*, *2*(4), 100042. doi:10.1016/j.latcb.2021.100042

Leong, K., & Sung, A. (2018). Fintech (financial technology): What is it and how to use technologies to create business value in fintech way? *International Journal of Innovation, Management and Technology*, *9*(2), 74–78. doi:10.18178/ijimt.2018.9.2.791

Lindenberg, N. (2014). *Definition of green finance*.

Lin, Z., Liao, X., & Jia, H. (2022). Could green finance facilitate low-carbon transformation of power generation? Some evidence from China. *International Journal of Climate Change Strategies and Management*, *15*(2), 141–158. doi:10.1108/IJCCSM-03-2022-0039

Little, L. R., Hobday, A. J., Parslow, J., Davies, C. R., Grafton, R. Q., Little, L. R., Hobday, A. J., Parslow, J., Davies, C. R., & Grafton, R. Q. (2015). Funding climate adaptation strategies with climate derivatives. *CliRM*, *8*, 9–15. doi:10.1016/j.crm.2015.02.002

Liu, Y. B., Deng, W. F., Luo, K., & Tang, M. Y. (2023). *Impact of Environmental Taxation on Financial Performance of Energy-Intensive Firms: The Role of Digital Transformation*. Hindawi.

Liu, C., & Wu, S. S. (2023). Green finance, sustainability disclosure and economic implications. *Fulbright Review of Economics and Policy*, *3*(1), 1–24. doi:10.1108/FREP-03-2022-0021

Liu, H., Yao, P., Latif, S., Aslam, S., & Iqbal, N. (2022). Impact of Green financing, Fintech, and financial inclusion on energy efficiency. *Environmental Science and Pollution Research International*, *29*(13), 1–12. doi:10.100711356-021-16949-x PMID:34705207

Liu, Q., Zou, L., Yang, X., & Tang, J. (2019). Survival or die: A survival analysis on peer-to-peer lending platforms in China. *Accounting and Finance*, *59*(S2), 2105–2131. doi:10.1111/acfi.12513

Liu, Z., Song, J., Wu, H., Gu, X., Zhao, Y., Yue, X., & Shi, L. (2021). Impact of Financial Technology on Regional Green Finance. *Computer Systems Science and Engineering*, *39*(3), 391–401. doi:10.32604/csse.2021.014527

Liu, Z., Yin, Y., Liu, W., & Dunford, M. (2015). Visualizing the intellectual structure and evolution of innovation systems research: A bibliometric analysis. *Scientometrics*, *103*(1), 135–158. doi:10.100711192-014-1517-y

Long, S., Lucey, B., Kumar, S., Zhang, D., & Zhang, Z. (2022). Climate finance: What we know and what we should know? *Journal of Climate Finance*, *1*, 100005. doi:10.1016/j.jclimf.2023.100005

LSEG. (2020). *London leads the world's Sustainable Finance Ecosystem*. LSEG. https://www2.lseg.com/sustainablefinance

Luciani, T. C., Distasio, B. A., Bungert, J., Sumner, M., & Bozzo, T. L. (2016). U.S. Patent Application No. 14/843,455.

Luo, X., Ge, L., & Wang, C. (2022). Crowdfunding for microfinance institutions: the new hope? *MIS Quarterly*, *46*, 1.

Luo, D., Mishra, T., Yarovaya, L., & Zhang, Z. (2021). Investing during a Fintech Revolution: Ambiguity and return risk in cryptocurrencies. *Journal of International Financial Markets, Institutions and Money*, *73*, 101362. doi:10.1016/j.intfin.2021.101362

Luqmani, A., Leach, M., & Jesson, D. (2017, September). Factors behind sustainable business innovation: The case of a global carpet manufacturing company. *Environmental Innovation and Societal Transitions*, *24*, 94–105. doi:10.1016/j.eist.2016.10.007

Lusardi, A., & Mitchell, O. S. (2011). Financial literacy around the world: An overview. *Journal of Pension Economics and Finance*, *10*(4), 497–508. doi:10.1017/S147474721100448 PMID:28553190

MacAskill, S., Roca, E., Liu, B., Stewart, R. A., & Sahin, O. (2021). Is there a green premium in the green bond market? Systematic literature review revealing premium determinants. *Journal of Cleaner Production*, *280*, 124491. doi:10.1016/j.jclepro.2020.124491

Macchiavello, E., & Siri, M. (2020). *Sustainable Finance and FinTech: Can Technology Contribute to Achieving Environmental Goals? A Preliminary Assessment of 'Green FinTech*. SSRN Electronic Journal. doi:10.2139srn.3672989

Macchiavello, E., & Siri, M. (2022). Sustainable finance and Fintech: Can technology contribute to achieving environmental goals? *European Company and Financial Law Review*, *19*(1), 128–174. doi:10.1515/ecfr-2022-0005

Mahesh, A. & Bhat, G. (2021). Digital Payment Service in India - A Case Study of Unified Payment Interface. *International Journal of Case Studies in Business, IT, and Education (IJCSBE)*, *5*(1), 256-265. doi:. doi:10.5281/zenodo.5091207

Maiti, M., & Ghosh, U. (2023, February 1). Next-Generation Internet of Things in Fintech Ecosystem. *IEEE Internet of Things Journal*, *10*(3), 2104–2111. doi:10.1109/JIOT.2021.3063494

Manocha, S., Kejriwal, R., & Upadhyaya, A. (2019). The Impact of Demonetization on Digital Payment Transactions: A Statistical Study Proceedings of International Conference on Advancements in Computing & Management (ICACM). *SSRN*. https://ssrn.com/abstract=3446558 or doi:10.2139/ssrn.3446558

Mantegna, R. N. (1999). Hierarchical structure in financial markets. *European Physical Journal. B, Condensed Matter and Complex Systems*, *11*(1), 193–197. doi:10.1007100510050929

Martinazzi, S. (2017). *The age of fintech: providing a liquid and efficient secondary market for security-based crowdfunding with distributed ledger technologies.*

Masiero, S., & Ravishankar, M. N. (2019). Exploring Hybridity in Digital Social Entrepreneurship. *IFIP Advances in Information and Communication Technology*, *551*, 295–306. doi:10.1007/978-3-030-18400-1_24

Mathur, P., Gupta, N., & Agarwal, M. (2022). *Are banking & and financial institutions ready for the transformation? An analysis of FinTech adoption challenges using DEMATEL.*

Ma, Y., & Liu, D. (2017). Introduction to the special issue on Crowdfunding and FinTech. *Financial Innovation*, *3*(1), 1–4. doi:10.118640854-017-0058-9

Mbaabu, M. K. (2020). *Phygital Banking and Customer Experience in Commercial Banks in Kenya* [Doctoral dissertation, University of Nairobi].

Mckinsey & Company (2022), *McKinsey's Global Banking Annual Review*. Retrieved on 10 July, 2023)

Mckinsey & Company. (2020). *The 2020 Mckinsey global payments report*. McKinsey. https://www.mckinsey.com/~/media/mckinsey/industries/financial%20services/our%20insights/accelerating%20winds%20of%20change%20in%20global%20payments/2020-mckinsey-global-payments-report-vf.pdf

Medhat, W., Hassan, A., & Korashy, H. (2014). Sentiment analysis algorithms and applications: A survey. *Ain Shams Engineering Journal*, *5*(4), 1093–1113. doi:10.1016/j.asej.2014.04.011

Meghana, K., & Tripathi, S. (2018). Digital Payment System for Economic Sustainability. A Case Study of Gujarat Narmada Fertilizers and Chemicals Ltd in India. *Scientific Quarterly* *4*(44). doi: www.oamquarterly.polsl.pl doi:10.29119/1899-6116.2018.44.8

Mehrban, S., Nadeem, M. W., Hussain, M., Ahmed, M. M., Hakeem, O., Saqib, S., & Khan, M. A. (2020). Towards secure FinTech: A survey, taxonomy, and open research challenges. *IEEE Access : Practical Innovations, Open Solutions*, *8*, 23391–23406. doi:10.1109/ACCESS.2020.2970430

Mehrotra, A., & Menon, S. (2021, January). The second round of FinTech trends and challenges. In *2021 2nd International Conference on Computation, Automation and Knowledge Management (ICCAKM)* (pp.–243–248). IEEE. 10.1109/ICCAKM50778.2021.9357759

Mensah, J. (2019). Sustainable development: Meaning, history, principles, pillars, and implications for human action. *Literature review, 5*(1). 10.1080/23311886.2019.1653531

Mention, A. L. (2019). The future of fintech. *Research Technology Management*, *62*(4), 59–63. doi:10.1080/08956308.2019.1613123

Merriam, S. B. (1998). Merriam S 1998 S1.pdf. In Qualitative Research and Case Study Applications in Education.

Mhlanga, D. (2020). Industry 4.0 in finance: The impact of artificial intelligence (ai) on digital financial inclusion. *International Journal of Financial Studies*, *8*(3), 45. doi:10.3390/ijfs8030045

MicroSave. (2022). *Library.* MicroSave. https://www.microsave.net/library/

Migliorelli, M. (2021). What Do We Mean by Sustainable Finance? Assessing Existing Frameworks and Policy Risks. *Sustainability*, *13*(2), 975. doi:10.3390u13020975

Migozzi, J., Urban, M., & Wójcik, D. (2023, March). "You should do what India does": FinTech ecosystems in India reshaping the geography of finance. *Geoforum*, *103720*, 103720. doi:10.1016/j.geoforum.2023.103720

Millington, T., & Niranjan, M. (2021). Construction of minimum spanning trees from financial returns using rank correlation. *Physica A*, *566*, 125605. doi:10.1016/j.physa.2020.125605

Mills, E. (2012). The greening of insurance. *Science*, *338*(6113), 1424–1425. doi:10.1126cience.1229351 PMID:23239720

Mirza, A. A. I., Muhamed, N. A., & Kamarubahrin, A. F. (2021). Islamic Insurtech Conceptual Framework: A Proposal. Ihtifaz. *Journal of Islamic Economics, Finance, and Banking*, *4*(2), 131–143.

Mishra, PSant, T. G. (2023). Examine the level of environmental, social and governance disclosure in sustainability report – a study of the Indian banking sector. International Journal of Innovation Science, (ahead-of-print). https://doi.org/10.1108/IJIS-08-2022-0136

Mishra, A., & Ray, B. (2018). Need of skill development in hand made carpet industry: A socio-economic perspective. *Journal of the Textile Association*, *79*(1), 24–27.

Moed, H. F., Markusova, V., & Akoev, M. (2018). Trends in Russian research output indexed in Scopus and Web of Science. *Scientometrics*, *116*(2), 1153–1180. doi:10.100711192-018-2769-8

Mogaji, E., & Nguyen, N. P. (2022). The dark side of mobile money: Perspectives from an emerging economy. *Technological Forecasting and Social Change*, *185*, 122045. doi:10.1016/j.techfore.2022.122045

Mohammadhosseini, H., & Awal, A. A. (2013). PHYSICAL AND MECHANICAL PROPERTIES OF CONCRETE CONTAINING FIBERS FROM INDUSTRIAL CARPET WASTE. *IJRET: International Journal of Research in Engineering and Technology, 2*(12), 464-468. https://citeseerx.ist.psu.edu/document?repid=rep1&type=pdf&doi=696db3c274267eff4b37a07641ffb5b63f0c4fb5

Mondego, D. Y., & Gide, E. (2020). Exploring the factors that have impact on Consumers'trust in Mobile Payment Systems nn Australia. *JISTEM-Journal of Information Systems and Technology Management, 17*, e202017009. doi:10.4301/S1807-1775202017009

Montoya, F. G., Alcayde, A., Baños, R., & Manzano-Agugliaro, F. (2018). A fast method for identifying worldwide scientific collaborations using the Scopus database. *Telematics and Informatics*, *35*(1), 168–185. doi:10.1016/j.tele.2017.10.010

Moravcikova, D., & Kliestikova, J. (2017). Brand building with using phygital marketing communication. Journal of Economics. *Business and Management*, *5*(3), 148–153.

Morgan, P. J., & Long, T. Q. (2020). Financial literacy, financial inclusion, and savings behavior in Laos. *Journal of Asian Economics*, *68*, 101197. doi:10.1016/j.asieco.2020.101197

Mosteanu, N. R., & Faccia, A. (2020). Digital systems and new challenges of financial management–FinTech, XBRL, blockchain and cryptocurrencies. *Quality - Access to Success*, *21*(174), 159–166.

Mouna, A., & Jarboui, A. (2022). Understanding the link between government cashless policy, digital financial services and socio-demographic characteristics in the MENA countries. *The International Journal of Sociology and Social Policy*, *42*(5–6), 416–433. doi:10.1108/IJSSP-12-2020-0544

mSTAR. (2019). *India Digital Financial Inclusion Report- Journey Map.* USAID, fhi360.

Muganyi, T., Yan, L., & Sun, H. P. (2021). Green finance, Fintech and environmental protection: Evidence from China. *Environmental Science and Ecotechnology*, *7*, 100107. doi:10.1016/j.ese.2021.100107 PMID:36160697

Mumtaz, M. Z., & Yoshino, N. (2021). Greenness index: IPO performance and portfolio allocation. *Research in International Business and Finance*, *57*, 101398. doi:10.1016/j.ribaf.2021.101398

Musau, S., Muathe, S., & Mwangi, L. (2018). Financial inclusion, bank competitiveness and credit risk of commercial banks in Kenya. *International Journal of Financial Research*, *9*(1), 203. doi:10.5430/ijfr.v9n1p203

Mustajbasic, A. (2018). *Introducing an e-marketplace and phygital store to the Swiss market.*

Muthaiyah, S., & Zaw, T. O. K. (2020). Digital know-how and FinTech readiness. In *Understanding Digital Industry* (pp. 1–4). Routledge. doi:10.1201/9780367814557-01

Naeem, M. A., Karim, S., Rabbani, M. R., Bashar, A., & Kumar, S. (2022). Current state and future directions of green and sustainable finance: a bibliometric analysis. *Qualitative Research in Financial Markets*. doi:10.1108/QRFM-10-2021-0174/FULL/PDF

Nakamoto, S. (2019). *Bitcoin: A peer-to-peer electronic cash system*. Manubot.

Namvar, E. (2014). An introduction to peer-to-peer loans as investments. *Journal of Investment Management First Quarter.*

Naranje, A. G. (2023). Future Of Digital Payment System in India: An Overview. *International Journal for Multidisciplinary Research International Conference on Multidisciplinary Research & Studies.*

Nassiry, D. (2018). *The role of FinTech in unlocking green finance: Policy insights for developing countries*. Econstor. https://www.econstor.eu/handle/10419/190304

Nassiry, D. (2018).*The role of fintech in unlocking green finance: policy insights for developing countries*. ADB. https://www.adb.org/sites/default/files/publication/464821/adbi-wp883.pdf

Nath, H., & Boro, D. (2022). Use and Awareness of Digital Payment in Rural Areas: Special reference to Lakhimpur District, Assam. *IJFANS, 11*. www.ijfans.org, Vol.11, Iss. 7

Navickas, V., Kontautiene, R., Stravinskiene, J., Bilan, Y., Navickas, V., Kontautiene, R., Stravinskiene, J., & Bilan, Y. (2021). Paradigm shift in the concept of corporate social responsibility: COVID-19. *Green, 3*(2), 138–152. doi:10.3934/GF.2021008

Nemteanu, M. S., Dinu, V., & Dabija, D. C. (2021). Job insecurity, job instability, and job satisfaction in the context of the COVID-19 pandemic. *Journal of Competitiveness, 13*(2), 65–82. doi:10.7441/joc.2021.02.04

Nenavath, S. (2022). Impact of FinTech and green finance on environmental quality protection in India: By applying the semi-parametric difference-in-differences (SDID). *Renewable Energy, 193*, 913–919. doi:10.1016/j.renene.2022.05.020

Nenavath, S., & Mishra, S. (2023). Impact of green finance and Fintech on sustainable economic growth: Empirical evidence from India. *Heliyon, 9*(5), e16301. doi:10.1016/j.heliyon.2023.e16301 PMID:37234625

Nguyen, C., & Wald, J. K. (2022, May 16). Debt maturity and the choice between bank loans and public bonds. *Review of Quantitative Finance and Accounting, 59*(1), 239–272. doi:10.100711156-022-01067-7

Niankara, I. (2023). The impact of financial inclusion on digital payment solution uptake within the Gulf Cooperation Council Economies. *International Journal of Innovation Studies, 7*(1), 1-17. doi:10.1016/j.ijis.2022.09.004

Nicholls, A. (n.d.). *Policies, Initiatives, and Regulations Related to Sustainable Finance*. Asian Development Bank. https://www.adb.org/sites/default/files/institutional-document/691951/ado2021bp-policies-initiatives-regulations.pdf

Nikhitha, U., & Shalini, R. (). Adoption of digital payment system: A study conducted in the state of Karnataka. Intern*ational Research Journal of Modernization in Engineering Technology and Science 5*(4).

Nordhaus, W. D. (2011). The architecture of climate economics: Designing a global agreement on global warming. *Bulletin of the Atomic Scientists*, *67*(1), 9–18. doi:10.1177/0096340210392964

Nordhaus, W. D. (2018). Projections and Uncertainties about Climate Change in an Era of Minimal Climate Policies †. *American Economic Journal. Economic Policy*, *10*(3), 333–360. doi:10.1257/pol.20170046

Noreen, M., Mia, M. S., Ghazali, Z., & Ahmed, F. (2022). Role of Government Policies to Fintech Adoption and Financial Inclusion: A Study in Pakistan. *Universal Journal of Accounting and Finance*, *10*(1), 37–46. doi:10.13189/ujaf.2022.100105

NSO. (2020). *Sustainable Development Goals National Indicator Framework Progress Report* . GoI, Ministry of Statistics & Programme Implementation .

Nudurupati, S. S., Budhwar, P., Pappu, R. P., Chowdhury, S., Kondala, M., Chakraborty, A., & Ghosh, S. K. (2022). Transforming sustainability of Indian small and medium-sized enterprises through circular economy adoption. *Journal of Business Research*, *149*, 250–269. doi:10.1016/j.jbusres.2022.05.036

O'Mahony, T., & O'Mahony, T. (2020). State of the art in carbon taxes: a review of the global conclusions. *Green Finance, 2*(4), 409–423. doi:10.3934/GF.2020022

OECD. (2022). *Aggregate Trends of Climate Finance Provided and Mobilised by Developed Countries in 2013-2020*. OECD. https://www.oecd.org/climate-change/finance-usd-100-billion-goal/aggregate-trends-of-climate-finance-provided-and-mobilised-by-developed-countries-in-2013-2020.pdf

Olowookere, D. (2019). Role of fintech in accelerating financial inclusion in Nigeria. *Business Post Nigeria*. https://businesspost.ng/featureoped/role-of-fintech-in-acceleratingfinancial-inclusion-in-nigeria/

Omarini, A. E. (2018). Fintech and the future of the payment landscape: The mobile wallet ecosystem. A challenge for retail banks? *International Journal of Financial Research*, *9*(4), 97–116. doi:10.5430/ijfr.v9n4p97

Omarova, S. T. (2020). Technology v technocracy: Fintech as a regulatory challenge. *Journal of Financial Regulation*, *6*(1), 75–124. doi:10.1093/jfr/fjaa004

Ozili, P. K. (2018). Impact of digital finance on financial inclusion and stability. *Borsa Istanbul Review*, *18*(4), 329–340. doi:10.1016/j.bir.2017.12.003

Ozili, P. K. (2021). Financial inclusion research around the world: A review. *The Forum for Social Economics*, *50*(4), 457–479. doi:10.1080/07360932.2020.1715238

Ozili, P. K. (2021). Has financial inclusion made the financial sector riskier? *Journal of Financial Regulation and Compliance*, *29*(3), 237–255. doi:10.1108/JFRC-08-2020-0074

P., V. (2021). 11 Indian Green Startups working for the climate. *Medium*. https://medium.com/climate-conscious/11-indian-green-startups-working-for-the-climate-583169f83862

Pacelli, V., Miglietta, F., & Foglia, M. (2022). The extreme risk connectedness of the new financial system: European evidence. *International Review of Financial Analysis*, *84*, 102408. doi:10.1016/j.irfa.2022.102408

Pal, J., Chandra, P., Kameswaran, V., Parameshwar, A., Joshi, S., & Johri, A. (2018, April). Digital payment and its discontents: Street shops and the Indian government's push for cashless transactions. In *Proceedings of the 2018 CHI Conference on Human Factors in Computing Systems* (pp. 1–13). IEEE. 10.1145/3173574.3173803

Pant, S. K. (2020). Fintech: Emerging Trends. *Telecom Business Review, 13*(1).

Papoutsi, A., & Sodhi, M. M. S. (2020). Does disclosure in sustainability reports indicate actual sustainability performance? *Journal of Cleaner Production*, *260*, 121049. doi:10.1016/j.jclepro.2020.121049

Parvathy, V., & Durairaj, D. (2023). Upi System: Utilisation and User Reaction toward Cost-Free Digital Payment Platform among Mobile Payment Users in Chennai. *Resmilitaris, 13*(3), 357-369.

Pástor, Ľ., Stambaugh, R. F., & Taylor, L. A. (2021). Sustainable investing in equilibrium. *Journal of Financial Economics*, *142*(2), 550–571. doi:10.1016/j.jfineco.2020.12.011

Patel, R., Kumar, S., Bouri, E., & Iqbal, N. (2023). Spillovers between green-and dirty cryptocurrencies and socially responsible investments around the war in Ukraine. *International Review of Economics & Finance*, *87*, 143–162. doi:10.1016/j.iref.2023.04.013

Patki, A., & Sople, V. (2020). Indian banking sector: Blockchain implementation, challenges and way forward. *Journal of Banking and Financial Technology*, *4*(1), 65–73. doi:10.100742786-020-00019-w

Pawłowska, M., Staniszewska, A., & Grzelak, M. (2022). *Does fintech promote the sustainable development of renewable energy enterprises?*

Pawłowska, M., Staniszewska, A., & Grzelak, M. (2022). Impact of Fintech on Sustainable Development. Financial Sciences. *Nauki o Finansach*, *27*(2), 49-66.

Pee, L. G., & Pan, S. L. (2022). Climate-intelligent cities and resilient urbanisation: Challenges and opportunities for information research. *International Journal of Information Management*, *63*, 102446. doi:10.1016/j.ijinfomgt.2021.102446

Pentland, A., & Shrier, D. L. (Eds.). (2016). *Frontiers of financial technology: Expeditions in future commerce, from blockchain and digital banking to prediction markets and beyond.* VisionaryFuture.

Phadke, S. (2020). *FinTech future: The digital DNA of finance*. Sage Publications Pvt. Limited. doi:10.4135/9789353885687

Pham, M. H., & Doan, T. P. L. (2020). The impact of financial inclusion on financial stability in Asian countries. *Journal of Asian Finance, Economics and Business*, *7*(6), 47–59. doi:10.13106/jafeb.2020.vol7.no6.047

Phan, D. H. B., Narayan, P. K., Rahman, R. E., & Hutabarat, A. R. (2020). Do financial technology firms influence bank performance? *Pacific-Basin Finance Journal*, *20*, 1–13. doi:10.1016/j.pacfin.2019.101210

Philippon, T. (2016). *The fintech opportunity (No. w22476)*. National Bureau of Economic Research. doi:10.3386/w22476

Phu, G. N. (2023). Factors Affecting the Use of Best Available Techniques and the Impact on Business Sustainability. *International Journal of Asian Business and Information Management*, *14*(1), 1–18. doi:10.4018/IJABIM.325651

Pourmoradian, S., Shoari, A. V., Omarzadeh, D., Sharifi, A. N. S., & Hosseini, S. S. (2021). An Integrated Approach to Assess Potential and Sustainability of Handmade Carpet Production in Different Areas of the East Azerbaijan Province of Iran. *Sustainability (Switzerland)*, *13*(4), 1–21. doi:10.3390u13042251

Prakash, P. (2020). Financial Inclusion Plan- Progress and Prospects. *IJRAR*, *7*(1).

Pritchard, A. (1969). Statistical bibliography or bibliometrics. *The Journal of Documentation*, *25*, 348.

Priya, P. K., & Anusha, K. (2019). Fintech issues and challenges in India. *International Journal of Recent Technology and Engineering*, *8*(3), 904–908.

Purkayastha, N. N., & Tuzlukaya, Ş. E. (2020). Determination Of The Benefits And Risks Of Peer-To-Peer (P2p) Lending: A Social Network Teory Approach. *Copernican Journal of Finance & Accounting*, *9*(3), 131–143. doi:10.12775/CJFA.2020.016

Puschmann, T., Hoffmann, C. H., & Khmarskyi, V. (2020). How Green FinTech Can Alleviate the Impact of Climate Change-The Case of Switzerland. *Sustainability*, *12*(24), 10691. doi:10.3390u122410691

PwC. (2020). *The Future of Banking: From Digital to Phygital*. PWC. https://www.pwc.in/assets/pdfs/publications/2020/the-future-of-banking-from-digital-to-phygital.pdf

Rabbani, M. R. (2022). Fintech innovations, scope, challenges, and implications in Islamic Finance: A systematic analysis. *International Journal of Computing and Digital Systems*, *11*(1), 1–28.

Rajesh Barik, P. S. (2019). Analyzing the progress and prospects of financial inclusion in India. *Journal of Public Affairs*.

Rajeswari, P., & Vijai, C. (2021). Fintech industry in India: the revolutionised finance sector. *Eur. J. Mol. Clin. Med, 8*(11).

Ramadani, V., Agarwal, S., Caputo, A., Agrawal, V., & Dixit, J. K. (2022, April 18). Sustainable competencies of social entrepreneurship for sustainable development: Exploratory analysis from a developing economy. *Business Strategy and the Environment, 31*(7), 3437–3453. doi:10.1002/bse.3093

Rambaud, S. C., & Gázquez, A. E. (2022). A RegTech approach to Fintech sustainability: The case of Spain. *European Journal of Risk Regulation, 13*(2), 333–349. doi:10.1017/err.2021.62

Rana, N. P., Luthra, S., & Rao, H. R. (2023). Assessing challenges to the mobile wallet usage in India: An interpretive structural modelling approach. *Information Technology & People, 36*(4), 1533–1554. doi:10.1108/ITP-07-2021-0535

Rasiwala, F. S., & Kohli, B. (2021, January). Artificial Intelligence in FinTech. *International Journal of Business Intelligence Research, 12*(1), 48–65. doi:10.4018/IJBIR.20210101.oa3

Rastogi, S., Panse, C., Sharma, A., & Bhimavarapu, V. M. (2021). Unified Payment Interface (UPI): A Digital Innovation and Its Impact on Financial Inclusion and Economic Development. *Universal Journal of Accounting and Finance., 9*(3), 518–530. doi:10.13189/ujaf.2021.090326

Ray, T. (2020). *Scopes and Impact of Cloud Computing on Banking & FinTech.*

RBI. (2021-22). *Trend and Progress of Banking in India.* New Delhi: RBI.

Reich, G. (2021). People love digital banking but will they surrender all their data? *The Financial Brand.* https://thefinancialbrand.com/news/open-banking/people-love-digital-banking-but-will-they-surrender-all-their-data-121891/

Ren, B., & Lucey, B. (2022). A clean, green haven?—Examining the relationship between clean energy, clean and dirty cryptocurrencies. *Energy Economics, 109*, 105951. doi:10.1016/j.eneco.2022.105951

Ren, B., & Lucey, B. (2022). Do clean and dirty cryptocurrency markets herd differently? *Finance Research Letters, 47*, 102795. doi:10.1016/j.frl.2022.102795

Reserve Bank of India. (2020). *FinTech: The Force of Creative Disruption.* RBI. https://rbidocs.rbi.org.in/rdocs/Bulletin/PDFs/7FINTECHEED4C43FC31D43C9B9D7F8F31D01B08E.PDF

Reserve Bank of India. (2021).*Green Finance in India: Progress and Challenges.* RBI. https://rbidocs.rbi.org.in/rdocs/Bulletin/PDFs/04AR_2101202185D9B6905ADD465CB7DD280B88266F77.PDF

Rešovský, M., Horváth, D., Gazda, V., & Siničáková, M. (2013). Minimum spanning tree application in the currency market. *Biatec, 21*(7), 21–23.

Rise. (2021). *Rise FinTech Insights climate fintech.* Barclays. https://rise.barclays/content/dam/thinkrise-com/documents/Rise-FinTech-Insights-climate-fintech-2021-DIGITAL.pdf

Ritchie, H. (2018). *Plastic Pollution*. Our World in Data. https://ourworldindata.org/plastic-pollution

Riva, F., Magrizos, S., Rubel, M. R. B., & Rizomyliotis, I. (2022). Green consumerism, green perceived value, and restaurant revisit intention: Millennials' sustainable consumption with moderating effect of green perceived quality. *Business Strategy and the Environment, 31*(7), 2807–2819. doi:10.1002/bse.3048

Robert Cull, T. E. (2014). Financial Inclusion and Development: Recent Impact Evidence. *Focus Note, 92*, 1.

Roh, T., Yang, Y. S., Xiao, S., & Park, B. I. (2022). What makes consumers trust and adopt fintech? An empirical investigation in China. *Electronic Commerce Research*, •••, 1–33. doi:10.100710660-021-09527-3

Romānova, I., & Kudinska, M. (2016). Banking and fintech: A challenge or opportunity? In Contemporary issues in finance: Current challenges from across *Europe, 98*, 21–35.

Romānova, I., & Kudinska, M. (2016). Banking and Fintech: A challenge or opportunity? In *Contemporary Issues in Finance: Current Challenges from across Europe*. Emerald Group Publishing Limited. doi:10.1108/S1569-375920160000098002

Rossolini, M., Pedrazzoli, A., & Ronconi, A. (2021). Greening crowdfunding campaigns: An investigation of message framing and effective communication strategies for funding success. *International Journal of Bank Marketing, 39*(7), 1395–1419. doi:10.1108/IJBM-01-2021-0039

Roszkowska, P. (2021). Fintech in financial reporting and audit for fraud prevention and safeguarding equity investments. *Journal of Accounting & Organizational Change, 17*(2), 164–196. doi:10.1108/JAOC-09-2019-0098

Rouibah, K., Lowry, P. B., & Hwang, Y. (2016). The effects of perceived enjoyment and perceived risks on trust formation and intentions to use online payment systems: New perspectives from an Arab country. *Electronic Commerce Research and Applications, 19*, 33–43. doi:10.1016/j.elerap.2016.07.001

S. B. F. N. Network. (2023). *Developing sustainable finance roadmaps*. Sustainable Banking and Finance Network. https://www.sbfnetwork.org/wp-content/assets/toolkit/SBFN_Sustainable_Finance_Roadmap-Toolkit_Guide.pdf

Sachdeva, M. (2021). India Ranks 1st in Digital payment transactions globally. *In Shorts*. https://inshorts.com/en/news/india-ranks-1st-in-digital-payment-transactions-globally-report-1617259436829

Saha, A. K., Barua, S., & Nath, S. D. (2021). Blockchain for financial technology: Challenges and opportunities for India. The Impact of Artificial Intelligence on Governance. *Economics and Finance, I*, 247–261.

Salampasis, D., & Mention, A. L. (2018). *FinTech: Harnessing Innovation for Financial Inclusion. Handbook of Blockchain* (Vol. 2). Digital Finance, and Inclusion. doi:10.1016/b978-0-12-812282-2.00018-8

Saon Ray, P. M. (2022). *Digital Financial Inclusion and Literacy from a G20 Perspective*. Asian Development Bank Institute.

Sarin, S., Haon, C., Belkhouja, M., Mas-Tur, A., Roig-Tierno, N., Sego, T., & Carley, S. (2020). Uncovering the knowledge flows and intellectual structures of research in Technological Forecasting and Social Change: A journey through history. *Technological Forecasting and Social Change*, *160*, 120210. doi:10.1016/j.techfore.2020.120210

Satpathy, I. B., Patnaik, B. C. M., & Das, P. K. (2015). Banishing Financial Untouchability of the Poor through PMJDY- A Tryst with New Destiny. *Mediterranean Journal of Social Sciences*. doi:10.5901/mjss.2015.v6n2p184

Saunila, M., Ukko, J., & Rantala, T. (2018). Sustainability as a driver of green innovation investment and exploitation. *Journal of Cleaner Production*, *179*, 631–641. doi:10.1016/j.jclepro.2017.11.211

Saura, J. R., Palos-Sanchez, P., & Grilo, A. (2019). Detecting Indicators for Startup Business Success: Sentiment Analysis Using Text Data Mining. *Sustainability*, *11*(3). 917. doi:10.3390/SU11030917

Savitha, B., Hawaldar, I. T., & Kumar, K. N. (2022, November). Continuance intentions to use FinTech peer-to-peer payments apps in India. *Heliyon*, *8*(11), e11654. doi:10.1016/j.heliyon.2022.e11654 PMID:36411928

Schalatek, L. (2012). Democratizing climate finance governance and the public funding of climate action. *Democratization*, *19*(5), 951–973. doi:10.1080/13510347.2012.709690

Schindler, J. W. (2017). *FinTech and financial innovation: Drivers and depth*.

Schneider, T. E. (2011). Is environmental performance a determinant of bond pricing? Evidence from the U.S. pulp and paper and chemical industries. *Contemporary Accounting Research*, *28*(5), 1537–1561. doi:10.1111/j.1911-3846.2010.01064.x

Schoenmaker, D. & Schramade, W. (2019). *Principles of Sustainable Finance*. Oxford University Press.https://papers.ssrn.com/sol3/papers.cfm?abstract_id=3282699

Schueffel, P. (2016). Taming the Beast: A scientific definition of fintech. *Journal of Innovation Management*, *4*(4), 32–54. doi:10.24840/2183-0606_004.004_0004

Schulz, K., & Feist, M. (2021). Leveraging blockchain technology for innovative climate finance under the Green Climate Fund. *Earth System Governance*, *7*, 100084. doi:10.1016/j.esg.2020.100084

Schumacher, K. (2022). *Environmental, Social, and Governance (ESG) Factors and Green Productivity: The Impacts of Greenwashing and Competence Greenwashing on Sustainable Finance and ESG Investing*. SSRN Electronic Journal. doi:10.2139/SSRN.4303609

Segall, R. S., & Sankarasubbu, V. (2022). Using Open-Source Software for Business, Urban, and Other Applications of Deep Neural Networks, Machine Learning, and Data Analytics Tools. *International Journal of Artificial Intelligence and Machine Learning*, *12*(1), 1–28. doi:10.4018/IJAIML.307905

SFWG. (2018). *Third Sustainable Finance Working Group (SFWG)*. DEA. https://dea.gov.in/sites/default/files/Third%20Sustainable%20Finance%20Working%20Group%20%28SFWG%29.pdf

Shah, P. (2019). *How fintech is revolutionising with blockchain technology*.

Shah, K., Mare, S., & Anderson, R. (2019). Understanding mobile money grievances from tweets. In *ACM International Conference Proceeding Series*. ACM. doi: 10.1145/3287098.3287123

Shanker, S., & Barve, A. (2021). Analysing sustainable concerns in diamond supply chain: A fuzzy ISM-MICMAC and DEMATEL approach. *International Journal of Sustainable Engineering*, *14*(5), 1269–1285. doi:10.1080/19397038.2020.1862351

Sharma, A., Kumari, R., & Goel, N. (2022). Universal Health Coverage (UHC): Case Study on World's Health Emerging Strategy after the COVID-19 Pandemic. In Handbook of Research on Global Networking Post COVID-19 (pp. 328-341). IGI Global.

Sharma, M., & Elmiligi, H. (2022). Behavioral biometrics: Past, present and future. *Recent Advances in Biometrics*, 69.

Shashikala, K. (2019). Digital disruption in the banking industry. *International Journal of Social and Economic Research*, *9*(3), 56–61. doi:10.5958/2249-6270.2019.00019.9

Shetty, K. U., & Kulal, A. (2017). Financial Inclusion through Mobile Banking in India. *SSRN 3768366*.

Shihadeh F., & Liu, B. (2019). Does financial inclusion influence the banks risk and performance? Evidence from global prospects. *Academy of Accounting and Financial Studies Journal, 23*(3).

Shihadeh, F. (2020). The influence of financial inclusion on banks' performance and risk: New evidence from MENAP. *Banks and Bank Systems*, *15*(1), 59–71. doi:10.21511/bbs.15(1).2020.07

Shihadeh, F. (2021). Financial inclusion and banks' performance: Evidence from palestine. *Investment Management and Financial Innovations*, *18*(1), 126–138. doi:10.21511/imfi.18(1).2021.11

Siddiqui, T. A., & Siddiqui, K. I. (2020). FinTech in India: An analysis on impact of telecommunication on financial inclusion. *Strategic Change*, *29*(3), 321–330. doi:10.1002/jsc.2331

Siemroth, C., & Hornuf, L. (2023). Why Do Retail Investors Pick Green Investments? A Lab-in-the-Field Experiment with Crowdfunders. *Journal of Economic Behavior & Organization*, *209*, 74–90. doi:10.1016/j.jebo.2023.02.023

Siew, R. Y. J. (2015). A review of corporate sustainability reporting tools (SRTs). *Journal of Environmental Management*, *164*, 180–195. doi:10.1016/j.jenvman.2015.09.010 PMID:26379255

Singh, S. K., Singh, S. S., & Singh, V. L. (2023). Predicting adoption of next generation digital technology utilizing the adoption-diffusion model fit: The case of mobile payments interface in an emerging economy. *ACCESS Journal: Access to Science, Business, Innovation in Digital Economy*, *4*(1), 130-148. doi:10.46656/access.2023.4.1(10)

Singh, A. K., & Sharma, P. (2023). A study of Indian Gen X and Millennials consumers' intention to use FinTech payment services during COVID-19 pandemic. *Journal of Modelling in Management*, *18*(4), 1177–1203. doi:10.1108/JM2-02-2022-0059

Singh, K., & Misra, M. (2022). The evolving path of CSR: Toward business and society relationship. *Journal of Economic and Administrative Sciences*, *38*(2), 304–332. doi:10.1108/JEAS-04-2020-0052

Singh, V. K., Singh, P., Karmakar, M., Leta, J., & Mayr, P. (2021). The journal coverage of Web of Science, Scopus and Dimensions: A comparative analysis. *Scientometrics*, *126*(6), 5113–5142. doi:10.100711192-021-03948-5

Sinha, S., Pandey, K. R., & Madan, N. (2018, March). Fintech and the demand side challenge in financial inclusion. *Enterprise Development & Microfinance*, *29*(1), 94–98. doi:10.3362/1755-1986.17-00016

Smith, R. D. (2009). *The spread of the credit crisis: view from a stock correlation network.* arXiv preprint arXiv:0901.1392.

Sreepriya, J., Suprabha, K. R., & Prasad, K. (2023). Does GRI compliance moderate the impact of sustainability disclosure on firm value? *Society and Business Review*, *18*(1), 152–174. doi:10.1108/SBR-06-2022-0172

Srivastav, S. (2020). *Blockchain in Fintech: A Catalyst for Disruption in Finance World.*

Srivastava, A. (2022, July 8). Digital Financial Inclusion. *International Journal of Innovation in the Digital Economy*, *13*(1), 1–12. doi:10.4018/IJIDE.303611

Srouji, J. (2020). Digital Payments, the Cashless Economy, and Financial Inclusion in the United Arab Emirates: Why Is Everyone Still Transacting in Cash? *Journal of Risk and Financial Management*, *13*(11), 260. doi:10.3390/jrfm13110260

Statista. (2022). *Green bonds worldwide.* Statista. https://www-statista-com.eu1.proxy.openathens.net/study/108882/green-bonds-worldwide/

Stolbov, M., & Shchepeleva, M. (2023). Does one size fit all? Comparing the determinants of the FinTech market segments expansion. *The Journal of Finance and Data Science*, *9*, 100095. doi:10.1016/j.jfds.2023.01.002

Stroebel, J., & Wurgler, J. (2021). What do you think about climate finance? *Journal of Financial Economics*, *142*(2), 487–498. doi:10.1016/j.jfineco.2021.08.004

Suhr, H. C. (2023). Designing Audience Participation and Gamification in Intermedia Performance: Conceptual Framework and Theoretical Implications Post COVID-19. *International Journal of Art, Culture, Design, and Technology*, *12*(1), 1–13. doi:10.4018/IJACDT.316966

Sun, W., Tian, C., & Yang, G. (2015). *Network analysis of the stock market.*

Sun, Y., & Grimes, S. (2016). The emerging dynamic structure of national innovation studies: A bibliometric analysis. *Scientometrics*, *106*(1), 17–40. doi:10.100711192-015-1778-0

Su, X. (2021). Can green investment win the favor of investors in China? Evidence from the return performance of green investment stocks. *Emerging Markets Finance & Trade*, *57*(11), 3120–3138. doi:10.1080/1540496X.2019.1710129

Tabak, B. M., Silva, I. B. D. R., & Silva, T. C. (2022). Analysis of connectivity between the world's banking markets: The COVID-19 global pandemic shock. *The Quarterly Review of Economics and Finance*, *84*, 324–336. doi:10.1016/j.qref.2022.03.002 PMID:35310015

Taghizadeh-Hesary, F., & Yoshino, N. (2019). The way to induce private participation in green finance and investment. *Finance Research Letters*, *31*, 98–103. doi:10.1016/j.frl.2019.04.016

Taherdoost, H. (2023, February 13). Smart Contracts in Blockchain Technology: A Critical Review. *Information*, *14*(2), 117. doi:10.3390/info14020117

Tan, X., Dong, H., Liu, Y., Su, X., & Li, Z. (2022). Green bonds and corporate performance: A potential way to achieve green recovery. *Renewable Energy*, *200*, 59–68. doi:10.1016/j.renene.2022.09.109

Tariq, A., & Hassan, A. (2023). Role of green finance, environmental regulations, and economic development in the transition towards a sustainable environment. *Journal of Cleaner Production*, *413*, 137425. doi:10.1016/j.jclepro.2023.137425

Taylor, M. C. R., Wilson, C., Holttinen, E., & Morozova, A. (2020). *Institutional arrangements for Fintech regulation and supervision*. International Monetary Fund. doi:10.5089/9781513520308.063

Thakkar, J., & Thakkar, P. (2023). Digital Payments Revolution: A Study of Awareness, Acceptance, and Usage of Unified Payments Interface Technology Among Selected Women in India. *2022 OPJU International Technology Conference on Emerging Technologies for Sustainable Development (OTCON)*, Raigarh, Chhattisgarh, India. 10.1109/OTCON56053.2023.10114004

The Economic Times. (2023). Banks open more branches to cash in on credit growth. *The Economic Times*. economictimes.indiatimes.com: https://economictimes.indiatimes.com/industry/banking/finance/banking/banks-open-more-branches-to-cash-in-on-credit-growth/articleshow/97330007.cms

Thiry, M. C. (2004). A carpet of green. *AATCC Review*, *4*(7), 9–13.

Tian, H., Siddik, A. B., Pertheban, T. R., & Rahman, M. N. (2023). Does Fintech innovation and green transformational leadership improve green innovation and corporate environmental performance? A hybrid SEM–ANN approach. *Journal of Innovation & Knowledge*, *8*(3), 100396. doi:10.1016/j.jik.2023.100396

Times of India. (30 April, 2023), *The future of financial services in India* Monica Hovespain in Voices, Economy, TOI accessed on 22 July, 2023.

TN, N., & Shailendra Kulkarni, M. (2022). Zero click attacks–a new cyber threat for the e-banking sector. *Journal of Financial Crime*.

Tolliver, C., Keeley, A. R., & Managi, S. (2020). Drivers of green bond market growth: The importance of Nationally Determined Contributions to the Paris Agreement and implications for sustainability. *Journal of Cleaner Production*, *244*, 118643. doi:10.1016/j.jclepro.2019.118643

*Transforming India's Digital Payment Landscape*. (n.d.). Press Information Bureau. https://pib.gov.in/FeaturesDeatils.aspx?NoteId=151163

Tripathy, K. K., Paliwal, M., & Singh, A. (2022, May 8). Women's social entrepreneurship and livelihood innovation: An exploratory study from India. *Service Business*, *16*(4), 863–881. doi:10.100711628-022-00493-w

Truong, P. (2019). *Insight and its importance in the transactional marketing era*.

UN Enviornment. (2017). *Roadmap for Sustainable Finance*. World Bank. https://sustainabledevelopment.un.org/content/documents/2451121283121120171533333RoadmapforaSustainableFinancialSystem.pdf

UN. (n.d.). *THE 17 GOALS*. UN. https://sdgs.un.org/goals

United Nations. (2015). *Transforming our world: the 2030 Agenda for Sustainable Development*. UN.

US EPA. (2022). *Climate Change Indicators: Global Greenhouse Gas Emissions*. EPA. https://www.epa.gov/climate-indicators/climate-change-indicators-global-greenhouse-gas-emissions

Uyyala, P., & Yadav, D. C. (2023). The advanced proprietary AI/ML solution as Anti-fraudTensorlink4cheque (AFTL4C) for Cheque fraud detection. *The International journal of analytical and experimental modal analysis, 15*(4), 1914-1921.

Vaganova, O. (2021, March 8). Growth Points Of Fintech Industry In The Perception Of Financial Market Transformation. *European Proceedings of Social and Behavioural Sciences*. doi:10.15405/epsbs.2021.03.54

Vagra, D. (2017). *Fintech, the new era of financial services*. Research Gate. doi:10.14267/VEZTUD.2017.11.03

Vajid, A., & Farooqi, A. W. (2022). ISSUES AND CHALLENGES TO THE FINTECH INDUSTRY IN INDIA. [JEBR]. *EPRA International Journal of Economic and Business Review*, *10*(12), 16–22. doi:10.36713/epra12006

Van Eck, N. J., & Waltman, L. (2011). Text mining and visualization using VOSviewer. *arXiv preprint arXiv:1109.2058*.

van Niekerk, M. G., & Phaladi, N. H. (2021). Digital financial services: Prospects and challenges. *Potchefstroom Electronic Law Journal, 24*, 1–25. doi:10.17159/1727-3781/2021/v24i0a10744

Van Tichelen, B. (2019). *The role and opportunities of Phygital in the digital omni-channel strategy*. Louvain School of Management.

Varma, A. (2019). Fintech Adoption Choices of Small Businesses: A Technology Organization Environment (TOE) Framework study. *Accounting and Finance Research, 8*(2), 86. doi:10.5430/afr.v8n2p86

Vijai, C. (2019). *FinTech in India–opportunities and challenges. SAARJ Journal on Banking & Insurance Research* (Vol. 8). SJBIR.

Vinitha, K. & Shanmugam, V. (2017). Factors Influencing Consumer's Intention to Adopt Digital Payment-Conceptual Model. *Indian Journal of Public Health Research & Development*. doi:. doi:10.5958/0976-5506.2017.00181.4

Viswanathan, R. (2014). RBI report on financial inclusion: A review. *Economic and Political Weekly, 49*(9).

Vo, D. H., Nguyen, N. T., & Thi-Hong Van, L. (2021). Financial inclusion and stability in the Asian region using bank-level data. *Borsa Istanbul Review, 21*(1), 36–43. doi:10.1016/j.bir.2020.06.003

Volz, U. (2018). *Fostering Green Finance for Sustainable Development in Asia*. (ADBI Working Paper Series). Asian Development Bank Institute. www.adbi.org

Wang, M., Li, X., & Wang, S. (2021). Discovering research trends and opportunities of green finance and energy policy: A data-driven scientometric analysis. *Energy Policy, 154*, 112295. doi:10.1016/j.enpol.2021.112295

Wang, Z., Shahid, M. S., Binh An, N., Shahzad, M., & Abdul-Samad, Z. (2022). Does green finance facilitate firms in achieving corporate social responsibility goals? *Economic research-. Ekonomska Istrazivanja, 35*(1), 5400–5419. doi:10.1080/1331677X.2022.2027259

WEFORUM. (2020), *Phygital: a banking strategy for the new isolation economy*. World Economic Forum. Accessed on 12 July, 2023

Wilburn, K., & Wilburn, R. (2014). The double bottom line: Profit and social benefit. *Business Horizons, 57*(1), 11–20. doi:10.1016/j.bushor.2013.10.001

Wonglimpiyarat, J. (2018). Challenges and dynamics of FinTech crowd funding: An innovation system approach. *The Journal of High Technology Management Research, 29*(1), 98–108. doi:10.1016/j.hitech.2018.04.009

Woodyard, A. S., & Grable, J. E. (2018). Insights into the Users of Robo-Advisory Firms. *Journal of Financial Service Professionals, 72*(5).

World Commission on Environment. (1987). *Report of the World Commission on Environment and Development: Our Common Future Towards Sustainable Development 2. Part II. Common Challenges Population and Human Resources 4*. WCE.

Wüstenhagen, R., & Menichetti, E. (2012). Strategic choices for renewable energy investment: Conceptual framework and opportunities for further research. *Energy Policy*, *40*(1), 1–10. doi:10.1016/j.enpol.2011.06.050

Wylde, V., Rawindaran, N., Lawrence, J., Balasubramanian, R., Prakash, E., Jayal, A., & Platts, J. (2022). Cybersecurity, data privacy and blockchain: A review. *SN Computer Science*, *3*(2), 127. doi:10.100742979-022-01020-4 PMID:35036930

Xiao, S., & Adekola, T. A. (2021). Investment Robo-Advisors: Some Reflections on China's Regulatory Experience. *Banking & Finance Law Review*, *37*(1), 127–148.

Xie, J., Ifie, K., & Gruber, T. (2022). The dual threat of COVID-19 to health and job security–Exploring the role of mindfulness in sustaining frontline employee-related outcomes. *Journal of Business Research*, *146*, 216–227. doi:10.1016/j.jbusres.2022.03.030 PMID:35340762

Xu, R., Yao, D., & Zhou, M. (2023). Does the development of digital inclusive finance improve the enthusiasm and quality of corporate green technology innovation? *Journal of Innovation & Knowledge*, *8*(3), 100382. doi:10.1016/j.jik.2023.100382

Yadav, U. S., Tripathi, R., & Tripathi, M. A. (2022). Digital Analysis of theTransformation of Institutions in theKnowledge and Innovation Systemof the Handmade Carpet Industry. *SEDME (Small Enterprises Development,Management & Extension Journal)*, *49*(1). doi:10.1177/0970846422109690

Yan, T. C., Schulte, P., & Chuen, D. L. K. (2018). *InsurTech and FinTech: banking and insurance enablement. Handbook of Blockchain* (Vol. 1). Digital Finance, and Inclusion.

Yazan, B. (2015). Three Approaches to Case Study Methods in Education: Yin, Merriam, and Stake. *Qualitative Report*, *20*(2), 134–152. doi:10.46743/2160-3715/2015.2102

Yeow, K. E., & Ng, S. H. (2021). The impact of green bonds on corporate environmental and financial performance. *Managerial Finance*, *47*(10), 1486–1510. doi:10.1108/MF-09-2020-0481

Ye, W., Wong, W. K., Arnone, G., Nassani, A. A., Haffar, M., & Faiz, M. F. (2023). Crypto currency and green investment impact on global environment: A time series analysis. *International Review of Economics & Finance*, *86*, 155–169. doi:10.1016/j.iref.2023.01.030

Yin, R. K. (2009). *Case study research: Design and methods*. Sage.

Yin, R. K. (1994). Discovering the future of the case study method in evaluation research. *Evaluation Practice*, *15*(3), 283–290. doi:10.1016/0886-1633(94)90023-X

Youssef, M. (2022). What drives herding behavior in the cryptocurrency market?q. *Journal of Behavioral Finance*, *23*(2), 230–239. doi:10.1080/15427560.2020.1867142

Yu, E. P., Van Luu, B., & Chen, C. H. (2020). Greenwashing in environmental, social and governance disclosures. *Research in International Business and Finance*, *52*, 101192. doi:10.1016/j.ribaf.2020.101192

Yuniarti, S., & Rasyid, A. (2020, March). Consumer Protection in Lending Fintech Transaction in Indonesia: Opportunities and Challenges. In Journal of Physics: Conference Series, 1477(5), 052016. IOP Publishing.

Zhang, D., Zhang, Z., & Managi, S. (2019). A bibliometric analysis on green finance: Current status, development, and future directions. *Finance Research Letters*, *29*, 425–430. doi:10.1016/j.frl.2019.02.003

Zhang, Y. (2023). Impact of green finance and environmental protection on green economic recovery in South Asian economies: Mediating role of Fintech. *Economic Change and Restructuring*, *56*(3), 2069–2086. doi:10.100710644-023-09500-0

Zhang-Zhang, Y., Rohlfer, S., & Rajasekera, J. (2020). An eco-systematic view of cross-sector fintech: The case of Alibaba and Tencent. *Sustainability*, *12*(21), 8907. doi:10.3390u12218907

Zhao, G., Zhou, P., & Wen, W. (2021). Feed-in tariffs, knowledge stocks and renewable energy technology innovation: The role of local government intervention. *Energy Policy*, *156*, 112453. doi:10.1016/j.enpol.2021.112453

Zhou, G., Zhu, J., & Luo, S. (2022). The impact of Fintech innovation on green growth in China: Mediating effect of green finance. *Ecological Economics*, *193*, 107308. doi:10.1016/j.ecolecon.2021.107308

Zieba, M., & Johansson, E. (2022). Sustainability reporting in the airline industry: Current literature and future research avenues. *Transportation Research Part D, Transport and Environment*, *102*, 103133. doi:10.1016/j.trd.2021.103133

Ziolo, M., Bak, I., & Cheba, K. (2020). The Role of Sustainable Finance in Achieving Sustainable Development Goals: Does It Work? *Technological and Economic Development of Economy*, *27*(1), 45–70. doi:10.3846/tede.2020.13863

# About the Contributors

**Kuldeep Singh** is a Professor at the Faculty of Management Studies, CMS Business School, JAIN (Deemed to be University), Bangalore, India. His research area is Financial Management and Corporate Social Responsibility (CSR). He obtained his Doctorate in Finance from the Indian Institute of Information Technology, Allahabad, India, in 2022. Dr. Singh possesses expertise in various statistical methods and analytical techniques, including Inferential statistics, Mediation-Moderation analysis, Structural Equation Modeling, Time Series Analysis, forecasting through regression modeling, PLS-SEM, Difference-in-Difference (DiD) analysis, Propensity Score Matching, Interpretive Structural Modeling (ISM-MICMAC), Analytic Hierarchy Process (AHP), Systematic Literature Review, among others. In recognition of his scholarly work, he was honored with the Best Paper Award at the 6th Management Doctoral Colloquium, IIT Kharagpur in 2020. Dr. Singh has also contributed to the academic community by publishing several research papers in renowned journals and publishers. Furthermore, he has presented his research findings at esteemed international conferences such as IEEE and the Academy of Management (AOM).

**Rebecca Abraham** is a Finance Professor at the H. Wayne Huizenga School of Business and Entrepreneurship. She obtained her Doctorate in Business Administration-Finance from the U.S. International University in 1989. After serving as an adjunct instructor in the Department of Management Science at the National University, Dr. Abraham joined the Farquhar Center of Nova Southeastern University in the Fall of 1989. Throughout her career, Dr. Abraham has taught a wide range of courses at both undergraduate and graduate levels, including corporate finance, investments, portfolio theory, financial management, business strategy and policy, quantitative methods, microeconomics, and macroeconomics. Her dedication to teaching excellence was recognized when she received the first Farquhar Center Award for Teaching Excellence in 2000, as well as the Teacher of the Year Award from the Huizenga School in 2006, highlighting her exceptional service to students. Dr. Abraham has made significant contributions to her field through extensive publications in reputable journals. She is a member of the Editorial Review Board of Personality and Individual Differences and has authored a book chapter in a prestigious journal. Together with Dr. Robert Trippi, formerly of California State University-Long Beach, she has pioneered a methodology for determining implicit interest rates in option prices. Her research work has also been featured in the Conference Proceedings of the Decision Sciences Institute and the Association of Management.

**Prasanna Kolar** is an Assistant Professor in the College of Agriculture at KL University, Vijayawada, A.P., India. With a strong educational background and a Ph.D. in Agricultural Economics from Jawaharlal Nehru Krishi Vishwa Vidyalaya, Jabalpur, India, he has established himself as a knowledgeable and accomplished researcher in his field. Dr. Kolar has also qualified in ASRB NET in Agricultural Economics and KSET in Economics, showcasing his 2 expertise in these subjects. Throughout his career, Dr. Kolar has made significant contributions to the field of agricultural economics through extensive research and publications. His work has garnered wide recognition, with numerous research papers published in prestigious national and international journals that have received high ratings from the National Academy of Agricultural Sciences (NAAS), as well as indexing in Scopus and the Web of Science. In addition to his scholarly achievements, Dr. Prasanna Kolar actively engages in various sustainability and agricultural conferences, seminars, webinars, and training programs. Notably, he presented his research at various conferences, including prestigious IEEE conferences. His research areas include finance, marketing, development economics, micro and macroeconomics, international economics, statistical data analysis, linear programming, regression models, time series, cross-sectional and panel data analysis, and more. Through the dissemination of his findings to a wide range of experts and scholars, Dr. Kolar not only shares his knowledge but also plays a vital role in advancing the collective understanding and fostering the development of the agricultural economics and sustainability field.

* * *

**Biju A. V.** is an Assistant Professor at the Department of Commerce, School of Business Management and Legal Studies, University of Kerala. His research interests include digital payments, the crypto market, ESG, green bonds, and behavioural economics. He is a Research Sans Frontier (RSF) member in Dubai; this research association aims to contribute to society through quality research and building a bridge between industry and academia. He takes guest lectures at the University of Wollongong, Dubai, and Jain University, Cochin. He is the managing editor of the Journal of Commerce and Business Researcher, published by the Department of

Commerce, University of Kerala. He also serves as a review member of the Journal of the Knowledge Economy, SN Business and Economics, the International Journal of Applied Management Science, the International Journal of E-business Research (IJEBR), and the International Journal of Business Analytics (IJBAN). He received the best paper award from the IIM Nagpur conference in 2022. His papers have appeared in Quality & Quantity, Employee Responsibilities and Rights, IJHCITP, Springer Digital Finance, etc.

**Jehad Aldehayyat** is an associate professor of Strategic Management College of Business and Economics, Al-Hussein Bin Talal University, Jordan. He received a doctorate degree in The University of Huddersfield, West Yorkshire U.K. Currently he is working in digitalization strategic decision making. His primary research interest in strategic planning and strategic decision making within a variety of organizational contexts. His Work appears in the International Journal of Hospitality Management, Strategic Change, and Management Decision.

**Sreelekshmi G.** is a doctoral student at the Department of Commerce, School of Business Management and Legal Studies, University of Kerala. Keenly interested in sustainable finance, after completing her B.Com. and M.Com. with first position in both the programmes from the University of Kerala, she is pursuing research on the topic of green bonds under the guidance of Dr. Biju A. V. under the UGC JRF scheme.

**Vijaya G. S.**, BE (E& EE), MBA, PHD is currently working as Professor in Decision Science Department at CMS Business School, JAIN (Deemed-to-be University), Bengaluru, India. She has worked in reputed Indian institutions and at Al Yamamah University, Riyadh, Kingdom of Saudi Arabia in various capacities both in teaching and administration. Under her guidance six students have been awarded PhD and She has more than two decades of Post Graduate teaching experience and three years of Industry experience. She is a Life Member of Indian Society for Technical Education, International Association of Engineers (IAENG) and Quality Circle Forum of India. She has Published 40 plus articles in refereed and peer reviewed National and International journals and book chapters. She has presented papers at IIM Bengaluru, IIM Kozhikode, Management Training Institute, Steel Authority of India Limited, Ranchi, International Institute of Social and Economic Sciences (IISES), Venice, Italy, World conference 2022 held at Valencia, Spain and World Conference 2023 held at London, UK to name a few.

**Sridevi Gopakumar** is currently a full time PhD Scholar under the guideship of Dr. D. Madhava Priya. After completing her MBA in Marketing and HR with a CGPA of 9.68 from SRM University, Chennai she took up a lucrative corporate career but her eagerness to learn and explore new terrains motivated her to pursue her research. She is currently pursuing her research in the field of sustainability marketing.

**Nisha Goyal** is an Associate Professor of Finance at School of Commerce and Management Studies, Dayananda Sagar University. She has about 12 years of teaching and research experience in reputed management institutions. She holds a PhD from Malaviya National Institute of Technology, Jaipur in 2017 and qualified UGC NET-JRF in 2012. Her research work is published in reputed international publishers like Emerald, Wiley and Science direct. She actively participated in various national and international conferences. She is a regular reviewer for Emerald publishing, Taylor and Francis and Inderscience journals. Her research work has achieved more than 1,000 citations of her work with h-index 9 as on 2023. Her research interest includes Corporate Finance, Behavioral Finance and Financial literacy, Sustainable Finance.

**V. V. Devi Prasad Kotni** is currently working as Associate Professor in GITAM School of Business, GITAM Deemed-to-be University, Visakhapatnam. He has a total of 19 years of experience of which 4 years industry experience and 15 years of academic experience. He published around 20 publications in Scopus/ABDC/UGC Care indexed journals. He travelled across the world and presented papers in USA, Australia, Malaysia and Thailand sponsored by government of India. He completed one UGC Major Research Project (as co-investigator) and one UGC Minor Research Project (as principal investigator). He was awarded AICTE – Career Award for Young Teacher Research grant in 2013 (as principal investigator). He completed two consultancy projects as project leader. He procured a total of INR 19,87,399/- from various funding agencies through research and consultancy.

**Gaurav Kumar** is Assistant Professor at the Dr. B. R. Ambedkar National Institute of Technology (NIT) Jalandhar. He has done post-doctoral research in the area of Financial Data Analytics at University College Dublin (UCD), Ireland. He has obtained a Ph.D. degree from the Indian Institute of Technology (IIT), Kharagpur, and an MBA degree from the Indian Institute of Foreign Trade (IIFT), Delhi. He has studied the liquidity of midcap stocks as an area of research for his doctoral thesis. He holds an engineering degree in Computer science from the National Institute of Technology (NIT), Allahabad. He has industry experience in SAP ERP consulting while working for Tata Consultancy Services (TCS). He has received many awards and grants including UGC Junior Research Fellowship (JRF). His research work is presented at various international conferences at American Economic Association (USA), ICMA centre (London), Corvinus University (Hungary), La Trobe University (Melbourne, Australia). Recently, he has published in top-tier journals such as European Journal of Finance, Journal of Behavioural and Experimental Finance, and Asian Journal of Economics. His broad research interest includes Stock markets, Banking, Corporate Finance and Financial Analytics.

**Sunil Kumar** is an Assistant Professor at the GITAM School of Business, GITAM (Deemed to be University), Visakhapatnam, A.P., India. He has over seven years of teaching experience. He earned his PhD from the Jamia Millia Islamia (A Central University), New Delhi in the area of NGO Management. He has qualified UGC-NET-JRF in Management. His academic qualifications include BA, MBA, DCA and PhD. He has published papers in journals of repute indexed and listed in Scopus, Web of Science, ABDC and UGC care, etc. He is a life member of Indian Commerce Association.

**Reenu Kumari** is Associate Professor in the Department of Business and Management Studies, Meerut Institute of Engineering and Technology, Meerut, Uttar Pradesh, (India). She has received Ph.D from Indian Institute of Technology, Roorkee in 2017. She has qualified UGC NET (JRF) in 2011. She has thirteen year experience in teaching as well as research also. Her area of specialization is Finance & Accounting. Her are of interest FDI, Education, Economic Growth, Digitalization and Trade Openness. She has written and published many research papers in the national & international Journal and Conferences. She has reviewer in various journals including Sage, Emerald, Inderscience, and Elsevier. International Journal of Emerging Markets (IJoEM), Management Research Review (MRR), International Journal of Comparative Management (IJoCM), the Third PAN-IIM World Management Conference, Human Development and Capabilities (JoHDC), the social science Journal (SSJ), Transnational Corporations Review (TCR), South Asian Journal of business studies. She has taken various guest lecturers on research methodology in repute institutions.

**Sandhya M.** is currently working in Govt. First Grade College Kaup, having 25 years of experience in the teaching field. She is a life member of the All India Accounting Association. She has trained several students especially students of professional courses. Her primary research interest is Finance and corporate sustainability reporting.

**Pooja Mishra** is a Research Scholar at the Institute of Business Management, GLA University. She has completed her MBA from Banasthali University and has 8 years of Corporate Experience. Her main research interests are in Financial Management, Green Finance, Sustainable Finance, Fintech, Business Ethics, and Corporate Finance. She has publisher her research work in the Scopus, peer-reviewed and ESCI journals.

**Parthasarathi Narayanasamy** is a full-time doctoral student at the Loyola Institute of Business Administration in Chennai. Pondicherry University conferred upon him an MBA with a concentration in marketing. His journey with youth and socially marginalized individuals inspired him to conduct research in the field of Social Entrepreneurship for Social Transformation.

**Brahmadev Panda** is an assistant professor at Rajagiri Business School, Kochi. He has around eight years of teaching experience. He has published research papers in many national and international journals of repute. His area of research interest includes corporate finance, governance and financial market.

**Bhartrihari Pandiya** is currently working as an Assistant Professor at National Forensic Sciences University, Gandhinagar, Gujarat. Previously, he has served Presidency College, Bangalore and GLA University, Mathura. He has a total of 8 years of teaching and research experience. He has earned his doctoral degree from IIIT Allahabad in the area of Employer Branding and completed his MBA from NIT Silchar. He has published 18 research papers in ABDC/ SCOPUS and Web of Science journals apart from presenting his research in reputed conferences like IEEE IEEM Singapore, Pan IIM and Pan IIT etc. His teaching and research areas include Human Resource Management, Organizational behaviour, Crowdshipping etc.

**Sujit Kumar Patra** is an Associate Professor at GITAM School of Business, GITAM (Deemed to be University) Visakhapatnam, Andhra Pradesh, India. He has been a teacher for 17 years. His graduate and doctoral degrees are from Sambalpur University in Odisha. He was eligible for the UGC-NET in 2018. He has published papers in indexed journals in Scopus, WOS, SCI, and ABDC.

**Divya Prabhu**, an Educator and Researcher by passion is a Ph.D holder from JAIN (Deemed to be University) Bangalore, India. She holds an MBA and a BCom from Mangalore University with first rank in both the programmes. With experiences one year in industry and twelve years in education, her research interests include banking, finance, quality management, technology etc. Currently she is working as an Assistant Professor at MPM GFGC, Karkala, Udupi, Karnataka in India.

**Madhava Priya** is a Assistant Dean – Students' Attendance & Discipline & Chair – International Relations and Assistant Professor in Finance teaching Finance Courses at LIBA. She has over 5 years of corporate experience in capital market in various roles and 7 years of experience in teaching and 6 years in research. She has also been trainer for Depository Operations in Capital Market. Her areas of interest include Financial Management, Financial Markets, Behavioural Finance and Security analysis and Portfolio Management. Dr. D. Madhava Priya has a B.C.A., from Madras University, Chennai, an M.B.A., form Anna University, Chennai, M.Phil. in Management form Madurai Kamaraj University, Madurai, P.G.Diploma in NGO management., form Madurai Kamaraj University, Madurai, Ph.D in Management Sciences., from University of Madras. While working on her doctoral thesis she was awarded the Research scholarship by WFI- Ingolstadt and AUDI, Germany. She also has Capital Market, Commodities Market, Derivatives Market and NSDL Depository Operations Certification in Financial Markets from National Stock Exchange.

**Vinaya R.** is a Researcher, Educator, ambitious, passionate, responsible, and professional, who completed Master of Commerce in accounting and taxation from Bangalore University, Bangalore, Master of Business administration in Finance from Karnataka State Open University, Mysuru. Currently pursuing PhD from Dayananda Sagar University, Bengaluru. Area of Specialization - Finance.

**Gowtham Ramkumar** is working as an Assistant Professor in the Department of Commerce, School of Commerce, Finance and Accountancy, Christ (Deemed to be University), Bangalore. He completed his Doctorate of Philosophy in Commerce. He completed his Doctorate of Philosophy in Commerce, especially Taxation, at the Department of Commerce, SRM Institute of Science and Technology, Kattankulathur, Chennai. His area of teaching interests includes Taxation, Accounting and Finance and Research interests includes survey based methods in finance and applications of data science technologies in businesses. He also worked as Assistant Professor at the Department of Commerce, Madras Christian College.

**Ashwani Sharma** is an assistant professor at Department of Master of Business Administration at Dewan Institute of Management Studies, Meerut, India. He Holds a Ph.D (Commerce) degree from CCS University Meerut, received MBA Degree from AKTU University Lucknow and is certified in Digital marketing by Google. He has 12 years experience in teaching and research also. His area of Interest is Digitalisation, Cashless Economy, marketing, economics, new technology and strategies adoption. He has published national and international research paper and also active on digital platform. He has also a copy right ownership of Design Thinking model for start-ups. He has always tried to expand his research areas according to the scenario.

**Priyanka Yadav** is assistant professor at NFSU gandhinagar in general mgt. She holds her phd from DOMS, IIT ROORKEE. She holds masters in commerce and finance. Her teaching interests are security analysis, portfolio management, financial mgt, corporate law. She has presented several papers at national and international conferences and has published several papers in good quality national and international journals. Before joining NFSU, she has worked with various Institutes of repute like FMS, DELHI UNIVERSITY, SRCC, COMPETITION COMMISSION OF INDIA, to name a few.

# Index

## N



## O



## P



## R



## S



## T



## U



## W

www.ingramcontent.com/pod-product-compliance
Lightning Source LLC
LaVergne TN
LVHW081332021026
849161LV00008BA/2103